Studies in
Business-Cycle
Theory

Studies in Business-Cycle Theory

Robert E. Lucas, Jr.

The MIT Press
Cambridge, Massachusetts
London, England

This book was set in Times Roman by DEKR Corp. and printed and bound by The Murray Printing Co. in the United States of America.

Library of Congress Cataloging in Publication Data

Lucas, Robert E.
  Studies in business-cycle theory.

  Bibliography: p.
  Includes index.
  1. Business cycles—Addresses, essays, lectures.
I. Title.
HB3711.L83   338.5'42   81-692
ISBN 0-262-12089-5   AACR2

To my wife Rita
We have shared everything, good
times and bad, since long before I
began thinking about the issues
treated here, so it is only natural and
right that we share this too.

Contents

Acknowledgments

I was raised in a political family in the sense that we spent hundreds of hours together arguing over how we thought our society worked and how we thought it ought to work. By the time I was old enough to realize that not everyone grows up this way, I had already accumulated so much of this rather specialized expertise that it seemed easiest just to keep on going. For this, as for so much else, I am grateful to my parents.

Most of my professional life has been spent at two institutions: the University of Chicago and Carnegie-Mellon University. It would be impossible to list all of the teachers, colleagues, and students who have made these environments so exciting and productive for me. Their individual influences are evident in the introduction to this collection and in the acknowledgments and citations in the individual papers. Richard M. Cyert, who was Dean of the Graduate School of Industrial Administration when I was hired and for most of my years there, placed his bets early on, and his support and encouragement helped me to take a longer term view of my research than most younger scholars feel they can afford. More than he knew, for we have always dealt with each other as equals, Allan Meltzer served as a personal and professional example as well as a friend and helpful colleague. These are debts of a different character from those that are acknowledged on a paper-by-paper basis but they are surely no less important, and I am glad to have this chance to express my gratitude.

The National Science Foundation has supported my work with an uninterrupted succession of grants. There is no good substitute for this kind of assistance, and I am very grateful for it.

A glance at my more technical papers should generate sympathy and appreciation for the excellent secretarial help I have benefited from over the years. I thank Mary Jo McClure and Alyce Monroe, who did most of the work, and also Eleanor Balochik, Altheia Chaballa, Wilhemina Healy, and Monica Malkus.

Studies in
Business-Cycle
Theory

Introduction

This volume contains fourteen of my papers on business cycles, including collaborations with Leonard Rapping and Edward Prescott, written between 1967 and the present. Each paper was written under its own set of stimuli, with the result that there are many inconsistencies of style, method, and substance among them. Yet the collection does have some coherence, induced not by an initial plan but by a stability in the set of substantive questions to which they are addressed together with an evolution in my thought on the methods by which these questions might usefully be treated. The aim of this introduction is to define this coherence by describing how these papers came to be written and by sketching the scientific and rhetorical problems to which each was an attempted solution.

My work, in conjunction with that of many others, on business cycles has received a good deal of professional and popular attention for what are thought to be its novel implications for national economic policy, to the point where one occasionally reads of a *rational-expectations school* on policy matters. I think this scholastic terminology suits debates over social policy, and I will have no regrets if it should displace technocratic language suggesting that economics can affect policy solely through the engineering of scientific consensus. It is not, however, a useful terminology in discussing research on business cycles. John Muth's hypothesis of rational expectations is a technical model-building principle, not a distinct, comprehensive macroeconomic theory. Recent research utilizing this principle has reinforced many of the policy recommendations of Milton Friedman and other postwar monetarists but has contributed few, if any, original policy proposals. My own research has been concerned almost exclusively with the attempt to discover a useful theoretical explanation of business cycles.

Macroeconomists in the 1960s did not think of their efforts as directed toward finding an "explanation of business cycles." Earlier economists who had thought of their research in this way were viewed as simply out of date, as Romanovs of the Keynesian Revolution. We thought of this problem as being, in a general way, solved, and our research was focused on refining the various pieces, or sectors, of an overall theory whose main outlines were fairly widely agreed upon. Research during the 1970s forced me and many others progressively further away from this view and toward a general-equilibrium point of view that seemed to me essentially the same in substance, however different in method, as the view taken by many pre-Keynesian theorists. This change in my views as to the nature of the scientific problem posed by business cycles, and the consequent shift in my own position from an attempted contributor to Keynesian macroeconomics to that of severe critic is also evident in these papers.

The remainder of this introduction is simply an account, in chronological order, of the writing of these papers. It is not an intellectual autobiography, for I worked on several other problem areas over this period. It is not a substitute for, or summary of, these papers. Unavoidably, I think, in a new introduction to previously published material, I find myself writing for those who are familiar with much of my work.

My first research directly related to business cycles was a joint project undertaken in collaboration with Leonard Rapping, "Real Wages, Employment, and Inflation," on the determination of aggregate employment and wages in the US economy. Our objective at the time, as is clear enough from the introduction to our paper and such defensive efforts as note 3, was not to challenge the current, Keynesian orthodoxy but rather to contribute to it by constructing a "microeconomic foundation" for the wage-price sector of macroeconometric models. Our strategy in attempting this was to try to rationalize the employment decisions of individual households and firms in a manner modeled after Friedman and Modigliani's work on the household consumption decision, Eisner and Jorgenson's work on the investment decision of business firms, or Friedman and Meltzer's work on the demand for money. We were aware, of course, that working toward a competitive-equilibrium account of the cyclical behavior of employment would be viewed in some circles as quixotic or even subversive, but we supposed that the basis for this widespread view was no deeper than the belief that such an account was not possible to devise. Since each of us had had some classroom success in discussing the behavior of employment over the cycle in price-theoretical terms, the task did not seem all that forbidding, and we proceeded with it.

The empirical task we faced, as we saw it, was to rationalize household and firm behavior through the large employment decline of 1929 to 1933 and the rapid increase in World War II, and to do so in a way that was consistent with the fairly well-established real-wage inelasticity of "long-run" labor supply. "Rationalizing" meant to us reconciling these observations with intelligent behavior on agents' parts. Evidently, this could not be carried out at the level of the static, one-period indifference diagram of the sort we use to explain, for example, the secular decline in hours worked per worker per week. (This is chapter 2 of Keynes's *General Theory*.) Instead, we adopted a two-period setup in which expected future prices, in addition to current prices, could play a role.

From the household's point of view, in such a framework and under competition, the candidates as inducers of employment changes were (besides spontaneous taste shifts, which we did not seriously consider) price, wage, and wealth changes. Unless leisure were treated as an inferior good, in contradiction to much secular and cross-section evidence, a wealth-induced decline in employment would necessarily be associated with happiness, not with depression! For cyclical purposes, this left price and wage changes, or, more particularly, the intertemporal substitution effects of these changes. Section 2 of our paper is simply the working out of the implications of this observation at a technical level sufficiently precise to be of use econometrically.

This stylized picture of the way households vary hours of work in response to changes in perceived current and future wages and prices is at the center of everything that follows in this volume. (Indeed, in some respects it later came to seem to me more complicated than necessary, and so has been stylized further.) This picture leaves unanswered many serious questions of substance, some of which have been treated in subsequent papers and others of which still seem to be unsatisfactorily resolved. (I shall return to questions in both these categories.) Yet there is a real sense in which this picture seems to me not the best account of employment fluctuations, but rather the *only* account; its main attraction to me from the first has been the absence of serious alternatives.

The time pattern of hours that an individual supplies to the market is something that, in a very clear sense, he *chooses*. Understanding employment fluctuations must involve, at some point, understanding how this choice is made or what combination of preference characteristics and changing opportunities gives rise to the patterns we observe. At some level of detail, there is no question that social convention and institutional structures affect these patterns, but conventions and institutions do not simply come out of the blue, arbitrarily imposing themselves on individual agents. On the contrary, institutions and customs are designed precisely in order to aid in matching preferences and opportunities satisfactorily. Taking into account theoretically, if it could be done, the complicated arrangements we observe in actual labor and product markets would not be a step toward constructing an *alternative* model to the one Rapping and I used, but toward an extension or elaboration. In order for such an extension to account for observed employment fluctuations, *in addition to* whatever other institutional features it succeeded in explaining, it would have to explain why, given their opportunities, people *prefer* arrangements involving erratic employment patterns. Ignoring this simple point seems to me simply bad social science: an attempt to explain important aspects of human behavior without reference either to what people like or what they are capable of doing.

In general, then, I see no way to account for observed employment patterns that does not rest on an understanding of the intertemporal substitutability of labor. The literature contains innumerable examples of possible additional, supplementary considerations, but to my knowledge no alternatives.

There are, certainly, other ways to capture intertemporal substitutability in an explicit model besides the one Rapping and I chose. Some of these can be, and have been, examined within a competitive framework. We were concerned in formulating our model with the degree of richness in the mix of activities considered: work versus "leisure"; work, leisure, and job search; schooling, sleeping, eating, and so on. Evidently there is no natural limit to this sort of activity breakdown, and different breakdowns will be useful for different purposes. In selecting a two-activity breakdown, we thought that our principal decision was whether to try to interpret measured unemployment theoretically as an activity. For reasons given in the paper, we decided not to do so, but for other purposes and data sets it is useful to try other two-activity breakdowns (work/search, for example) or multiactivity formulations, and there is by now a sizable literature, stemming from the original work of McCall and Mortensen, exploring various possibilities. I am arguing, then, not that the specific form of Rapping's and my formulation of the labor supply response to current and expected wage and price movements was the first, best, or only formulation, but rather that the essential mechanics of these various formulations are the same, and that all rest on intertemporal substitution of labor.

In any formulation, intertemporal substitution involves current hours supplied responding to something with the dimensions of a real interest rate or real rate of return. An expected price inflation affects behavior in our model because it lowers the real return on labor supplied today for purposes of consuming tomorrow. If today's labor is transformed into tomorrow's consumption via the holding of interest-bearing bonds *and* if the expected inflation induces a one-for-one increase in the nominal interest rate on these bonds, then the real rate of return relevant for the current-hour's decision will not be affected by inflationary expectations in any way. Rapping and I simply evaded this difficulty by acknowledging it as a possibility but noting that interest rates do not seem to adjust in this way, for reasons we did not explore. This was the right decision, I think, since there was no hope of resolving this difficulty at the partial-equilibrium level at which we were working. Yet the question keeps coming up in other contexts and is still largely unresolved. Indeed, when any macroeconomist employs a *Lucas* (really, of course, *Lucas-Rapping*) *supply function,* he too is evading this issue (as well as the responsibility for doing so!).

The other central unresolved issue in our paper, but one on which much progress has been made since, was its treatment of expectations formation. Milton Friedman's (1968) presidential address to the American Economic Association was published while we were working on our paper, and we were disturbed that his reasoning appeared conclusive and that it contradicted the prediction of our model (as it did the predictions of *all* Phillips-curve models). Our last three sentences dealt with this puzzle in a way that did not resolve it but was well designed to require no retractions or apologies later on.

"Unemployment in the Great Depression" is included here because it contains an important correction to the original paper and remains a useful summary of which aspects of labor-market behavior in the 1930s can be explained by existing theory and which cannot. The paper is a reply to Albert Rees's comments, but the reader interested in adjudicating this argument obviously will have to read Rees's views as well.

The best thing that happened to Rapping's and my paper was that Edmund Phelps came across it and a number of related papers by others at a time when he himself was working on similar problems. The volume he assembled has become known, fairly enough, as the Phelps volume (1970). To celebrate the signing of the contract with the publisher, Phelps hosted a conference in Philadelphia. Fortunately for subsequent developments, if not for the coherence of our discussion, he imposed as a ground rule for the conference that no author could discuss his own paper, but instead certain basic questions presented by Phelps in the form of an agenda, to which none of the papers had provided an adequate answer.

Rapping and I had been thinking in the sectoral terms typical of at least the more econometrically oriented macroeconomic tradition. We viewed ourselves as constructing a model of the "wage-price sector," potentially suitable for combining with other models of other "sectors" to provide a model of the entire economy. Most other participants at the conference viewed their work in the same terms. (Armen Alchian did not attend.) Phelps, as is evident from his introductory essay to the volume, was thinking in general-equilibrium terms and used his list of questions to focus our discussion in this direction. If one agent is fooled into imagining relative prices are moving in his favor, is his action not offset by another with the opposite misapprehension? (This is not a direct quote from Phelps's list, which I have long since lost.) Why formulate price expectations as adaptive in the *levels* (as Rapping and I had done)? How can the price expectations relevant for labor-market decisions differ from those relevant for bond-market decisions? Is it possible, in short, to describe an entire economy operating in a mutually consistent way that is led into large-scale employment fluctuations via informational imperfections alone? It was clear that none of the papers in the volume had succeeded in doing this, though most presupposed that it was possible to do so.

Phelps's introductory essay dealt with this general-equilibrium issue in an informal but concrete way. Much of our discussion at the conference involved questions that seemed to stand in the way of casting this argument in modern mathematical form.

"Expectations and the Neutrality of Money" was an attempt to do this. This paper's ties to the Phelps essay turned out to be stronger than I had foreseen when I began work on it. The initial idea simply was to situate some Lucas-Rapping households in a monetary economy, subject the system to stochastic shocks to the money supply, and see what would happen. Samuelson's intergenerational monetary economy offered a convenient analytical setting because it both fit the two-period consumer maximization problem Rapping and I had studied and the function of "money" in it was so clearly defined. The idea of defining an equilibrium as a point in a space of functions of a few "state variables" was one that Prescott and I had utilized in "Investment under Uncertainty." This analytical device had forced Prescott and me to be precise as to the meaning of terms like *information and expectations* and led us to formulate and utilize Muth's rational-expectations hypothesis in exactly the way I then used it in "Expectations and the Neutrality of Money." In short, the needed ingredients for a general-equilibrium formulation seemed to be readily at hand.

The original formulation I tried involved a one-sector system with monetary shocks as the only source of uncertainty. With new money injected by proportional transfers, I learned (embarrassingly, to my surprise) that monetary shocks, whether anticipated or not, acted exactly like neutral monetary movements, for which agents could then perfectly correct. It was sufficiently easy to alter the model to introduce nonneutralities via, for example, an inflation tax or by transfers to the working young generation, but the real effects of such shocks then would have arisen not from the substitution effects that operate in Rapping's and my framework, but rather from the income or wealth effects ruled out on empirical grounds in the preceding section.

At this point, it became clear to me why Phelps had imagined an island economy, with traders scattered and short on useful, system-wide information. It is exactly this feature that permits all producers simultaneously to believe they have gained relative to others as the consequence of a monetary shock. Incorporating this "island" feature into a general-equilibrium system turned out to be more difficult analytically than I had expected. On the other hand, the "fit" between the workings of the completed model and the conjecture of Friedman, Phelps, Rapping and me, and others turned out to be perfect.

This "fit" came as something of a relief. I had already been persuaded, it is true, by the arguments of Friedman and Phelps that a natural-rate hypothesis was valid and consistent with the main features of the observed business cycle, but the form this persuasion took was the conviction that an artificial, model society could be constructed in which these conjectures were verifiably valid. Had this construction not been possible, the possibility that I simply had attempted it in the wrong way would have remained the most attractive conclusion, but the degree of persuasion would have been weakened. In general, I believe that one who claims to understand the principles of flight can reasonably be expected to be able to make a flying machine, and that understanding business cycles means the ability to make them too, in roughly the same sense. I viewed the Phelps volume as now being off the ground.

Despite (or perhaps because of) its highly abstract character, "Expectations and the Neutrality of Money" influenced my research along three difference directions. First, it was clear that Rapping's and my original view that our supply theory could be combined fairly easily with an IS-LM-type aggregate-demand theory was not working out as planned. Though the theory of household behavior remained unchanged in these two papers, the change from adaptive to rational expectations implied that the behavior of a single sector no longer could be worked out without reference to that sector's interaction with the rest of the system.

Second, the construction of an explicit model economy undergoing what was in some sense a business cycle made it possible to see whether the econometric methods we were then using to learn what is true in the actual economy, about which we know so little, would give us the correct answers in a model economy about which we know everything. Here the answer was very clearly negative. (This is section 4 of "Expectations and the Neutrality of Money.") This observation, in itself, proved little about actual business cycles, but it suggested some sharp questions about econometric methods that could be posed and studied in a way that was largely independent of the abstract context in which they originally arose.

Third, the apparent novelty of the model of "Expectations and the Neutrality of Money," in combination with the unhappy experience that the substantively original ideas in my own economic thought invariably had proved to be wrong, renewed my interest in the vast pre-Keynesian literature on business-cycle theory. There I found not the obstinate resistance to evident fact described by Keynes, and repeated as "history" by two or three generations of Keynesians, but a sophisticated literature, however unaided by modern theoretical technology, emphasizing the recurrent character of business cycles, the necessity of viewing these recurrences as mistakes, and attempts to rationalize these mistakes as intelligent responses to movements in nominal "signals" of movements in the underlying "real" events we care about and want to react to. If Wesley Mitchell could view agents as "signal processors" in 1913, then I saw no reason to regard my own adoption of this viewpoint in 1972 as unduly speculative.

Each of these three directions is in evidence in the remaining papers of this volume. Each appears in a form that I have found to be more persuasive, to others, than the technically more demanding form it assumes in "Expectations and the Neutrality of Money." Certainly one cannot be at all surprised or resentful over the fact that to persuade people of something one has to put it in a way that speaks to their concerns, and in a language that they find congenial. Yet it is a mistake, I think, to conclude that these abstract "toy models" are a step that can be dispensed with, or that one can go directly to the formulation of useful, simple linear models or to reading Mitchell with new under-standing without their assistance. It is, at least for me, the working out of these highly abstract but explicit models that is the *source* of ideas for constructing new econometric models, criticizing old ones, or reading the classics from a fresh viewpoint.

If the theory of "Expectations and the Neutrality of Money" was the correct way to formulate the Friedman-Phelps natural-rate hy-pothesis, then it was evident that the econometric methods then being applied to test this hypothesis were entirely missing the point. More-over, though the negative sample correlations between inflation rates and unemployment rates could be defined to be a "trade-off," it was clear that there might be no way to base welfare-improving social policy on this correlation. The limited size of the audience that that paper could ever hope for had been brought home to me rather clearly by a withering rejection from the journal to which it was first submitted. I was very pleased, therefore, to be asked to read papers before two conferences, both of which offered assignments sufficiently broad to permit me to treat the points I wanted to make.

"Econometric Testing of the Natural Rate Hypothesis" was prepared for a conference evaluating the wage-price sectors of the large-scale econometric models, to which I was invited (I assumed) as a spokesman for the deviant Friedman-Phelps viewpoint. The paper's objectives were to make clear, with a minimum of technical complication, exactly why the standard distributed-lag tests of the Friedman-Phelps hypothesis could not decide the issue and to indicate in a general way the kind of test from which one could learn something. [The first of these objectives already had been attained, though I did not know this at the time, by Thomas Sargent (1971). Sargent's subsequent application (1973) of the rational-expectations hypothesis to the Fisherian equation linking nominal interest rates to expected inflation rates, written about the same time, accomplished the second.]

"Econometric Policy Evaluation: A Critique" was prepared for the initial meeting of Karl Brunner and Allan Meltzer's Carnegie-Rochester conference series. The assignment encouraged me to write on a broader and more general theme than I would have chosen left to my own devices; this worthwhile series has provided similar stimulus to other young scholars many times since. The paper also reflects the influence of Edward Prescott, who recently had returned to Carnegie-Mellon from the University of Pennsylvania and was instructing me on many aspects of the art of large-scale econometric modeling.

In following Lawrence Klein's work, I had been struck with the impression that as the short-term forecasting abilities of his models steadily improved, he himself evidently was becoming less and less interested in both economic and econometric theory. I recall (but cannot recall its location) an illustration of his in which the *same* price equation is derived from a competitive model, a pure-monopoly model, and a behavioral markup pricing model! The point was clear: Pick the "story" that suits your prejudices, but do not be deluded that this choice matters operationally. The theoretical work that I and others had been engaged in on the optimizing basis of distributed-lag investment functions had been leading me to this same position; though our "stories" were getting better and better, this "progress" seemed to be leading to no improvements in the performance of econometric investment functions.

The prestige of theoretical work is so secure in our profession that its proponents too rarely find themselves on the defensive, and casting meaningless epithets like ad hoc becomes a devastating criticism of empirical work. The cost of this attitude is not that econometric work fails to get done—someone has to do it—but that contact between theorists and working econometricians becomes unpleasant, with the result that the two groups tend to stick to themselves and the necessary interaction between theory and fact tends not to take place. Yet examples, such as Klein's price equation, and the general challenge posed by the forecasting successes of relatively atheoretical models needed to be taken seriously, I thought; for if the practical questions for which people look to economists for answers can be answered without recourse to economic theory, why do we need the theory?

The general-equilibrium approach taken in "Expectations and the Neutrality of Money" suggested a clear answer to this question. In that model economy, it is evident that changes in the rule governing monetary policy alters coefficients in what one would ordinarily have thought of as structural equations in the econometric sense, regardless of the stability of these coefficients over a past sample period. Once the reasons for this are understood, it is not difficult to see that the same parameter instability must arise in the actual economy. "Econometric Policy Evaluation" simply spelled these reasons out, in as many different contexts as I could conceive. I was pleased that this case for the crucial role of theory in evaluating policy was entirely consistent with the possibility of successful ex ante short-term forecasting with relatively atheoretical econometric models, since a simple denial of this success (which was still done then in some circles) was becoming an increasingly untenable position.

I view "Econometric Policy Evaluation" as a contribution to this important question of the relation of theory to econometric work, but sometimes it is read as though it resolved the issue much more decisively than can ever be the case. The paper stressed the importance of identifying structural parameters that are invariant under the kinds of policy changes one is interested in evaluating; and in all of the paper's examples, only the parameters describing "tastes" and "tech-

nology'' were treated as having this property. This presumption seems
a sound one to me, but it must be defended on empirical, not logical,
grounds, and the nature of such a defense presumably would vary with
the particular application one has in mind. That is, utility theory does
not *tell* us that utility functions are invariant under changes in the
behavior of prices; its application *assumes* this. The stability of, say,
empirical Engel curves over so wide a range of circumstances reflects
well on Engel's judgment and is an amazing piece of good luck for us,
as empirical scientists, but there is no way that Engel could have
assured himself logically that this would be the case.

Although the standard, distributed-lag tests of the natural-rate hypothesis appeared to be entirely discredited, it seemed inconceivable
that there could be no way to distinguish empirically between two
hypotheses as different in their implications as a stable Phillips trade-
off and a natural rate of unemployment. If the coefficients in a distributed-lag Phillips curve do not bear on the question, some other tests
must. In 1970, I had experimented with models along the lines of that
used illustratively in "Econometric Testing of the Natural Rate Hypothesis" using US time series, but had not succeeded in finding a
maintainable "maintained" hypothesis within which the natural-rate
hypothesis could be nested. Leonard Rapping had thought for some
time that cross-country comparisons would be useful, especially if the
high-inflation Latin American countries were included, and we had
looked at plots of decade-averaged unemployment rates against averaged inflation rates. Major cross-country conceptual differences in the
measurement of unemployment, however, made these plots impossible
to interpret, or so we thought, and this project, too, was abandoned.

A linearized version of the model in "Expectations and the Neutrality of Money" suggested a cross-country test that did not utilize
measured unemployment rates. This was carried out in "Some International Evidence on Output-Inflation Tradeoffs" but with nominal
income rather than money used as the "forcing variable" so as to
avoid having to take a position on the international transmission of
demand shocks. By this time, Rapping had become interested in other
issues, so I proceeded on my own. This was unfortunate, since Rapping would have caught the more glaring of the econometric errors
that mar this paper. Despite these mistakes, however, the paper's
main conclusions have stood up well. In an unpublished paper, Jose

Alberro replicated these results with correct econometric methods and with a much larger sample of countries. Since then, of course, Sargent, Robert Barro, and others have devised time-series tests of the natural-rate hypothesis suited to data for a single country, so that the empirical burden on my cross-country tests has been considerably lightened.

"Capacity, Overtime, and Empirical Production Functions" is an entirely real, neoclassical piece, with no tight connection with the rest of the volume. It was written earlier, as a paper invited by the American Economic Association, presumably on the basis of my credentials as an investment theorist. Yet it is an outgrowth of the Phelps volume, as are many of the other papers in this volume. Phelps had insisted at the Philadelphia conference on the importance of the puzzle raised by the lack of systematic countercyclical wage movements and, in his paper with Sidney Winter, attempted to deal with it. The outcome of an exercise I assigned to a masters class at Carnegie-Mellon reminded me of the unsatisfactory performance of fitted, aggregate-production functions, however one fiddled with "corrections" for measurement error and the like. It occurred to me that these two puzzles both involved the failure of the law of diminishing returns to reveal to itself in the time series, and hence might best be treated as a single problem. That is what this paper does.

Obviously, there is a large gap between the highly abstract model of "Expectations and the Neutrality of Money" and an econometric model capable of giving reliable, quantitative assessments of the consequences of alternative monetary- and fiscal-policy rules. Much of my work over the past decade has been directed toward trying to narrow this gap. The diversity among the three papers now to be discussed illustrates how hard fought even a little progress is, and how uncertain I am of even the general shape that a solution to this ill-posed problem is likely to take.

For technical reasons, "Expectations and the Neutrality of Money" abstracted from all forms of serial correlation (or capital, or "persistence") and focused only on initial shocks. Despite what I had thought was careful footnoting of my reasons for doing this, the "persistence" question later emerged as what some seemed to view as a major difficulty with business-cycle theories utilizing rational expectations. Most of this was simply a confusion over whether serial independence is an inherent feature of such models (which it clearly is not) or whether it is a technically hard feature to relax (which, outside linear contexts, it seems to be).

Prescott's and my "Equilibrium Search and Unemployment" began as an attempt to move from the model of "Expectations and the Neutrality of Money" toward a more McCall-Mortensen-Phelps-like "island" model that would illustrate one mechanism by which initial-demand shocks could induce a distributed-lag response (see McCall, 1965). In this model, a match between a worker and his "market" is a kind of capital, due to an assumed fixed cost of switching from one market to another. The model went through many formulations in an attempt to find one that was tractable. The simplifying device we finally hit on exploits the constancy of the expected present value of job search (λ in the paper) in an essential way, an assumption that evidently cannot be reconciled with economy-wide demand fluctuations! We ended up with an interesting theory of something, I think, but not a theory of business cycles. Even so, the model is a conclusive counterexample (if one is needed) to the idea that a persistent response to shocks is not possible in a rational-expectations equilibrium.

"Expectations and the Neutrality of Money" and "Equilibrium Search and Unemployment" are technically difficult because in both models the decision problem faced by agents is made fully explicit and (in the former paper) the incompleteness of information possessed by any single agent implies that the system as a whole does not solve a grand maximum problem. The practical necessity of modeling the individual's decision problem, as opposed to his decision rules, is the main theme of "Econometric Policy Evaluation," and I did not wish to evade the argument of that paper. Similarly, finding a dynamic program to which the business cycle is a solution would seem to me uncomfortably close to discovering a social purpose served by business cycles, yet I was convinced that business cycles have no social purpose.

These considerations are much too loose to add up to anything like an "impossibility theorem." I raise them here only to indicate the technical difficulties discouraging the introduction of more interesting dynamics into a theory at the level of "Expectations and the Neutrality of Money." The relative ease of manipulating the linear system of "Some International Evidence on Output-Inflation Tradeoffs" (which is just a linearization of the model of "Expectations and the Neutrality of Money'') suggested that a formulation with agents' demands written as functions of expected future prices (the latter formed rationally) might provide a useful compromise framework within which progress might be made. This is the route taken in ''An Equilibrium Model of the Business Cycle.''

This model introduced lags due to capital accumulation, an accelerator effect, and the gradual diffusion of information. This yielded a second-order system potentially consistent with the second-order autoregressive character typical of many economic time series (Nerlove's law). The paper evidently does not quite work: there are too many compromises of convenience granted per unit of convenience received. These are sure symptoms of a poor match between the mathematical framework being utilized and the substantive question being posed.

In spite of this, I reprint the paper without apology, for it is the only paper here that attempts to capture the interaction between monetary shocks and the accelerator effect, which seems to be, at the empirical level, so central in observed behavior over the cycle. The volatility of business investment over the cycle is at least as severe a paradox as the cyclical behavior of employment, since the principal characteristic of optimal investment behavior (as we understand it theoretically) is the way it *smooths* reactions to transient shocks. Volatile cyclical investment must be explicable, exactly as it volatile cyclical employment, only as a repeated *mistake*. This observation suggests that these two aspects of behavior have a common explanation. ''An Equilibrium Model of the Business Cycle'' was an attempt to provide one.

The model sketched in ''Understanding Business Cycles'' is, of course, that of the last-mentioned paper. Isn't it remarkable how simple it all becomes in plain English? Yet how deceptive this simplicity is: The description of inventory behavior in ''Understanding Business Cycles'' is as coherent as the description of accelerator effects, yet the latter is a verbal transcription of a fully worked-out model while the former is only conjecture. There is nothing dishonest in this—I think the conjectures are good ones—but this example illustrates the sense in which theorizing at this verbal level is limited to conveying the state of theory to the casually interested or perhaps stimulating oneself or others toward genuine developments in theory.

''Understanding Business Cycles'' was another paper invited by Brunner and Meltzer. I took it as an opportunity to try to state for the first time exactly what, to my thinking, the empirical problem posed by business cycles was and what it would mean to solve it. Naturally, my earlier papers recognized to some extent which qualitative facts, because of their central importance, required explanation; but for the most part these were second-hand facts for me, picked up from Phelps or Allan Meltzer or "common knowledge" around Chicago and Carnegie-Mellon. I was beginning to be concerned that the particular theoretical line I was following might be focused on explaining "coffee-break" facts only.

The basic source for "my" facts, not very surprisingly, turned out to be Friedman and Schwartz's *Monetary History* (1963). As a student, I had thought this monograph was made unduly difficult by its failure to use any explicit, general theoretical framework to give structure to the complicated history of US economic time series, and therefore I had paid it only casual attention. Now, thoroughly disillusioned with standard macroeconomic theory, I appreciated the book's relatively atheoretical approach. From Friedman and Schwartz, it is a short and direct step back to the work of Wesley Mitchell (1913). These connections were not pursued from genealogical interest, but because they are helpful in organizing one's thinking about the implications of the evidence. It is the similarity from cycle to cycle of comovements among series, as documented by Mitchell, that leads one to a single-shock view of business cycles. *Given* this, Friedman and Schwartz have no alternative but to identify this single shock with monetary instability. What are the other candidates?

The final four papers in this volume are a miscellany. Each was prepared in response to an invitation to write on a specific topic for a specific occasion, and none would have been written otherwise. Yet each contains something of interest not said elsewhere, so all seemed worth including.

"Unemployment Policy" is mainly an expression of exasperation at the way certain words are used in our profession. It is what Rapping and I would have said in our original paper if we had had the nerve. Expressions of exasperation tend to be better, I think, when directed at a specific target, so I much prefer the review of the OECD report, *Towards Full Employment and Price Stability*. It was fun to write; I hope it is fun to read. It is also, of course, terribly unfair: there must be many "committee jobs" of this sort that would have served the same purpose.

"Rules, Discretion, and the Role of the Economic Advisor" is the only paper in this volume directed at macroeconomic policy, and really the only policy paper I have written. One of the virtues of coming down on the side of rules versus authority is, I suppose, that one only gets one such paper per lifetime. In my case, I only got a fraction, since I simply took the particular set of rules I advocated from Milton Friedman. This must have been a disappointment to those in attendance who believed that rational expectations imply an entirely new point of view on policy; that was why I thought it worth writing.

The final paper, "Methods and Problems in Business-Cycle Theory," was completed earlier this year. I am struck by the rather "literary" tone it shares with the other papers grouped toward the back. Much of its concern is with words and the way people use them in support of the scientific or policy positions they advocate. Given the level of popular, and even not so popular, economic debate at the present time, this concern seems to me unavoidable.

At times such as the 1960s in the United States, when a broad scientific consensus has been reached and is widely acknowledged and accepted by nonprofessionals (these two conditions are of course related), it is possible to use a shared verbal shorthand to convey fairly complicated ideas. Looseness of language is not harmful, because when forced to make a loose statement precise, one economist will do so in about the same way as any other. During times like the present, when consensus has broken down, such looseness becomes a barrier in professional debate, and it becomes impossible for the public to distinguish language that summarizes serious underlying analysis from language that is just talk. In such a situation, it does not seem to me fruitful simply to wade into the current verbal debate, letting one's words take on whatever unknown meanings other participants may assign. Instead, one needs to try to go behind terms like *theory* or *equilibrium* or *unemployment* to get at the specific constructs or facts they are being used to summarize.

It is best, I think, to resist the temptation to conclude this introduction with a summing-up. The study of business cycles is a complex social process; there is no reason to believe that evaluating the contribution to it of any individual contributor will reveal a great deal of unity.

If there is a single, main theme to this introduction, it is a sense of having severely limited theoretical options, which I feel very strongly but do not perceive to be very widely shared. The nature of the questions to which we want answers, the level of theorizing at which there seems to be any real hope of obtaining reliable answers, and the equipment at hand for theorizing at this level combine to make genuine progress painfully slow. Since business cycles have plagued capitalist societies in essentially unchanging form for at least two centuries, it does not seem unreasonable to attribute some of this slow progress to the difficulty of the problem itself, rather than to some easily corrected flaw in our viewpoint. Politically, this is not an especially encouraging conclusion, but scientifically it is a heartening one.

References

Friedman, Milton. "The Role of Monetary Policy." *American Economic Review* 58 (March 1968):1–17.

Friedman, Milton, and Anna J. Schwartz. *A Monetary History of the United States, 1867–1960*. Princeton: Princeton University Press and N.B.E.R., 1963.

McCall, John. "The Economics of Information and Optimal Stopping Rules." *Journal of Business* 38 (1965):300–317.

Mitchell, Wesley C. *Business Cycles*. Berkeley: University of California Press, 1913.

Phelps, Edmunds S., et al., *Microeconomic Foundations of Employment and Inflation Theory*. New York: Norton, 1970.

Sargent, Thomas J. "A Note on the 'Accelerationist' Controversy." *Journal of Money, Credit and Banking* 3 (1971):721–725.

Sargent, Thomas J. "Interest Rates and Prices in the Long Run." *Journal of Money, Credit and Banking* 5 (1973):385–449.

Real Wages, Employment, and Inflation

Introduction

The aggregate labor-supply function is a cornerstone of both neoclassical growth theory and short-run Keynesian-type employment theory. Yet no empirical estimates of the parameters of this function, comparable to estimated aggregate consumption, investment, or money demand functions, are available.[1] Despite this lack of evidence, economists have found it necessary to proceed on the basis of certain widely accepted assumptions. In the growth literature, it is generally assumed that population growth is exogenous and that the supply of labor from any fixed population is an inelastic function of the real wage rate. In the short-run literature, on the other hand, it is commonly assumed that the labor supply is infinitely elastic at some rigid real or money wage rate. Our purpose in this paper is to construct a model of the labor market which reconciles these apparently divergent views of labor supply and to test the model on annual aggregate, U.S. time series covering the period 1929–65.

Wherever possible, we will motivate our assumptions by reference to the microeconomic labor-market literature. Yet, as with any aggre-

Reprinted from *Journal of Political Economy* 77 (September/October 1969):721–754 by permission of The University of Chicago Press. Copyright 1969 by The University of Chicago Press.

We wish to thank Professors T. McGuire, A. Meltzer, W. Oi, E. Phelps, and A. Rees who commented on an earlier draft of this study. Their willingness to comment on our work should not be interpreted as an endorsement of our views. Indeed, at least one of the readers substantially disagreed with us, but because his disagreement aided us in clarifying our thinking we feel obliged to acknowledge his assistance.

gate study of a single sector of the economy, it will be necessary to gloss over much of the richness of detail provided by the many studies of particular features of labor-market behavior. We will not compensate for this loss by offering a full econometric model of the economy, but in the next section we sketch the structure of our labor-market model and its relation to the other sectors of the economy. There remains, nevertheless, an inevitable arbitrariness in our selection of two functions—the labor-supply function and a marginal productivity condition for labor—to be estimated as a simultaneous equation system.

In addition to our primary aim of understanding the workings of the U.S. labor market, this study has as a secondary purpose the rationalization in supply-and-demand terms of the observed correlation between unemployment rates and the rate of inflation, or Phillips curve. Recent attemps to give a theoretical basis to the Phillips curve have been based largely on a view of the labor market as dominated by collective bargaining, where bargaining outcomes bear no explicit relation to supply-and-demand forces.[2] While we offer no crucial test of the two views, we shall show that a competitive market theory is rich in implications and is consistent with the U.S. experience.

The remainder of the paper is organized as follows. In section 1, a model of the production-employment sector is discussed in general terms and related to the rest of the economy. In section 2, an aggregate labor-supply function is developed. The demand side of the market is treated in section 3 and the role of measured unemployment in section 4. The model is then stated in full in section 5, with tests reported in the next section. Section 7 is a summary of our conclusions.

1 Structure of the Model

The results reported in section 6, below, are estimates of a two-equation model of the U.S. labor market, where the two equations are the labor-supply function and a marginal productivity condition for labor. The time series on which our tests were conducted are, as are all economic time series, subject to both short- and long-run forces. It is thus impossible, however desirable, to construct and test on these series either a "short-run model" or a "long-run model" of the labor market: an adequate model must contain both a short and a long run. There are, then, three features which we feel a model of the labor market (or, more broadly, the production-employment sector) should possess. First, it should incorporate the neoclassical feature that for fixed capital stock the aggregate supply schedule (relating the price of goods to real output) will become perfectly inelastic over a long period of stable aggregate demand. Second, the model should imply an elastic short-run aggregate supply function consistent with the observed fluctuations in real output and employment in the face of shifting aggregate demand. Finally, the transition from short-run to long-run labor-market equilibrium should be described in full.

The models tested in this paper share these three features. In implementing the models empirically, however, it is necessary to introduce a number of complications which obscure these central features. To aid in interpreting the results, we devote the remainder of this section to a simple prototype of the more complex models actually tested. In doing this, we consider the two functions actually estimated, together with the aggregate production function which was *not* estimated, as a bloc of equations determining the aggregate supply function.

Let m_t be employed persons per household in period t, k_t be capital per household, and y_t be real output per household. Let w_t be the real wage rate, and let Δp_t be the percentage rate of price increase from $t - 1$ to t. We assume an aggregate production function with constant returns to scale, which can be written:

$$y_t/m_t = f(k_t/m_t), \qquad f' > 0, \quad f'' < 0. \tag{1}$$

With competitive labor markets and continuous profit maximization on the part of firms, equation (1) implies the marginal productivity condition for labor:

$$w_t = f(k_t/m_t) - (k_t/m_t)f'(k_t/m_t). \tag{2}$$

Equations (1) and (2) can be solved for the short-run (that is, capital fixed) output supply and labor demand functions if one wishes; their content is the same in either form. To (1) and (2) we add a labor-supply function:

$$m_t = S(w_t, w_{t-1}, \Delta p_t, m_{t-1}), \tag{3}$$

where S is an increasing function of w_t, Δp_t, and m_{t-1}, and a decreasing function of w_{t-1}. In section 2 we discuss in some detail a Fisherian model motivating this labor-supply function. For the present, our interest is in the properties of the production-employment sector characterized by (1)–(3).

The supply function (3) is *not* homogeneous of degree zero in *current* prices and money wages, p_t and $w_t p_t$. Hence in the short run, the model exhibits a form of the "money illusion" postulated in many modern, Keynesian models. If wages and prices were to remain stable over a long period, however, (3) could be solved for a long-run labor supply (relative to population) which depends only on the *real* wage rate.

Eliminating w_t, m_t and their lagged values from (1)–(3) yields the aggregate supply function:

$$y_t = F(y_{t-1}, k_t, k_{t-1}, \Delta p_t). \tag{4}$$

The derivative of F with respect to p_t is positive, so that the short-run aggregate supply function has an upward slope—although it will not be perfectly elastic with respect to the price level. If prices are stable over a long period, and if the difference equation (4) is stable, the supply function becomes perfectly inelastic. In summary, the model (1)–(3) does possess the features discussed at the beginning of this section.

In discussing (1)–(3), we have regarded the labor market as being in *short-run* equilibrium at each time t. This assumption is not inconsistent with observed fluctuations in employment, nor does it "define away" unemployment.[3] The main result of postulating a short-run equilibrium is that measured unemployment, or the measured labor force, will not enter in an important way into the model. We do, however, attempt to account for movements in measured unemployment by using our model to suggest an answer to the question: "What question do respondents to the employment survey think they are answering when asked if they are seeking work?" This is discussed in detail in section 4.

A second general remark is necessitated by the presence of the inflation rate Δp_t in the aggregate supply function (4). This would appear to offer the possibility that, by pursuing a systematic policy of inflation, the government can raise real output arbitrarily without limit. We do *not* accept this implication. As we shall see in the next section, if such a policy were followed the model (1)–(3) would cease to hold.

Before turning from the general structure of the labor market to the behavior of individual suppliers and demanders of labor (sections 2, 3, and 4), we should perhaps raise the broader question of whether a competitive supply-demand mechanism of the sort proposed above, or of *any* kind, can account for labor-market behavior. Posed in such general terms, an a priori discussion of this question is pointless, but two specific noncompetitive forces on wages and employment are sufficiently important to warrant special mention: collective bargaining and the military draft.

Clearly, the model sketched above is an inaccurate view of wage and employment determination in a single, unionized industry. In such an industry, the union imposes a higher-than-competitive wage rate, limited by the labor-demand elasticity it faces and the effectiveness of its strikes. Labor supply to the industry is irrelevant, since the excess supply which must exist is not able to bid down wages. A labor-market model for such an industry will thus consist of a demand function for labor and a "wage setting equation." One is tempted to generalize this view of a unionized industry to the economy as a whole, and, indeed, many economists have yielded to this temptation. Over the period covered by our study, however, at most 25 percent of the labor force was employed under collective bargaining arrangements, so that this generalization makes no sense. Those who cannot find work in the unionized sector will be supplied to the nonunion sector, depressing wages there. As a result, there will be important distortions in the *relative* wage structure, but we have found neither theoretical presumption nor empirical evidence to indicate that the effect of unionism on *aggregate* wage rates is sizable (or even of predictable direction).[4]

Since the military is included in our wages and employment data, with the government treated exactly as a private employer, it is also important to consider the impact of the military draft. Ideally, one should deduct those coerced into the military (a figure which would differ from total draftees) from employment and from "population," deduct their pay from compensation of employees, and deduct their product from GNP—in short, redo the national accounts. We have not attempted this but have instead introduced a wartime dummy variable to control for the effects of the draft during World War II—the only period in our sample where draftees form a substantial fraction of total employment. This is discussed further in section 2.

2 Aggregate Supply of Labor

By the supply of labor, we mean the quantity of man-hours supplied to the *market* economy per year.[5] There are several ways in which this quantity can vary in response to changes in the real wage rate. The wage rate may influence the size of the population through its effect on the child-bearing decision, it may affect the fraction of a given population supplied to the labor force (that is, the participation rate), or it may alter the number of hours supplied per year per labor-force member. We will examine only the last two responses—hours and participation rates—and attempt to explain changes in total labor supply for a population of fixed size and with a fixed age and sex composition.[6]

The relationship of labor supplied to the real wage, referred to in the preceding paragraph, is implied by the familiar utility analysis of the goods-leisure choice facing a single household in a competitive market. For a household facing fluctuating money wages and goods prices, this trade-off at *current* prices captures only one facet of the labor-supply decision. Equally important will be choices involving substitution between *future* goods and leisure and *current* goods and leisure. Consider, for example, the decision facing a worker who has been laid off (or who, in our terms, is confronted with a fall in the wage at which he can find work). Since accepting work at a lower wage may involve, say, an investment in search or in moving to another community, the decision on current labor supply will differ depending on the wage he anticipates in the near future. If the current fall in wages is regarded as temporary, he may accept leisure now (be unemployed). If it is regarded as permanent, he may accept work elsewhere.

To examine these features of the labor-supply choice more systematically, we shall utilize an extended version of the utility analysis of a representative household, involving four commodities: current goods consumption ($\overline{C}$) and labor supply ($\overline{N}$), and "future" consumption and labor supply ($\overline{C}^*$ and $\overline{N}^*$). The household is assumed to maximize utility:[7]

$$U(\overline{C}, \overline{C}^*, \overline{N}, \overline{N}^*), \qquad U_1, U_2 > 0, \quad U_3, U_4 < 0, \tag{5}$$

subject to the constraint that the present value of consumption cannot exceed the present value of income. Present values are computed using a nominal interest rate r, at which the household may lend any amount up to its current assets or borrow any amount up to that which may be secured by future income. The initial nonhuman assets, fixed in money terms, are $\overline{A}$, and present and future goods, prices, and money wage rates are P, P^*, W, and W^*. Thus, U is maximized subject to:

$$P\overline{C} + \frac{P^*}{1+r}\,\overline{C}^* \leq \overline{A} + W\overline{N} + \frac{W^*}{1+r}\,\overline{N}^*. \tag{6}$$

We assume that for all positive prices a unique maximum is attained at which $\overline{C}, \overline{C}^*, \overline{N}, \overline{N}^* > 0$. Then the solution to the maximum problem gives each of these decision variables as a function of the four "prices" in (6) and $\overline{A}$. In particular, we have the current labor-supply function:

$$\overline{N} = F\left(W, \frac{W^*}{1+r}, P, \frac{P^*}{1+r}, \overline{A}\right). \tag{7}$$

The function F is homogeneous of degree zero in its five arguments, so that if the current price level P is chosen as a deflator, (7) is equivalent to:

$$\overline{N} = F\left[\frac{W}{P}, \frac{W^*}{P(1+r)}, 1, \frac{P^*}{P(1+r)}, \frac{\overline{A}}{P}\right], \tag{8}$$

The theory's implications for the signs of the derivatives of F are, in general, ambiguous, as one would expect, but on the presumption that future goods and leisure are substitutes for current leisure, that leisure is not inferior, and on the presumption that the asset effect is small, there is a presumption that:[8]

$$\partial F/\partial \mp W/P) > 0, \qquad \partial F/\partial\left(\frac{W^*}{P(1+r)}\right) < 0,$$

$$\partial F/\partial\left(\frac{P^*}{P(1+r)}\right) < 0, \qquad \partial F/\partial(\overline{A}/P) < 0. \tag{9}$$

This simple theory of a single household suggests an aggregate labor-supply function relating total man-hours supplied annually, N_t, deflated by an index of the number of households, M_t, to the empirical counterparts of the arguments of F. Let W_t be an index of money wages, P_t the GNP deflator, r_t a nominal interest rate, and A_t the market value of assets held by the household sector. Let W_t^* and P_t^* be (unobservable) indexes of the anticipated prices of the composite goods "future labor" and "future consumption" based on information available at t. Then, based on (8), we postulate the log-linear relationship:

$$\ln(N_t/M_t) = \beta_0 + \beta_1 \ln(W_t/P_t) - \beta_2 \ln\left[\frac{W_t^*}{P_t(1 + r_t)}\right]$$

$$- \beta_3' \ln\left[\frac{P_t^*}{P_t(1 + r_t)}\right] - \beta_4 \ln\left(\frac{A_t}{P_t M_t}\right), \tag{10}$$

where (cf. [9]) β_1, β_2, β_3', and β_4 are positive, and β_0 may have either sign.[9] Letting $w_t = W_t/P_t$, $w_t^* = W_t^*/P_t^*$, $a_t = A_t/P_t$, and $\beta_3 = \beta_2 + \beta_3' > 0$, and observing that $\ln(1 + r_t) \sim r_t$, (10) may be rearranged to give the more easily interpreted:

$$\ln(N_t/M_t) = \beta_0 + \beta_1 \ln(w_t) - \beta_2 \ln(w_t^*)$$
$$+ \beta_3[r_t - \ln(P_t^*/P_t)] - \beta_4 \ln(a_t/M_t). \tag{11}$$

Thus labor supply is assumed to depend on current and expected real wages, on the expected real interest rate, $r_t - \ln(P_t^*/P_t)$, and on asset holdings. The presence of both current and anticipated future wage rates in this function is very much in the spirit of modern labor economics in which the laborer is viewed as a capitalist and the decision to transfer one's supply from one market to another (which is how one typically accepts a wage cut or obtains a higher than normal increase in our economy) is recognized as an investment decision. The presence of the real interest rate (which was suggested earlier by Patinkin [1965, p. 129]) reflects the ability to transfer consumption from one period to another.

An alternative way to view the wage response indicated by (11) is in terms of a current real wage consisting of "permanent" and "transitory" components.[10] Thus the terms involving wages on the right of (11) may be written $\beta_1 \ln(w_t/w_t^*) + (\beta_1 - \beta_2) \ln(w_t^*)$. The variable w_t^* has the natural interpretation as a permanent or normal real wage rate; the elasticity of labor supply with respect to this wage may have either sign, admitting the possibility of a backward-bending supply curve. The variable $\ln(w_t/w_t^*)$ is then the ratio of current to permanent wages. If $w_t > w_t^*$, or if current wages are abnormally high, more labor is supplied than would be implied by the long-run labor-supply function. If $w_t < w_t^*$, workers are off the long-run supply curve to the left.[11]

As indicated above, there is some reason to believe that the asset effect on labor supply is minor (that β_4 is near 0), and for this reason this variable was originally excluded from our tests. Later we introduced some rather unsatisfactory "proxies," with generally poor results.[12] These results are reported in the Appendix, but for the present a_t/M_t will be dropped from the discussion. Similarly, while results with a nominal interest rate, r_t, are reported in the Appendix, our most satisfactory models exclude this variable, and it will be dropped from the discussion which follows.[13] Finally, it is often alleged that during World War II appeals to patriotism increased the supply of labor to both the military and nonmilitary sectors. To account for this, some of our tests in the Appendix introduce a zero-one dummy variable, D_t, equal to one for 1941–45 and zero otherwise.[14] Each of these variables, r_t, $\ln(a_t/M_t)$, and D_t, figures in (11) in a similar way, so that the reader should have no difficulty in determining the effect on the model of adding any, or any combination, of them.

To complete the construction of an operational supply hypothesis, it is necessary to postulate a mechanism by which the real wage and price anticipations, w_t^* and P_t^*, are formed. A full analysis of this problem involves two elements: the formulation in t of forecasts for periods $t + 1, t + 2, \ldots$, and the construction of an index number based on these forecasts. Since we know in advance that this problem has no neat or illuminating solution, there is little incentive to conduct this analysis. Instead, we simply postulate the adaptive scheme:

$$\frac{w_t^*}{w_{t-1}} = \left(\frac{w_t}{w_{t-1}^*}\right)^\lambda e^{\lambda'}, \tag{12}$$

where $0 < \lambda < 1$, and where $e^{\lambda'}$ is added to permit an anticipated trend in real wages.

In logs, (12) becomes:

$$\ln(w_t^*) = \lambda \ln(w_t) + (1 - \lambda)\ln(w_{t-1}^*) + \lambda'. \tag{13}$$

Similarly, we assume that price anticipations are formed adaptively, with the *same* reaction parameter λ:

$$\ln(P_t^*) = \lambda \ln(P_t) + (1 - \lambda)\ln(P_{t-1}^*) + \lambda''. \tag{14}$$

Since we will allude to the trend term λ'' at several points when interpreting our theoretical model and when evaluating our empirical results, we might mention that this term depends on major political and military events as well as the past development of prices. Its determination will not be examined in our study.

Using a Koyck transformation to eliminate w_t^* and P_t^* between (11), (13), and (14) (with r_t and a_t/M_t deleted from [11] as discussed above), we obtain:

$$\ln(N_t/M_t) = (\beta_0\lambda - \lambda'\beta_2 - \lambda''\beta_3) + (\beta_1 - \lambda\beta_2)\ln(w_t)$$
$$- (1 - \lambda)\beta_1\ln(w_{t-1}) + (1 - \lambda)\beta_3\ln(P_t/P_{t-1})$$
$$+ (1 - \lambda)\ln(N_{t-1}/M_{t-1}). \tag{15}$$

Estimates of the parameters of (15) and its variants are reported in section 6.[15]

Since the labor-supply equation (15) is not homogeneous in current money wages and current prices, we might say that there is "money-illusion" in the supply of labor. We should stress, however, that this behavior is not "irrational," nor does it stem from ignorance concerning the course of prices. In (15), "money-illusion" results not from a myopic concentration on money values but from our assumption that the suppliers of labor are adaptive on the level of prices, expecting a return to normal price levels regardless of current prices, and from the empirical fact that the nominal interest rate does not change in proportion to the actual rate of inflation. With these expectations, it is to a supplier's advantage to increase his current supply of labor and his current money savings when prices rise.[16]

Since (15) rests on the expectations hypotheses (13) and (14) fully as much as on the utility theory underlying (11), it is evident that one can expect (15) to obtain *only* in any economy where wages and prices might plausibly be forecast as (13) and (14) assume. In particular, a marked and sustained change in the trend rate of inflation (from one value of λ'' to another) will lead households using (14) to consistently over- or underforecast prices, in which case some other forecasting scheme would presumably be adopted. We think (13) and (14) are plausible for the period 1929–65 in the United States, although the average inflation rate is somewhat higher in the latter part of the period than in the former. But we wish to emphasize that the theory underlying (15) shows that it is altogether illegitimate to insert an arbitrary, fixed value of $\ln(P_t/P_{t-1})$ into (15) to obtain estimated long-run effects of inflation on labor supply.

3 Aggregate Marginal Productivity Condition for Labor

We assume an aggregate production function with constant elasticity of substitution, with constant returns to scale and labor-augmenting technological change. Let y_t be the real gross national product, N_t the employment variable used in the preceding section, K_t the economy's real capital stock, and Q_t an index of labor quality (in practice, a years-of-school-completed index).[17] Then:

$$y_t = [a(Q_t N_t)^{-b} + c(K_t)^{-b}]^{-1/b}, \tag{16}$$

where a and c are positive, and $b > -1$. Then $\sigma = 1/(1 + b)$ is the elasticity of substitution. The marginal productivity condition for labor implied by (16) and profit maximization under competition can be written in the form:[18]

$$w_t = aQ_t \left(\frac{y_t}{Q_t N_t}\right)^{1+b}. \tag{17}$$

Taking logs and rearranging, (17) implies:

$$\ln(N_t) + \ln(Q_t) - \ln(y_t) = \sigma \ln(a) + \sigma[\ln(w_t) - \ln(Q_t)]. \tag{18}$$

Equation (17) is not a specialization of the marginal productivity condition (2); rather, it is obtained from (2) using the equality $k_t/m_t = f^{-1}(y_t/m_t)$ given by (1). The content of (16) and (17) is, of course, the same as the content of (16) and the form of (2) obtained from (16). The main virtue of (17) (or [18]) from our point of view is that it enables us to have some control over simultaneous equations problems in estimating the supply function without requiring time series on K_t.

Equation (18) is operational, and estimates of its parameters have been obtained. The use of (18), however, rests on the hypothesis that labor is a freely variable input. To the contrary, there is a good deal of evidence that varying labor entails adjustment costs and that this leads firms to adjust gradually to the level implied by (18) rather than attempting to maintain it continually through time.[19] We shall not pursue the analysis of the maximum problem suggested by this remark but rather simply observe that it suggests a relation involving current *and* lagged output and employment, and the current real wage, which reduces to (18) under stationary levels of output and employment. Retaining the assumption of log linearity, this may be written:

$$\ln(Q_t N_t) = c_0 - c_1 \ln\left(\frac{w_t}{Q_t}\right) + c_2 \ln(y_t)$$
$$+ c_3 \ln(y_{t-1}) + c_4 \ln(Q_{t-1} N_{t-1}), \tag{19}$$

where $c_0, \ldots, c_4$ satisfy:

$$c_0 = (1 - c_4)\sigma \ln(a), \qquad c_1 = (1 - c_4)\sigma, \qquad c_2 + c_3 = 1 - c_4. \qquad (20)$$

Monotonic convergence at fixed wage rates implies:

$$0 < c_4 < 1, \qquad (21)$$

which implies that c_1 is positive. Using the last equality of (20) to eliminate c_3 puts (19) into the form:

$$\ln\left(\frac{Q_t N_t}{y_t}\right) = c_0 - c_1 \ln\left(\frac{W_t}{Q_t}\right) + c_4 \ln\left(\frac{Q_{t-1} N_{t-1}}{y_{t-1}}\right)$$
$$+ (c_2 - 1)\ln\left(\frac{y_t}{y_{t-1}}\right). \qquad (22)$$

Estimates of the parameters of (22) are reported in section 6.

It is natural to interpret the presence of real output, y_t, in (22) as a measure of the impact of aggregate demand on the labor market. This interpretation is, however, fallacious, as should be clear from the discussion in section 1. A fall (for example) in aggregate demand will involve a shift to the left in the *schedule* relating real output, y_t, and the price level, P_t. This event will appear to individual firms as a price decline or demand shift, and in response firms will vary output and labor input *simultaneously*. Our hypothesis states that, as this adjustment takes place, (22) will remain valid; it does *not* state that labor demand will respond to exogenous shifts in output.

In our empirical work, however, output is treated as an exogenous variable, which gives rise to a simultaneous equations problem. This difficulty cannot be resolved by obtaining labor demand as a function of capital stock, wages, and the price level. It is true that such an equation is entitled to be called a demand function for labor, as (22) is not, but since the price level is no more exogenous than is the level of real output a simultaneity problem would persist. In short, there is, in our view, no way to set up an aggregate labor-market model in which employment and wages are affected by other variables in the economy but do not in turn affect them.

4 Measured Unemployment

The government generates an unemployment series based on the number of persons who answer "yes" to the question: "Are you actively

seeking work?''[20] There is a strong temptation to assume that respondents to this survey take the question to mean, "Are you seeking
work at the current wage rate?''—but it is important to recognize that
this assumption is simply a hypothesis the truth of which is far from
obvious. In our model, it has been implicitly assumed that this interpretation is *not* correct, since the current way is assumed to equate
quantity demanded and quantity supplied exactly each period. In this
section, we offer an alternative hypothesis about what it is people
mean when they classify themselves as unemployed.

Our theory of the *market* behavior of suppliers of labor is developed
in section 2. We now return to this theory to see if it can also suggest
a hypothesis about responses to the employment survey, but before
doing so we make some general observations about wage rates and
unemployment. First, an unemployed worker does not generally know
what *his* current wage rate is. To find out, he must engage in a search
over a variety of employment possibilities (and there are always *some*),
always balancing the gains from further search against the gains from
accepting a job at the best wage his search has turned up to date. As
a guide in this search process, he must use some notion of his "normal" wage rate, based on wages in occupations in which he has
formerly worked, wages of comparably skilled and aged workers, and
so forth. The normal wage rate serves as a guide to job search. Once
the searcher becomes convinced that his normal wage rate is lower
than he originally thought, he may "bid" his money wage rate down
by changing occupations or moving to a new location. Indeed, it is
occupational or locational change which is the principal means
whereby individuals can, in fact, cut their money wages. The search
process may extend over a wide geographic area and may include
search among many different potential occupations. It is not only a
search for information concerning current job availabilities but concerning the future course of job development as well. Because information is limited and costly to acquire, and because action on the
basis of acquired information sometimes requires large resource investments in moving and retraining, the suppliers of labor will adjust
slowly.[21]

In the above discussion we speak as though everyone has a reasonable firm view of his "normal" wage rate. This of course is an oversimplification. However, those unemployed persons who can speak
with the least ambiguity about *their* normal wage rates are those

workers, primarily industrial, who have been *laid off,* as opposed to dismissed, from jobs formerly held. The term lay off has an explicit connotation of a temporary deviation from a normal or "permanent" situation.

These observations, none of which is original with us, suggest strongly that the labor force as measured by the employment survey consists of those who are employed *plus* those who are unemployed but would accept work at what they regard as their normal wage rates (or, equivalently, in their normal occupation). In section 2, we pointed out that the index w_t^* of anticipated future wages can be interpreted as a (trend corrected) measure of normal or permanent wages. According to (13), suppliers will regard the current real wage as normal (that is, will not revise their estimates of the height of the trend line of wages) provided $w_t = w_{t-1}^*$. Similarly, a normal price level may, using (14), be defined as P_t such that $P_t = P_{t-1}^*$. Using these definitions of normal wages and prices, we may evaluate the right side of (11) at these prices to define *normal labor supply* N_t^*:

$$\ln(N_t^*/M_t) = \beta_0 + \beta_1 \ln(w_{t-1}^*) - \beta_2 \ln(w_t^*)$$
$$+ \beta_3[r_t - \ln(P_t^*/P_{t-1}^*)] - \beta_4 \ln(a_t/M_t). \tag{23}$$

Then from (11) and (23):

$$\ln\left(\frac{N_t^*}{N_t}\right) = \beta_1 \ln\left(\frac{w_{t-1}^*}{w_t}\right) + \beta_3 \ln\left(\frac{P_{t-1}^*}{P_t}\right). \tag{24}$$

Since $\ln(N_t^*/N_t) \approx (N_t^* - N_t)/N_t^*$, the left side of (24) is a kind of unemployment rate. There are two reasons, however, why it might differ from the measured unemployment rates, U_t. First, many persons in the normal work force, N_t^*, may not report themselves as actively seeking work, especially teen-agers and women. Second, there is a frictional component of measured unemployment which cannot be captured by a variable which, like our N_t^*, is defined in terms of a representative household. Since there is good reason to believe that frictional unemployment varies positively with the nonfrictional component, it will not simply appear in (24) as an additive constant.[22] To summarize these two forces, we assume that U_t and $\ln(N_t^*/N_t)$ are linearly related:

$$U_t = g_0 + g_1 \ln(N_t^*/N_t), \qquad g_0, g_1 > 0, \tag{25}$$

then combining (24) and (25):

$$U_t = g_0 + g_1\beta_1 \ln \left(\frac{w_{t-1}^*}{w_t}\right) + g_1\beta_3 \ln \left(\frac{P_{t-1}^*}{P_t}\right). \tag{26}$$

Finally, using the Koyck transformation to eliminate w_t^* and P_t^* between (26), (13), and (14), we obtain:

$$U_t = (\lambda g_0 + \lambda' g_1\beta_1 + \lambda'' g_1\beta_3) - g_1\beta_1 \ln \left(\frac{w_t}{w_{t-1}}\right)$$

$$- g_1\beta_3 \ln \left(\frac{P_t}{P_{t-1}}\right) + (1 - \lambda)U_{t-1}. \tag{27}$$

Equation (27) will be added to (15) and (22) to form the three-equation system which is discussed further below. In our view, it adds nothing to the theory of labor-market behavior contained in (15) and (22), but it has independent interest because of its resemblance to the now famous Phillips curve. (Indeed, defining a Phillips curve as any equality linking an inflation rate and unemployment with a negative correlation, (27) *is* a Phillips curve.) The derivation of (27) from the labor-supply theory of section 2, together with a behavioral hypothesis introduced in this section, leads to some strong warnings as to the empirical performance one should expect from this Phillips curve and the policy implications one should draw from it.

First, the trend rates of change in real wages and prices (λ' and λ'') appear in the constant term of (27). Hence, there is no reason to expect stability of the Phillips curve across countries with different inflation rates or rates of productivity change, or in time series on a single country where these trends change sharply. Similarly, changes in the trend rate of inflation will induce a counteracting shift in the Phillips curve, so that (27) in no sense exhibits a "trade-off" offering arbitrarily low unemployment rates to a country which will tolerate sufficiently high rates of inflation. (It should be emphasized, of course, that these assertions about the way in which households perceive and adjust to changes in trend rates of inflation are not supported empirically by this study. We *test* (13) and (14), which refer to reactions to deviations from trend rates of change, and *assume* that expected trends would be revised, given sufficient cause.)

If we are correct in assuming that the expected trend rate of inflation, λ'', would eventually adjust to a sustained actual rate of inflation, then there is an important sense in which there is a relevant trade-off between unemployment today and unemployment tomorrow, a proposition suggested by Friedman (1968). To illustrate the point, consider figure 1. Assume that there has been a *sustained* rate of inflation of 2 percent so that the expected trend rate of inflation, λ'', equals 0.02. Let U_t^* be the steady state value of U_t from (27). This value is g_0 when $\lambda' = \Delta \ln w_t$. Now let $\Delta \ln P_t$ rise to 0.03, and let it be maintained at this new level. From figure 1 we see that unemployment will fall to U_1^*, but now the suppliers of labor are consistently underestimating the price level (recall, $P_{t-1}^* < P_t$ when $\Delta \ln P_t > 0$). Consequently, λ'' will eventually rise to 0.03, and then unemployment will return to U^* (see [27]). If, on the other hand, a sustained 2 percent inflation is followed by a *sustained* 1 percent inflation, unemployment will *increase* to U_2^*, but eventually it will return to U^*. It appears that a policy designed to sustain an inflation can temporarily reduce unemployment, but unless the higher rate of increase in prices can be permanently maintained a subsequent attempt to return to the original rate of inflation will result in an offset to the initial employment gains.[23]

5 Summary Statement of the Model
In this section, the model developed in sections 2–4 is restated in econometric form with a uniform notation. The restrictions on the

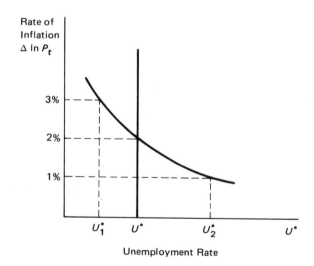

Figure 1

regression coefficients implied by the theory are summarized, and estimation is discussed.

The marginal productivity condition for labor, corresponding to (22), is:

$$\ln \left(\frac{Q_t N_t}{y_t}\right) = \beta_{10} - \beta_{11} \ln \left(\frac{w_t}{Q_t}\right) + \beta_{12} \ln \left(\frac{Q_{t-1} N_{t-1}}{y_{t-1}}\right)$$

$$+ \beta_{13} \ln \left(\frac{y_t}{y_{t-1}}\right) + u_{1t}, \tag{28}$$

where:

$$\beta_{11} > 0, \qquad 0 < \beta_{12} < 1, \tag{29}$$

and where u_{1t} is a random error.

The labor supply function corresponding to (15) is:

$$\ln \left(\frac{N_t}{M_t}\right) = \beta_{20} + \beta_{21} \ln(w_t) - \beta_{22} \ln(w_{t-1})$$

$$+ \beta_{23} \ln \left(\frac{P_t}{P_{t-1}}\right) + \beta_{24} \ln \left(\frac{N_{t-1}}{M_{t-1}}\right) + u_{2t}, \tag{30}$$

where:[24]

$$0 < \beta_{21} < \frac{\beta_{22}}{\beta_{24}}, \qquad \beta_{22} > 0, \quad \beta_{23} > 0, \quad 0 < \beta_{24} < 1, \tag{31}$$

and where u_{2t} is a random error.

The unemployment-rate function, corresponding to (27), is:

$$U_t = \beta_{30} - \beta_{31} \ln \left(\frac{w_t}{w_{t-1}}\right) - \beta_{32} \ln \left(\frac{P_t}{P_{t-1}}\right) + \beta_{33} U_{t-1} + u_{3t}, \tag{32}$$

where:

$$\beta_{31} > 0, \quad \beta_{32} > 0, \quad 0 < \beta_{33} < 1, \tag{33}$$

$$\beta_{31}/\beta_{32} = \beta_{21}/\beta_{23}, \qquad \beta_{33} = \beta_{24}, \tag{34}$$

and where u_{3t} is a random error.

The error vectors (u_{1t}, u_{2t}, u_{3t}), $t = 1, \ldots, T$, are assumed to be independent and identically distributed, with a finite covariance matrix, and a mean vector $(0, 0, 0)$. The variables Q_t, y_t, M_t, and P_t are taken to be exogenous;[25] the endogenous variables are N_t, w_t, and U_t. All three equations are overidentified.

The reduced-form equations for w_t and N_t/M_t implied by (28) and (30) are:

$$
\left.\begin{array}{l} \ln(w_t) \\[2em] \ln\left(\dfrac{N_t}{M_t}\right) \end{array}\right\} =
\begin{array}{l}
\pi_{i0} + \pi_{i1}\ln(w_{t-1}) + \pi_{i2}\,ln\left(\dfrac{P_t}{P_{t-1}}\right) \\[1.5em]
+ \pi_{i3}\ln\left(\dfrac{y_t}{M_t}\right) + \pi_{i4}\ln(Q_t) + \pi_{i5}\ln\left(\dfrac{Q_{t-1}N_{t-1}}{y_{t-1}}\right) \\[1.5em]
+ \pi_{i6}\,ln\left(\dfrac{y_t}{y_{t-1}}\right) + \pi_{i7}\ln\left(\dfrac{N_{t-1}}{M_{t-1}}\right) + \epsilon_{it},
\end{array}
$$

$$(35)$$

$$(36)$$

where $i = 1$ for (35) and $i = 2$ for (36). The restrictions on $\pi_{i0}, \ldots,$ $\pi_{i7}, \pi_{20}, \ldots, \pi_{27}$ implied by (29) and (31) are:

$$\pi_{11} > 0, \quad \pi_{12} < 0, \quad \pi_{13} > 0, \quad \pi_{15} > 0, \quad \pi_{17} > 0, \tag{37}$$

and:

$$\pi_{21} < 0, \quad \pi_{22} > 0, \quad \pi_{13} > 0, \quad \pi_{15} > 0, \quad \pi_{17} > 0. \tag{38}$$

In addition, the hypothesis that the difference equations (35) and (36) are stable, which was first introduced in the discussion of section 1, requires that the real parts of the roots of

$$x^2 - (\pi_{11} + \pi_{27})x + (\pi_{11}\pi_{27} - \pi_{17}\pi_{21}) = 0 \tag{39}$$

be less than one in absolute value. (If all the information in the structure were imposed on the reduced form, this quadratic would have one zero root and one nonzero real root.)

The estimated reduced-form coefficients will, under our assumptions, be consistent estimators of the true coefficients and asymptotically normally distributed when estimated by ordinary least squares. We have estimated the coefficients of (28), (30), and (32) using two-stage least squares, which involves using only (35) of the reduced form. The estimated structural coefficients will also be asymptotically normal. In addition to the coefficients and their standard errors, we report the multiple correlation coefficient and the Durbin–Watson statistic. The latter is included as a rough measure of serial correlation, although nothing is known about its distribution in models such as ours.

6 Results

In this section, we report estimates of the parameters of equations (28), (30), (32), (35), and (36), and tests of the hypotheses (29), (31), (33), (34), (37), and (38).[26] These estimates were obtained from aggregate, U.S. time series covering the years 1930–65. Employment is man-hours engaged in production per year in the civilian and government sectors. The money wage rate is compensation per man-hour, a measure which includes wages and salaries, and public and private fringes. The price level is the GNP implicit price deflator. Real output is GNP in constant dollars. Labor quality is an index of years of school completed. Population is an index of the number of households, corrected for changes in age-sex composition.[27]

The estimated reduced-form coefficients (equations [35] and [36]) appear in lines 4 and 5 of table 1. The five hypotheses (37) on the coefficients of the equation for $\ln(w_t)$, (35), are *all* confirmed at the .005 level using the relevant one-tail test of significance. Of the five hypotheses (38) on the coefficients of the equation for $\ln(N_t/M_t)$, (36), only one is confirmed at the .05 level: $\hat{\pi}_{17} > 0$ as predicted. The other four are neither confirmed nor contradicted, the estimated coefficients being insignificantly different from zero. Good fits were obtained on both equations; serial correlation appears to be absent. The two roots of the quadratic (39) are complex conjugates with real parts equal to 0.68, confirming (but with no statistical significance) the predicted stability of these difference equations. In summary, of the ten sign implications placed by the theory on the reduced form, six are confirmed at the .05 level; four are neither confirmed nor contradicted. Equation (35) strikingly outperforms (36).

The estimated structural coefficients (equations [28] and [30] appear on lines 1 and 2 of table 1. Tests on these coefficients are not, of course, independent of the reduced form tests just discussed, since the predictions on the structure imply those on the reduced form. But the converse of this statement is *not* true, so that a comparison of the estimates with (29) and (31) does provide additional information as to the validity of the model.

The three predictions (29) on the marginal productivity condition (28) are confirmed at the .005 level. The fit on this equation is good, and there appears to be no evidence of serial correlation. The coefficient on $\Delta \ln y_t$ is also different from zero, indicating that one cannot

Table 1 Labor Market Model 1 Reduced Form, Supply, Demand, and Unemployment Rate Estimates Using Two-Stage Least-Squares Procedures (Time Series 1930–65)

Equation and Dependent Variable	Independent Variables												
	Constant	$\ln w_t$	$\ln w_{t-1}$	$\Delta \ln P_t$	$\ln(N/M)_{t-1}$	$\ln(w_t/Q_t)$	$\ln(NQ/y)_{t-1}$	$\ln(\dot{w}_t/w_{t-1})$	$\Delta \ln y_t$	U_{t-1}	$\ln Q_t$	$\ln(y/M)_t$	R^2 and d^a
Supply: $\ln(N/M)_t$	3.81 (.93)**	1.40 (.51)**	−1.39 (.51)**	0.74 (.17)**	0.64 (.09)**	—	—	—	—	—	—	—	0.798 1.56
First order condition on labor: $\ln(NQ/y)_t$	−2.21 (.70)**	—	—	—	—	−0.46 (.12)**	0.58 (.11)**	—	−0.21 (.04)**	—	—	—	0.993 1.84
Unemployment rate function: U_t	0.042 (.010)**	—	—	−0.59 (.08)**	—	—	—	−0.41 (.24)*	—	0.80 (.05)**	—	—	0.925 1.50
Reduced form wage: $\ln w_t$	−15.65 (3.50)**	—	0.44 (.17)**	−0.22 (.07)**	−1.15 (.45)**	—	1.24 (.44)**	—	−1.22 (.45)**	—	0.27 (.55)	1.25 (.44)**	0.997 2.26
Reduced form employment: $\ln(N/M)_t$	11.60 (3.50)**	—	0.08 (.17)	0.06 (.07)	0.91 (.45)*	—	−0.39 (.44)	—	0.80 (.45)	—	−1.02 (.55)*	0.02 (.44)	0.976 1.73

Note: N = man-hours per year, M = population over fourteen years of age with constant age-sex distribution, Q = index of labor quality as measured by years of school completed, U = fraction of the labor force unemployed, w = real compensation per man-hour, P = implicit GNP deflator, y = real GNP.

a. All R^2 are adjusted for degrees of freedom.

* One-tail significance at .05 test level (except for intercepts $\Delta \ln y_t$ and $\ln Q_t$ which are two-tail tests).

** One-tail significance at .005 test level (except for intercepts $\Delta \ln y_t$ and $\ln Q_t$ which are two-tail tests).

add an additional (to [20]) restriction on the coefficients in this equation without a significant loss in explanatory power.

The five predictions (31) on the labor-supply function (30) are also all confirmed at the .005 level. The fit on this equation is reasonably good. There is some slight indication of positive serial correlation.

Estimates of the employment-rate function (32) are reported on line 3 of table 1. Three of the four predictions (33), which are independent of any implications tested elsewhere, are confirmed at the .005 level; the fourth is confirmed at the .05 level. The estimated ratios $\hat{\beta}_{31}/\hat{\beta}_{32}$ and $\hat{\beta}_{21}/\hat{\beta}_{23}$, which are predicted to be equal in (34), are, respectively, 0.70 and 1.89. To get a rough idea of the significance of this difference, one may use the approximation

$$ SE\left(\frac{\hat{\beta}_{31}}{\hat{\beta}_{32}}\right) \approx \frac{SE(\hat{\beta}_{31})}{\hat{\beta}_{32}} , $$

where $SE(\ )$ denotes standard error, which is valid for large samples and similarly for the standard error of $\hat{\beta}_{21}/\hat{\beta}_{23}$. This gives standard error estimates of 0.41 and 0.69, respectively. Hence it seems unlikely that the observed difference is significant at the .05 level. Finally, $\hat{\beta}_{33}$ and $\hat{\beta}_{24}$, whose equality is also predicted in (34), are, respectively, 0.80 and 0.64 with standard errors of .05 and .09, respectively. In summary, (32) is a satisfactory Phillips curve, and, further, the predicted link between (32) and the rest of the model appears to be consistent with the data.

In reviewing these results, the reader should be aware, as we are, that the absence of small sample tests and the arbitrary nature of the choice of significance levels makes the test results less easy to interpret than our rather formal summary might suggest. Further, as discussed below, many variants of the basic model were also tested. Finally, many predictions of "our" theory are also predictions of virtually any plausible theory (for example, the prediction that unemployment rates are positively correlated with their own lagged values). But we wish to emphasize that the configuration of signs predicted by (29), (31), and (33) is only one of $(2)^6(3)^3 = 1728$ possible outcomes. The theory has thus provided us with an extremely sharp prediction on the way the variables examined are related, and these predicted relationships have been confirmed by the 1930–65 data.

As a second, informal, way of evaluating our results as well as an aid in interpreting them, it will be useful to compare them with results of previous studies with which ours overlap. First, from the estimated supply-function parameters, one may compute long- and short-run elasticities with respect to the real (or money) wage rate. The estimated long-run elasticity is $(1 - \hat{\beta}_{24})^{-1}(\hat{\beta}_{21} - \hat{\beta}_{22}) = (1.40 - 1.39)/0.36 = 0.03$, or essentially zero. This finding indicates that the neoclassical growth model assumption of a zero labor-supply elasticity is approximately correct. Further, the Keynesian-type assumption of a relatively elastic short-run supply schedule is also confirmed, using the estimate $\hat{\beta}_{21} = 1.40$.

From the marginal productivity condition for labor, the statistic $(1 - \hat{\beta}_{12})^{-1}\hat{\beta}_{11} = 0.46/0.42 = 1.09$ is an estimate of the aggregate elasticity of substitution. This estimate is broadly consistent with the variety of cross-sectional estimates which are available and generally higher than other time-series estimates.[28] Since aggregation introduces increased possibilities for substitution in consumption between goods of different factor intensities as well as substitution in production of each good, this latter result is perhaps not surprising. The long-run elasticity of employment with respect to output has been constrained in (28) to be unity. The short-run elasticity has been left free to vary, however, and is estimated to be $1 - \hat{\beta}_{13} = 0.79$. In the sense that labor inputs appear to be quasi-fixed with respect to short-run output changes, this finding is consistent with those of Wilson and Eckstein (1964), Kuh (1966), and McGuire (1968), although since different variables are controlled for in each case this fact provides little information.

The estimated reduced-form equation for the real wage rate provides a third point of contact with earlier studies.[29] The effect of inflation on real wages has been a subject of concern to economists for some time. This concern has been motivated by interest in the wage-lag doctrine according to which real wages fall during inflationary periods. Hamilton (1952), Hansen (1925), and Mitchell (1903), each studying a different historical period, all argued for the wage-lag hypothesis, and all of these writers suggest that the wage lag results from some form of "money-illusion" or contract fixity.

Mitchell (1903), and later Lerner (1956), both argued that the decline in real wages during the Civil War was a result of monetary inflation. Later Kessel and Alchian (1959) reinterpreted the northern experience in the Civil War, arguing that real, not monetary factors, account for the decline in real wages between 1860 and 1865 (without, however, controlling simultaneously for real and monetary variables). Examining a different historical period, these writers (Kessel and Alchian 1960) were again unable to uncover any evidence in support of the wage-lag hypothesis. For the post-World War II inflation, they examined profit rates in high labor cost industries relative to profit rates in low labor cost industries, and they could not find a systematic difference in the behavior of profits in the two groups of industries. Our empirical results are not consistent with these findings. For the period 1930–65, we find that the partial effect of inflation on real wages is negative and quantitatively significant. A 10 percent increase in prices will result in a 2.2 percent decline in real wages, and this result is based on a model which controls for real factors in the form of the variable output per capita, (y_t/M_t).[30]

To this point, we have been concerned exclusively with a single model, which has been found to be consistent with the 1929–65 data we used, and, in a general way, consistent with several previous related empirical studies. As remarked at several points above, this model is but one variant of the class of models suggested by our theory. Other variants are obtained by adding different combinations of asset variables, nominal interest rates, and a dummy variable to control for wartime phenomena. In addition, models based on a different price-and-wage expectations hypothesis were tested. These results are tabulated and discussed briefly in the Appendix.

There are three important reasons for including these additional results. First, since our discussion of the tests in this section emphasizes the small probability that our predictions could have been confirmed "by chance," we are anxious to make clear that the predicted configuration of coefficient signs is confirmed in all the variants estimated. Second, our selection of the model reported in this section as the "best" of those estimates was made on informal and tenuous grounds. Finally, many coefficient estimates vary rather widely depending on which other variables are included, so that the standard errors reported in table 1 overstate considerably the accuracy of these estimates.

7 Summary and Conclusions

The aim of this study has been to construct and test an aggregative model of the U.S. labor market. On the demand side of this market, we employed a variant of the widely used marginal productivity condition based on a constant elasticity of substitution production function. The aggregate supply function tested was suggested by a Fisherian two-period model of a representative household. This theory views suppliers of labor as reacting primarily to three variables: an anticipated "normal" or "permanent" real wage rate, which corresponds to the wage rate in the usual one-period analysis of the labor-leisure choice and has a negligible effect on labor supply; the deviation of the current real wage from this normal rate, which has a strong, positive effect on labor supply; and the deviation of the price level from its perceived "normal" trend, which also has a strong positive effect on labor supply.

This labor-supply theory has been shown to resolve two apparent contradictions in the economic theory of labor markets. First, as stressed in the introduction and in section 1, it is consistent both with the observed wage inelasticity of labor supply in the long run and with short-run fluctuations in employment, which require an elastic labor supply. Second, by regarding the labor-supply choice as depending on a multiperiod decision problem, "money illusion," in the sense of a supply function which is *not* homogeneous of zero degree in *current* money wages and prices, is reconciled with rational behavior on the part of households.

As a corollary to the supply theory utilized in this paper, the survey-measured labor force (as used to compute unemployment rates) is viewed *not* as an effective market supply, part of which cannot find employment, but rather as the supply of labor which *would be forthcoming* at perceived normal wages and prices. Measured unemployment (more exactly, its nonfrictional component) is then viewed as consisting of persons who regard the wage rates at which they could currently be employed as temporarily low and who therefore choose to wait or search for improved conditions rather than to invest in moving or occupational change. The view that nonfrictional unemployment is, in this sense, "voluntary" does not of course imply that high measured-unemployment rates are socially costless. Rather, it implies that economic fluctuations are costly, not simply because they induce idleness but because they lead workers as well as capitalists to make investments (in moving, training, and so forth) on the basis of perceived rates of return which cannot in fact be sustained.

We conclude with a brief mention of two problems which we regard as central to an understanding of labor markets and which our study *cannot* be used to answer. One is tempted to use our estimated structural equations to study the dynamics of the labor-market response to changes in prices and output. As we have stressed at several points above, however, this question is illegitimate: movements over time in labor-market variables will be determined simultaneously with changes in other sectors. Thus, while we know that our model is consistent with a gradual approach to full employment equilibrium, we cannot say whether or not the speed of approach is consistent with the observed business cycle. Second, our model emphasizes the crucial role of expectations formation, while testing only the very crudest expectations model. We have used an adaptive scheme which will clearly hold only under reasonably stable rates of price increase. To define what is meant by reasonable stability, and to discover how expectations are revised when such stability ceases to obtain, seem to us to be a crucial, unresolved problem.

Appendix   Additional Results

As indicated in section 6, several versions of the basic model have been tested. We refer to the model reported in section 6 as model 1; models 2 through 9 are described below.

Our basic model omits interest rates, real nonhuman assets per family, and the wartime zero-one dummy variable from the supply equation. Given our expectations assumption, each variable must be introduced by using both the current and one-period lagged value. In models (2) through (4), each variable is introduced separately.

We have also experimented with an alternative expectations hypothesis. Models (5) through (8) are the same as models (1) through (4) except that anticipated real wages and prices are formed in the following simple ways:

$$\ln w_t^* = \lambda \ln w_t + (1 - \lambda)\ln w_{t-1} + \lambda', \tag{A1}$$

and

$$\ln P_t^* = \mu \ln P_t + (1 - \mu)\ln P_{t-1} + \mu', \tag{A2}$$

where $0 \le \lambda \le 1$, and $0 \le \mu \le 1$, and λ' and μ' are the expected trend rates of growth. Substituting (A1) and (A2) into the labor-supply equation (11), we obtain a different equation from (15). In particular, except for w_{t-1} and P_{t-1}, there are no other lagged independent variables nor does the lagged dependent variable appear. With this formulation there remains considerable statistical evidence as indexed by the d statistic of serial correlation in the residuals.

Model (9) is the same as model (1) except that a time variable is added to the first-order condition and both reduced forms. We interpret this variable as an index of technical change.

Space limitations prevent us from discussing each estimated model in as complete a detail as we have done for model (1). However, tables similar to table 1 are contained in the Lucas–Rapping chapter in Phelps *et al.* (in press), and each reader is free to tabulate or summarize those aspects of our results which he thinks are most relevant. We have chosen to summarize our statistical results by stressing the estimated short- and long-run elasticity of labor supply and the effect of inflation on the supply of labor. The relevant supply elasticities for all of the models—(1) through (9)—are summarized in table A1. We will also summarize the overall "goodness-of-fit" of our models by tabulating the number (and proportion) of statistically significant reduced-form estimates as well as a separate tabulation for the structural estimates. This is done in table A2.

When the Moody's Aaa interest rate and its lagged value are added to the supply equation (model [2]), the short- and long-run supply elasticity is practically unchanged as compared to that obtained in model (1). And since the estimated effect of inflation is also unchanged, it would appear that omitting the interest rate variable does not seriously bias the remaining coefficient estimates. However, we do not

Table A1 Some Highlights of Supply Equation Estimates for Models (1) through (9)

Model	Short-Run Labor Supply Elasticity	Long-Run Labor Supply Elasticity	Effect of Inflation on Labor Supply	Variables Held Constant
1	1.40**	0.03	0.74**	$(N/M)_{t-1}$
2	1.35**	0.03	0.70**	$(N/M)_{t-1}, r_t, r_{t-1}$
3	0.78**	0.12	0.49**	$(N/M)_{t-1}, D_t, D_{t-1}$
4	1.12*	0.58	0.68**	$(N/M)_{t-1}, a_t/M_t, a_{t-1}/M_{t-1}$
5	3.93**	0.03	1.14**	—
6	3.59**	0.04	1.03**	r_t
7	2.11**	0.10	0.55*	D_t
8	2.93**	−0.07	1.04**	a_t/M_t
9	1.13*	0.01	0.72**	$(N/M)_{t-1}$

* One-tail significance at .05 level.
** One-tail significance at .005 level.

Table A2 Summary of Estimates for Models (1) through (9)

Model	No. of Significant Reduced Form Estimates Compared to Total	No. of Significant Structural Estimates Compared to Total
1	6/10	9/9
2	5/14	9/11
3	5/14	10/11
4	1/14	8/11
5	5/8	7/7
6	7/10	7/8
7	6/10	8/8
8	3/10	7/8
9	6/10	9/9

attach special importance to this result because we have serious reservations concerning the meaning of the Aaa rate as an index of the rate relevant to households.

When the current and lagged interest rate variables are replaced by the current and lagged wartime dummy variable (model [3]), the results are broadly consistent with our supply theory. But there is an important difference between model (3) and model (1) in that the estimated short-run real wage elasticity and the inflation-elasticity estimates are smaller in model (3) than in model (1). While the point estimates are significantly different in an economic sense, they are not significantly different from each other as the 5 percent t-test level. The point estimates on the dummy coefficient indicate a quantitatively important wartime effect—the supply of labor rose by 12 percent because of the war. This may reflect a patriotism effect.

We have made no attempt to construct our own nonhuman household-wealth series. Instead we have used three different readily available series on nominal, nonhuman wealth—and deflated these series by the implicit GNP deflator and by our population index to obtain (a_t/M_t) in (11). Model (4) is based on the Meltzer wealth series.[31] The Meltzer wealth series was obtained directly from Professor Meltzer (1963). This series is for reproducible wealth less government reproducible wealth plus government debt. It covers the period 1930–58, and, therefore, models (4) and (8) are based on only twenty-nine observations. In model (4) the addition of nonhuman wealth per capita increases the estimated long-run supply elasticity. However, this finding is based on a model in which the estimated asset coefficients are insignificantly different from zero in both the structural equations and the reduced forms.

Estimates of the real wage and inflation coefficients for models (5)–(8) are summarized in table A1. On the whole, the assumption that only the present and the recent past influence the formation of expectations generates larger estimates of short-run supply elasticities than were previously obtained.

Model (9) yields supply elasticities similar to model (1). An examination of the estimated first-order condition indicates that all of the production-function conclusions are practically unchanged when a time variable is added.

In table A2 we show the ratio of the number of significant reduced-form and structural coefficients to the total number estimated. In this summary, we omit all of the coefficients for which our theory does not predict the signs. This includes the estimated coefficients for the intercept, the change-in-income variable, the labor-quality variable, and the time variable.

The summary results in table A2 suggest to us that among a broad class of models using the same general body of time-series data, "significant" results are almost always obtained. And, broadly speaking, conclusions concerning the effect of transitory and permanent wage changes as well as inflation on the supply of labor remain intact regardless of which model we use.

Notes

1. Leaving aside studies of the relative supply of labor to individual industries or firms, most of the empirical work on the supply of labor can be separated into three categories. Studies of hours of work per unit of time per member of the labor force have found a negative relationship between wage rates and hours supplied, especially for male members of the labor force. This result is reported by Lewis (1956), Finegan (1962), Jones (1963), Kosters (1966), and Rosen (1969). A second group of studies has examined the relationship between participation rates and wage rates. These have largely been cross-sectional studies, and they have reported a positive wage-rate effect for women and a small negative effect for men. The reader will find these results in studies by Douglas (1934), Long (1958), Mincer (1962, pp. 63–105), Bowen and Finegan (1965), and Cain (1966). To the best of our knowledge, no attempt has been made to combine all of the existing hours per head and participation-rate studies in such a way as to infer an aggregate supply of labor schedule for a population fixed in terms of its demographic characteristics.

The above-mentioned studies represent attempts to isolate the long-run effect of a permanent change in real wages on labor supply. On the other hand, a third class of labor-supply studies has investigated the short-run cyclical behavior of labor supply as measured by participation rates and their relationship to unemployment rates. These studies suggest a procyclical behavior in the supply of labor. See Mincer's summary of these studies (1966) and recent papers by Black and Russell (1966), Tella (1966), and Cain and Mincer (1969).

2. A bargaining interpretation of the Phillips relationship is given by Eckstein and Wilson (1962) and Perry (1964). Others have attempted to motivate the Phillips curve by appealing to an "out-of-equilibrium" adjustment function. This was the original motivation suggested by Phillips (1958) and later Lipsey (1960), and this view is extended in a recent paper by Phelps (1968). For a discussion of the Phillips relationship and the joint influence of collective bargaining and monetary-fiscal policy, see Bronfenbrenner and Holzman (1963). See also Bronfenbrenner's discussion of government wage-price guidelines (1967).

3. Historically, much has been made of the distinction between "voluntary" and "involuntary" unemployment. When formulated carefully, however, this distinction turns out to be purely formal and serves only to obscure the important distinction between models in which labor-market equilibrium implies a particular (full employment) level of output *independent of the level of aggregate demand* and models in which this implication does not hold. Our model is in the latter class. Without attempting a definitive review of the post-Keynesian literature, we wish to point out that many writers appear to treat labor markets as being in equilibrium throughout the cycle. Patinkin (1965, p. 341) interprets Modigliani (1951, pp. 186–239) in this way and attributes to Lange (1945) this interpretation of Keynes. After seeking to differentiate himself from those who insist on labor suppliers being "on their supply curves" at each point in time, he himself attributes "rigidities" to the fact that "individual decisions . . . respond only 'stickily' to market changes" (p. 343). Similarly Rees (1951) attributes wage rigidities to the *unwillingness* of employers to cut money wages. Of course, Patinkin is correct in asserting that it is not *necessary* to construct models in which labor markets are continuously cleared, but, as his discussion of the Keynesian literature makes clear, the continuous-equilibrium view is in no sense a radical departure from the views of earlier theorists, nor does it have, in itself, any obvious normative consequences.

4. While the effect of collective bargaining on *relative* union/nonunion wage rates has been established (at various points in time) by Lewis (1963), the bargaining effect on the aggregate wage rate (weighted average of union and nonunion rates) remains uncertain and, indeed, largely unexplored. Since successful union activity will reduce employment in the unionized sector, releasing workers to the rest of the economy, there is not even a presumption

that the union effect on the aggregate wage rate is positive. For example, if the demand elasticity for labor is unity in both sectors (union and nonunion) and if labor is inelastically supplied, unions will have *no* effect on either aggregate employment or the average wage rate. Even if one assumes an inelastic labor demand in the unionized sector, the union effect on wages at the peak of union power (the 1950s, when 25 percent of the work force was unionized and the relative union/nonunion wage was, according to Lewis, 1.15) is estimated at less than 4 percent. Since the percentage of the labor force covered by collective bargaining agreements has varied from 9 percent in 1929 to a high of about 25 percent in 1953, time-series analyses of the impact of bargaining on real wages has been possible. The few empirical studies we have examined suggest that collective bargaining may have a modest upward impact on aggregate real wages, but most of the observed secular and cyclical variation in this series is explained by competitive market forces. This conclusion is suggested by Rees (1959) in his study of real wages in manufacturing for the period 1889–1957, and by Cagan (1968) who also examined the manufacturing wage data for the period 1890–1961.

5. Our analysis will be restricted to the household decision problem involving the choice between market work and leisure. This is admittedly an oversimplification of a more complex decision problem involving choices among market work, leisure, homework, and schoolwork. Our approach obviates the need for discussion of an implicit homework wage rate, and it also permits us to suppress the formal introduction of an explicit schoolwork wage rate. For a fuller statement of these issues, see Mincer (1962), Cain (1966), and Kosters (1966). It should also be stressed that since we are defining *leisure* to include *all* uses of time except remunerative labor, this term covers a variety of activities: for example, schooling, job seeking, retirement, and housework.

6. We are aware that in treating the population as exogenous we are failing to explain the single most important factor accounting for the secular growth in the U.S. labor force (on this point see Easterling 1965). Yet this assumption does not in any way lessen the usefulness of our model in understanding the dynamics of labor supply and in separating short- from long-run labor supply responses to once-and-for-all real wage rate changes.

7. Liviatan has shown (1966) that the common procedure of collapsing an *n*-period decision problem into a two-dimensional problem raises the usual index number problems. These problems are neither more nor less severe than those which arise when, say, the price level is measured by an index, a procedure quite common in economics.

8. To obtain information on the signs of the partial derivatives of the labor-supply function F given in (7) from the hypothesis that the household maximizes (5) subject to (6), we follow the standard procedure of expressing each derivative as the sum of two terms: a Slutsky, or substitution, term and a term representing the asset (income) effect of a price change. Let $K(N, W)$ denote the substitution effect of a wage change on current labor supply, and so forth.

Then:

$$\partial F/\partial W = K(N,W) + N\frac{\partial F}{\partial A} ,$$

$$\partial F/\partial \left(\frac{W^*}{1+r}\right) = K\left(N, \frac{W^*}{1+r}\right) + N^*\frac{\partial F}{\partial A} ,$$

$$\partial F/\partial P = K(N, P) - C\frac{\partial F}{\partial A} ,$$

$$\partial F/\partial \left(\frac{P^*}{1+r}\right) = K\left(N, \frac{P^*}{1+r}\right) - C^*\frac{\partial F}{\partial A} ,$$

The only implication of the utility maximization hypothesis for the signs of the individual terms is: $K(N, W) > 0$. The additional hypothesis that consumption in both periods and future leisure each are substitutes for current leisure implies that the other three substitution terms are negative. Finally, we suppose that $\partial F/\partial A$ is negative but negligible. Combining these hypotheses yields (9).

9. The implication of our theory is that a change in the wage rate will elicit a particular labor-supply response from the household. As a practical matter, of course, there is no single wage rate. Instead, wages vary according to occupation, education, sex, race, geography, and religion. When labor-supply responses vary with these characteristics, relative as well as absolute real wages will influence the aggregate supply of labor. It is assumed that over our sample period, changes in the relative wage structure are such that equation (10) remains a good approximation of the true relation among the included variables.

10. The distinction between the labor-supply effect of a permanent as opposed to a transitory real wage-rate change serves as the basis of Friedman's (1962) explanation of the unusually large increase in the supply of labor during World War II. To the best of our knowledge, Friedman was the first to suggest the empirical usefulness of the permanent-transitory wage-rate distinction when studying the supply of labor. In studying the labor supply of married women, Mincer (1962), Cain (1966), and Cain and Mincer (1969) have distinguished between the effect of permanent and transitory variables on the supply of married women. But their model and objectives are different from ours. We do not address ourselves to the problems of the intrahousehold allocation of leisure and work, and it is difficult to compare directly our model with models primarily designed to explain the labor-supply behavior of the female member of the household. Nonetheless, we should stress that they have distinguished between the effect of permanent and transitory variables on the supply of female labor.

11. Like Friedman's original permanent income hypothesis (1957), this view of labor supply has life-cycle as well as business-cycle implications. For example, the theory "predicts" that workers will concentrate their labor

supply in years of peak earnings, consuming leisure in larger than average amounts in childhood and old age. A systematic development and testing of such implications is beyond the scope of this paper.

12. Our assumption that the nonhuman asset effect is small is consistent with some but not all of the available literature. Using a nonemployment income variable which includes reported income from owned assets, transfer payments, and other items, Bowen and Finegan (1965) obtained a negative and significant coefficient when regressing participation rates on this variable. They obtained this result for the years 1940, 1950, and 1960 and for several different age-sex groups. But another cross-sectional study by Kosters (1966) who used the 1960 0.1 percent sample was considerably less successful in identifying a nonemployment income effect on male hours of work. Kosters discusses the measurement problems occasioned by the use of census nonemployment income data as a proxy for income from nonhuman assets.

13. In the model reported in section 6 and in many of those reported in the Appendix, either the asset variable or the nominal interest rate or both has been excluded from the regression equation for labor supply. In these cases the link between (9) and the version of (11) with r_t and $\ln(a_t/M_t)$ omitted needs clarification. A household's nonhuman wealth will consist of claims to future income, partly fixed in money terms and partly in real terms. (For the representative household, A is, of course, positive.) An increase in future prices P^* will then induce an increase, less than proportional, in the current market value of assets. In regressions which include an asset variable which measures market value, this capital gain or loss effect of price changes will be controlled for. Since the gain in assets is positively related to P^*, and assets are negatively related to current labor supply, the negative effect of P^* on current labor supply will be *accentuated* in regressions omitting $\ln(a_t/M_t)$. Hence β_3 is positive, whether or not an asset variable appears in (11). When the interest rate r_t is omitted, a similar issue is raised. The nominal rate may vary with P_t^*/P_t, so that β_3 is biased toward zero in regressions with r_t excluded. There is some theoretical ground for believing this effect to be present, but there is little evidence that nominal interest rates adjust to expected inflation with sufficient speed to maintain a constant real rate. Indeed, the evidence indicates a very slow adjustment. Fisher (1930, p. 418), who empirically investigated the relationship between interest rates and the change in prices for the United States and Great Britain, concluded: "The results suggest no direct and consistent connection of any real significance exists between P' [*the actual rate of price change*] and i [*the rate of interest*]." (The definitions in brackets were supplied by us.) A more recent study by Sargent (1969) corroborates Fisher's findings.

14. Insofar as D_t indexes patriotism, it reflects a rightward shift in the supply function, resulting in increased employment and lower average wages (other things equal). We will also regard D_t as an admittedly imperfect control for the effect of the draft. As a measure of the effect of the draft, it has a positive effect on employment and an uncertain effect on the wage rate. If all of the

reluctant military personnel are from the nonmarket sector, the draft is simply a leftward shift in market demand with a depressing effect on wages. On the other extreme, if all of the coerced military personnel are from the nonmilitary market sector, the effect on average wages will depend on both the elasticity of labor demand in the nonmilitary sector and the difference between military pay rates and market rates. The effect of D_t will thus depend in an unknown way on patriotism and draft forces. It is our judgment that the net effect on wages will be negative; the effect on employment is positive.

15. One need not view (12) and (13) as exact equations. We will subsequently introduce an error term in (15) and assume that the errors are serially independent. Under this assumption, error terms in (12) and (13) are necessarily serially dependent, and this dependence is broken by the Koyck transformation.

16. The assumption that price expectations are formed on the (trend corrected) *level* of prices as opposed to their rate of change is crucial to the predictions of our model, since it accounts for the "switch" in sign on the coefficients of the inflation term in passing from (11) to (14). The appropriateness of this assumption is, of course, an empirical question, but we wish to point out that the route we have taken has a long history. To illustrate, we quote first from Hicks (1946, pp. 270–71): "In order to explain the rigidity of wages, we have to assume in the parties to the wage bargain some sense of normal prices, hardly distinguished (perhaps) from 'just' prices. The rigidity of wages extends over precisely that time—it may be quite a long time—during which the parties concerned persuade themselves that changes in related prices (whether prices of the products of labour, or of the things labour buys) are temporary changes. Once they become convinced that these changes are permanent changes, there *is* a tendency for wages to change; in situations of extreme instability, when they have lost their sense of normal prices, negotiators have recourse to automatic sliding scales and the rigidity of money wages ceases altogether." Our treatment differs from Hicks' in its asymmetrical handling of suppliers and demanders. A still closer forerunner of our model is provided by Tobin (1952, p. 581): "Labor may have inelastic price expectations; a certain 'normal' price level, or range of price levels, may be expected to prevail in the future, regardless of the level of current prices. With such expectations, it is clearly to the advantage of wage earners to have, with the same current real income, the highest possible money income. For the higher their money incomes the greater will be their money savings and, therefore, their expected command over future goods."

In his celebrated study of hyperinflation, Cagan (1956) assumed that the expected rate of price change was an exponentially weighted average of past inflation rates. Since his application involved monthly inflation rates comparable to the rate of price change per decade in our sample, there is no inconsistency between his practice and ours. Previous studies which used expectations adaptive on price *levels* include Nerlove's study of the supply of farm products (1958), and Lewis's study of union/nonunion wage determination (1963). More recent studies, such as Sargent (1969), have used hypotheses permitting both "extrapolative" (like Cagan's) and "regressive" (like ours) components in the expected inflation rate. In short, there is no empirical consensus on the formation of price expectations, nor indeed should there be, since inflation policies of governments vary over countries and over time and households are obliged to vary the way they form expectations accordingly.

17. While our basic model includes only labor-embodied technical change, we do not rule out other sources of technical change. In the Appendix we present results based on a constant elasticity of substitution production function which contains not only labor-embodied technical change but a neutral source of technical advance introduced by multiplying equation (16) by $e^{\alpha t}$.

18. See Arrow *et al.* (1961).

19. The investment in firm specific on-the-job training is perhaps the single most important factor making it costly for firms to continuously adjust their work forces. Both Oi (1962) and Becker (1964) develop this argument to explain the quasi-fixity of labor inputs. Schramm (1967) treats labor and capital inputs symmetrically as partially fixed factors and finds that in the manufacturing sector lagged values of *both* variables affect current input decisions. There is also considerable evidence to suggest that the employment/output ratio rises during downturns and falls during upturns, an observation implying labor adjustment costs. However, there are wide differences among studies in the estimates of the short-run elasticity of labor inputs with respect to output. Using post-World War II quarterly data, estimates between 0.30 and 0.55 have been obtained by Wilson and Eckstein (1964) and Kuh (1965, 1966), but the estimated elasticity is quite sensitive to what is held constant in the regressions. McGuire (1968) has carefully documented this fact and has obtained estimates in the range 0.8 and 0.9 on quarterly data.

20. The unemployment series most often used is based on a census survey. Presently, unemployment is defined as follows: "Unemployed persons comprise all persons who did not work during the survey week, who made specific efforts to find a job within the past four weeks, and who were available for work during the survey week (except for temporary illness). Also included as unemployed are those who did not work at all, were available for work, and (*a*) were waiting to be called back to a job from which they had been laid off; or (*b*) were waiting to report to a new wage or salary job within 30 days" (quoted from U.S. Department of Labor 1968, p. 48).

21. Perhaps the clearest statement of the view that unemployment is essentially employment at job search can be found in Alchian and Allen (1967, pp. 494–524) and Mortensen (in press). While Alchian and Allen emphasize information lacunae and search costs as the source of lagged wage adjustments, another paper by Holt and David (1966) stresses a kind of psychological resistance to wage cuts in the form of an aspiration-level model which is combined with a search process to generate unemployment. The Alchian–Allen model is closely related to an earlier paper on information by Stigler (1961), while the Holt–David view is very much in the spirit of Simon's work (1957).

22. The argument that frictional unemployment and nonfrictional unemployment do not additively determine aggregate unemployment is developed by Gaver and Rapping (1966) in terms of a stochastic job-search model with jobs being simultaneously created and destroyed.

23. Our argument that there is no *long*-run employment-inflation trade off is based on theoretical considerations. In another study (Lucas and Rapping, in press), we attempt to empirically verify this position within the framework of a more general price expectations model than equation (14).

24. The prediction that $\beta_{21} > 0$ follows from considerations raised in section 1 rather than in section 2: since β_{21} is the short-run labor-supply elasticity, it must be positive for the aggregate supply function of goods to have the upward slope assumed in section 2. The inequality $\beta_{21} < \beta_{22}/\beta_{24}$ follows from $\beta_2 > 0$, which is implied by the argument of section 2. Also note that since $\beta_{22} > 0$ follows from other predictions in (31), (31) contains five (not six) independent restrictions.

25. We have already discussed the assumption that y_t and P_t are exogenous. On the other hand, we think of M_t and Q_t as predetermined variables. The current population and its quality are the result of past decisions which, of course, depend in part on past real wage rates.

26. Formally, we regard (28), (30), and (32), together with the assumptions on the error vectors, as a maintained hypothesis, and we wish to test the hypothesis that the parameters β_{11}, β_{12}, β_{21}, β_{22}, β_{24}, β_{31}, β_{32}, and β_{33} lie in that subset of nine-dimensional space satisfying (29), (31), (33), and (34). (The matter is further complicated if we test rather than assume the serial independence of the errors.) In lieu of a generally accepted test of hypotheses of this sort, we shall summarize and evaluate our results from several points of view using the customary "*t*-statistics" as measures of precision. Hence our conclusion that our model is "consistent with the 1929–65 data . . . and with several related empirical studies" should be regarded as a careful but informal conclusion on our part, *not* as a consequence of any single, formal, statistical test.

27. The data used in this study are available upon request. The series on measured unemployment is from Lebergott (1964) and the Manpower Report (U.S. Department of Labor 1967, p. 201). The Moody's Aaa rate (used later) is from the President's Economic Report (Council of Economic Advisers 1967, p. 272). Gross national product, the implicit GNP deflator, compensation per full-time equivalent employee, and persons engaged were all taken from Survey of Current Business sources (U.S. Department of Commerce 1966, pp. 2, 90, 102, 110, 158). The man-hour series is the product of the number of persons engaged in production reported by the Department of Commerce times annual hours worked per year by full-time employees for the whole economy as reported by Denison (1962, p. 85). Denison's series was extended beyond 1958 by regressing his series on the Bureau of Labor Statistics (BLS) weekly manufacturing hours series (U.S. Department of Labor Statistics 1966, p. 44) for the years 1929–58. Then, this regression equation was used in conjunction

with known BLS manufacturing hours data to predict hours for the whole economy for 1959–65. Compensation per man-hour was obtained by dividing annual compensation per full-time equivalent employee by annual man-hours worked by full-time employees. The index of labor quality is taken from Denison (1962, p. 85). His data were available from 1929–58 and were extended by a simple linear extrapolation. The aggregate supply of labor, N_t, was deflated by a variable which accounts for changes in the total supply of labor due solely to changes in the total number of households *as well as* the joint age-sex distribution of the population. The nominal nonhuman asset variable, A_t (used later), should be deflated by an index of the number of households only. However, because our age-sex corrected population series was roughly proportional to the population over fourteen years of age, we deflated both N_t and A_t by the same index, M_t. In constructing M_t, let L_{0i} = the labor force in the zero period of the ith age-sex group, and let P_{0i} = the population of the ith group again in the zero period. Then we define our population index as

$$M_t = \sum_{i=1}^{n} \left(\frac{L_{0i}}{L_0}\right)\left(\frac{P_{1i}}{P_{0i}}\right)$$

where

$$L_0 = \sum_{i=1}^{n} L_{0i}.$$

This index has two simple and equivalent interpretations. First, it is a weighted average of the percentage increase in the population of each age-sex cohort, the weights being the percentage of the base year labor force who are members of the particular age-sex group. Second, writing the index as

$$M_t = \frac{1}{L_0} \sum_{i=1}^{n} \left(\frac{L_{0i}}{P_{0i}}\right) P_{1i},$$

we interpret it as the relative increase in the labor force that would have occurred because of the change in population if the base period participation rates had remained unchanged. The index i covers six age-sex groups—males and females separately for age groups 14–20, 20–65, and 65 and over. We used the 1947–49 arithmetic average of reported participation rates taken from the Manpower Report (U.S. Department of Labor 1965, p. 202). The figures include the armed forces and institutional population. The population data are taken from Current Population Reports (U.S. Department of Commerce), and these data include estimates of overseas military personnel. Prior to 1940 it was assumed that there were 150,000 overseas personnel; subsequent to that date the above sources included overseas personnel.

28. Both the time-series and cross-section CES production function studies are summarized and discussed by Nerlove (1965). Additional CES time-series production-function estimates can be found in a study by Lucas (1964).

29. One should be cautious in interpreting this equation. In particular, although the coefficient of ln Q_t is apparently near zero, this should *not* be interpreted

to mean that changes in labor quality do not affect real wages, since our real income variable already includes the secular wage effect of improvements in labor quality as well as other sources of technical change. For this reason there is an important sense in which our model does not "explain" the secular growth in real wages. Similarly, note that the population variable like the income variable also affects real wage movements but is left unexplained in our model.

30. Kessel and Alchian (1962) have argued that even when inflation is fully anticipated, real wages may still decline, ceteris paribus, because firms will shift to more capital-intensive processes which reduces the demand for labor.

31. Similar results were obtained with the Ando–Brown (1964, p. 20) and Chow (1966) series. Upon request, results using these series are available.

References

Alchian, A., and Allen, W. *University Economics*. Belmont, Calif.: Wadsworth, 1967.

Ando, A., and Brown, E. C. "Lags in Fiscal Policy." *Stabilization Policies*. Englewood Cliffs, N.J.: Prentice-Hall, 1964.

Arrow, K. J.; Chenery, H. B.; Minhas, B. S.; and Solow, R. M. "Capital-Labor Substitution and Economic Efficiency." *Rev. Econ. and Statis.* 43 (August 1961):225–250.

Becker, G. S. *Human Capital: A Theoretical and Empirical Analysis with Special Reference to Education*. New York: Nat. Bur. Econ. Res., 1964.

Black, S. W., and Russell, R. R. "The Estimation of Potential Labor Force and GNP." Paper presented at the Econometric Society meetings, Winter 1966, at New York.

Bowen, W. G., and Finegan, T. A. "Labor Force Participation and Unemployment." In *Employment Policy and the Labor Market*, edited by A. M. Ross. Berkeley: Univ. Calif., 1965.

Bronfenbrenner, M. "A Guidepost-Mortem." *Indus. Labor Relations Rev.* 20 (July 1967):637–650.

Bronfenbrenner, M., and Holzman, F. D. "Survey of Inflation Theory." *A.E.R.* 53 (September 1963):593–661.

Cagan, P. "The Monetary Dynamics of Hyperinflation," in *Studies in the Quantity Theory of Money*, edited by M. Friedman. Chicago: Univ. of Chicago Press, 1956.

Cagan, P. "Theories of Mild, Continuing Inflation: A Critique and Extension," in *Inflation: Its Causes, Consequences, and Control*, edited by S. W. Rousseas. New York, 1968.

Cain, G. *Married Women in the Labor Force: An Economic Analysis*. Chicago: Univ. of Chicago Press, 1966.

Cain, G., and Mincer, J. "Urban Poverty and Labor Force Participation: Comment." *A.E.R.* 59 (March 1969):185–194.

Chow, G. C. "On the Long-Run and Short-Run Demand for Money." *J.P.E.* 74 (April 1966):111–132.

Council of Economic Advisers. *Economic Report of the President, January 1967*. Washington: Government Printing Office, 1967.

Denison, E. F. *The Sources of Economic Growth in the United States and the Alternatives before Us,* Supplementary Paper no. 13, published by Committee for Economic Development, 1962.

Douglas, P. H. *The Theory of Wages.* New York: Macmillan, 1934.

Easterling, R. A. Comments on paper by J. Mincer. In *Prosperity and Unemployment,* edited by R. A. Gordon and M. S. Gordon. New York: Wiley, 1966.

Eckstein, O., and Wilson, T. "Determination of Wages in American Industry." *Q.J.E.* 76 (August 1962):379–414.

Finegan, T. A. "Hours of Work in the United States." *J.P.E.* 70 (October 1962):452–470.

Fisher, I. *Theory of Interest.* New York: Macmillan, 1930.

Friedman, M. *A Theory of the Consumption Function.* Chicago: Aldine, 1957.

Friedman, M. *Price Theory: A Provisional Text.* Chicago: Aldine, 1962.

Friedman, M. "The Role of Monetary Policy." *A.E.R.* 58 (March 1968):1–18.

Gaver, D., and Rapping, L. A. "A Stochastic Process Model of the United States Labor Market." Unpublished paper, Carnegie-Mellon Univ., 1966.

Hamilton, E. J. "Prices and Progress." *J. Econ. Hist.* 12 (Fall 1952):325–349.

Hansen, A. "Factors Affecting the Trend of Real Wages." *A.E.R.* 15 (March 1925):27–42.

Hicks, J. R. *Value and Capital.* Oxford: Clarendon Press, 1946.

Holt, C., and David, M. "The Concept of Job Vacancies in a Dynamic Theory of the Labor Market." In *The Measurement and Interpretation of Job Vacancies,* edited by R. Ferber. New York: Nat. Bur. Econ. Res., 1966.

Jones, E. B. "New Estimates of House of Work per Week and Hourly Earnings, 1900–1957." *Rev. Econ. and Statis.* 45 (November 1963):374–386.

Kessel, R. A., and Alchian, A. A. "Real Wages in the North During the Civil War: Mitchell's Data Reconsidered." *J. Law and Econ.* 20 (October 1959):95–114.

Kessel, R. A. "The Meaning and Validity of the Inflation-Induced Lag of Wages Behind Prices." *A.E.R.* 50 (March 1960):43–66.

Kessel, R. A. "Effects of Inflation." *J.P.E.* 70 (December 1962):521–537.

Kosters, M. *Income and Substitution Effects in a Family Labor Supply Model.* RAND no. P-3339. Santa Monica, Calif.: RAND Corp., 1966.

Kuh, E. "Cyclical and Secular Labor Productivity in United States Manufacturing." *Rev. Econ. and Statis.* 47 (February 1965):11–30.

Kuh, E. "Measurement of Potential Output." *A.E.R.* 56 (September 1966):762.

Lange, O. *Price Flexibility and Employment.* Bloomington, Ind.: Principia, 1945.

Lebergott, S. *Manpower in Economic Growth: The American Record Since 1800.* New York: McGraw-Hill, 1964.

Lerner, E. M. "Inflation in the Confederacy, 1961–65." In *Studies in the Quantity Theory of Money,* edited by M. Friedman. Chicago: Univ. of Chicago Press, 1956.

Lewis, H. G. "Hours of Work and Hours of Leisure." Proceedings of the Indus. Relations Res. Assoc., 1956:196–207.

Lewis, H. G. *Unionism and Relative Wages in the United States: An Empirical Inquiry.* Chicago: Univ. of Chicago Press, 1963.

Lipsey, R. G. "The Relationship between Unemployment and the Rate of Change of Money Wage Rates in the U.K., 1862–1957." *Economica* 27 (February 1960):1–31.

Liviatan, N. "Multiperiod Future Consumption as an Aggregate." *A.E.R.* 56 (September 1966):828–840.

Long, C. D. *The Labor Force Under Changing Income and Employment.* Princeton, N.J.: Princeton Univ. Press, 1958.

Lucas, R. E., Jr. "Substitution between Labor and Capital in U.S. Manufacturing, 1929–1958." Ph.D. dissertation, University of Chicago, 1964.

Lucas, R. E., Jr., and Rapping, L. A. "Price Expectations and the Phillips Curve." *A.E.R.,* in press.

McGuire, T. W. "An Empirical Investigation of the U.S. Manufacturing Production Function in the Post-War Period." Ph.D. dissertation, Stanford University, 1968.

Meltzer, A. H. "The Demand for Money: The Evidence from the Time Series." *J.P.E.* 71 (June 1963):219–247.

Mincer, J. "Labor Force Participation of Married Women." In *Aspects of Labor Economics,* edited by H. G. Lewis. A conference of the Universities–National Bureau Committee for Economic Research. Princeton, N.J.: Princeton Univ. Press, 1962.

Mincer, J. "Labor Force Participation and Unemployment: A Review of Recent Evidence." In *Prosperity and Unemployment,* edited by R. A. Gordon and M. S. Gordon. New York: Wiley, 1966.

Mitchell, W. C. *A History of the Greenbacks.* Chicago: Univ. of Chicago Press, 1903.

Modigliani, F. "Liquidity Preference and the Theory of Interest and Money." In *Readings in Monetary Theory,* edited by F. A. Lutz and L. W. Mints. New York: Blakistan, 1951.

Mortensen, D. T. "A Theory of Wage and Employment Dynamics." In *The New Microeconomics in Employment and Inflation Theory,* E. Phelps *et al.* New York: Norton, in press.

Nerlove, M. *Dynamics of Supply: Estimation of Farmers' Response to Price.* Baltimore: Johns Hopkins Press, 1958.

Nerlove, M. "Notes on Recent Empirical Studies of the CES and Related Production Functions." Technical report no. 13, Institute for Mathematical Studies in the Social Sciences, July 1965, at Stanford University.

Oi, W. "Labor as a Quasi-fixed Factor of Production." *J.P.E.* 70 (December 1962):538–55.

Patinkin, D. *Money, Interest, and Prices.* New York: Harper & Row, 1965.

Perry, G. "The Determinants of Wage Rate Changes." *Rev. Econ. Studies* 31 (October 1964):287–308.

Phelps, E. "Money Wage Dynamics and Labor Market Equilibrium." *J.P.E.* 76, pt. 2 (August 1968):687–711.

Phelps, E., *et al. The New Microeconomics in Employment and Inflation Theory.* New York: Norton, in press.

Phillips, A. W. "The Relation between Unemployment and the Rate of Change of Money Wage Rates in the United Kingdom, 1861–1957." *Economica* 25 (November 1958):283–299.

Rees, A. "Wage Determination and Involuntary Unemployment." *J.P.E.* 59 (April 1951):143–153.

Rees, A. "Patterns of Wages, Price and Productivity." In *Wages, Prices, Profits and Productivity*, edited by C. Myers. New York: American Assembly, Columbia Univ., 1959.

Rosen, S. "On the Interindustry Wage and Hours Structure." *J.P.E.* 77, no. 2 (March/April 1969):249–273.

Sargent, T. "Price Expectations and the Interest Rate." *Q.J.E.* 83 (February 1969):127–141.

Schramm, Richard. "Optimal Adjustment of Factors of Production and the Study of Investment Behavior." Ph.D. dissertation, Carnegie-Mellon Univ., 1967.

Simon, H. A. *Models of Man*. New York: Wiley, 1957.

Stigler, G. "The Economics of Information." *J.P.E.* 69 (June 1961):213–225.

Tella, A. "Hidden Unemployment 1953–62: Comment." *A.E.R.* 56 (December 1966): 1235–41.

Tobin, J. "Money Wage Rates and Employment." In *The New Economics*, edited by S. E. Harris. New York: Knopf, 1952.

U.S., Department of Commerce, Bureau of the Census. *Current Population Reports*, C.3, no. 186, and P.25, nos. 98, 114, 310, 311, and 321.

U.S., Department of Commerce, Office of Business Economics. *The National Income and Product Accounts of the United States, 1929–1965: Statistical Tables: A Supplement to the Survey of Current Business*. Washington: Government Printing Office, 1966.

U.S., Department of Labor. *Manpower Report of the President*. Washington: Government Printing Office, 1965 and 1967.

U.S., Department of Labor, Bureau of Labor Statistics. *Employment and Earnings*. Vol. 14, no. 7. Washington: Government Printing Office, 1968.

U.S., Department of Labor Statistics. *Employment and Earnings Statistics for the United States, 1909–66*. Bulletin no. 1312–4. Washington: Government Printing Office, 1966.

Wilson, T. A., and Eckstein, O. "Short-Run Productivity Behavior in U.S. Manufacturing." *Rev. Econ. and Statis.* 46 (February 1964):53–64.

Unemployment in the Great Depression: Is There a Full Explanation?

Introduction

Professor Rees's reactions to our econometric study of the U.S. labor market, recently published in this *Journal* (1970), raise a bewildering variety of issues. Many of these issues have to do with "important implications for policy" which "lurk close . . . to the surface," as Rees sees it, of our study. These implications, whatever they may be, remain submerged after one has read Rees's remarks. We shall not attempt to guess at their nature or respond to them.

There are, however, two substantive issues raised by Rees which deserve further discussion. Rees asserts that "in this [that is, our] model unemployment arises from the recalcitrance of suppliers and not from deficiencies in demand." This highly misleading statement is corrected in section 1 of this note. Rees also raises the important empirical question of whether our theory does succeed in accounting for labor-market behavior during the period 1929–39. Further study on our part indicates that Rees's skepticism on this point is well founded: our hypothesis accounts for much, but *not* all, of the observed labor-market rigidity during this period. These results are reported in section 2.

1 Aggregate Demand and Unemployment

Near the end of his paper, Rees observes: "It should be stressed that although real GNP enters the Lucas-Rapping model as an exogenous variable, it does not appear in the unemployment rate function. Measured unemployment depends only on price changes, the relation of current to past wages, and past unemployment. Again this brings out that in this model unemployment arises from the recalcitrance of suppliers and not from deficiencies in aggregate demand.''

The first two sentences of this paragraph refer to equation (32) in Lucas-Rapping (1969). They are accurate, as inspection of (32) verifies. The third sentence, however, simply does not follow. Our unemployment-rate function (32) is one of three structural equations in a three-equation system. To determine the effect on unemployment of a variable classed as exogenous to the labor market, as is real GNP in our scheme, one must examine the *reduced-form* equation for unemployment. While we did not exhibit this equation in Lucas-Rapping (1969), it is readily determined from (32) and the reduced form for real wages, equation (35) as reported in our previous paper.

Since reported unemployment is a function of real wages in equation (32) and since real wages are a function of real GNP per household in equation (35), we obtain (1) below by combining these two equations:

$$U_t = -\beta_{31}\pi_{13}\ln(y_t/M_t) + \text{other terms,} \tag{1}$$

where U_t is unemployment as a fraction, and y_t/M_t is real GNP per household. Since β_{31} and π_{13} are predicted to be positive, the predicted effect of real output on the unemployment rate is negative, as one would expect. Quantitatively, using our table 1 (1969) estimates, the effect is about $-.51$, meaning that for, say, a 10 percent decline in real output per capita, the unemployment rate rises by 5.1 percentage points.

Clearly, there is no reason to interpret our model as viewing unemployment as generated within the labor market independently of aggregate demand. On the contrary, as we promised in section 1 of our 1969 study, our model is "consistent with the observed fluctuations in real output and employment [and, we now add, in *un*employment] in the face of shifting aggregate demand." Of course, Rees is correct in his assertion that our model implies a zero rate of unemployment if workers were willing to sell apples or shine shoes. (Is there any theory which does *not* carry this implication?) But to infer from this observation that antidepression policy should be limited to, or even involve, exhortations to workers to behave in this way is fantastic. The only aggregative economic policy implications we see for events like the Great Depression are the standard ones: if possible, avoid the aggregate-demand shifts which cause them; failing this, pursue corrective demand policies to make them as brief as possible.

In our view, then, the assumption that the labor market is cleared has no implications, in itself, for cyclical policy. Any attempt to convince us (and, we hope, our readers) otherwise must involve a serious effort to draw these implications from our model *as we stated it,* not plays on words like "voluntary," "recalcitrant," and so forth.

2 Labor Supply in the Depression

The second substantive issue Rees raises concerns the plausibility of our view of household-decision making during the depression years. After accurately paraphrasing our view that "the current wage rate is viewed by the unemployed as below the wage rate they could normally expect, leading to their temporary withdrawal from the labor supply," Rees asks: "How long does it take workers to revise their expectations of normal wages in light of the facts? Unemployment was never below 14 percent of the labor force btween 1931 and 1939, and was still about 17 percent of the labor force in 1939, a decade after the depression began."

Now, the depression did not, of course, involve a once-and-for-all change in "the facts" as seen by workers at the time. Hence, there is no self-evident contradiction between an expectations model and the facts cited by Rees. Nevertheless, the question is of interest and, more important, answerable in terms of our model. We shall rephrase the question and deal with it in the remainder of this section.

From our point of view, the relevant facts for the labor-supply decision are current real wages and prices, w_t and P_t, and "normal" real wages and prices w_t^* and P_t^*. Since the latter variables are weighted averages of past actual values, the weights being unknown parameters, these time series could not be calculated prior to estimation. Accordingly, we used a Koyck transformation to eliminate these variables, introducing lagged real wages, prices, and employment as additional explanatory variables. This transformed labor-supply function was used in estimation and testing.

While this widely used procedure is econometrically acceptable, it does obscure the link between the estimated labor-supply function and the hypothetical household-decision problem on which it is based. That is, one cannot readily match up our econometric results with one's intuition on the labor-supply decision or with evidence from other sources. To remedy this, we should have used the estimated adaptation parameter to calculate series on normal wages and prices and displayed the latter alongside the actual series. We shall next do this.

Normal and actual prices, according to our theory, are related by $\ln(P_t^*) = \lambda \ln(P_t) + (1 - \lambda)\ln(P_{t-1}^*) + \lambda''$ (eq. [14] in our 1969 paper). Normal and actual real wages are linked in the same way, with the same adaptation parameter λ but with a possibly different trend, λ' instead of λ''. From our estimated labor-supply function, $\lambda = .36$. Using this value, together with postulated trends, we have used (14) to calculate a series of "normal prices." [1] Similarly, a normal *money*-wage series has been obtained.[2] These results are displayed in table 1.

Examining table 1, one sees that money wages and prices fell noticeably below their "normal levels" in 1930, fell further below in subsequent years, and remained below through 1933.[3] This occurred *not* because of any unreasonable stubbornness (on the part of our hypothetical household) in revising the normal levels: these normal values fell through 1933, although at a rate slower than the rate of decline of actual wages and prices. Qualitatively, then, our theory is consistent with the early depression years. Quantitatively, the fit is also fairly good: applying the estimated coefficients of our unemployment-rate function (32) to the wage and price changes in table 1, one would predict a rise of .17 in the unemployment rate from 1929 to 1933. From table 1, the observed increase was .22.

On the other hand, from 1934 until World War II, the picture is quite different. By 1934, according to table 1, actual wages and prices had returned to their normal levels. In part, this is due to falling expectations "in light of the facts," as Rees puts it. In part, it is the result of the astonishing wage-price increases from 1933 to 1934. Whatever the cause, the expectations model we used implies that in 1934 the unemployment rate should have been at its 1929 or 1930 level, as opposed to the observed 22 percent level. To make matters worse, our theory continues to "miss" for the remainder of the depression years, accounting for the observed drift toward lower unemployment during this period but failing entirely to explain why this drift proceeded at so slow a pace.[4]

Table 1 Wages and Prices during the Depression

Year	Unemploy-ment Rate U_t	Money Wage Rate W_t ($)	"Normal" Money Wage Rate W_t^* ($)	GNP Deflator P_t(1958 = 1)	"Normal" GNP Deflator P_t^*
1928	.04	.55	.56	.50	.51
1929	.03	.56	.57	.51	.51
1930	.09	.56	.58	.49	.50
1931	.16	.53	.57	.45	.48
1932	.24	.48	.55	.40	.45
1933	.25	.46	.52	.39	.43
1934	.22	.51	.53	.42	.43
1935	.20	.52	.53	.43	.43
1936	.17	.53	.54	.43	.43
1937	.14	.57	.56	.44	.44
1938	.19	.58	.57	.44	.44
1939	.17	.58	.59	.43	.44
1940	.15	.60	.60	.44	.44
1941	.10	.66	.63	.47	.45
1942	.05	.76	.68	.53	.48
1943	.02	.84	.75	.57	.51
1944	.01	.90	.81	.58	.54
1945	.02	.98	.88	.60	.56

The reason these errors were not detected in our statistical tests is clear (in retrospect). The lagged employment variable in our labor-supply function (Lucas-Rapping [1969], eq. [30]) and the lagged un-employment rate in (32) were included essentially as "proxies" for geometric sums of past prices and wages. Apparently, the coefficients of these variables are biased upward due to *other* sources of persist-ence (auto-correlation) in the employment- and unemployment-rate series. In summary, our theory postulated lags in the adjustment of price-wage expectations as the *only* source of "rigidity" or of the persistence of unemployment. In fact, other important sources of rigidity were present in the Great Depression. (For the post–World War II period, however, the assertion that lags in price-wage expec-tations are sufficient to account for *all* observed labor-market rigidity remains valid.)[5]

The fact that our model explains less than it originally appeared to should not, however, obscure the fact that the evidence for our aggregate-labor-supply theory is essentially as strong as before. To underscore this point, we refer to model 5, reported briefly in tables A1 and A2 of Lucas-Rapping (1969) and in full in Lucas-Rapping (1970). This model is identical to that reported in table 1 of the text of Lucas-Rapping (1969) and criticized above, except that it does *not* include lagged employment as an explanatory labor-supply variable. This model, then, does not confound other sources of rigidity with the expectations effect; yet it confirms the importance of the latter very strongly.

It would also be misleading to conclude this paper without discussing the possibility that "traditional" theory can account for the residual rigidities unexplained by our model. Clearly the "theory" embodied in Rees's figure 1 fails to account for the drastic wage decline of the 1929–33 period as well as for the fact that the wage increase of 1934 failed to restore full employment. Similarly, the Phillips model of wage adjustment to excess labor supply fails to explain the 11 percent wage *increase* of 1933–34 in the face of a 25 percent rate of unemployment. In short, once one attempts to obtain a quantitative explanation for wage-price rigidity in terms of individual and market behavior, there *is* no traditional theory to return to.

Notes

1. To calculate the series P_t^* from an estimated λ and the series P_t, one must supply a trend value, λ'', and an initial value for P_t^*. We took actual and normal prices to be equal in 1923. The trend λ'' was selected so as to make forecasts developed from P_t^* come out correct *on average* for the period 1923–45. The same practice was followed with wage rates. To extend the price and wage series used in Lucas-Rapping (1969) back to 1923, we used the implicit GNP deflator from Kendrick (1961) and the wage series from Rees (1959).

2. Since the same adaptation parameter applies to prices and wages, and since our expectations hypotheses are expressed in logs, one may work interchangeably with real or money wages.

3. We caution against a possible misinterpretation of table 1. The table does *not* imply that any worker in 1933 compared his best offer of \$.46 per hour to his normal offer of \$.52 and chose to be unemployed. Taken literally, it says that a "representative household" made this wage comparison and chose to work 25 percent less than its normal amount. In fact, of course, the abnormally low wage offers which lead to unemployment are not evenly distributed over the labor force. The figure \$.46 is the average wage of those who found jobs

and accepted them. Presumably, the average "best offer" for those who did not work was considerably lower. For a labor-market model similar in concept to ours but which captures some of the important effects of labor-force heterogeneity, the reader is referred to Mortensen (1970).

4. Alchian (1970) recognized this problem and offers an interesting discussion of it. He conjectures that recovery was retarded by the succession of New Deal price- and wage-fixing measures. Whether such explanations are quantitatively adequate remains an open question.

5. This assertion is based on an unpublished Carnegie-Mellon working paper by Charles Hedrick (1971). Hedrick finds that our labor-supply function (1969) fits the 1950–70 period well, and that coefficient estimates from this period are remarkably similar to those we obtained for the period 1930–65. Further, he finds that the coefficient of the lagged dependent variable in this equation reflects expectation lags *only*.

References

Alchian, Armen. "Information Costs, Pricing, and Resource Unemployment." In *Microeconomic Foundation of Employment and Inflation Theory,* edited by E. S. Phelps. New York: Norton, 1970.

Hedrick, Charles. "Expectations and Labor Supply." GSIA Working Paper. Mimeographed. Pittsburgh: Carnegie-Mellon Univ., 1971.

Kendrick, John W. *Productivity Trends in the United States.* Princeton, N.J.: Princeton Univ. Press, 1961.

Lucas, R. E., Jr., and Rapping, L. A. "Real Wages, Employment, and Inflation." *J.P.E.* 77 (September/October 1969): 721–754.

Lucas, R. E., Jr. "Real Wages, Employment, and Inflation." In *Microeconomic Foundations of Employment and Inflation Theory,* edited by E. S. Phelps. New York: Norton, 1970.

Mortensen, Dale T. "A Theory of Wage and Employment Dynamics." In *Microeconomic Foundations of Employment and Inflation Theory,* edited by E. S. Phelps. New York: Norton, 1970.

Rees, A. "Patterns of Wages, Prices and Productivity." In *Wages, Prices, Profits and Productivity,* edited by C. Meyers. New York: American Assembly, Columbia Univ., 1959.

Rees, A. "On Equilibrium in Labor Markets." *J.P.E.* 78 (March/April 1970):306–310.

Expectations and the Neutrality of Money

1 Introduction

This paper provides a simple example of an economy in which equilibrium prices and quantities exhibit what may be the central feature of the modern business cycle: a systematic relation between the rate of change in nominal prices and the level of real output. The relationship, essentially a variant of the well-known Phillips curve, is derived within a framework from which all forms of "money illusion" are rigorously excluded: all prices are market clearing, all agents behave optimally in light of their objectives and expectations, and expectations are formed optimally (in a sense to be made precise below).

Exchange in the economy studied takes place in two physically separated markets. The allocation of traders across markets in each period is in part stochastic, introducing fluctuations in relative prices between the two markets. A second source of disturbance arises from stochastic changes in the quantity of money, which in itself introduces fluctuations in the nominal price level (the average rate of exchange between money and goods). Information on the current state of these real and monetary disturbances is transmitted to agents only through prices in the market where each agent happens to be. In the particular framework presented below, prices convey this information only imperfectly, forcing agents to hedge on whether a particular price movement results from a relative demand shift or a nominal (monetary) one.

Reprinted from *Journal of Economic Theory* 4 (April 1972):103–124 by permission. Copyright 1972 by Academic Press.
I would like to thank James Scott for his helpful comments.

This hedging behavior results in a nonneutrality of money, or broadly speaking a Phillips curve, similar in nature to that which we observe in reality. At the same time, classical results on the long-run neutrality of money, or independence of real and nominal magnitudes, continue to hold.

These features of aggregate economic behavior, derived below within a particular, abstract framework, bear more than a surface resemblance to many of the characteristics attributed to the U.S. economy by Friedman [3 and elsewhere]. This paper provides an explicitly elaborated example, to my knowledge the first, of an economy in which some of these propositions can be formulated rigorously and shown to be valid.

A second, in many respects closer, forerunner of the approach taken here is provided by Phelps. Phelps [8] foresees a new inflation and employment theory in which Phillips curves are obtained within a framework which is neoclassical except for "the removal of the postulate that all transactions are made under complete information." This is precisely what is attempted here.

The substantive results developed below are based on a concept of equilibrium which is, I believe, new (although closely related to the principles underlying dynamic programming) and which may be of independent interest. In this paper, equilibrium prices and quantities will be characterized mathematically as *functions* defined on the space of possible states of the economy, which are in turn characterized as finite dimensional vectors. This characterization permits a treatment of the relation of information to expectations which is in some ways much more satisfactory than is possible with conventional adaptive expectations hypotheses.

The physical structure of the model economy to be studied is set out in the following section. Section 3 deals with preference and demand functions; and in section 4, an exact definition of equilibrium is provided and motivated. The characteristics of this equilibrium are obtained in section 5, with certain existence and uniqueness arguments deferred to the appendix. The paper concludes with the discussion of some of the implications of the theory, in sections 6, 7, and 8.

2 The Structure of the Economy

In order to exhibit the phenomena described in the introduction, we shall utilize an abstract model economy, due in many of its essentials to Samuelson [10].[1] Each period, N identical individuals are born, each of whom lives for two periods (the current one and the next). In each period, then, there is a constant population of $2N$: N of age 0 and N of age 1. During the first period of life, each person supplies, at his discretion, n units of labor which yield the same n units of output. Denote the output consumed by a member of the younger generation (its producer) by c^0, and that consumed by the old by c^1. Output cannot be stored but can be freely disposed of, so that the aggregate production–consumption possibilities for any period are completely described (in per capita terms) by:

$$c^0 + c^1 \leq n, \qquad c^0, c^1, n \geq 0. \tag{1}$$

Since n may vary, it is physically possible for this economy to experience fluctuations in real output.

In addition to labor-output, there is one other good: fiat money, issued by a government which has no other function. This money enters the economy by means of a beginning-of-period transfer to the members of the older generation, in a quantity proportional to the pretransfer holdings of each. No inheritance is possible, so that unspent cash balances revert, at the death of the holder, to the monetary authority.

Within this framework, the only exchange which can occur will involve a surrender of output by the young, in exchange for money held over from the preceding period, and altered by transfer, by the old.[2] We shall assume that such exchange occurs in two physically separate markets. To keep matters as simple as possible, we assume that the older generation is allocated across these two markets so as to equate total monetary demand between them. The young are allocated stochastically, fraction $\theta/2$ going to one and $1 - (\theta/2)$ to the other. Once the assignment of persons to markets is made, no switching or communication between markets is possible. Within each market, trading by auction occurs, with all trades transacted at a single, market clearing price.[3]

The pretransfer money supply, per member of the older generation, is known to all agents.[4] Denote this quantity by m. Posttransfer balances, denoted by m', are not generally known (until next period) except to the extent that they are "revealed" to traders by the current period price level. Similarly, the allocation variable θ is unknown, except indirectly via price. The development through time of the nominal money supply is governed by

$$m' = mx, \tag{2}$$

where x is a random variable. Let x' denote next period's value of this transfer variable, and let θ' be next period's allocation variable. It is assumed that x and x' are independent, with the common, continuous density function f on $(0, \infty)$. Similarly, θ and θ' are independent, with the common, continuous symmetric density g on $(0, 2)$.

To summarize, the state of the economy in any period is entirely described by three variables m, x, and θ. The motion of the economy from state to state is independent of decisions made by individuals in the economy, and is given by (2) and the densities f and g of x and θ.

3 Preferences and Demand Functions

We shall assume that the members of the older generation prefer more consumption to less, other things equal, and attach no utility to the holding of money. As a result, they will supply their cash holdings, as augmented by transfers, inelastically. (Equivalently, they have a unit elastic demand for goods.) The young, in contrast, have a nontrivial decision problem, to which we now turn.

The objects of choice for a person of age 0 are his current consumption c, current labor supplied, n, and future consumption, denoted by c'. All individuals evaluate these goods according to the common utility function:

$$U(c, n) + E\{V(c')\}. \tag{3}$$

(The distribution with respect to which the expectation in (3) is taken will be specified later.) The function U is increasing in c, decreasing in n, strictly concave, and continuously twice differentiable. In addition, current consumption and leisure are not inferior goods, or:

$$U_{cn} + U_{nn} < 0 \quad \text{and} \quad U_{cc} + U_{cn} < 0. \tag{4}$$

The function V is increasing, strictly concave and continuously twice differentiable. The function $V'(c')c'$ is increasing, with an elasticity bounded away from unity, or:

$$V''(c')c' + V'(c') > 0, \tag{5}$$

$$\frac{c'V''(c')}{V'(c')} \leq -a < 0. \tag{6}$$

Condition (5) essentially insures that a rise in the price of future goods will, ceteris paribus, induce an increase in current consumption or that the substitution effect of such a price change will dominate its income effect.[5] The strict concavity requirement imposed on V implies that the left term of (6) be negative, so that (6) is a slight strengthening of concavity. Finally, we require that the marginal utility of future consumption be high enough to justify at least the first unit of labor expended, and ultimately tend to zero:

$$\lim_{c' \to 0} V'(c') = +\infty, \tag{7}$$

$$\lim_{c' \to \infty} V'(c') = 0. \tag{8}$$

Future consumption, c', cannot be purchased directly by an age 0 individual. Instead, a known quantity of nominal balances λ is acquired in exchange for goods. If next period's price level (dollars per unit of output) is p' and if next period's transfer is x', these balances will then purchase $x'\lambda/p'$ units of future consumption.[6] Although it is purely formal at this point, it is convenient to have some notation for the distribution function of (x', p'), conditioned on the information currently available to the age-0 person: denote it by $F(x', p' \mid m, p)$, where p is the current price level. Then the decision problem facing an age-0 person is:

$$\max_{c,n,\lambda \geq 0} \left\{ U(c,n) + \int V \left(\frac{x'\lambda}{p'} \right) dF(x', p' \mid m, p) \right\} \tag{9}$$

subject to:

$$p(n - c) - \lambda \geq 0. \tag{10}$$

Provided the distribution F is so specified that the objective function is continuously differentiable, the Kuhn–Tucker conditions apply to this problem and are both necessary and sufficient. These are:

$$U_c(c,n) - p\mu \leq 0, \quad \text{with equality if } c > 0, \tag{11}$$
$$U_n(c,n) + p\mu \leq 0, \quad \text{with equality if } n > 0, \tag{12}$$
$$p(n - c) - \lambda \geq 0, \quad \text{with equality if } \mu > 0, \tag{13}$$
$$\int V' \left(\frac{x'\lambda}{p'} \right) \frac{x'}{p'} dF(x', p' \mid m, p) - \mu \leq 0, \quad \text{with equality if } \lambda > 0, \tag{14}$$

where μ is a nonnegative multiplier.

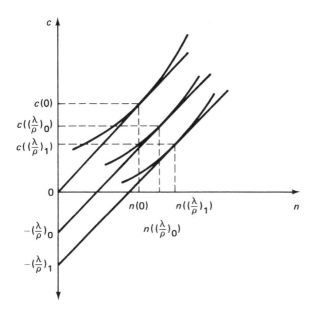

Figure 1

We first solve (11)–(13) for c, n, and $p\mu$ as functions of λ/p. This is equivalent to finding the optimal consumption and labor supply for a fixed acquisition of money balances. The solution for $p\mu$ will have the interpretation as the *marginal cost* (in units of foregone utility from consumption and leisure) of holding money. This solution is diagrammed in Fig. 1.

It is not difficult to show that, as Fig. 1 suggests, for any $\lambda/p > 0$ (11)–(13) may be solved for unique values of c, n, and $p\mu$. As λ/p varies, these solution values vary in a continuous and (almost everywhere) continuously differentiable manner. From the noninferiority assumptions (4), it follows that as λ/p increases, n increases and c decreases. The solution value for $p\mu$, which we denote by $h(\lambda/p)$ is, positive, increasing, and continuously differentiable. As λ/p tends to zero, $h(\lambda/p)$ tends to a positive limit, $h(0)$.

Substituting the function h into (14), one obtains

$$h\left(\frac{\lambda}{p}\right)\frac{1}{p} \geq \int V'\left(\frac{x'\lambda}{p'}\right)\frac{x'}{p'}\,dF(x',p'\,|\,m,p), \qquad (15)$$

with equality if $\lambda > 0$. After multiplying through by p, (15) equates the marginal cost of acquiring cash (in units of current utility foregone) to the marginal benefit (in units of expected future utility gained). Implicitly, (15) is a demand function for money, relating current nominal quantity demanded, λ, to the current and expected future price levels.

4 Expectations and a Definition of Equilibrium

Since the two markets in this economy are structurally identical, and since within a trading period there is no communication between them, the economy's general (current period) equilibrium may be determined by determining equilibrium in each market separately. We shall do so by equating nominal money demand (as determined in section 3) and nominal money supply in the market which receives a fraction $\theta/2$ of the young. Equilibrium in the other market is then determined in the same way, with θ replaced by $2 - \theta$, and aggregate values of output and prices are determined in the usual way by adding over markets. This will be carried out explicitly in section 6.

At the beginning of the last section, we observed that money will be supplied inelastically in each market. The total money supply, after transfer, is Nmx. Following the convention adopted in section 1, $Nmx/2$ is supplied in each market. Thus in the market receiving a fraction $\theta/2$ of the young, the quantity supplied per demander is $(Nmx/2)/(\theta N/2) = mx/\theta$. Equilibirum requires that $\lambda = mx/\theta$, where λ is quantity demanded per age-0 person. Since $mx/\theta > 0$, substitution into (15) gives the equilibrium condition

$$h\left(\frac{mx}{\theta p}\right)\frac{1}{p} = \int V'\left(\frac{mxx'}{\theta p'}\right)\frac{x'}{p'}\,dF(x',p'\,|\,m,p). \qquad (16)$$

Equation (16) relates the current period price level to the (unknown) future price level, p'. To "solve" for the market clearing price p (and hence to obtain the current equilibrium values of employment, output, and consumption) p and p' must be linked. This connection is provided in the definition of equilibrium stated below, which is motivated by the following considerations.

First, it was remarked earlier that in some (not very well defined) sense the *state* of the economy is fully described by the three variables (m, x, θ). That is, if at two different points in calendar time the economy arrives at a particular state (m, x, θ) it is reasonable to expect it to behave the same way both times, regardless of the route by which the state was attained each time. If this is so, one can express the equilibrium price as a function $p(m, x, \theta)$ on the space of possible states and similarly for the equilibrium values of employment, output, and consumption.

Second, if price can be expressed as a function of (m, x, θ), the *true* probability distribution of next period's price, $p' = p(m', x', \theta') = p(mx, x', \theta')$ is known, conditional on m, from the known distributions of x, x', and θ'. Further information is also available to traders, however, since the current price, $p(m, x, \theta)$, yields information on x. Hence, on the basis of information available to him, an age-0 trader should take the expectation in (16) [or (15)] with respect to the joint distribution of (m, x, x', θ') conditional on the values of m and $p(m, x, \theta)$, or treating m as a parameter, the joint distribution of (x, x', θ') conditional on the value of $p(m, x, \theta)$. Denote this latter distribution by $G(x, x', \theta \mid p(m, x, \theta))$.[7]

We are thus led to the following

Definition.   An equilibrium price is a continuous, nonnegative function $p(\cdot)$ of (m, x, θ), with $mx/\theta p(m, x, \theta)$ bounded and bounded away from zero, which satisfies:

$$
h\left[\frac{mx}{\theta p(m, x, \theta)}\right] \frac{1}{p(m, x, \theta)}
$$
$$
= \int V'\left[\frac{mxx'}{\theta p(m\xi, x', \theta')}\right] \frac{x'}{p(m\xi, x', \theta')} \, dG(\xi, x', \theta' \mid p(m, x, \theta)). \quad (17)
$$

Equation (17) is, of course, simply (16) with p replaced by the value of the function $p(\cdot)$ under the current state, (m, x, θ), and p' replaced by the value of the *same* function under next period's state (mx, x', θ). In addition, we have dispensed with unspecified distribution F, taking the expectation instead with respect to the well-defined distribution G.[8]

In the next section, we show that (17) has a unique solution and develop the important characteristics of this solution. The more difficult mathematical issues will be relegated to the appendix.

5   Characteristics of the Equilibrium Price Function

We proceed by showing the existence of a solution to (17) of a particular form, then showing that there are no other solutions, and finally by characterizing the unique solution. As a useful preliminary step, we show:

Lemma 1. *If $p(\cdot)$ is any solution to (17), it is monotonic in x/θ in the sense that for any fixed m, $x_0/\theta_0 > x_1/\theta_1$ implies $p(m, x_0, \theta_0) \neq p(m, x_1, \theta_1)$.*

Proof. Suppose to the contrary that $x_0/\theta_0 > x_1/\theta_1$ and $p(m, x_0, \theta_0) = p(m, x_1, \theta_1) = p_0$ (say). Then from (17),

$$h\left(\frac{mx_0}{\theta_0 p_0}\right)\frac{1}{p_0} = \int V'\left[\frac{mx_0 x'}{\theta_0 p(m\xi, x', \theta')}\right]\frac{x'}{p(m\xi, x', \theta')}\, dG(\xi, x', \theta' \,|\, p_0).$$

and

$$h\left(\frac{mx_1}{\theta_1 p_0}\right)\frac{1}{p_0} = \int V'\left[\frac{mx_1 x'}{\theta_1 p(m\xi, x', \theta')}\right]\frac{x'}{p(m\xi, x', \theta')}\, dG(\xi, x', \theta' \,|\, p_0).$$

Since h is strictly increasing while V' is strictly decreasing, these equalities are contradictory. This completes the proof.

In view of this Lemma, the distribution of (x, x', θ') conditional on $p(m, x, \theta)$ is the same as the distribution conditional on x/θ for *all* solution functions $p(\cdot)$, a fact which vastly simplifies the study of (17).

It is a plausible conjecture that solutions to (17) assume the form $p(m, x, \theta) = m\varphi(x/\theta)$, where φ is a continuous, nonnegative function.[9] If this is true, the function φ satisfies [multiplying (17) through by mx/θ and substituting]:

$$h\left[\frac{x}{\theta\varphi(x/\theta)}\right]\frac{x}{\theta\varphi(x/\theta)}$$
$$= \int V'\left[\frac{xx'}{\theta\xi\varphi(x'/\theta')}\right]\frac{xx'}{\theta\xi\varphi(x'/\theta')}\, dG\left(\xi, x', \theta' \,\bigg|\, \frac{x}{\theta}\right). \tag{18}$$

Let us make the change of variable $z = x/\theta$, and $z' = x'/\theta'$, and let $H(z, \theta)$ be the joint density function of z and θ and let $\tilde{H}(z, \theta)$ be the density of θ conditional on z. Then (18) is equivalent to:

$$h\left[\frac{z}{\varphi(z)}\right]\frac{z}{\varphi(z)}$$
$$= \int V'\left[\frac{\theta'}{\theta}\frac{z'}{\varphi(z')}\right]\frac{\theta'}{\theta}\frac{z'}{\varphi(z')}\, \tilde{H}(z, \theta)\, H(z', \theta')\, d\theta\, dz'\, d\theta'. \tag{19}$$

Equations (17) and (19) are studied in the appendix. The result of interest is:

Theorem 1. *Equation (19) has exactly one continuous solution $\varphi(z)$ on*

(0, ∞) *with z/φ(z) bounded. The function φ(z) is strictly positive and continuously differentiable. Further, mφ(x/θ) is the unique equilibrium price function.*

Proof.   See the appendix.

We turn next to the characteristics of the solution function φ. It is convenient to begin this study by first examining two polar cases, one in which $\theta = 1$ with probability one, and a second in which $x = 1$ with probability one.

The first of these two cases may be interpreted as applying to an economy in which all trading place in a single market, and no non-monetary disturbances are present. Then z is simply equal to x and, in view of Lemma 1, the current value of x is fully revealed to traders by the equilibrium price. It should not be surprising that the following classical neutrality of money theorem holds.

Theorem 2.   *Suppose $\theta = 1$ with probability one. Let y^* be the unique solution to*

$$h(y) = V'(y). \tag{20}$$

Then $p(m, x, \theta) = mx/y^*$ is the unique solution to (17).

Proof.   We have observed that h is increasing and V' is decreasing, tending to 0 as y tends to infinity by (8). By (7), $h(0) < V'(0)$. Hence (20) does have a unique solution, y^*. It is clear that $\varphi(z) = z/y^*$ satisfies (19). By Theorem 1, it is the only solution and mx/y^* is the unique solution to (17).

The second polar case, where x is identically 1, may be interpreted as applying to an economy with real disturbances but with a perfectly stable monetary policy. In this case, $z = 1/\theta$, so that the current market price reveals θ to all traders. It is convenient to let $\Psi(\theta) = [\theta\varphi(1/\theta)]^{-1}$ so that (19) becomes:

$$h[\Psi(\theta)]\Psi(\theta) = \int V'\left[\frac{\theta'}{\theta}\ \Psi(\theta)\right]\ \frac{\theta'}{\theta}\ \Psi(\theta')g(\theta')\,d\theta'. \tag{21}$$

Denote the right side of (21) by $m(\theta)$. Then

$$m'(\theta) = \int \left[V''\frac{\theta'}{\theta}\ \Psi(\theta') + V'\right]\left[\frac{-\theta'\Psi(\theta)}{\theta^2}\right]g(\theta')\,d\theta'$$

(suppressing the arguments of V'' and V'). The *elasticity* of $m(\theta)$ is therefore

$$\frac{\theta m'(\theta)}{m(\theta)} = -\int w(\theta, \theta')(V')^{-1} \left[V'' \frac{\theta'}{\theta} \Psi(\theta') + V' \right] d\theta',$$

where

$$w(\theta, \theta') = \left[\int V' \frac{\theta'}{\theta} \varphi(\theta')g(\theta') \, d\theta' \right]^{-1} \left[V' \frac{\theta'}{\theta} \Psi(\theta')g(\theta') \right].$$

Clearly, $w(\theta, \theta') \geq 0$ and $\int w(\theta, \theta')d\theta' = 1$. From (5) and (6)

$$0 < (V')^{-1} \left[V'' \frac{\theta'}{\theta} \varphi(\theta') + V' \right] < 1.$$

Hence $-[\theta m'(\theta)/m(\theta)]$ is a mean value of terms between 0 and 1, so that

$$-1 < \frac{\theta m'(\theta)}{m(\theta)} < 0. \tag{22}$$

Now differentiating both sides of (21), we have

$$[h'(\Psi)\Psi + h]\Psi'(\theta) = m'(\theta),$$

which using (22) and the fact that h is increasing implies

$$-1 < \frac{\theta \Psi'(\theta)}{\Psi(\theta)} < 0. \tag{23}$$

Recalling the definition of $\Psi(\theta)$ in terms of $\varphi(\theta)$, it is readily seen that (23) implies

$$0 < \frac{z\varphi'(z)}{\varphi(z)} < 1.$$

We summarize the discussion of this case in

Theorem 3. *Suppose* $x = 1$ *with probability one. Then* (17) *has a unique solution* $p(m, x, \theta) = m\varphi(1/\theta)$, *where* φ *is a continuously diffentiable function, with an elasticity between zero and one.*

If the factor disturbing the economy is exclusively monetary, then current price will adjust *proportionally* to changes in the money supply. Money is neutral in the short run, in the classical sense that the equilibrium level of real cash balances, employment, and consumption will remain unchanged in the face even of unanticipated monetary changes. These, in words, are the implications of Theorem 2. If, on the other hand, the forces disturbing the economy are exclusively real, the money supply being held fixed, disturbances will have real consequences. Those of the young generation who find themselves in a market with few of their cohorts (in a market with a low θ, or a high z-value) obtain what is in effect a lower price of future consumption. Theorem 3, resting on the assumptions of income and substitution effects set out in section 3, indicates that they will distribute all of this gain to the future, holding higher real balances. This attempt is partially frustrated by a rise in the current price level.

Returning to the general case, in which both x and θ fluctuate, it is clear that the current price informs agents only of the *ratio* x/θ of these two variables. Agents cannot discriminate with certainty between real and monetary changes in demand for the good they offer, but must instead make inferences on the basis of the known distributions $f(x)$ and $g(\theta)$ and the value of x/θ revealed by the current price level. It seems reasonable that their behavior will somehow mix the strategies described in Theorems 2 and 3, since a high x/θ value indicates a high x *and* a low θ.

Unfortunately this last statement, aside from being imprecise, is not true, as one can easily show by example.[10] Hence we wish to impose additional restrictions on the densities f and g, with the aim of assuring that, first, for any fixed $\bar{\theta}$, $\Pr\{\theta \le \bar{\theta} \mid x/\theta = z\}$ is an increasing function of z, and, second, that for any fixed $\bar{x}$, $\Pr\{x \le \bar{x} \mid x/\theta = z\}$ is a decreasing function of z. Using $\tilde{H}(z, \theta)$ as above to denote the density of θ conditional on $x/\theta = z$ the first of these probabilities is

$$F(z,\bar{\theta}) = \int_0^{\bar{\theta}} \tilde{H}(z, \theta)\, d\theta,$$

while the second, in terms of the same function F, is $F(z, \bar{x}/z)$. The desired restriction is then found (by differentiating with respect to z) to be:

$$0 < F_z(z, \theta) < \frac{\theta \tilde{H}(z, \theta)}{z} \tag{24}$$

for all (z, θ). We proceed, under (24), with a discussion analogous to that which precedes Theorem 3.

Let

$$m(\theta) = \int V' \left[\frac{\theta'}{\theta} \frac{z'}{\varphi(z')} \right] \frac{\theta'}{\theta} \frac{z'}{\varphi(z')} H(z', \theta') \, dz' \, d\theta',$$

where, as in the proof of Theorem 3, $m(\theta)$ is positive with an elasticity between -1 and 0.

Then (19) may be written

$$h \left[\frac{z}{\varphi(z)} \right] \frac{z}{\varphi(z)} = \int m(\theta) H(z, \theta) \, d\theta. \tag{25}$$

Denote the right side of (25) by $G(z)$. Then integrating by parts,

$$G(z) = m(2) - \int m'(\theta) F(z, \theta) \, d\theta$$

where it will be recalled that 2 is the upper limit of the range of θ. Then

$$G'(z) = -\int m'(\theta) F_z(z'\theta) \, d\theta > 0,$$

by the first inequality of (24). Continuing,

$$\frac{zG'(z)}{G(z)} = -\frac{z \int m'(\theta) F_z(z, \theta) \, d\theta}{\int m(\theta) \tilde{H}(z, \theta) \, d\theta}$$

$$= \int w(z, \theta) \left[-\frac{\theta m'(\theta)}{m(\theta)} \right] \left[\frac{zF_z(z, \theta)}{\theta \tilde{H}(z, \theta)} \right] d\theta,$$

where $w(z, \theta) = [\int m(\theta) \tilde{H}(z, \theta) d\theta]^{-1} m(\theta) \tilde{H}(z, \theta)$. Hence, applying (24) again,

$$0 > \frac{z\varphi'(z)}{\varphi(z)} < 1. \tag{26}$$

We summarize the discussion of this case in

Theorem 4.   *Suppose the function $F(z, \theta)$, obtained from the densities $f(x)$ and $g(\theta)$, satisfies the restriction (24). Then (17) has a unique solution $p(m, x, \theta) = m\varphi(x/\theta)$, where φ is a continuously differentiable function, with an elasticity between zero and one.*

Theorems 2–4 indicate that, within this framework, monetary changes have real consequences only because agents cannot discriminate perfectly between real and monetary demand shifts. Since their ability to discriminate should not be altered by a proportional change in the *scale* of monetary policy, intuition suggests that such scale changes should have no real consequences. We formalize this as a corollary to Theorem 4:

Corollary.   *Let the hypotheses of Theorem* 4 *hold, but let the transfer variable be* $y = \lambda x$, *where* λ *is a positive constant. Then the equilibrium price is* $p(m, y, \theta) = m\varphi(y/\lambda\theta) = m\varphi(x/\theta)$, *where* φ *is as in Theorem* 4.

Proof.   In the derivation of (19), let $z = y/\lambda\theta = x/\theta$.

6   Positive Implications of the Theory

In the previous section we have studied the determination of price in one of the markets in this two market economy: the one which received a fraction $\theta/2$ of producers. Excluding the limiting case in which the disturbance is purely monetary, this price function was found to take the form $m\varphi(x/\theta)$, where $\varphi(x/\theta)$ is positive with an elasticity between zero and one. Recalling the study of the individual producer–consumer in section 3, this price function implies an equilibrium employment function $n(x/\theta)$, where $n'(x/\theta) > 0$.[11] That is, increases in demand induce increases in real output. Since the two markets are identical in structure, equilibrium price in the other market will be $m\varphi(x/(2 - \theta))$ and employment will be $n(x/(2 - \theta))$. In short, we have characterized behavior in all markets in the economy under all possible states.

With this accomplished, it is in order to ask whether this behavior does in fact resemble certain aspects of the observed business cycle. One way of phrasing this question is: how would citizens of this economy describe the ups and downs they experience?[12]

Certainly casual observers would describe periods of higher than average x-values (monetary expansions) as "good times" even, or perhaps especially, in retrospect. The older generation will do so with good reason: they receive the transfer, and it raises their real consumption levels to higher than average levels. The younger generation will similarly approve a monetary expansion as it occurs: they perceive it only through a higher-than-average price of the goods they are selling which, on average, means an increase in their real wealth. In the future, they will, of course, be disappointed (on average) in the real consumption their accumulated balances provide. Yet there is no reason for them to attribute this disappointment to the previous expansion; it would be much more natural to criticize the current inflation.

This criticism could be expected to be particularly severe during periods, which will regularly arise, when inflation continues at a higher than average rate while real output declines.[13] To summarize, in spite of the symmetry between ups and downs built into this simple model, *all* participants will agree in viewing periods of high real output as better than other periods.[14]

Less casual observers will similarly be misled. To see why, we consider the results of fitting a variant of an econometric Phillips curve on realizations generated by the economy described above. Let Y_t denote real GNP (or employment) in period t, and let P_t be the implicit GNP deflator for t. Consider the regression hypothesis

$$\ln Y_t = \beta_0 + \beta_1(\ln P_t - \ln P_{t-1}) + \epsilon_t, \tag{27}$$

where $\epsilon_1, \epsilon_2, \ldots$ is a sequence of independent, identically distributed random variables with 0 mean. Certainly a positive estimate for β_1 would, provided the estimated residuals do not violate the hypothesis, be interpreted as evidence for the existence of a "trade-off" between inflation and real output. By this point, it should be clear intuitively that there is no such trade-off in the model under study, yet $\hat{\beta}_1$ will turn out to be positive. We next develop the latter point more explicitly.

We have:

$$Y_t = \frac{1}{2} \theta_t Nn \left(\frac{x_t}{\theta_t}\right) + \frac{1}{2} (2 - \theta_t)Nn \left(\frac{x_t}{2 - \theta_t}\right) \tag{28}$$

and,

$$P_t Y_t = \frac{1}{2} \theta_t Nn \left(\frac{x_t}{\theta_t}\right) m_t \varphi \left(\frac{x_t}{\theta_t}\right) + \frac{1}{2} (2 - \theta_t)Nn \left(\frac{x_t}{2 - \theta_t}\right) m_t \varphi \left(\frac{x_t}{2 - \theta_t}\right). \tag{29}$$

Let $\mu = E[\ln(x)] = \int \ln(x) f(x) \, dx$. Regarding the logs of the right sides of (28) and (29) as functions of $\ln(x_t)$ and θ_t, expanding these about $(\mu, 1)$ and discarding terms of the second order and higher we obtain the approximations:

$$\ln(Y_t) = \ln(N) + \ln(n(\mu)) + \eta_n[\ln x_t - \mu], \tag{30}$$

and

$$\ln(P_t) - \ln(P_{t-1}) = \eta_\varphi \ln x_t + (1 - \eta_\varphi) \ln x_{t-1}, \tag{31}$$

where η_n and η_φ are the elasticities of the functions n and φ, respectively, evaluated at μ.

Using (30) and (31), one can compute the approximate[15] probability limit of the estimated coefficient $\hat{\beta}_1$ of (27). It is the covariance of $\ln(Y_t)$ and $\ln(P_t/P_{t-1})$, divided by the variance of the latter, or

$$\frac{\eta_n \eta_\varphi}{1 - 2\eta_\varphi + 2\eta_\varphi^2} > 0.$$

The estimated residuals from this regression will exhibit negative serial correlation. By adding $\ln(Y_{t-1})$ as an additional variable, however, this problem is eliminated and a near perfect fit is obtained [cf. (30) and (31)]. The coefficient on the inflation rate remains positive.[16]

To summarize this section, we have deliberately constructed an economy in which there is *no* usable trade-off between inflation and real output. Yet the econometric evidence for the existence of such trade-offs is much more convincing here than is the comparable evidence from the real world.

7 Policy Considerations

Within the framework developed and studied in the preceding sections, the choice of a monetary policy is equivalent to the choice of a density function f governing the stochastic rate of monetary expansion. Densities f which are concentrated on a single point correspond to fixing the rate of monetary growth at a constant percentage rate k. Following Friedman, we shall call such a policy a *k-percent rule*. Any other policy implies random fluctuations about a constant mean. Since (as far as I know) no critic of a k-percent rule consciously advocates a randomized policy in its stead, there is little interest pursuing a study of monetary policies within the restricted class available to us in this context. We can, however, show that *if* a k-percent rule is followed the competitive allocation will be Pareto-optimal. This demonstration will occupy the remainder of this section.

For the case of a constant money supply ($x \equiv 1$) there is an equilibrium price function $m\varphi(1/\theta)$, the properties of which are given in Theorem 3. Corresponding to this price function are functions $\bar{c}(\theta)$, $\bar{n}(\theta)$ which give the equilibrium values of consumption and labor supply of the young for each possible state of the world, θ. Since product is exhausted, these imply an average per capita consumption level for the old in the same market:[17]

$$\bar{c}'(\theta) = \theta[\bar{n}(\theta) - \bar{c}(\theta)].$$

By the Corollary to Theorem 4, this allocation rule $\{\bar{c}(\theta), \bar{n}(\theta), \bar{c}'(\theta)\}$ will be followed if monetary policy follows any k-percent rule. We wish to compare the efficiency of this rule to alternative (nonmarket) allocation rules $\{c(\theta), n(\theta), c'(\theta)\}$.

The individuals whose tastes are to be taken into account are the successive generations inhabiting the model economy. If we continue to ignore calendar time (to treat present and future generations symmetrically) each generation can be indexed by the states of nature (θ, θ') which prevail during its lifetime. This leads to the notion that one allocation is superior to another in a Pareto sense if it is preferred *uniformly* over all possible states, or to the following

Definition. An allocation rule $\{\bar{c}(\theta), \bar{n}(\theta), \bar{c}'(\theta)\}$ is Pareto-optimal if it satisfies

$$c(\theta) + \frac{1}{\theta} c'(\theta) \leq n(\theta), \qquad c(\theta), n(\theta), c'(\theta) \geq 0 \qquad\qquad (32)$$

(is feasible) for all $0 < \theta < 2$, and if there is no feasible allocation rule $\{c(\theta), n(\theta), c'(\theta)\}$ such that

$$U[c(\theta), n(\theta)] \geq U[\bar{c}(\theta)\bar{n}(\theta)], \qquad\qquad (33)$$
$$c'(\theta) \geq \bar{c}'(\theta), \qquad\qquad (34)$$

for all θ, with strict inequality in either (33) or (34) over some subset of $(0, 2)$ assigned positive probability by $g(\theta)$.

We then have:

Theorem 5. *The equilibrium $\{\bar{c}(\theta), \bar{n}(\theta), \bar{c}'(\theta)\}$, which arises under a k-percent rule, is Pareto-optimal.*

Proof. Suppose, to the contrary, that an allocation $\{c(\theta), n(\theta), c'(\theta)\}$ satisfying (32)–(34) exists. Recall from sections 3 and 5 that the problem

$$\max_{c,n,\lambda} \left\{ U(c,n) + \int V\left[\frac{\lambda}{m\varphi(1/\theta')}\right] g(\theta') \, d\theta' \right\},$$

subject to

$$m\varphi\left(\frac{1}{\theta}\right)[n - c] - \lambda \geq 0$$

is uniquely solved by $\bar{c}(\theta)$, $\bar{n}(\theta)$ and $\lambda = m/\theta$. Hence $\bar{c}'(\theta) = [\varphi(1/\theta)]^{-1}$.
Now using (32), if

$$\lambda(\theta) = [n(\theta) - c(\theta)]m\varphi\left(\frac{1}{\theta}\right) = \frac{m}{\theta}\varphi\left(\frac{1}{\theta}\right)c'(\theta),$$

then $c(\theta)$, $n(\theta)$, $\lambda(\theta)$ is feasible for this problem. Since (if it differs from
the equilibrium) it cannot be optimal for this problem,

$$U[\bar{c}(\theta), \bar{n}(\theta)] + \int V\left[\frac{1}{\theta\varphi(1/\theta')}\right] g(\theta')\,d\theta'$$

$$> U[c(\theta), n(\theta)] + \int V\left[\frac{(1/\theta)\,\varphi(1/\theta)c'\,(\theta)}{\varphi\,(1/\theta')}\right] g(\theta')\,d\theta'.$$

By (33), this implies

$$\int \left\{V\left[\frac{1}{\theta\varphi(1/\theta')}\right] - V\left[\frac{(1/\theta)\,\varphi(1/\theta)c'(\theta)}{\varphi(1/\theta')}\right]\right\} g(\theta')\,d\theta > 0. \tag{35}$$

But by (34), $c'(\theta) \geq \bar{c}'(\theta)$, so that

$$V\left[\frac{(1/\theta)\varphi(1/\theta)c'(\theta)}{\varphi(1/\theta')}\right] \geq V\left[\frac{\varphi(1/\theta)\bar{c}'(\theta)}{\theta\varphi(1/\theta')}\right] = V\left[\frac{1}{\theta\varphi(1/\theta')}\right].$$

This contradicts (35), contradicting the assumed superiority of $\{c(\theta),$
$n(\theta)\ c'(\theta)\}$, and completes the proof.

Two features of this discussion should perhaps be reemphasized.
First, Theorem 5 does *not* compare resource allocation under a k-
percent rule to allocations which result from other monetary policies.
In general, the latter allocations will be randomized, in the sense that
allocation for given θ will be stochastic. It *does* compare allocation
under a k-percent rule to other nonrandomized (and thus nonmarket)
allocation rules. Second, our discussion of optimality takes the market
and information structure of the economy as a physical *datum*. Obviously, if the two markets can costlessly be merged, superior resource
allocation can be obtained.

8 Conclusion

This paper has been an attempt to resolve the paradox posed by Gurley [4], in his mild but accurate parody of Friedmanian monetary theory: "Money is a veil, but when the veil flutters, real output sputters." The resolution has been effected by postulating economic agents free of money illusion, so that the Ricardian hypothetical experiment of a fully announced, proportional monetary expansion will have no real consequences (that is, so that money *is* a veil). These rational agents are then placed in a setting in which the information conveyed to traders by market prices is inadequate to permit them to distinguish real from monetary disturbances. In this setting, monetary fluctuations lead to real output movements in the same direction.

In order for this resolution to carry any conviction, it has been necessary to adopt a framework simple enough to permit a precise specification of the information available to each trader at each point in time, and to facilitate verification of the rationality of each trader's behavior. To obtain this simplicity, most of the interesting features of the observed business cycle have been abstracted from, with one notable exception: the Phillips curve emerges not as an unexplained empirical fact, but as a central feature of the solution to a general equilibrium system.

Appendix Proof of Theorem 1

We first show the existence of a unique solution to (19). Define $\Psi(z)$ by

$$\Psi(z) = h\left[\frac{z}{\varphi(z)}\right]\frac{z}{\varphi(z)}.$$

Let G_1 be the inverse of the function $h(x)x$, so that $z/\varphi(z) = G_1[\Psi(z)]$. The function $G_1(x)$ is positive for all $x > 0$, and satisfies

$$\lim_{x \to 0} G_1(x) = 0, \tag{A1}$$

and

$$0 < \frac{xG_1'(x)}{G_1(x)} < 1. \tag{A2}$$

Let $G_2(x) = V'(x)x$. $G_2(x) > 0$ for all $x > 0$ and, repeating (5) and (6),

$$0 < \frac{xG_2'(x)}{G_2(x)} \le 1 - a < 1. \tag{A3}$$

In terms of the functions Ψ, G_1, and G_2 (19) becomes

$$\Psi(z) = \int G_2 \left[G_1(\Psi(x')) \frac{\theta'}{\theta} \right] \tilde{H}(z, \theta) H(z', \theta') \, d\theta \, d\theta' \, dz'. \tag{A4}$$

Let S denote the space of bounded, continous functions on $(-\infty, \infty)$, normed by

$$\|f\| = \sup_z |f(z)|.$$

Define the operator T on S by

$$Tf = \ln \int G_2 \left[G_1(e^{f(z')}) \frac{\theta'}{\theta} \right] \tilde{H}(z, \theta) H(z', \theta') \, d\theta \, d\theta' \, dz'.$$

In terms of T, (A4) is

$$\ln \Psi = T \ln \Psi. \tag{A5}$$

We have:

Lemma 2.   *T is a contraction mapping: for any f, $g \in S$,*

$$\|Tf - Tg\| \le (1 - a)\|f - g\|.$$

Proof.

$$\|Tf - Tg\| = \sup_z \left| \ln \int w(\theta, z, \theta', z') \frac{G_2[G_1(e^{f(z')})(\theta'/\theta)]}{G_2[G_1(e^{g(z')})(\theta'/\theta)]} \, d\theta \, d\theta' \, dz' \right|,$$

where

$$w(\theta, z, \theta', z')$$
$$= [\textstyle\int G_2 \tilde{H}(z, \theta) H(z', \theta') \, d\theta \, d\theta' \, dz']^{-1} [G_2 \tilde{H}(z, \theta) H(z', \theta')].$$

Since $w(\theta, z, \theta', z') > 0$ and $\int w \, d\theta \, d\theta' \, dz' = 1$ we have, continuing,

$$\|Tf - Tg\| \le \sup_{z, \theta', \theta} \left| \ln G_2 \left[G_1(e^{f(z)}) \frac{\theta'}{\theta} \right] - \ln G_2 \left[G_1(e^{g(z)}) \frac{\theta'}{\theta} \right] \right|. \tag{A6}$$

Now

$$\frac{\partial}{\partial x} \ln G_2 \left[G_1(e^x) \frac{\theta'}{\theta} \right] = \left[\frac{G_1(e^x)(\theta'/\theta)G_2'[G_1(e^x)(\theta'/\theta)]}{G_2[G_1(e^x)(\theta'/\theta)]} \right] \left[\frac{e^x G_1'(e^x)}{G_1(e^x)} \right].$$

By (A3), the first of these factors is between 0 and $1 - a$. By (A2), the second factor is between 0 and 1. Since these observations are valid for all (x, θ, θ'), application of the mean value theorem to the right side of (A6) gives

$$\|Tf - Tg\| = (1 - a)\|f - g\|,$$

which completes the proof.

It follows from Lemma 2 and the Banach fixed point theorem that the equation $Tf = f$ has a unique bounded, continuous solution f^*. Then $\Psi(z) = e^{f^*(z)}$ is the unique solution to (A4). Clearly $\Psi(z)$ is positive, bounded, and bounded away from zero. It follows that $G_1[\Psi(z)]$ has these properties, and hence that $\varphi(z) = z/(G_1[\Psi(z)])$ is the function referred to in Theorem 1.

Clearly $m\varphi(x/\theta)$ is an equilibrium price function [satisfies (17)]. In view of Lemma 1, any solution $p(m, x, \theta)$ must satisfy:

$$h \left[\frac{mx}{\theta p(m,x,\theta)} \right] \frac{mx}{\theta p(m,x,\theta)}$$
$$= \int V' \left[\frac{m\xi x'}{\theta' p(m\xi,x',\theta')} \frac{\theta'x}{\theta\xi} \right] \frac{m\xi x'}{\theta' p(m\xi,x',\theta')} \, dG \left(\xi,x',\theta' \Big| \frac{\xi}{\theta} \right).$$

Now let $\Psi(m, x, \theta) = h[mx/(\theta p(m, x, \theta))] \, mx/[\theta p(m, x, \theta)]$. Proceeding as before, one finds that there is only one bounded solution $\Psi(m, x, \theta)$. This proves Theorem 1.

Notes

1. The usefulness of this model as a framework for considering problems in monetary theory is indicated by the work of Cass and Yaari [1, 2].

2. This is not quite right. If members of the younger generation were risk preferrers, they could and would exchange claims on future consumption among themselves so as to increase variance. This possibility will be ruled out in the next section.

3. This device of viewing traders as randomly allocated over distinct markets serves two purposes. First, it provides a setting in which information is imperfect in a specific (and hence analyzable) way. Second, random variation

in the allocation of traders provides a source of *relative* price variation. This could as well have been achieved by postulating random taste or technology shifts, with little effect on the structure of the model.

4. This somewhat artificial assumption, like the absence of capital goods and the serial independence of shocks, is part of an effort to keep the laws governing the transition of the economy from state to state as simple as possible. In general, I have tried to abstract from all sources of *persistence* of fluctuations, in order to focus on the nature of the initial disturbances.

5. The restrictions (4) and (5) are similar to those utilized in an econometric study of the labor market conducted by Rapping and myself, [5]. Their function here is the same as it was in [5]: to assure that the Phillips curve slopes the "right way."

6. There is a question as to whether cash balances in this scheme are "transactions balances" or a "store of value." I think it is clear that the model under discussion is not rich enough to permit an interesting discussion of the distinctions between these, or other, motives for holding money. On the other hand, *all* motives for holding money require that it be held for a positive time interval before being spent: there is no reason to use money (as opposed to barter) if it is to be received for goods and then *instantaneously* exchanged for other goods. There is also the question of whether money "yields utility." Certainly the answer in this context is *yes,* in the sense that if one imposes on an individual the constraint that he cannot hold cash, his utility under an optimal policy is lower than it will be if this constraint is removed. It should be equally clear, however, that this argument does *not* imply that real or nominal balances should be included as an argument in the individual preference functions. The distinction is the familiar one between the utility function and the *value* of this function under a particular set of choices.

7. The assumption that traders use the correct conditional distribution in forming expectations, together with the assumption that all exchanges take place at the market clearing price, implies that markets in this economy are *efficient,* as this term is defined by Roll [9]. It will also be true that price expectations are *rational* in the sense of Muth [7].

8. The restriction, embodied in this definition, that price may be expressed as a function of the state of the economy appears innocuous but in fact is very strong. For example, in the models of Cass and Yaari without storage, the state of the economy never changes, so the only sequences satisfying the definition used here are constant sequences (or stationary schemes, in the terminology of [1]).

9. To decide whether it is plausible that m should factor out of the equilibrium price function, the reader should ask himself: what are the consequences of a *fully announced* change in the quantity of money which does not alter the distribution of money over persons? To see why only the *ratio* of x to θ affects price, recall that x/θ *alone* determines the demand for goods facing each individual producer.

10. For example, let x take only the values 1 and 1.05 and let θ be either 0.5 or 1.5. Then a *decrease* of x/θ from 2.0 to 0.7 implies (with certainty) an increase in x from 1 to 1.05. It is not difficult to construct continuous densities f and g which exhibit this sort of behavior.

11. The analysis of section 3 showed that if age-0 consumers wish to accumulate more real balances, they will finance this accumulation in part by supplying more labor. In section 5 it was shown that equilibrium per capita real balances, $[\theta\varphi(x/\theta)]^-x$, rise with x/θ. These two facts together imply $n'(x/\theta) > 0$.

12. The following discussion, while I hope it is suggestive, is not intended to be a substitute for econometric evidence.

13. The term "regularly arise" is appropriate. The *current* real output level, relative to "normal," depends only on the current monetary expansion. The current inflation rate, however, depends on the current *and* previous period's monetary expansion. Thus a large expansion followed by a modest contraction will occur (though perhaps infrequently) and will result in the situation described in the text.

14. This unanimity rests, of course, on the assumption that new money is introduced so as *never* to subject cash holders to a real capital loss. If transfers were, say, randomly distributed over young and old, there would be a group among the old which perceives monetary expansion as harmful.

15. Because (30) and (31) are approximations.

16. It is interesting to note that if one formulates a distributed lag version of the Phillips curve, as Rapping and I have done in [6], one will obtain a positive estimated *long-run* real output-inflation trade-off *even if* a model of the above sort is valid.

17. The unequal distribution of money acquired during the first year of life (due to varying θ values) creates two classes among the old. In general, then, no one will actually obtain the average consumption $\bar{c}'(\theta)$. But a reallocation which receives the unanimous consent of the old in the market receiving a fraction θ of producers is possible if and only if average consumption is increased. For our purposes, then, we can ignore the distribution of actual consumption about this average.

References

1. D. Cass and M. E. Yaari, A Re-examination of the Pure Consumption Loans Model, *J. Polit. Econ.* **74** (1966).

2. D. Cass and M. E. Yaari, "A Note on the role of Money in Providing Sufficient Intermediation," Cowles Foundation Discussion Paper No. 215, 1966.

3. M. Friedman, The role of monetary policy, *Amer. Econ. Rev.* **58** (1968).

4. J. G. Gurley, review of M. Friedman, "A Program for Monetary Stability," *Rev. Econ. Stat.* **43** (1961), 307–308.

5. R. E. Lucas, Jr., and L. A. Rapping, Real wages, employment and inflation, *J. Polit. Econ.* **77** (1969).

6. R. E. Lucas, Jr., and L. A. Rapping, Price Expectations and the Phillips Curve, *Amer. Econ. Rev.* **59** (1969).

7. J. F. Muth, Rational expectations and the theory of price movements, *Econometrica* **29** (1961).

8. E. S. Phelps, introductory chapter *in* E. S. Phelps, *et al.*, "Microeconomic Foundations of Employment and Inflation Theory," Norton, New York, 1969.

9. R. Roll, The efficient market model applied to U.S. Treasury bill rates, University of Chicago doctoral dissertation, 1968.

10. P. A. Samuelson, An exact consumption-loan model of interest with or without the contrivance of money, *J. Polit. Econ.* **66** (1958).

Econometric Testing of the Natural Rate Hypothesis

1 Introduction

A growing number of economists are questioning the widely accepted view that empirical Phillips curves provide even a rough summary of the inflation–real output "trade-offs" available to society. The main source of this skepticism is the notion that the observed Phillips curve results from the way agents form and respond to price and wage expectations, and that attempts to move along the curve to increase output may be frustrated by changes in expectations that shift the curve. The objective of this paper will be to consider some of the issues involved in capturing this "expectations theory" or "natural rate hypothesis"[1] in an explicit, testable econometric model.

Before addressing these issues, however, it is well to acknowledge, or rather to emphasize, the degree to which the existence of an inflation–real output trade-off is grounded in accepted econometric methodology. It is an observed fact that, in U.S. time series, inflation rates and unemployment are negatively correlated. This remains true (with the obvious sign change) if unemployment is replaced with de-trended

Reprinted from *The Econometrics of Price Determination Conference,* ed. Otto Eckstein, Washington, D.C.: Board of Governors of the Federal Reserve System, 1972, pp. 50–59, by permission.

The author of this paper, who is Professor of Economics, Graduate School of Industrial Administration, Carnegie-Mellon University, has benefited from discussions with colleagues at Carnegie-Mellon University—particularly Leonard Rapping, Allan Meltzer, and Martin Bronfenbrenner—and at the University of Washington, especially Allan Hynes.

real output, if price inflation is replaced by money wage inflation, and so forth. It follows that this short-run (whatever this ambiguous qualification means) trade-off will be exhibited in *any* econometric model estimated from these time series, regardless of its complexity, lag structure, or theoretical motivation. These basic points should not be obscured by the instability and arbitrariness of so many empirical Phillips curves: when stable, well-motivated Phillips curves are found (and they will be) they will continue to exhibit the same trade-offs as do the current versions.

These observations raise a dual challenge to proponents of a natural rate hypothesis. The first involves econometric testing: if one rejects the use of observed correlation, as already discussed, as a test of the existence of a usable trade-off, what is the alternative? Or is the natural rate hypothesis to be judged solely on "theoretical grounds"? The second involves policy evaluation: if one cannot evaluate alternative economic policies by extrapolating along estimated regression lines, what alternatives exist? Or is the goal of quantitative policy evaluation to be abandoned?

The answers to these questions will depend, of course, on the way the natural rate hypothesis is translated into explicit theory. Since this process has scarcely begun, and is certain to involve much controversy, we shall proceed tentatively, using simple examples. Section 2 reviews the theoretical link between wage–price expectations and the observed inflation–real output trade-off. Sections 3 and 4 consider alternative models of expectations formation, or the link between expected and actual prices. In Section 3, it is argued that the standard hypothesis of "adaptive expectations" leads to an inadequate formulation of the natural rate hypothesis. Section 4 considers the alternative of "rational expectations," originally proposed by Muth, observing that this assumption *does* lead to the natural rate hypothesis. In Sections 4 and 5, econometric testing and policy evaluation under rational expectations are discussed. Section 6 summarizes conclusions.

2 Expectations and Aggregate Supply

It is natural (to an economist) to view the cyclical correlation between real output and prices as arising from a volatile aggregate demand schedule that traces out a relatively stable, upward-sloping supply curve.[2] This point of departure leads to something of a paradox, since the absence of money illusion on the part of firms and consumers appears to imply a vertical aggregate supply schedule, which in turn implies that aggregate demand fluctuations of a purely nominal nature should lead to price fluctuations only. The paradox may be resolved by the adoption of a refined view of the decision problem facing agents, in which short-run supply behavior under available information differs from long-run behavior under perfect information. This resolution was suggested by Hicks (and by many others since) as indicated by the following passage from *Value and Capital*:[3] "In order to explain the rigidity of wages, we have to assume in the parties to the wage bargain some sense of normal prices, hardly distinguished (perhaps) from "just" prices. The rigidity of wages extends over precisely that time— it may be quite a long time—during which the parties concerned persuade themselves that changes in related prices (whether prices of the products of labor, or of the things labor buys) are temporary changes. Once they become convinced that these changes are permanent changes, there is a tendency for wages to change."

Recently several models have been developed that attempt to capture the supply behavior described verbally by Hicks. This analysis involves two distinct parts: the analysis of the optimal response to given current and expected prices and wages, and the study of the relation of expected to actual prices. The first part is straightforward, and will be reviewed in the remainder of this section. The second, discussed at length in the following sections, is largely unsettled.

In [7], Rapping and I obtained Hicksian labor supply behavior from a two-period consumer decision model. The consumer's objects of choice are four: (1) current consumption of goods; (2) current leisure; (3) future goods; and (4) future leisure. Current prices and wages are known; the consumer has precise (but not necessarily correct) expectations of future prices. This decision problem leads to a labor supply function relating quantity supplied to current *and* expected future prices and wages, or which, in other terminology, permits the supply response to *permanent* wage or price changes to differ from the response to *transitory* changes.

This labor supply response is transmitted through firms to goods markets, leading to an aggregate supply function that is vertical with respect to permanent price changes (consistent with the absence of money illusion) but that slopes upward with respect to transitory price movements (consistent with observed price–output correlations).

Thus, letting y_t be the log of real output in t, P_t be the log of the price level, and P_t^* be the log of an index of expected future prices, one obtains an aggregate supply function:[4]

$$y_t = a(P_t - P_t^*) \tag{1}$$

This rationalization of the Phillips trade-off, or in less current language, of price "rigidity," has been present (though not necessarily dominant) in the literature for many years. It may be supplemented by consideration of the firm's inventory problem (which involves the same sort of intertemporal substitution as the consumer's supply problem), by considering activities of workers other than simply work and "leisure" (for example, school, job search, and so forth), and in other ways as well. In short, whereas this rationalization need not be regarded as the *only* way to account for rigid prices, neither should it be regarded as particularly novel.

To this point, two tacit assumptions have been applied to the relationship of P_t^* to P_t. The first is that the initial or first-period response of P_t^* to a change in P_t is less than proportional. If this were not so, the short-run supply schedule (Equation 1) would have a slope inconsistent with observed price–output correlations. The second is that under perfectly constant prices, $P_t^* = P_t$. If this were not so, there would be no sense in which Equation 1 could be said to be based on the hypothesis of rational behavior. There are, of course, many distinct ways to link expected and actual prices that satisfy these two assumptions. More important, these two assumptions, together with Equation 1, do *not* imply the existence of a natural output level or even a modest skepticism about the existence of output–inflation trade-offs. On the contrary, Equation 1 is consistent with the most extreme inflationism (and has, no doubt, been used to defend it).

The crucial issue, then, is the nature of the relationship between expected and actual prices. Two alternative approaches are discussed in the following sections.

3 Aggregate Supply under Adaptive Expectations

In the previous section it was argued that Equation 1 is a theory of aggregate supply, albeit in primitive form, once the relation between actual prices, P_t, and expected prices, P_t^*, is made explicit. In this section, we pursue the implications of adjoining to Equation 1 the hypothesis of *adaptive expectations*.

To begin at the simplest level, suppose that P_t^* and P_t are related by:

$$P_t^* = \lambda P_t + (1 - \lambda)P_{t-1}^*, \qquad 0 < \lambda < 1 \tag{2}$$

Combining Equations 1 and 2 by using a Koyck transformation:

$$y_t = a(1 - \lambda)(P_t - P_{t-1}) + (1 - \lambda)y_{t-1} \tag{3}$$

Equation 3 is a perfectly serviceable supply theory, and this serviceability has earned it wide use in applied econometric work. At first sight, it also seems to embody the important features of the expectations theory sketched in the preceding section. First, since the coefficient $a(1 - \lambda)$ on the current inflation rate is positive, it predicts a short-run inflation–output trade-off in the right direction. Second, it predicts that a once-and-for-all change in the price *level* will have *no* long-run effect on real output.

On reflection, however, Equation 3 if taken seriously promises *un-limited* real output gains from a well-chosen inflationary policy. Even a once-and-for-all price increase, while yielding no output expansion in the limit, will induce increased output over the (infinity of) transition periods. Moreover, a sustained inflation will yield a permanently increased level of output. Further, the implications regarding output are true for any positive value of $a(1 - \lambda)$ so that, since we know a short-run trade-off is present in the U.S. time series, this long-run possibility concerning output cannot be refuted by experience within the framework given by Equation 3. In short, restricting oneself to expectations formation hypotheses of the form (2) leads to a supply theory possessing *none* of the attributes associated with the leading verbal view of the natural rate hypothesis.

An elegant generalization of the adaptive scheme (2), proposed by Jorgenson,[5] appears to offer a way out of this dilemma. To develop this approach, let L denote the lag operator on a time series x_t defined by; $Lx_t = x_{t-1}$. Let $u(L)$ and $v(L)$ be polynomials in the lag operator. Then Equation 2 is the special case of

$$v(L)P_t^* = u(L)P_t \tag{4}$$

with $v(L) = 1 - (1 - \lambda)L$ and $u(L) = \lambda$. Other specifications of $u(L)$ and $v(L)$ can lead to a wide variety of price expectations hypotheses. Now multiplying Equation 1 through by $v(L)$ and combining with

Equation 4, one obtains the supply theory:

$$v(L)y_t = a[v(L) - u(L)]P_t \tag{5}$$

If $[v(L) - u(L)]k = 0$ for any constant k (it is easy to see that Equation 2 satisfies this restriction) and if the roots of the ordinary polynomial $v(x)$ are greater than unity in absolute value (that is, if the difference, Equation 4, is stable), then a once-and-for-all price level change will have no real output effect in the long run. Other restrictions on $u(L)$ and $v(L)$ can assure that a constant inflation rate has no long-run output effect, or that a constant rate of price acceleration has no long-run effect, and so on.

Thus, the absence of a long-run real output–inflation trade-off can, within this framework, be expressed as an ordinary linear hypothesis and subjected to statistical hypothesis testing. This apparently promising route has been pursued, with mixed success, in several empirical studies.[6]

Unfortunately, the deficiencies of Equation 2 as a formalization of the expectations hypothesis carry over, albeit in obscure form, to the more elaborate Equation 4. First, Equations 4 and 5 still imply that real output gains will follow an inflationary policy over an infinitely long period of adjustment, and these interim gains may be made as large as desired. Second, Equations 4 and 5 still imply that sustained gains in real output will result from *some* inflation policy, although not necessarily from one so simple as a once-and-for-all change in the inflation rate.

The conclusions of this section and the preceding one can be summarized very simply. The supply model (Equation 1) developed in Section 2 says that inflation will yield higher real output *on average* only if price expectations fall below actual prices *on average*. The adaptive expectation schemes reviewed in this section do not rule out this possibility of systematically biased expectations; hence they necessarily permit both short- and long-run Phillips-like trade-offs between inflation and real output.

4 Aggregate Supply under Rational Expectations
In the preceding section, the hypothesis of adaptive expectations was rejected as a component of the natural rate hypothesis on the grounds that, under *some* policy

$$E\{P_t - P_t^*\} \tag{6}$$

is non-zero. If the impossibility of a non-zero value for Expression 6 is taken as an essential feature of the natural rate theory, one is led simply to adding the assumption that Expression 6 is zero as an additional axiom, or to assume that expectations are *rational* in the sense of Muth [9].[7] Indeed, with aggregate supply described by Equation 1, rational expectations are *equivalent* to the existence of a natural output rate.

To use Expression 6 with any meaning, one must specify the distribution with respect to which the mean value is taken. This involves two major steps: (1) the inclusion in the model of an aggregate demand side (so that the distributions of actual and expected prices may be simultaneously determined) and (2) a specification of what is meant by a *policy*. Without taking these steps, one cannot go beyond the obvious link between Expression 6 and the natural rate hypothesis to consider the issues of testing and policy raised in the introduction. Of necessity, we proceed with an extremely simple illustrative example.

For an aggregate demand schedule, we use the rectangular hyperbola

$$y_t + P_t = x_t \tag{7}$$

where x_t (the log of nominal GNP) is viewed as a shift parameter. By a *policy* we shall mean a (possibly randomized) *rule* giving the current value of x_t as a function of the state of the system.[8] For concreteness, let us consider the particular policy (in this sense):

$$x_t = \rho_1 x_{t-1} + \rho_2 x_{t-2} + \epsilon_t \tag{8}$$

where $\{\epsilon_t\}$ is a sequence of independent random variables that are distributed identically and normally, each with mean zero and variance σ^2.

Again with a view to retaining simplicity we take the next period's price, P_{t+1}, as the variable of which P_t^* is a forecast.[9] Assume that P_t^* is equal to its mean value plus a forecast error, η_t, which shares the properties of ϵ_t but which is distributed independently of ϵ_t.

The state of the system at time t is now entirely described by the values of three variables: x_t, x_{t-1}, and η_t. Accordingly, one is led to define a *solution* of the system to be a set of functions P_t, y_t, P_t^* of x_t, x_{t-1}, and η_t which satisfy Equations 1 and 7 identically in these arguments. Given a solution, the expectation in Expression 6 now has content, and we can define a solution characterized by rational expectations as satisfying:

$$P_t^* = E\{P_{t+1} | x_t, x_{t-1}, \eta_t\} + \eta_t \tag{9}$$

Equations 1, 7, 8, and 9 constitute a system of equations in the unknown *functions* y_t, P_t, and P_t^*. The analysis of such systems is, in general, quite difficult but in the present linear model one can conjecture the form of the solution and calculate it directly, as follows.[10]

Let us first eliminate y_t between Equations 1 and 7, to obtain:

$$(1 + a)P_t - aP_t^* = x_t \tag{10}$$

We shall seek linear solutions P_t and P_t^* to Equations 9 and 10:

$$P_t = \pi_1 x_1 + \pi_2 x_{t-1} + \pi_3 \eta_t \tag{11}$$
$$P_t^* = \pi_4 x_t + \pi_5 x_{t-1} + \pi_6 \eta_t \tag{12}$$

Now substituting from Equations 11 and 12 into 10, and observing that the result is an identity in x_t, x_{t-1}, and η_t we have:

$$(1 + a)\pi_1 - a\pi_4 = 1 \tag{13}$$
$$(1 + a)\pi_2 - a\pi_5 = 0 \tag{14}$$
$$(1 + a)\pi_3 - a\pi_6 = 0 \tag{15}$$

Similarly, substituting from Equations 11 and 12 into 9, and using Equation 8 to compute $E\{x_{t+1} | x_t, x_{t-1}, \eta_t\}$, one obtains:

$$\pi_4 = \rho_1 \pi_1 + \pi_2 \tag{16}$$
$$\pi_5 = \pi_1 \rho_2 \tag{17}$$
$$\pi_6 = 1 \tag{18}$$

Equations 13 to 18 are six independent, linear restrictions on π_1, . . . π_6, and are readily solved for these parameter values in terms of ρ_1, ρ_2, and a. This gives the solution functions Equations 11 and 12; the solution for y_t is obtained from Equation 11 and the Identity 7.

The properties of these solutions may be discussed by reference to the solution for real output, calculated as above:

$$y_t = \frac{a(1 + a)(1 - \rho_1) - \rho_2 a^2}{(1 + a)[1 + a(1 - \rho_1)] - \rho_2 a^2} x_t$$
$$- \frac{\rho_2 a^2}{(1 + a)[1 + a(1 - \rho_1)] - \rho_2 a^2} x_{t-1} - \left(\frac{1}{1 + a}\right) \eta_t \tag{19}$$

The coefficient of x_t in Equation 19 is empirically between zero and 1: this, of course, is the observed "trade-off." This range of values is not predicted by the theory (that is, does not hold for all values of a, ρ_1, and ρ_2) but is consistent with "reasonable" parameter values.

The unconditional mean[11] of y_t is zero, since this is the mean of x_t and η_t, under all stable demand policies (ρ_1 and ρ_2). Thus, as anticipated earlier, the model implies a natural output rate that cannot be bettered on average. But one need not limit analysis to this observation. For *any* choice of the policy parameters (ρ_1, ρ_2, or σ^2) one may readily compute the time series properties of prices and real output. Thus, under perfectly stable demand ($\rho_1 = \rho_2 = \sigma^2 = 0$) real output will vary unsystematically due to the expectations error, η_t. Less obviously, real output will vary in the *same* unsystematic way under the simple random walk policy ($\rho_1 = 1$, $\rho_2 = 0$, σ^2 arbitrary) with the price level pursuing a random walk. (These superficially different policies share an important feature: any demand shift is "permanent." The tendency for demand to return to "normal," essential under the Hicksian view for price rigidity, is absent.) One could multiply these examples, but this is unnecessary to support the main point of this section: The rational expectations version of the natural rate hypothesis leads to a tractable model, fully capable of supporting quantitative policy evaluations.[12]

Before continuing, however, one particular "policy" deserves discussion. Under Equation 19, it is clear that the choice of an expansionary policy (a high ϵ_t) in the current period will increase current-period real output. As far as I know, the existence of a usable trade-off in this trivial sense is disputed by no one. The issue, then, is whether the recommendation to exploit this trade-off in the current period amounts to a *policy,* as that term is usually used. Certainly, if one views a policy as a *rule* describing a response to given values of state variables ("indicators"), this recommendation is *not* a policy: One cannot call for demand to be higher than average on average.

5 Testing the Natural Rate Hypothesis

Section 4 has developed a particular form of the natural rate hypothesis, and argued that it provides a workable theory, capable of aiding in the quantitative evaluation of a wide variety of policies. We now turn to an equally important question: How (if at all) can models of this class be tested?

Let us first discuss the wrong test, which is of interest in this case since it is universally believed to be the correct one.[13] From *ad hoc* estimation of Equation 19, without supporting theory, one would normally use the *sum* of the coefficients of x_t and x_{t-1} as a measure of the long-run effect of a once-and-for-all demand shift. The hypothesis that such a shift will not affect real output in the long run thus becomes the linear restriction that this sum of coefficients be zero. This test, or any of its many variants, has been to date the "standard" test of the natural rate view. Yet, it is clear from Equation 19 that *no such restriction is implied by the rational expectations version of the theory.*[14]

This paradox is easily resolved by the methods of the preceding section. A once-and-for-all move to a new, fixed demand level implies a change in the policy *parameters,* the consequences of which have been discussed. This policy cannot be evaluated by simply summing parameters implied by some previous, now irrelevant policy.

To develop the valid test, we discuss inference in this model more generally. The model consists of the policy function (Equation 8), plus the solutions for y_t, P_t, and P_t^*. Of the solutions, one is redundant in view of Identity 7. The solution for P_t^* is not usable, since its dependent variable is unobservable. We are left, then, with a two-equation model consisting of Equations 8 and 19. This model is recursive, so that ordinary least squares yield consistent, asymptotically normal estimates of the four slope parameters.

Under rationality of expectations, however, there are but three independent parameters in the system: a, ρ_1, and ρ_2. This fact leads us to several asymptotically valid tests. For concreteness, consider the following procedure. Obtain consistent estimators of ρ_1 and ρ_2 from Equation 8. Treating these as true values, Equation 19 is, under the null hypothesis, nonlinear in the single unknown parameter a. A standard Chi-square test, using a comparison of the sum of squared errors from Equation 19 estimated with and without this restriction, can then be used to evaluate the hypothesis.

I have dwelt on the mechanics of this test in order to leave no doubt as to the point of this section: the natural rate hypothesis restricts the *relationship* of policy parameters to behavioral parameters. It cannot be tested on a behavioral relationship (Phillips curve, supply function, and so on) alone.

This discussion can also lend insight into the conditions necessary for a successful test. An essential prerequisite is reliable estimates of the parameters governing policy. This suggests seeking periods when policies are relatively easy to describe in simple ways, such as periods of very stable demand, periods when demand fluctuates in some simple way, and so on. On the other hand, one need not wait for an experiment so clean as the "perfectly anticipated inflation" of the textbooks. What is required is a period in which policy has a stable, demonstrable stochastic structure, *not* one in which policy variables maintain stable realizations.

6 Conclusions

The example studied in this paper is far from being an operational econometric embodiment of the natural rate hypothesis. Nevertheless, it has led to a number of conclusions, the most important of which seem to me to be the following.

First, the hypothesis that agents form expectations adaptively (with adjustment parameters fixed) does *not* lead to the hypothesis of a natural rate of output. On the contrary, the two hypotheses are mutually contradictory. It follows that econometric models utilizing the adaptive hypothesis cannot provide a test of the natural rate view.

Second, the hypothesis of rational expectations *does* lead to the natural rate theory. Indeed, if imperfect expectations are the *only* source of price rigidity, the two hypotheses are equivalent.

Third, the natural rate hypothesis, correctly formulated, has *no* implications for the coefficients of distributed lag Phillips curves, or for any other single-equation expression of the empirical inflation–real output "trade-off."

Fourth, a valid test of the natural rate hypothesis involves a test of a restriction on the parameters "across equations" of a complete simultaneous equations model. The existence of a natural rate is thus a "systems property," like stability or identifiability.

Fifth, the natural rate hypothesis is consistent with quantitative policy evaluation. Under this hypothesis evaluation is performed *not* by extrapolating along estimated regression lines but by recomputing the parameters of the system under alternative policy proposals.

Notes

1. With no pretense of precision, let us define the natural rate hypothesis as the hypothesis that different time paths of the general price level will be associated with time paths of real output that do not differ *on average*. The term "expectations theory" was used in Lucas-Rapping [8]. Friedman [2] and Phelps [10] use the term "natural rate"; the latter usage will be followed here.

2. The issue of whether to treat observed prices and quantities as market clearing arouses more controversy than it deserves. I prefer thinking of markets as cleared partly because of logical difficulties with the leading alternative view (see Gordon and Hynes [3]), and partly because it leads the theory into the crucial questions of intertemporal substitution and expectations and away from the mechanical "auctioneer" of the standard dynamics.

3. Hicks ([5], pp. 270–71).

4. That is, one obtains an aggregate supply function that, other things being equal, increases as the expected inflation rate falls. Here, and elsewhere in the paper, we ignore the control variables that give content to the "other things being equal" qualification, and ignore all constant and trend terms. To facilitate the analysis of Section 4, we shall also assume log-linearity throughout.

5. In Jorgenson [6]. Jorgenson applies the term "rational" to distributed lags of the form (4). Since we shall use this term for an unrelated expectations hypothesis in the next section, we refer to Equation 4 and its special case Equation 2 as "adaptive."

6. The tests of Lucas-Rapping [8], Cagan [1], and Gordon [4] are essentially tests of linear restrictions on the coefficients of Equation 4. In addition to those actually carrying out such tests, many others have treated them as "the" test of the natural rate hypothesis. (See, for example, Tobin [12], Solow [11], and Phelps [10].)

7. My concern in this paper will be to show that rational expectations can lead to workable, testable cycle models. For the argument that this hypothesis is also plausible and consistent with a variety of evidence, the reader is referred to Muth [9].

8. In fact, of course, aggregate demand shifts result from many causes, only some of which would typically be called "policies." The assumption that policy works on aggregate demand directly is adopted here only for convenience; it does not affect the essentials of the argument.

Nor is the notion that "policies" in this overly broad sense may be randomized intended to be flippant, any more than the inclusion of error terms in investment functions is intended to suggest coin-tossing managers. The error in Equation 8 reflects merely governmental and private decisions not systematically related to the other variables of the model.

9. In practice, P_t^* is an index of expected prices over a number of future periods. It should be noted that this obviously relevant question ("Of what

future prices is P_t^* a forecast?'') simply did not arise under adaptive expectations, which should have alerted us that something was amiss.

10. The solution method used here closely parallels Muth's. The main difference is in what superficially appears to be a fine mathematical point. Muth defines solutions to be elements of the space of sequences of realizations, as opposed to being elements of the space of functions of current state variables. The definition used here is much more restrictive.

11. The reader will recall (compare Note 4) that we are ignoring constant and trend terms. Thus y_t is strictly interpreted as the percentage deviation of real output from its natural rate.

12. Provided, of course, that the policy satisfies the regularity conditions set out earlier in this section. Certainly, suppliers following Equation 1 could be "gamed" into higher production by an aggregate demand sequence that kept them in continual surprise; the point is that such a sequence could not be generated by a policy rule that responds to the state of the economy in a stationary way.

13. See the references cited in Note 6.

14. The restriction *could* be satisfied by the coefficients of Equation 19 but only due to a purely coincidental relationship between policy parameters and the parameter a reflecting intertemporal substitution possibilities.

References

1. Cagan, Phillip. "Theories of Mild, Continuing Inflation: A Critique and Extension," *Inflation: Its Causes, Consequences and Control,* ed. Stephen W. Rousseas. New York: New York University Press, 1968.

2. Friedman, Milton. "The Role of Monetary Policy," *The American Economic Review,* Vol. 58 (March 1968), pp. 1–17.

3. Gordon, Donald F., and Hynes, Allan. "On the Theory of Price Dynamics," *The New Microeconomics in Employment and Inflation Theory,* eds. E. S. Phelps *et al.* New York: W. W. Norton, 1970.

4. Gordon, Robert J. "The Recent Acceleration of Inflation and Its Lessons for the Future," *Brookings Papers on Economic Activity,* eds. Arthur M. Okun and George L. Perry, Vol. 1 (1970), pp. 8–14.

5. Hicks, J. R. *Value and Capital.* Oxford: Clarendon Press, 1946.

6. Jorgenson, Dale W. "Rational Distributed Lag Functions," *Econometrica,* Vol. 34 (January 1966), pp. 135–149.

7. Lucas, R. E., Jr., and Rapping, L. A. "Real Wages, Employment and Inflation," *Journal of Political Economy,* Vol. 77 (September/October 1969), pp. 721–754.

8. Lucas, R. E., Jr., and Rapping, L. A. "Price Expectations and the Phillips Curve," *The American Economic Review,* Vol. 59 (June 1969), pp. 342–350.

9. Muth, John F. "Rational Expectations and the Theory of Price Movements," *Econometrica,* Vol. 29 (July 1961), pp. 315–335.

10. Phelps, E. S. "Inflation, Expectations and Economic Theory." Paper presented at the Queen's University Conference on Inflation and the Canadian Experience, June 1970.

11. Solow, Robert M. Discussion of Robert J. Gordon's "The Recent Acceleration of Inflation and Its Lessons for the Future," *Brookings Papers on Economic Activity,* eds. Arthur M. Okun and George L. Perry, Vol. 1 (1970).

12. Tobin, James. Discussion of Phillip Cagan's "Theories of Mild, Continuing Inflation: A Critique and Extension." *Inflation: Its Causes, Consequences and Control,* ed. Stephen W. Rousseas. New York: New York University Press, 1968.

Econometric Policy Evaluation: A Critique

1 Introduction

The fact that nominal prices and wages tend to rise more rapidly at the peak of the business cycle than they do in the trough has been well recognized from the time when the cycle was first perceived as a distinct phenomenon. The inference that permanent inflation will therefore induce a permanent economic high is no doubt equally ancient, yet it is only recently that this notion has undergone the mysterious transformation from obvious fallacy to cornerstone of the theory of economic policy.

This transformation did not arise from new developments in economic theory. On the contrary, as soon as Phelps and others made the first serious attempts to rationalize the apparent trade-off in modern theoretical terms, the zero-degree homogeneity of demand and supply functions was re-discovered in this new context (as Friedman predicted it would be) and re-named the "natural rate hypothesis".[1] It arose, instead, from the younger tradition of the econometric forecasting models, and from the commitment on the part of a large fraction of economists to the use of these models for quantitative policy evaluation. These models have implied the existence of long-run unemployment-inflation trade-offs ever since the "wage-price sectors" were first incorporated and they promise to do so in the future although the "terms" of the trade-off continue to shift.[2]

Reprinted from *The Phillips Curve and Labor Markets,* vol. 1 of Carnegie-Rochester Conference Series on Public Policy, eds. Karl Brunner and Allan H. Meltzer, Amsterdam: North-Holland Publishing Company, pp. 19–46, by permission.

This clear-cut conflict between two rightly respected traditions—
theoretical and econometric—caught those of us who viewed the two
as harmoniously complementary quite by surprise. At first, it seemed
that the conflict might be resolved by somewhat fancier econometric
footwork. On the theoretical level, one hears talk of a "disequilibrium
dynamics" which will somehow make money illusion respectable
while going beyond the sterility of $dp/dt = k(p - p^e)$. Without underestimating the ingenuity of either econometricians or theorists, it seems
to me appropriate to entertain the possibility that reconciliation along
both of these lines will fail, and that one of these traditions is fundamentally in error.

The thesis of this essay is that it is the econometric tradition, or
more precisely, the "theory of economic policy" based on this tradition, which is in need of major revision. More particularly, I shall
argue that the features which lead to success in short-term forecasting
are unrelated to quantitative policy evaluation, that the major econometric models are (well) designed to perform the former task only, and
that simulations using these models can, in principle, provide *no* useful
information as to the actual consequences of alternative economic
policies. These contentions will be based not on deviations between
estimated and "true" structure prior to a policy change but on the
deviations between the prior "true" structure and the "true" structure
prevailing afterwards.

Before turning to details, I should like to advance two disclaimers.
First, as is true with any technically difficult and novel area of science,
econometric model building is subject to a great deal of ill-informed
and casual criticism. Thus models are condemned as being "too big"
(with equal insight, I suppose one could fault smaller models for being
"too little"), too messy, too simplistic (that is, not messy enough),
and, the ultimate blow, inferior to "naive" models. Surely the increasing sophistication of the "naive" alternatives to the major forecasting
models is the highest of tributes to the remarkable success of the
latter. I hope I can succeed in disassociating the criticism which
follows from any denial of the very important advances in forecasting
ability recorded by the econometric models, and of the promise they
offer for advancement of comparable importance in the future.

One may well define a critique as a paper which does not fully
engage the vanity of its author. In this spirit, let me offer a second
disclaimer. There is little in this essay which is not implicit (and

perhaps to more discerning readers, explicit) in Friedman [11], Muth [29] and, still earlier, in Knight [21]. For that matter, the criticisms I shall raise against currently popular applications of econometric theory have, for the most part, been anticipated by the major original contributors to that theory.[3] Nevertheless, the case for sustained inflation, based entirely on econometric simulations, is attended now with a seriousness it has not commanded for many decades. It may, therefore, be worthwhile to attempt to trace this case back to its foundation, and then to examine again the scientific basis of this foundation itself.

2   The Theory of Economic Policy

Virtually all quantitative macro-economic policy discussions today are conducted within a theoretical framework which I shall call "the theory of economic policy" (following Tinbergen [35]). The essentials of this framework are so widely known and subscribed to that it may be superfluous to devote space to their review. On the other hand, since the main theme of this paper is the inadequacy of this framework, it is probably best to have an explicit version before us.

One describes the economy in a time period t by a vector y_t of state variables, a vector x_t of exogenous forcing variables, and a vector ϵ_t of independent (through time), identically distributed random shocks. The motion of the economy is determined by a difference equation

$$y_{t+1} = f(y_t, x_t, \epsilon_t),$$

the distribution of ϵ_t, and a description of the temporal behavior of the forcing variables, x_t. The function f is taken to be fixed but not directly known; the task of empiricists is then to estimate f. For practical purposes, one usually thinks of estimating the values of a fixed parameter vector θ, with

$$f(y,x,\epsilon) \equiv F(y,x,\theta,\epsilon)$$

and F being specified in advance.

Mathematically, the sequence $\{x_t\}$ of forcing vectors is regarded as being "arbitrary" (that is, it is not characterized stochastically). Since the past x_t values are observed, this causes no difficulty in estimating θ, and in fact simplifies the theoretical estimation problem slightly. For forecasting, one is obliged to insert forecasted x_t values into F.

With knowledge of the function F and θ, policy evaluation is a straightforward matter. A *policy* is viewed as a specification of present and future values of some components of $\{x_t\}$. With the other components somehow specified, the stochastic behavior of $\{y_t, x_t, \epsilon_t\}$ from the present on is specified, and functionals defined on this sequence are well-defined random variables, whose moments may be calculated theoretically or obtained by numerical simulation. Sometimes, for example, one wishes to examine the mean value of a hypothetical "social objective function," such as

$$\sum_{t=0}^{\infty} \beta^t u(y_t, x_t, \epsilon_t)$$

under alternative policies. More usually, one is interested in the "operating characteristics" of the system under alternative policies. Thus, in this standard context, a "long-run Phillips curve" is simply a plot of average inflation–unemployment pairs under a range of hypothetical policies.[4]

Since one cannot treat θ as known in practice, the actual problem of policy evaluation is somewhat more complicated. The fact that θ is estimated from past sample values affects the above moment calculations for small samples; it also makes policies which promise to sharpen estimates of θ relatively more attractive. These considerations complicate without, I think, essentially altering the theory of economic policy as sketched above.

Two features of this theoretical framework deserve special comment. The first is the uneasy relationship between this theory of economic policy and traditional economic theory. The components of the vector-valued function F are behavioral relationships–demand functions; the role of theory may thus be viewed as suggesting forms for F, or in Samuelson's terms, distributing zeros throughout the Jacobian of F. This role for theory is decidedly secondary: microeconomics shows surprising power to rationalize individual econometric relationships in a variety of ways. More significantly, this micro-economic role for theory abdicates the task of describing the aggregate behavior of the system entirely to the econometrician. Theorists suggest forms for consumption, investment, price and wage setting functions separately; these suggestions, if useful, influence individual components of F. The aggregate behavior of the system then is what it is.[5] Surely this point of view (though I doubt if many would now endorse it in so bald a form) accounts for the demise of traditional "business cycle theory" and the widespread acceptance of a Phillips "trade-off" in the absence of *any* aggregative theoretical model embodying such a relationship.

Secondly, one must emphasize the intimate link between short-term forecasting and long-term simulations within this standard framework. The variance of short-term forecasts tend to zero with the variance of ϵ_t; as the latter becomes small, so also does the variance of estimated behavior of $\{y_t\}$ conditional on hypothetical policies $\{x_t\}$. Thus forecasting accuracy in the short-run implies reliability of long-term policy evaluation.

3 Adaptive Forecasting

There are many signs that practicing econometricians pay little more than lip-service to the theory outlined in the preceding section. The most striking is the indifference of econometric forecasters to data series prior to 1947. Within the theory of economic policy, more observations *always* sharpen parameter estimates and forecasts, and observations on "extreme" x_t values particularly so; yet even the readily available annual series from 1929–1946 are rarely used as a check on the post-war fits.

A second sign is the frequent and frequently important refitting of econometric relationships. The revisions of the wage-price sector now in progress are a good example.[6] The continuously improving precision of the estimates of θ within the fixed structure F, predicted by the theory, does not seem to be occurring in practice.

Finally, and most suggestively, is the practice of using patterns in recent residuals to revise intercept estimates for forecasting purposes. For example, if a "run" of positive residuals (predicted less actual) arises in an equation in recent periods, one revises the estimated intercept downward by their average amount. This practice accounts, for example, for the superiority of the actual Wharton forecasts as compared to forecasts based on the published version of the model.[7]

It should be emphasized that recounting these discrepancies between theory and practice is not to be taken as criticism of econometric forecasters. Certainly if new observations are better accounted for by new or modified equations, it would be foolish to continue to forecast using the old relationships. The point is simply that, econometrics textbooks notwithstanding, current forecasting practice is *not* conducted within the framework of the theory of economic policy, and the unquestioned success of the forecasters should *not* be construed as evidence for the soundness or reliability of the structure proposed in that theory.

An alternative structure to that underlying the theory of economic policy has recently been proposed (in [3] and [5]) by Cooley and Prescott. The structure is of interest in the present context, since optimal forecasting within it shares many features with current forecasting practice as just described. Instead of treating the parameter vector θ as fixed, Cooley and Prescott view it as a random variable following the random walk

$$\theta_{t+1} = \theta_t + \eta_{t+1},$$

where $\{\eta_t\}$ is a sequence of independent, identically distributed random variables.

Maximum likelihood forecasting under this alternative framework ("adaptive regression") resembles "exponential smoothing" on the observations, with observations in the distant past receiving a small "weight"—very much as in usual econometric practice; similarly, recent forecast errors are used to adjust the estimates. Using both artificial data and economic time series, Cooley and Prescott have shown (in [4]) that adaptive methods have good short-term forecasting properties when compared to even relatively sophisticated versions of the "fixed θ" regression model. As Klein and others have remarked, this advantage is shared by actual large-model forecasts (that is, model forecasts modified by the forecaster's judgment) over mechanical forecasts using the published versions of the model.[8]

Cooley and Prescott have proposed adaptive regression as a normative forecasting method. I am using it here in a positive sense: as an idealized "model" of the behavior of large-model forecasters. If the model is, as I believe, roughly accurate, it serves to reconcile the assertion that long-term policy evaluations based on econometric models are meaningless with the acknowledgment that the forecast accuracy of these models is good and likely to become even better. Under the adaptive structure, a small standard error of short-term forecasts is consistent with *infinite* variance of the long-term operating characteristics of the system.

4 Theoretical Considerations: General

To this point, I have argued simply that the standard, stable-parameter view of econometric theory and quantitative policy evaluation appears not to match several important characteristics of econometric practice, while an alternative general structure, embodying stochastic parameter drift, matches these characteristics very closely. This argument is, if accepted, sufficient to establish that the "long-run" implications of current forecasting models are without content, and that the short-term forecasting ability of these models provides no evidence of the accuracy to be expected from simulations of hypothetical policy rules.

These points are, I think, important, but their implications for the future are unclear. After all, the major econometric models are still in their first, highly successful, decade. No one, surely, expected the initial parameterizations of these models to stand forever, even under the most optimistic view of the stability of the unknown, underlying structure. Perhaps the adaptive character of this early stage of macro-economic forecasting is merely the initial groping for the true structure which, however ignored in statistical theory, all practitioners knew to be necessary. If so, the arguments of this paper are transitory debating points, obsolete soon after they are written down. Personally, I would not be sorry if this were the case, but I do not believe it is. I shall try to explain why, beginning with generalities, and then, in the following section, introducing examples.

In section 2, we discussed an economy characterized by

$$y_{t+1} = F(y_t, x_t, \theta, \epsilon_t).$$

The function F and parameter vector θ are derived from decision rules (demand and supply functions) of agents in the economy, and these decisions are, theoretically, optimal given the situation in which each agent is placed. There is, as remarked above, no presumption that (F, θ) will be easy to discover, but it *is* the central assumption of the theory of economic policy that once they *are* (approximately) known, they will remain stable under arbitrary changes in the behavior of the forcing sequence $\{x_t\}$.

For example, suppose a reliable model (F, θ) is in hand, and one wishes to use it to assess the consequences of alternative monetary and fiscal policy rules (choices of $x_0, x_1, x_2, \ldots$, where $t = 0$ is "now"). According to the theory of economic policy, one then simulates the system under alternative policies (theoretically or numerically) and compares outcomes by some criterion. For such comparisons to have any meaning, it is essential that the structure (F, θ) not vary system-atically with the choice of $\{x_t\}$.

Everything we know about dynamic economic theory indicates that this presumption is unjustified. First, the individual decision problem: "find an optimal decision rule when certain parameters (future prices, say) follow 'arbitrary' paths" is simply not well formulated. Only trivial problems in which agents can safely ignore the future can be formulated under such a vague description of market constraints. Even to obtain the decision rules underlying (F, θ) then, we have to attribute to individuals some view of the behavior of the future values of variables of concern to them. This view, in conjunction with other factors, determines their optimum decision rules. To assume stability of (F, θ) under alternative policy rules is thus to assume that agents' views about the behavior of shocks to the system are invariant under changes in the true behavior of these shocks. Without this extreme assumption, the kinds of policy simulations called for by the theory of economic policy are meaningless.

It is likely that the "drift" in θ which the adaptive models describe stochastically reflects, in part, the adaptation of the decision rules of agents to the changing character of the series they are trying to forecast.[9] Since this adaptation will be in most (though not all) cases slow, one is not surprised that adaptive methods can improve the short-term forecasting abilities of the econometric models. For longer term forecasting and policy simulations, however, ignoring the systematic sources of drift will lead to large, unpredictable errors.

5   Theoretical Considerations: Examples

If these general theoretical observations on the likelihood of systematic "parametric drift" in the face of variations in the structure of shocks are correct, it should be possible to confirm them by examination of the specific decision problems underlying the major components of aggregative models. I shall discuss in turn consumption, investment, and the wage-price sector, or Phillips curve. In each case, the "right-hand variables" will, for simplicity, be taken as "exogenous" (as components of $\{x_t\}$). The thought-experiments matching this assumption, and the adaptations necessary for simultaneous equations, are too well known to require comment.

5.1   Consumption

The easiest example to discuss with confidence is the aggregate consumption function since, due to Friedman [11], Muth [28] and Modigliani, Brumberg and Ando [2], [27], it has both a sound theoretical rationale and an unusually high degree of empirical success. Adopting Friedman's formulation, permanent consumption is proportional to permanent income (an estimate of a discounted future income stream),

$$c_{pt} = k y_{pt}; \tag{1}$$

actual consumption is

$$c_t = c_{pt} + u_t; \tag{2}$$

and actual, current income is

$$y_t = y_{pt} + v_t. \tag{3}$$

The variables u_t, v_t are independent temporally and of each other and of y_{pt}.

An empirical "short-run" marginal propensity to consume is the sample moment corresponding to $\mathrm{Cov}(c_t, y_t)/\mathrm{Var}(y_t)$, or

$$k \, \frac{\mathrm{Var}(y_{pt})}{\mathrm{Var}(y_{pt}) + \mathrm{Var}(v_t)} \, .$$

Now as long as these moments are viewed as subjective parameters in the heads of consumers, this model lacks content. Friedman, however, viewed them as true moments, known to consumers, the logical step which led to the cross-sectional tests which provided the most striking confirmation of his permanent income hypothesis.[10]

This central equating of a true probability distribution and the subjective distribution on which decisions are based was termed rational expectations by Muth, who developed its implications more generally (in [29]). In particular, in [28], Muth found the stochastic behavior of income over time under which Friedman's identification of permanent income as an exponentially weighted sum of current and lagged observations on actual income was consistent with optimal forecasting on the part of agents.[11]

To review Muth's results, we begin by recalling that permanent income is that constant flow y_{pt} which has the same value, with the subjective discount factor β, as the forecasted actual income stream:

$$y_{pt} = (1 - \beta) \sum_{i=0}^{\infty} \beta^i E(y_{t+i} \mid I_t) \tag{4}$$

where each expectation is conditioned on information I_t available at t.

Now let actual income y_t be a sum of three terms

$$y_t = a + w_t + v_t, \tag{5}$$

where v_t is transitory income, a is a constant, and w_t is a sum of independent *increments*, each with zero mean and constant variance. Muth showed that the minimum variance estimator of y_{t+i} for all $i =$ 1,2, . . . is $(1 - \lambda) \Sigma_{j=0}^{\infty} \lambda^j y_{t-j}$ where λ depends in a known way on the relative variances of w_t and v_t.[12] Inserting this estimator into (4) and summing the series gives the empirical consumption function

$$c_t = k(1 - \beta)y_t + k\beta(1 - \lambda) \sum_{j=0}^{\infty} \lambda^j y_{t-j} + u_t. \tag{6}$$

(This formula differs slightly from Muth's because Muth implicitly assumed that c_t was determined prior to realizing y_t. The difference is not important in the sequel.)

Now let us imagine a consumer of this type, with a current income generated by an "experimenter" according to the pattern described by Muth (so that the premises of the theory of economic policy are correct for a single equation consumption function). An econometrician observing this consumer over many periods will have good success describing him by (6) whether he arrives at this equation by the Friedman-Muth reasoning, or simply hits on it by trial-and-error. Next consider *policies* taking the form of a sequence of supplements $\{x_t\}$ to this consumer's income from time T on. Whether $\{x_t\}$ is specified deterministically or by some stochastic law, whether it is announced in advance to the consumer or not, the theory of economic policy prescribes the *same* method for evaluating its consequences: add x_t to the forecasts of y_t for each $t > T$, insert into (6), and obtain the new forecasts of c_t.

If the consumer knows of the policy change in advance, it is clear that this standard method gives incorrect forecasts. For example, suppose the policy consists of a constant increase, $x_t = \bar{x}$, in income over the entire future. From (4), this leads to an increase in consumption of $k\bar{x}$. The forecast based on (6), however, is of an effect in period t of

$$(\Delta c)_t = k\bar{x}\{(1 - \beta) + \beta(1 - \lambda) \sum_{i=0}^{t-T} \lambda^i\}.$$

Since this effect tends to the correct forecast, $k\bar{x}$, as t tends to infinity, one might conjecture that the difficulty vanishes in the "long run." To see that this conjecture is false, consider an exponentially growing supplement $x_t = \bar{x}a^t$, $1 < a < 1/\beta$. The true effect in $t - T$ is, from (1) and (4),

$$(\Delta c)_t = k\bar{x}\frac{(1 - \beta)a^t}{1 - a\beta}$$

The effect as forecast by (6) is

$$(\Delta c)_t = k\bar{x}\left\{(1 - \beta) + \beta(1 - \lambda)\sum_{j=0}^{t-T}\left(\frac{\lambda}{a}\right)^j\right\}a^t.$$

Neither effect tends to zero, as t tends to infinity; the ratio (forecast over actual) tends to

$$(1 - a\beta)\left\{1 + \frac{a\beta(1 - \lambda)}{(1 - \beta)(a - \lambda)}\right\},$$

which may lie on either side of unity.

More interesting divergences between forecasts and reality emerge when the policy is stochastic, but with characteristics known in advance. For example, let $\{x_t\}$ be a sequence of independent random variables, with zero mean and constant variance, distributed independently of u_t, v_t and w_t. This policy amounts to an increase in the variance of transitory income, lowering the weight λ in a manner given by the Muth formula. Average consumption, in fact and as forecast by (6), is not affected, but the variance of consumption is. The correct estimate of this variance effect requires revision of the weight λ; evidently the standard, fixed-parameter prediction based on (6) will again yield the wrong answer, and the error will not tend to vanish for large t.

The list of deterministic and stochastic policy changes, and their combination is inexhaustible but one need not proceed further to establish the point: for *any* policy change which is understood in advance, extrapolation or simulation based on (6) yields an incorrect forecast, and what is more, a *correctibly* incorrect forecast. What of changes in policy which are *not* understood in advance? As Fisher observes, "the notion that one cannot fool all of the people all of the time [need not] imply that one cannot fool all the people even some of the time."[13]

The observation is, if obvious, true enough; but it provides no support whatever for the standard forecasting method of extrapolating on the basis of (6). Our knowledge of consumption behavior is summarized in (1)–(4). For certain policy changes we can, with some confidence, guess at the permanent income recalculations consumers will go through and hope to predict their consumption responses with some accuracy. For other types of policies, particularly those involving deliberate "fooling" of consumers, it will not be at all clear how to apply (1)–(4), and hence impossible to forecast. Obviously, in such cases, there is no reason to imagine that forecasting with (6) will be accurate either.

5.2 Taxation and Investment Demand
In [15], Hall and Jorgenson provided quantitative estimates of the consequences, current and lagged, of various tax policies on the demand for producers' durable equipment. Their work is an example of the current state of the art of conditional forecasting at its best. The general method is to use econometric estimates of a Jorgensonian investment function, which captures all of the relevant tax structure in a single implicit rental price variable, to simulate the effects of alternative tax policies.

An implicit assumption in this work is that any tax change is regarded as a permanent, once-and-for-all change. Insofar as this assumption is false over the sample period, the econometric estimates are subject to bias.[14] More important for this discussion, the conditional forecasts will be valid *only* for tax changes *believed* to be permanent by taxpaying corporations.

For many issues in public finance, this obvious qualification would properly be regarded as a mere technicality. For Keynesian countercyclical policy, however, it is the very heart of the issue. The whole point, after all, of the investment tax credit is that it be viewed as temporary, so that it can serve as an inducement to firms to reschedule their investment projects. It should be clear that the forecasting methods used by Hall and Jorgenson (and, of course, by other econometricians) cannot be expected to yield even order-of-magnitude estimates of the effects of explicitly temporary tax adjustments.

To pursue this issue further, it will be useful to begin with an explicit version of the standard accelerator model of investment behavior. We imagine a constant returns industry in which each firm has a constant output-capital ratio λ. Using a common notation for variables at both the firm and industry level, let k_t denote capital at the beginning of year t. Output during t is λk_t. Investment during the year, i_t, affects next period's capital according to

$$k_{t+1} = i_t + (1 - \delta)k_t,$$

where δ is a constant physical rate of depreciation. Output is sold on a perfect market at a price p_t; investment goods are purchased at a constant price of unity. Profits (sales less depreciation) are taxed at the rate θ_t; there is an investment tax credit at the rate Ψ_t.

The firm is interested in maximizing the expected present value of receipts net of taxes, discounted at the constant cost of capital r. In the absence (assumed here) of adjustment costs, this involves equating the current cost of an additional unit of investment to the expected discounted net return. Assuming that the current tax bill is always large enough to cover the credit, the current *cost* of acquiring an additional unit of capital is $(1 - \Psi_t)$, independent of the volume of investment goods purchased. Each unit of investment yields λ units of output, to be sold next period at the (unknown) price p_{t+1}. Offsetting this profit is a tax bill of $\theta_{t+1}[\lambda p_{t+1} - \delta]$. In addition, $(1 - \delta)$ units of the investment good remain for use after period $t + 1$; with perfect capital goods markets, these units are valued at $(1 - \Psi_{t+1})$. Thus letting $E_t(\cdot)$ denote an expectation conditional on information up to period t, the expected discounted return per unit of investment in t is

$$\frac{1}{1 + r} E_t[\lambda p_{t+1}(1 - \theta_{t+1}) + \delta\theta_{t+1} + (1 - \delta)(1 - \Psi_{t+1})].$$

Since a change in next period's tax rate θ_{t+1} which is not anticipated in t is a "pure profit tax," θ_{t+1} and p_{t+1} will be uncorrelated. Hence, equating costs and returns, one equilibrium condition for the industry is

$$1 - \Psi_t = \frac{1}{1 + r} \{\lambda E_t(p_{t+1})[1 - E_t(\theta_{t+1})] + \delta E_t(\theta_{t+1})$$
$$+ (1 - \delta)[1 - E_t(\Psi_{t+1})]\}. \tag{7}$$

A second equilibrium condition is obtained from the assumption that the product market is cleared each period. Let industry demand be given by a linear function, with a stochastically shifting intercept a_t and a constant slope b, so that quantity demanded next period will be

$a_{t+1} - bp_{t+1}$. Quantity supplied will be λ times next period's capital. Then a second equilibrium condition is

$$\lambda[i_t + (1 - \delta)k_t] = a_{t+1} - bp_{t+1}.$$

Taking mean values of both sides,

$$\lambda[i_t + (1 - \delta)k_t] = E_t(a_{t+1}) - bE_t(p_{t+1}). \tag{8}$$

Since our interest is in the industry investment function, we eliminate $E_t(p_{t+1})$ between (7) and (8) to obtain:

$$i_t + (1 - \delta)k_t = \frac{1}{\lambda}E_t(a_{t+1}) - \frac{b}{\lambda^2}\left[\frac{r}{1 - E_t(\theta_{t+1})} + \delta\right]$$
$$+ \frac{b}{\lambda^2}\left[\frac{(1 + r)\Psi_t - (1 - \delta)E_t(\Psi_{t+1})}{1 - E_t(\theta_{t+1})}\right]. \tag{9}$$

Equation (9) gives the industry's "desired" stock of capital, $i_t + (1 - \delta)k_t$, as a function of the expected future state of demand and the current and expected future tax structure, as well as of the cost of capital r, taken in this illustration to be constant. The second and third terms on the right are the product of the slope of the demand curve for capital, $-b\lambda^{-2}$, and the familiar Jorgensonian implicit rental price; the second term includes "interest" and depreciation costs, net of taxes; the third includes the expected capital gain (or loss) due to changes in the investment tax credit rate.

In most empirical investment studies, firms are assumed to move gradually from k_t to the desired stock given by (9), due to costs of adjustment, delivery lags, and the like. We assume here, purely for convenience, that the full adjustment occurs in a single period.

Equation (9) is operationally at the same level as equations (1) and (4) of the preceding section: it relates current behavior to unobserved expectations of future variables. To move to a testable hypothesis, one must specify the time series behavior of a_t, θ_t and Ψ_t (as was done for income in consumption theory), obtain the optimal forecasting rule, and obtain the analogue to the consumption function (6). Let us imagine that this has been accomplished, and estimates of the parameters λ and b have been obtained. How would one use these estimates to evaluate the consequences of a particular investment tax credit policy?

The method used by Hall and Jorgenson is to treat the credit as a permanent or once-and-for-all change, or implicitly to set $E_t(\Psi_{t+1})$ equal to Ψ_t. Holding θ_t constant at θ, the effect of a change in the credit from 0 to Ψ (say) would be the same as a permanent lowering of the price of investment goods to $1 - \Psi$ or, from (9), an increase in the desired capital stock of $(b/\lambda^2)(r + \delta)/(1 - \theta)$. If the credit is in fact believed by corporations to be permanent, this forecast will be correct; otherwise it will not be.

To consider alternatives, imagine a stochastic tax credit policy which switches from 0 to a fixed number Ψ in a Markovian fashion, with transitions given by $\Pr\{\Psi_{t+1} = \Psi | \Psi_t = 0\} = q$ and $\Pr\{\Psi_{t+1} = \Psi | \Psi_t = \Psi\} = p$.[15] Then if expectations on next period's tax credit are formed rationally, conditional on the presence or absence of the credit in the current period, we have

$$E_t(\Psi_{t+1}) = \begin{cases} q\Psi & \text{if } \Psi_t = 0 \\ p\Psi & \text{if } \Psi_t = \Psi. \end{cases}$$

The third term on the right of (9) is then

$$\frac{b\Psi}{\lambda^2(1 - \theta)} [- q(1 - \delta)] \qquad \text{if } \Psi_t = 0,$$

$$\frac{b\Psi}{\lambda^2(1 - \theta)} [1 + r - p(1 - \delta)] \qquad \text{if } \Psi_t = \Psi.$$

The difference between these terms is given by the expression

$$\frac{b\Psi}{\lambda^2(1 - \theta)} [1 + r + (q - p)(1 - \delta)]. \qquad (10)$$

The expression (10) gives the increment to desired capital stock (and, with immediate adjustment, to current investment) when the tax credit is switched from zero to Ψ *in an economy where the credit operates, and is known to operate, in the stochastic fashion described above.* It does *not* measure the effect of a switch in policy from a no-credit regime to the stochastic regime used here. (The difference arises because even when the credit is set at zero in the stochastic regime, the possibility of capital loss, due to the introduction of the credit in the future, increases the implicit rental on capital, relative to the situation in which the credit is expected to remain at zero forever.)

By examining extreme values of p and q one can get a good idea of the quantitative importance of expectations in measuring the effect of the credit. At one extreme, consider the case where the credit is expected almost *never* to be offered (q near 0), but once offered, it is permanent (p near 1). The effect of a switch from 0 to Ψ is, in this case, approximately

$$\frac{b\Psi}{\lambda^2(1 - \theta)} [r + \delta],$$

using (10). This is the situation assumed, implicitly, by Hall and Jorgenson. At the other extreme, consider the case of a frequently imposed but always transitory credit (q near 1, p near 0). Applying (10), the effect of a switch in this case is approximately

$$\frac{b\Psi}{\lambda^2(1 - \theta)} [2 + r - \delta].$$

The ratio of effects is then $(2 + r - \delta)/(r + \delta)$. With $r = .14$ and $\delta = .15$, this ratio is about 7.[16] We are not, then, discussing a quantitatively minor issue.

For a more realistic estimate, consider a credit which remains "off" for an average period of 5 years, and when "switched on" remains for an average of one year. These assumptions correspond to setting $p \approx 0$ and $q = \frac{1}{5}$. The ratio of the effect (from (10)), under these assumptions versus those used by Hall and Jorgenson is now $[1 + r + \frac{1}{5}(1 - \delta)]/(r + \delta)$. With $r = .14$ and $\delta = .15$, this ratio is approximately 4.5. This ratio would probably be somewhat smaller under a more satisfactory lag structure[17], but even taking this into account, it appears likely that the potential stimulus of the investment tax credit may well be several times greater than the Hall-Jorgenson estimates would indicate.[18]

As was the case in the discussion of consumption behavior, estimation of a policy effect along the above lines presupposes a policy generated by a fixed, relatively simple *rule*, known by forecasters (ourselves) and by the agents subject to the policy (an assumption which is not only convenient analytically but consistent with Article 1, Section 7 of the U.S. Constitution). To go beyond the kind of order-of-magnitude calculations used here to an accurate assessment of the effects of the 1962 credit studied by Hall and Jorgenson, one would have to infer the implicit rule which generated (or was thought by corporations to generate) that policy, a task made difficult, or perhaps impossible, by the novelty of the policy at the time it was introduced. Similarly, there is no reason to hope that we can accurately forecast the effects of future *ad hoc* tax policies on investment behavior. On the other hand, there is every reason to believe that good quantitative assessments of counter-cyclical fiscal rules, which are built into the tax structure in a stable and well-understood way, can be obtained.

5.3 Phillips Curves

A third example is suggested by the recent controversy over the Phelps-Friedman hypothesis that permanent changes in the inflation rate will not alter the average rate of unemployment. Most of the major econometric models have been used in simulation experiments to test this proposition; the results are uniformly negative. Since expectations are involved in an essential way in labor and product market supply behavior, one would presume, on the basis of the considerations raised in section 4, that these tests are beside the point.[19] This presumption is correct, as the following example illustrates.

It will be helpful to utilize a simple, parametric model which captures the main features of the expectational view of aggregate supply—rational agents, cleared markets, incomplete information.[20] We imagine suppliers of goods to be distributed over N distinct markets i, $i = 1, \ldots, N$. To avoid index number problems, suppose that the same (except for location) good is traded in each market, and let y_{it} be the log of quantity supplied in market i in period t. Assume, further, that the supply y_{it} is composed of two factors

$$y_{it} = y_{it}^{P} + y_{it}^{c}.$$

where y_{it}^{P} denotes normal or permanent supply, and y_{it}^{c} cyclical or transitory supply (both, again, in logs). We take y_{it}^{P} to be unresponsive to all but permanent relative price changes or, since the latter have been defined away by assuming a single good, simply unresponsive to price changes. Transitory supply y_{it}^{c} varies with perceived changes in the *relative* price of goods in i:

$$y_{it}^{c} = \beta(p_{it} - p_{it}^{e}),$$

where p_{it} is the log of the actual price in i at t, and p_{it}^{e} is the log of the general (geometric average) price level in the economy as a whole, *as perceived in market i.*[21]

Prices will vary from market to market for each t, due to the usual sources of fluctuation in relative demands. They will also fluctuate over time, due to movements in aggregate demand. We shall not explore the sources of these price movements (although this is easy

enough to do) but simply postulate that the actual price in i at t consists
of two components:

$$p_{it} = p_t + z_{it}.$$

Sellers observe the actual price p_{it}; the two components cannot be
separately observed. The component p_t varies with time, but is common to all markets. Based on information obtained prior to t (call it
I_{t-1}) traders in all markets take p_t to be a normally distributed random
variable, with mean $\bar{p}_t$ (reflecting this past information) and variance
σ^2. The component z_{it} reflects relative price variation across markets
and time: z_{it} is normally distributed, independent of p_t and z_{js} (unless
$i = j$, $s = t$), with mean 0 and variance τ^2.

  The *actual* general price level at t is the average over markets of
individual prices,

$$\frac{1}{N} \sum_{i=1}^{N} p_{it} = p_t + \frac{1}{N} \sum_{i=1}^{N} z_{it}.$$

We take the number of markets N to be large, so that the second term
can be neglected, and p_t is the general price level. To form the supply
decision, suppliers estimate p_t; assume that this estimate p_{it}^c is the
mean of the true conditional distribution of p_t. The latter is calculated
using the observation that p_{it} is the sum of two independent normal
variates, one with mean 0 and variance τ^2; one with mean $\bar{p}_t$ and
variance σ^2. It follows that

$$p_{it}^e = E\{p_t | p_{it}, I_{t-1}\} = (1 - \theta)p_{it} + \theta\bar{p}_t,$$

where $\theta = \tau^2/(\sigma^2 + \tau^2)$.

  Based on this unbiased but generally inaccurate estimate of the
current general level of prices, suppliers in i follow

$$y_{it}^c = \beta[p_{it} - ((1 - \theta)p_{it} + \theta\bar{p}_t)] = \theta\beta[p_{it} - \bar{p}_t].$$

Now averaging over markets, and invoking the law of large numbers
again, we have the cyclical component of *aggregate* supply:

$$y_t^c = \theta\beta(p_t - \bar{p}_t).$$

Re-introducing the permanent components,

$$y_t = \theta\beta(p_t - \bar{p}_t) + y_{pt}. \tag{11}$$

   Though simple, (11) captures the main features of the expectational
or "natural rate" view of aggregate supply. The supply of goods is
viewed as following a trend path y_{pt} which is not dependent on nominal
price movements. Deviations from this path are induced whenever the
nominal price deviates from the level which was expected to prevail
on the basis of past information. These deviations occur because
agents are obliged to infer current general price movements on the
basis of incomplete information.
   It is worth speculating as to the sort of empirical performance one
would *expect* from (11). In doing so, we ignore the trend component
y_{pt}, concentrating on the determinants of p_t, β and θ. The parameter
β reflects intertemporal substitution possibilities in supply: technological factors such as storability of production, and tastes for substituting
labor supplied today for supply tomorrow. One would expect β to be
reasonably stable over time and across economies at a similar level of
development. The parameter θ is the ratio $\tau^2/(\sigma^2 + \tau^2)$. τ^2 reflects the
variability of relative prices within the economy; there is no reason to
expect it to vary systematically with demand policy. σ^2 is the variance
of the general price level about its expected level; it will obviously
increase with increases in the volatility of demand.[22] Similarly, $\bar{p}_t$, the
expected price level conditional on past information, will vary with
actual, average inflation rates.
   Turning to a specific example, suppose that actual prices follow the
random walk

$$p_t = p_{t-1} + \epsilon_t \tag{12}$$

where ϵ_t is normal with mean π and variance σ^2. Then $p_t = p_{t-1} + \pi$
and (11) becomes

$$y_t = \theta\beta(p_t - p_{t-1}) - \theta\beta\pi + y_{pt}. \tag{13}$$

Over a sample period during which π and σ^2 remain roughly constant,
and if y_{pt} can be effectively controlled for, (13) will appear to the
econometrician to describe a stable trade-off between inflation and
real output. The addition of lagged inflation rates will not improve the
fit, or alter this conclusion in any way. Yet is is evident from (13) that
a sustained increase in the inflation rate (an increase in π) will not
affect real output.
   This is not to say that a distributed lag version of (11) might not
perform better empirically. Thus let the actual rate of inflation follow

a first-order autoregressive scheme

$$\Delta p_t = \rho \, \Delta p_{t-1} + \epsilon_t$$

or

$$p_t = (1 + \rho)p_{t-1} - \rho p_{t-2} + \epsilon_t \qquad (14)$$

where $0 < \rho < 1$ and ϵ_t is distributed as before.

Then combining (11) and (14):

$$y_t = \theta\beta \, \Delta p_t - \theta\beta\rho \, \Delta p_{t-1} - \theta\beta\pi + y_{pt}. \qquad (15)$$

In econometric terms, the "long-run" slope, or trade-off, would be the *sum* of the inflation coefficients, or $\theta\beta(1 - \rho)$, which will not, if (14) is stable, be zero.

In short, one can imagine situations in which empirical Phillips curves exhibit long lags and situations in which there are no lagged effects. In either case, the "long-run" output-inflation relationship as calculated or simulated in the conventional way has *no* bearing on the actual consequences of pursuing a policy of inflation.

As in the consumption and investment examples, the ability to use (13) or (15) to forecast the consequences of a change in policy rests crucially on the assumption that the parameters describing the new policy (in this case π, σ^2 and ρ) are known by agents. Over periods for which this assumption is not approximately valid (obviously there have been, and will continue to be, many such periods) empirical Phillips curves will appear subject to "parameter drift," describable over the sample period, but unpredictable for all but the very near future.

6 Policy Considerations

In preceding sections, I have argued in general and by example that there are compelling empirical and theoretical reasons for believing that a structure of the form

$$y_{t+1} = F(y_t, x_t, \theta, \epsilon_t)$$

(F known, θ fixed, x_t "arbitrary") will not be of use for forecasting and policy evaluation in actual economies. For short-term forecasting, these arguments have long been anticipated in practice, and models with good (and improvable) tracking properties have been obtained by permitting and measuring "drift" in the parameter vector θ. Under adaptive models which rationalize these tracking procedures, however, long-run policy simulations are acknowledged to have infinite variance, which leaves open the question of quantitative policy evaluation.

One response to this situation, seldom defended explicitly today though in implicit form probably dominant at the most "practical" level of economic advice-giving, is simply to dismiss questions of the long-term behavior of the economy under alternative policies and focus instead on obtaining what is viewed as desirable behavior in the next few quarters. The hope is that the changes in θ induced by policy changes will occur slowly, and that conditional forecasting based on tracking models will therefore be roughly accurate for a few periods. This hope is both false and misleading. First, some policy changes induce immediate jumps in θ: for example, an explicitly temporary personal income tax surcharge will (cf. section 5.1) induce an *immediate* rise in propensity to consume out of disposable income and consequent errors in short-term conditional forecasts.[23] Second, even if the induced changes in θ are slow to occur, they should be counted in the short-term "objective function", yet rarely are. Thus econometric Phillips curves roughly forecast the initial phase of the current inflation, but not the "adverse" shift in the curve to which that inflation led.

What kind of structure might be at once consistent with the theoretical considerations raised in section 4 and with operational, accurate policy evaluation? One hesitates to indulge the common illusion that "general" structures are more useful than specific, empirically verified ones; nevertheless, a provisional structure, cautiously used, will facilitate the remainder of the discussion.

As observed in section 4, one cannot meaningfully discuss optimal decisions of agents under arbitrary sequences $\{x_t\}$ of future shocks. As an alternative characterization, then, let policies and other disturbances be viewed as stochastically disturbed functions of the state of the system, or (parametrically)

$$x_t = G(y_t, \lambda, \eta_t), \tag{16}$$

where G is known, λ is a fixed parameter vector, and η_t a vector of disturbances. Then the remainder of the economy follows

$$y_{t+1} = F(y_t, x_t, \theta(\lambda), \epsilon_t), \tag{17}$$

where, as indicated, the behavioral parameters θ vary systematically with the parameters λ governing policy and other "shocks." The econometric problem in this context is that of estimating the function $\theta(\lambda)$.

In a model of this sort, a *policy* is viewed as a change in the parameters λ, or in the function generating the values of policy variables at particular times. A change in policy (in λ) affects the behavior of the system in two ways: first by altering the time series behavior of x_t; second by leading to modification of the behavioral parameters $\theta(\lambda)$ governing the rest of the system. Evidently, the way this latter modification can be expected to occur depends crucially on the way the policy change is carried out. If the policy change occurs by a sequence of decisions following no discussed or pre-announced pattern, it will become known to agents only gradually, and then perhaps largely as higher variance of "noise." In this case, the movement to a new $\theta(\lambda)$, if it occurs in a stable way at all, will be unsystematic, and econometrically unpredictable. If, on the other hand, policy changes occur as fully discussed and understood changes in *rules*, there is some hope that the resulting structural changes can be forecast on the basis of estimation from past data of $\theta(\lambda)$.

It is perhaps necessary to emphasize that this point of view towards conditonal forecasting, due originally to Knight and, in modern form, to Muth, does not attribute to agents unnatural powers of instantly divining the true structure of policies affecting them. More modestly, it asserts that agents' responses become predictable to outside observers only when there can be some confidence that agents and observers share a common view of the nature of the shocks which must be forecast by both.

The preference for "rules versus authority" in economic policy making suggested by this point of view, is not, as I hope is clear, based on any demonstrable optimality properties of rules-in-general (whatever that might mean). There seems to be no theoretical argument ruling out the possibility that (for example) delegating economic decision-making authority to some individual or group might not lead to superior (by some criterion) economic performance than is attainable under some, or all, hypothetical rules in the sense of (16). The point is rather that this possibility cannot *in principle* be substantiated empirically. The only *scientific* quantitative policy evaluations available to us are comparisons of the consequences of alternative policy rules.

7 Concluding Remarks

This essay has been devoted to an exposition and elaboration of a single syllogism: given that the structure of an econometric model consists of optimal decision rules of economic agents, and that optimal decision rules vary systematically with changes in the structure of series relevant to the decision maker, it follows that any change in policy will systematically alter the structure of econometric models.

For the question of the short-term forecasting, or tracking ability of econometric models, we have seen that this conclusion is of only occasional significance. For issues involving policy evaluation, in contrast, it is fundamental; for it implies that comparisons of the effects of alternative policy rules using current macroeconometric models are invalid regardless of the performance of these models over the sample period or in ex ante short-term forecasting.

The argument is, in part, destructive: the ability to forecast the consequences of "arbitrary," unannounced sequences of policy decisions, currently claimed (at least implicitly) by the theory of economic policy, appears to be beyond the capability not only of the current-generation models, but of conceivable future models as well. On the other hand, as the consumption example shows, conditional forecasting under the alternative structure (16) and (17) is, while scientifically more demanding, entirely operational.

In short, it appears that policy makers, if they wish to forecast the response of citizens, must take the latter into their confidence. This conclusion, if ill-suited to current econometric practice, seems to accord well with a preference for democratic decision making.

Notes

1. See Phelps et al. [31], Phelps' earlier [30] and Friedman [13].

2. The earliest wage-price sector embodying the "trade-off" is (as far as I know) in the 1955 version of the Klein-Goldberger model [19]. It has persisted, with minimal conceptual change, into all current generation forecasting models. The subsequent shift of the "trade-off" relationship to center stage in policy discussions appears due primarily to Phillips [32] and Samuelson and Solow [33].

3. See in particular Marschak's discussion in [25] (helpfully recalled to me by T. D. Wallace) and Tinbergen's in [36], especially his discussion of "qualitative policy" in ch. 5, pp. 149–185.

4. See, for example, de Menil and Enzler [6], Hirsch [16] and Hymans [17].

5. The ill-fated Brookings model project was probably the ultimate expression of this view.

6. See, for example, Gordon [14].

7. A good account of this and other aspects of forecasting in theory and practice is provided by Klein [20]. A fuller treatment is available in Evans and Klein [9].

8. See Klein [20].

9. This is not to suggest that all parameter drift is due to this source. For example, shifts in production functions due to technological change are probably well described by a random walk scheme.

10. Of course, the hypothesis continues to be tested as new data sources become available, and anomalies continue to arise. (For a recent example, see Mayer [26]). Thus one may expect that, as with most "confirmed" hypotheses, it will someday be subsumed in some more general formulation.

11. In [12], Friedman proposes an alternative view to Muth's, namely that the weight used in averaging past incomes (λ) is the same as the discount factor used in averaging future incomes (β). It is Muth's theory, rather than Friedman's of [12], which is consistent with the cross-section tests based on relative variances mentioned above.

12. Let σ_v^2 be the variance of v_t and $\sigma_{\Delta w}^2$ be the variance of the increments of w_t, then the relationship is

$$\lambda = 1 + \frac{1}{2} \frac{\sigma_{\Delta w}^2}{\sigma_v^2} - \frac{\sigma_{\Delta w}}{\sigma_v} \sqrt{1 + \frac{1}{4} \frac{\sigma_{\Delta w}^2}{\sigma_v^2}} \ .$$

13. [10], p. 113.

14. In particular, the low estimates of 'α' (see [15], Table 2, p. 400), which should equal capital's share in value added, are probably due to a sizeable transitory component in a variable which is treated theoretically as though it were subject to permanent changes only.

15. A tax credit designed for stabilization would, of course, need to respond to projected movements in the shift variable a_t. In this case, the transition probabilities p and q would vary with indicators (say current and lagged a_t values) of future economic activity. Since my aim here is only to get an idea of the quantitative importance of a correct treatment of expectations, I will not pursue this design problem further.

16. The cost of capital of .14 and the depreciation rate of .15 (for manufacturing equipment) are annual rates from [15]. Since the ratio $(2 + r - \delta)/(r + \delta)$ is

not time-unit free, the assumption that all movement toward the new desired stock of capital takes place in one year is crucial at this point: by defining a *period* as shorter than one year this ratio will increase, and conversely for a longer period.

17. For the reason given in note 16.

18. It should be noted that this conclusion *reinforces* the qualitative conclusion reached by Hall and Jorgenson [15], p. 413.

19. Sargent [34] and I [23] have developed this conclusion earlier in similar contexts.

20. This model is taken, with a few changes, from my earlier [24].

21. This supply function for goods should be thought of as drawn up given a cleared labor market in i. See Lucas and Rapping [22] for an analysis of the factors underlying this function.

22. This implication that the variability in demand affects the slope of the "trade-off" is the basis for the tests of the natural rate hypothesis reported in [24], as well as those by Adie [1] and B. Klein [18].

23. This observation has been made earlier, for exactly the reasons set out in section 5.1, by Eisner [8] and Dolde [7], p. 15.

References

1. Adie, Douglas K., "The Importance of Expectations for the Phillips Curve Relation," Research Paper No. 133, Department of Economics, Ohio University (undated).

2. Ando, Albert and Franco Modigliani, "The Life Cycle Hypothesis of Saving; Aggregate Implications and Tests," *American Economic Review*, v. 53 (1963), pp. 55–84.

3. Cooley, Thomas F. and Edward C. Prescott, "An Adaptive Regression Model," International Economic Review, (June 1973), 364–371.

4. Cooley, Thomas F. and Edward C. Prescott, "Tests of the Adaptive Regression Model," *Review of Economics and Statistics*, (April 1973), 248–256.

5. Cooley, Thomas F. and Edward C. Prescott, "Estimation in the Presence of Sequential Parameter Variation," *Econometrica*, forthcoming.

6. de Menil, George and Jared J. Enzler, "Prices and Wages in the FRB-MIT-Penn Econometric Model," in Otto Eckstein, ed., *The Econometrics of Price Determination Conference* (Washington: Board of Governors of the Federal Reserve System and Social Science Research Council), 1972, pp. 277–308.

7. Dolde, Walter, "Capital Markets and the Relevant Horizon for Consumption Planning," Yale doctoral dissertation, 1973.

8. Eisner, Robert, "Fiscal and Monetary Policy Reconsidered," *American Economic Review*, v. 59 (1969), pp. 897–905.

9. Evans, Michael K. and Lawrence R. Klein, *The Wharton Econometric Forecasting Model*. 2nd, Enlarged Edition (Philadelphia: University of Pennsylvania Economics Research Unit), 1968.

10. Fisher, Franklin M., "Discussion" in Otto Eckstein, ed., *op. cit.* (reference [6]), pp. 113–115.

11. Friedman, Milton, *A Theory of the Consumption Function.* (Princeton: Princeton University Press), 1957.

12. Friedman, Milton, "Windfalls, the 'Horizon', and Related Concepts in the Permanent Income Hypothesis," in Carl F. Christ, *et. al.,* eds., *Measurement in Economics* (Stanford: Stanford University Press), 1963, pp. 3–28.

13. Friedman, Milton, "The Role of Monetary Policy," *American Economic Review,* v. 58 (1968), pp. 1–17.

14. Gordon, Robert J., "Wage-Price Controls and the Shifting Phillips Curve," *Brookings Papers on Economic Activity,* 1972, no. 2, pp. 385–421.

15. Hall, Robert E. and Dale W. Jorgenson, "Tax Policy and Investment Behavior," *American Economic Review,* v. 57 (1967), pp. 391–414.

16. Hirsch, Albert A., "Price Simulations with the OBE Econometric Model," in Otto Eckstein, ed., *op. cit.* (reference [6]), pp. 237–276.

17. Hymans, Saul H., "Prices and Price Behavior in Three U.S. Econometric Models," in Otto Eckstein, ed., *op. cit.* (reference [6]), pp. 309–322.

18. Klein, Benjamin, "The Effect of Price Level Unpredictability on the Composition of Income Change," unpublished working paper, April, 1973.

19. Klein, Lawrence R. and Arthur S. Goldberger, *An Econometric Model of the United States, 1929–1952.* (Amsterdam: North Holland), 1955.

20. Klein, Lawrence R., *An Essay on the Theory of Economic Prediction.* (Helsinki: Yrjo Jahnsson Lectures), 1968.

21. Knight, Frank H., *Risk, Uncertainty and Profit.* (Boston: Houghton-Mifflin), 1921.

22. Lucas, Robert E., Jr. and Leonard A. Rapping, "Real Wages, Employment, and Inflation," *Journal of Political Economy,* v. 77 (1969), pp. 721–754.

23. Lucas, Robert E., Jr., "Econometric Testing of the Natural Rate Hypothesis," in Otto Eckstein, ed., *op. cit.* (reference [6]), pp. 50–59.

24. Lucas, Robert E., Jr., "Some International Evidence on Output-Inflation Trade-Offs," *American Economic Review,* v. 63 (1973).

25. Marschak, Jacob, "Economic Measurements for Policy and Prediction," in William C. Hood and Tjalling G. Koopmans, eds., *Studies in Econometric Method,* Cowles Commission Monograph 14 (New York: Wiley), 1953, pp. 1–26.

26. Mayer, Thomas, "Tests of the Permanent Income Theory with Continuous Budgets," *Journal of Money, Credit, and Banking,* v. 4 (1972) pp. 757–778.

27. Modigliani, Franco and Richard Brumberg, "Utility Analysis and the Consumption Function: An Interpretation of Cross-Section Data," in K. K. Kurihara, ed., *Post-Keynesian Economics.* (New Brunswick: Rutgers University Press), 1954.

28. Muth, John F., "Optimal Properties of Exponentially Weighted Forecasts," *Journal of the American Statistical Association,* v. 55 (1960), pp. 299–306.

29. Muth, John F., "Rational Expectations and the Theory of Price Movements," *Econometrica,* v. 29 (1961), pp. 315–335.

30. Phelps, Edmund S., "Money Wage Dynamics and Labor Market Equilibrium," *Journal of Political Economy,* v. 76 (1968), pp. 687–711.

31. Phelps, Edmund S., *et al.*, *The New Microeconomics in Employment and Inflation Theory*. (New York: Norton), 1970.

32. Phillips, A. W., "The Relation Between Unemployment and the Rate of Change of Money Wage Rates in the United Kingdom, 1861–1957," *Economica*, v. 25 (1958), pp. 283–299.

33. Samuelson, Paul A. and Robert M. Solow, "Analytical Aspects of Anti-Inflation Policy," *American Economic Review*, v. 50 (1960), pp. 177–194.

34. Sargent, Thomas J., "A Note on the 'Accelerationist' Controversy," *Journal of Money, Credit, and Banking*, v. 3 (1971), pp. 721–725.

35. Tinbergen, Jan, *On the Theory of Economic Policy*. (Amsterdam: North Holland), 1952.

36. Tinbergen, Jan, *Economic Policy: Principles and Design*. (Amsterdam: North Holland), 1956.

Some International Evidence on Output-Inflation Tradeoffs

This paper reports the results of an empirical study of real output-inflation tradeoffs, based on annual time-series from eighteen countries over the years 1951–67. These data are examined from the point of view of the hypothesis that average real output levels are invariant under changes in the time pattern of the rate of inflation, or that there exists a "natural rate" of real output. That is, we are concerned with the questions (i) does the natural rate theory lead to expressions of the output-inflation relationship which perform satisfactorily in an econometric sense for all, or most, of the countries in the sample, (ii) what testable restrictions does the theory impose on this relationship, and (iii) are these restrictions consistent with recent experience?

Since the term "natural rate theory" refers to varied aggregation of models and verbal developments,[1] it may be helpful to sketch the key elements of the particular version used in this paper. The first essential presumption is that *nominal* output is determined on the aggregate demand side of the economy, with the division into real output and the price level largely dependent on the behavior of *suppliers* of labor and goods. The second is that the partial "rigidities" which dominate short-run supply behavior result from suppliers' lack of information on some of the prices relevant to their decisions. The third presumption is that inferences on these relevant, unobserved prices are made optimally (or "rationally") in light of the stochastic character of the economy.

Reprinted from *American Economic Review* 63 (June 1973):326–334 by permission.

As I have argued elsewhere (1972), theories developed along these
lines will *not* place testable restrictions on the coefficients of estimated
Phillips curves or other single equation expressions of the tradeoff.
They will not, for example, imply that money wage changes are linked
to price level changes with a unit coefficient, or that "long-run" (in
the usual distributed lag sense) Phillips curves must be vertical. They
will (as we shall see below) link supply parameters to parameters
governing the stochastic nature of demand shifts. The fact that the
implications of the natural rate theory come in this form suggests an
attempt to test it using a sample, such as the one employed in this
study, in which a wide variety of aggregate demand behavior is
exhibited.

In the following section, a simple aggregative model will be constructed using the elements sketched above. Results based on this
model are reported in Section 2, followed by a discussion and
conclusions.

1 An Economic Model

The general structure of the model developed in this section may be
described very simply. First, the aggregate price-quantity observations
are viewed as intersection points of an aggregate demand and an
aggregate supply schedule. The former is drawn up under the assumption of a cleared money market and represents the output-price level
relationship implicit in the standard IS-LM diagram. It is viewed as
being shifted by the usual set of demand-shift variables: monetary and
fiscal policies and variation in export demands. The supply schedule
is drawn under the assumption of a cleared labor market; its slope
therefore reflects labor and product market "rigidities."

The structure of this model, which is essentially that suggested in
Lucas and Leonard Rapping (1969), will be greatly simplified by an
additional special assumption: that the aggregate demand curve is unit
elastic.[2] In this case, the level of nominal output can be treated as an
"exogenous" variable with respect to the goods market, and the entire
burden of accounting for the breakdown of nominal income into real
output and price is placed on the aggregate supply side. In the next
subsection, 1.1, a supply model designed to serve this purpose is
developed. In subsection 1.2, solutions to the full (demand and supply)
model are obtained.

1.1 Aggregate Supply

All formulations of the natural rate theory postulate rational agents, whose decisions depend on *relative* prices only, placed in an economic setting in which they cannot distinguish relative from general price movements. Obviously, there is no limit to the number of models one can construct where agents are placed in this situation of imperfect information; the trick is to find tractable schemes with this feature. One such model is developed below.

We imagine suppliers as located in a large number of scattered, competitive markets. Demand for goods in each period is distributed unevenly over markets, leading to relative as well as general price movements. As a consequence, the situation as perceived by individual suppliers will be quite different from the aggregate situation as seen by an outside observer. Accordingly, we shall attempt to keep these two points of view separate, turning first to the situation faced by individual suppliers.

Quantity supplied in each market will be viewed as the product of a normal (or secular) component common to all markets and a cyclical component which varies from market to market. Letting z index markets, and using y_{nt} and y_{ct} to denote the logs of these components, supply in market z is:

$$y_t(z) = y_{nt} + y_{ct}(z) \tag{1}$$

The secular component, reflecting capital accumulation and population change, follows the trend line:

$$y_{nt} = \alpha + \beta t \tag{2}$$

The cyclical component varies with perceived, *relative* prices and with its own lagged value:

$$y_{ct}(z) = \gamma[P_t(z) - E(P_t \mid I_t(z))] \\ + \lambda y_{c,t-1}(z) \tag{3}$$

where $P_t(z)$ is the actual price in z at t and $E(P_t \mid I_t(z))$ is the mean current, general price level, conditioned on information available in z at t, $I_t(z)$.[3] Since y_{ct} is a deviation from trend, $|\lambda| < 1$.

The information available to suppliers in z at t comes from two sources. First, traders enter period t with knowledge of the past course of demand shifts, of normal supply y_{nt}, and of past deviations $y_{c,t-1}$,

$y_{c,t-2}, \ldots$. While this information does not permit exact inference of the log of the current general price level, P_t, it does determine a "prior" distribution on P_t, common to traders in all markets. We assume that this distribution is known to be normal, with mean $\overline{P}_t$ (depending in a known way on the above history) and a constant variance σ^2.

Second, we suppose that the actual price deviates from the (geometric) economy-wide average by an amount which is distributed independently of P_t. Specifically, let the percentage deviation of the price in z from the average P_t be denoted by z (so that markets are indexed by their price deviations from average) where z is normally distributed, independent of P_t, with mean zero and variance τ^2. Then the observed price in z, $P_t(z)$ (in logs) is the sum of independent, normal variates

$$P_t(z) = P_t + z \tag{4}$$

The information $I_t(z)$ relevant for estimation of the unobserved (by suppliers in z at t) P_t, consists then of the observed price $P_t(z)$ and the history summarized in $\overline{P}_t$.

To utilize this information, suppliers use (4) to calculate the distribution of P_t, conditional on $P_t(z)$ and $\overline{P}_t$. This distribution is (by straightforward calculation) normal with mean:

$$\begin{aligned} E(P_t \mid I_t(z)) &= E(P_t \mid P_t(z), \overline{P}_t) \\ &= (1 - \theta)P_t(z) + \theta\overline{P}_t \end{aligned} \tag{5}$$

where $\theta = \tau^2/(\sigma^2 + \tau^2)$, and variance $\theta\sigma^2$. Combining (1), (3), and (5) yields the supply function for market z:

$$\begin{aligned} y_t(z) &= y_{nt} + \theta\gamma[P_t(z) - \overline{P}_t] \\ &\quad + \lambda y_{c,t-1}(z) \end{aligned} \tag{6}$$

Averaging over markets (integrating with respect to the distribution of z) gives the aggregate supply function:

$$\begin{aligned} y_t &= y_{nt} + \theta\gamma(P_t - \overline{P}_t) \\ &\quad + \lambda[y_{t-1} - y_{n,t-1}] \end{aligned} \tag{7}$$

The *slope* of the aggregate supply function (7) thus varies with the fraction θ of *total* individual price variance, $\sigma^2 + \tau^2$, which is due to *relative* price variation. In cases where τ^2 is relatively small, so that individual price changes are virtually certain to reflect general price changes, the supply curve is nearly vertical. At the other extreme when general prices are stable (σ^2 is relatively small) the slope of the supply curve approaches the limiting value of γ.[4]

1.2 Completion and Solution of the Model

A central assumption in the development above is that supply behavior is based on the *correct* distribution of the unobserved current price level, P_t. To proceed, then, it is necessary to determine what this correct distribution is, a step which requires the completion of the model by inclusion of an aggregate demand side.

As suggested earlier, this will be done by postulating a demand function for goods of the form:

$$y_t + P_t = x_t \tag{8}$$

where x_t is an exogenous shift variable—equal to the observable log of nominal *GNP*. Further, let $\{\Delta x_t\}$ be a sequence of independent, normal variates with mean δ and variance σ_x^2.[5]

The relevant history of the economy then consists (at most) of y_{nt} (which fixes calendar time), the demand shifts $x_t, x_{t-1}, \ldots$, and past actual real outputs $y_{t-1}, y_{t-2}, \ldots$. Since the model is linear in logs, it is reasonable to conjecture a price solution of the form:[6]

$$
\begin{aligned}
P_t = {}& \pi_0 + \pi_1 x_t + \pi_2 x_{t-1} + \pi_3 x_{t-2} + \cdots \\
& + \eta_1 y_{t-1} + \eta_2 y_{t-2} + \cdots + \xi_0 y_{nt}
\end{aligned}
\tag{9}
$$

Then $\bar{P}_t$ will be the expectation of P_t, based on all information *except* x_t (the current demand level) or:

$$
\begin{aligned}
\bar{P}_t = {}& \bar{P}_0 + \pi_1(x_{t-1} + \delta) + \pi_2 x_{t-1} \\
& + \pi_3 x_{t-2} + \cdots + \eta_1 y_{t-1} \\
& + \eta_2 y_{t-2} + \cdots + \xi_0 y_{nt}
\end{aligned}
\tag{10}
$$

To solve for the unknown parameters π_i, η_j and ξ_0 we first eliminate y_t between (7) and (8), or equate quantity demanded and supplied. Then inserting the right sides of (9) and (10) in place of P_t and $\bar{P}_t$, one obtains an identity in $\{x_t\}$, $\{y_t\}$, and y_{nt}, which is then used to obtain the parameter values. The resulting solutions for price and output are:[7]

$$P_t = \frac{\theta \gamma \delta}{1 + \theta \gamma} - \lambda \beta + \frac{1}{1 + \theta \gamma} x_t$$

$$+ \frac{\theta \gamma}{1 + \theta \gamma} x_{t-1} - \lambda y_{t-1} - (1 - \lambda) y_{nt}$$

$$y_t = -\frac{\theta \gamma \delta}{1 + \theta \gamma} + \lambda \beta + \frac{\theta \gamma}{1 + \theta \gamma} \Delta x_t$$

$$+ \lambda y_{t-1} + (1 - \lambda) y_{nt}$$

In terms of ΔP_t and y_{ct}, and letting $\pi = \theta \gamma / (1 + \theta \gamma)$, the solutions are:

$$y_{ct} = -\pi \delta + \pi \Delta x_t + \lambda y_{c,t-1} \tag{11}$$
$$\Delta P_t = -\beta + (1 - \pi) \Delta x_t + \pi \Delta x_{t-1}$$
$$-\lambda \Delta y_{c,t-1} \tag{12}$$

Let us review these solutions for internal consistency. Evidently, P_t is normally distributed about $\bar{P}_t$. The conditional variance of P_t will have the constant (as assumed) variance $1/(1 + \theta \gamma)^2 \sigma_x^2$. Thus those features of the behavior of prices which were assumed "known" by suppliers in subsection 1.1 are, in fact, true in this economy.

To review, equations (11) and (12) are the *equilibrium values* of the inflation rate and real output (as a percentage deviation from trend). They give the intersection points of an aggregate demand schedule, shifted by changes in x_t, and an aggregate supply schedule shifted by variables (lagged prices) which determine expectations. In order to avoid the introduction of an additional, spurious "expectations parameter," one cannot solve for this intersection on a period-by-period basis; accordingly, we have adopted a method which yields equilibrium "paths" of prices and output. Otherwise, the interpretation of (11) and (12) is entirely conventional.

Not surprisingly, the solution values of inflation and the cyclical component of real output are indicated by (11) and (12) to be distributed lags of current and past changes in nominal output. A change in the nominal expansion rate, Δx_t, has an immediate effect on real output, and lagged effects which decay geometrically. The immediate effect on prices is one minus the real output effect, with the remainder of the impact coming in the succeeding period. We note in particular that this lag pattern may well produce periods of simultaneous inflation and below average real output. Though these periods arise because of supply shifts, the shifts result from lagged perception of demand changes, and *not* from autonomous changes in the cost structure of suppliers.

In addition to these features, the model does indeed assert the existence of a natural rate of output: the *average* rate of demand expansion, δ, appears in (11) with a coefficient equal in magnitude to the coefficient of the current rate, and with the opposite sign. Thus changes in the average rate of nominal income growth will have *no* effect on average real output. On the other hand, unanticipated demand shifts do have output effects, with magnitude given by the parameter π. Since this effect depends on "fooling" suppliers (in the sense of subsection 1.1), one expects that π will be larger the smaller the variance of the demand shifts. We next develop this implication explicitly.

From the definition of π in terms of θ and γ, and the definition of θ in terms of σ^2 and τ^2 we have

$$\pi = \frac{\tau^2 \gamma}{\sigma^2 + \tau^2(1 + \gamma)}$$

Combining with the expression for σ^2 obtained above, this gives

$$\pi = \frac{\tau^2 \gamma}{(1 - \pi)^2 \sigma_x^2 + \tau^2(1 + \gamma)} \tag{13}$$

For fixed τ^2 and γ, then, π takes the value $\gamma/(1 + \gamma)$ at $\sigma_x^2 = 0$ and tends monotonically to zero as σ_x^2 tends to infinity.

The prediction that the average deviation of output from trend, $E(y_{ct})$, is invariant under demand policies is not, of course, subject to test: the deviations from a *fitted* trend line must average to zero. Accordingly, we must base tests of the natural rate hypothesis (in this context) on (13): a relationship between an observable variance and a slope parameter.

2 Test Results

Testing the hypothesis advanced above involves two steps. First, within each country (11) and (12) should perform reasonably well. In particular, under the presumption that demand fluctuations are the major source of variation in ΔP_t and y_{ct}, the fits should be "good." The estimated values of π and λ should be between zero and one. Finally, since (11) and (12) involve five slope parameters but only two

theoretical ones, the estimated π and λ values obtained from fitting
(11) should work reasonably well in explaining variations in ΔP_t.

The main object of this study, however, is not to "explain" output
and price level movements within a given country, but rather to see
whether the terms of the output-inflation "tradeoff" vary across countries in the way predicted by the natural rate theory. For this purpose,
we shall utilize the theoretical relationship (13) and the estimated
values of π and σ_x^2. Under the assumption that τ^2 and γ are relatively
stable across countries, the estimated π values should decline as the
sample variance of Δx_t increases.

Descriptive statistics for the eighteen countries in the sample are
given in Table 1.[8] As is evident, there is no association between
average real growth rates and average rates of inflation: this fact seems
to be consistent with both the conventional and natural rate views of
the tradeoff. Since our interest is in comparing real output and price
behavior under different time patterns of nominal income, these statistics are somewhat disappointing. Essentially two types of nominal
income behavior are observed: the highly volatile and expansive policies of Argentina and Paraguay, and the relatively smooth and mod-

Table 1 Descriptive Statistics, 1952–67

Country	Mean Δy_t	Mean ΔP_t	Variance y_{ct}	Variance ΔP_t	Variance Δx_t
Argentina	.026	.220	.00096	.01998	.01555
Austria	.048	.038	.00104	.00113	.00124
Belgium	.034	.021	.00075	.00033	.00072
Canada	.043	.024	.00109	.00018	.00139
Denmark	.039	.041	.00082	.00038	.00084
West Germany	.056	.026	.00147	.00026	.00073
Guatemala	.046	.004	.00111	.00079	.00096
Honduras	.044	.012	.00042	.00084	.00109
Ireland	.025	.038	.00139	.00060	.00111
Italy	.053	.032	.00022	.00044	.00040
Netherlands	.047	.036	.00055	.00043	.00101
Norway	.038	.034	.00092	.00033	.00098
Paraguay	.054	.157	.00488	.03192	.03450
Puerto Rico	.058	.024	.00205	.00021	.00077
Sweden	.039	.036	.00030	.00043	.00041
United Kingdom	.028	.034	.00022	.00037	.00014
United States	.036	.019	.00105	.00007	.00064
Venezuela	.060	.016	.00175	.00068	.00127

erately expansive policies of the remaining sixteen countries. But if
the sample provides only two "points," they are indeed widely separated: the estimated variance of demand in the high inflation countries
is on the order of 10 times that in the stable price countries.

The first three columns of Table 2 summarize the performance of
equation (11) in accounting for movements in y_{ct}. The estimated values
for π all lie between zero and one; with the exceptions of Argentina
and Puerto Rico, so do the estimated λ values. The R^2s indicate that

Table 2 Summary Statistics by Country, 1953–67

Country	π	λ	R_y^2	$R_{\Delta P}^2$	R_ω^2
Argentina	.011	−.126	.018	.929	.914
	(.070)	(.258)			
Austria	.319	.703	.507	.518	—
	(.179)	(.209)			
Belgium	.502	.741	.875	.772	.661
	(.100)	(.093)			
Canada	.759	.736	.936	.418	—
	(.064)	(.075)			
Denmark	.571	.679	.812	.498	.282
	(.118)	(.110)			
West Germany	.820	.784	.881	.130	—
	(.136)	(.110)			
Guatemala	.674	.695	.356	.016	—
	(.301)	(.274)			
Honduras	.287	.414	.274	.521	.358
	(.152)	(.250)			
Ireland	.430	.858	.847	.499	.192
	(.121)	(.111)			
Italy	.622	.042	.746	.934	.914
	(.134)	(.183)			
Netherlands	.531	.571	.711	.627	.580
	(.111)	(.149)			
Norway	.530	.841	.893	.633	.427
	(.088)	(.096)			
Paraguay	.022	.742	.568	.941	.751
	(.079)	(.201)			
Puerto Rico	.689	1.029	.939	.419	—.
	(.121)	(.072)			
Sweden	.287	.584	.525	.648	.405
	(.166)	(.186)			
United Kingdom	.665	.178	.394	.266	.115
	(.290)	(.209)			
United States	.910	.887	.945	.571	.464
	(.086)	(.070)			
Venezuela	.514	.937	.755	.425	—
	(.183)	(.148)			

for many, or perhaps most countries, important output-determining variables have been omitted from the model. The R^2s for the inflation rate equation, (12), are given in column (4) of Table 2. In general, these tend to be lower than for equation (11), and not surprisingly the estimated coefficients from (12) (which are not shown) tend to behave erratically. Column (5) of Table 2 gives the fraction of the variance of ΔP_t explained by (12) when the coefficient estimates from (11) are imposed. (A "—" indicates a negative value.)[9]

With respect to its performance as an intracountry model of income and price determination, then, the system (11)–(12) passes the formal tests of significance. On the other hand, the goodness-of-fit statistics are generally considerably poorer than we have come to expect from annual time-series models.

In contrast to these somewhat mixed results, the behavior of the estimated π values across countries is in striking conformity with the natural rate hypothesis. For the sixteen stable price countries, π ranges from .287 to .910; for the two volatile price countries, this estimate is smaller by a factor of 10! To illustrate this order-of-magnitude effect more sharply, let us examine the complete results for two countries: the United States and Argentina. For the United States, the fitted versions of (11) and (12) are:

$$y_{ct} = -.049 + (.910)\Delta x_t + (.887)y_{c,t-1}$$
$$\Delta P_t = -.028 + (.119)\Delta x_t + (.758)\Delta x_{t-1}$$
$$\quad -(.637)\Delta y_{c,t-1}$$

The comparable results for Argentina are:

$$y_{ct} = -.006 + (.011)\Delta x_t - (.126)y_{c,t-1}$$
$$\Delta P_t = -.047 + (1.140)\Delta x_t - (.083)\Delta x_{t-1}$$
$$\quad + (.102)\Delta y_{c,t-1}$$

In a stable price country like the United States, then, policies which increase nominal income tend to have a large initial effect on real output, together with a small, positive initial effect on the rate of inflation. Thus the apparent short-term tradeoff is favorable, as long as it remains unused. In contrast, in a volatile price country like Argentina, nominal income changes are associated with equal, contemporaneous price movements with no discernible effect on real output. These results are, of course, inconsistent with the existence of even moderately stable Phillips curves. On the other hand, they follow directly from the view that inflation stimulates real output if, and only if, it succeeds in "fooling" suppliers of labor and goods into thinking *relative* prices are moving in their favor.

3   Concluding Remarks

The basic idea underlying the tests reported above is extremely simple, yet I am afraid it may have become obscured by the rather special model in which it is embodied. In this section, I shall try to restate this idea in a way which, though not quite accurate enough to form the basis for econometric work, conveys its essential feature more directly.

The propositions to be compared empirically refer to the effects of aggregate demand policies which tend to move inflation rates and output (relative to trend) in the same direction, or alternatively, unemployment and inflation in opposite directions. The conventional Phillips curve account of this observed co-movement says that the terms of the tradeoff arise from relatively stable structural features of the economy, and are thus independent of the nature of the aggregate demand policy pursued. The alternative explanation of the same observed tradeoff is that the positive association of price changes and output arises because suppliers misinterpret general price movements for relative price changes. It follows from this view, first, that changes in average inflation rates will not increase average output, and secondly, that the higher the *variance* in average prices, the less "favorable" will be the observed tradeoff.

The most natural cross-national comparison of these propositions would seem to be a direct examination of the association of average inflation rates and average output, relative to "normal" or "full employment." Unfortunately, there seems to be no satisfactory way to measure normal output. The deviation-from-fitted-trend method I have used *defines* normal output to be average output. The use of unemployment series suffers from the same difficulty, since one must somehow select the (obviously positive) rate to be denoted full employment.

Thus although the issue revolves around the relation between *means* of inflation and output rates, it cannot be resolved by examination of sample averages. Fortunately, the existence of a stable tradeoff also implies a relationship between *variances* of inflation and output rates, as illustrated in Figure 1. With a stable tradeoff, policies which lead to wide variation in prices must also induce comparable variation in

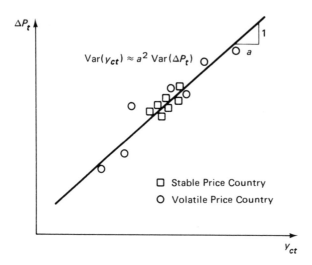

Figure 1

real output. If these sample variances do not tend to move together (and, as Table 1 shows, they do not) one can only conclude that the tradeoff tends to fade away the more frequently it is used, or abused.

This simple argument leads to a formal test if the output-inflation association is entirely contemporaneous. In fact, however, it involves lagged effects which make a direct comparison of variances, as just suggested, difficult in short time-series. Accordingly, it has been necessary to impose a specific, simple structure on the data. As we have seen, this structure accounts for output and inflation rate movements only moderately well, but well enough to capture the main phenomenon predicted by the natural rate theory: the higher the variance of demand, the more unfavorable are the terms of the Phillips tradeoff.

Notes

1. The most useful, general statements are those of Milton Friedman (1968) and Edmund Phelps. Specific illustrative examples are provided by Donald Gordon and Allan Hynes and Lucas (April 1972).

2. An explicit derivation of the price-output relationship from the IS-LM framework is given by Frederic Raines. Of course, this framework does not imply an elasticity of unity, though it is consistent with it. Since the unit elasticity hypothesis is primarily a matter of convenience in the present study, I shall comment below on the probable consequences of relaxing it.

3. A supply function for labor which varies with the ratio of actual to expected prices is developed and verified empirically by Lucas and Rapping (1969). The effect of lagged on actual employment is also shown. In our 1972 paper, in response to Albert Rees's criticism, we found that this persistence in employment cannot be fully explained by price expectations behavior. Both these effects—an expectations and a persistence effect—will be transmitted by firms to the goods market. In addition, they are probably augmented by speculative behavior on the part of firms (as analyzed for example, by Paul Taubman and Maurice Wilkinson).

For a general equilibrium model in which suppliers behave essentially as given by (3), see my 1972 papers.

4. This predicted relationship between a supply elasticity and the variance of a component of the price series is analogous to the link between the income elasticity of consumption demand and the variances of permanent and transitory income components which Friedman (1957) observes. As will be seen in Section 2, it works in empirical testing in much the same way as well.

5. This particular characterization of the "shocks" to the economy is not central to the theory, but to discuss rational expectations formation at all, *some* explicit stochastic description is clearly required. Independence is used here partly for simplicity, partly because it is empirically roughly accurate for most countries in the sample. The effect of autocorrelation in the shocks would, as can be easily traced out, be to add higher order lag terms to the solutions found below.

6. This solution method is adapted from Lucas (1972), which is in turn based on the ideas of John Muth.

7. If a demand function of the form $y_t = \xi P_t + x_t$ had been used, these solutions would assume the same form, with different expressions for the coefficients. If $\xi \neq 1$, however, x_t is an unobserved shock, unequal in general to observed nominal income. In this case, the model still predicts the time-series structure (moments and lagged moments) of the series y_{ct} and ΔP_t and is thus, in principle, testable. I have found empirical experimenting along these lines suggestive, but the series used are simply too short to yield results of any reliability.

8. The raw data on real and nominal GNP are from *Yearbook of National Accounts Statistics*, where series from many countries are collected and put on a uniform basis. The choice of countries is by no means random: the eighteen used are all the countries from which continuous series are available. The sample could thus be broadened considerably by use of sources from individual countries. To obtain the variables used in the tests, the logs of real and nominal output, y_t and x_t, are logs of the series in the source. The log of the price level, P_t, is the difference $x_t - y_t$; y_{ct} is the residual from the trend line $y_t = a + bt$, fit by least squares from the sample period. The moments given in Table 1 are maximum likelihood estimates based on these series. The estimates reported in Table 2 are by ordinary least squares.

9. The loss of explanatory power when these coefficients are imposed on (12) can be assessed formally by an approximate Chi-square test. By this measure, the loss is significant at the .05 level for Paraguay only. As Table 2 shows, however, this test is somewhat deceptive: for several countries the least squares estimates of (12) are so poor that there is little explanatory power to lose, and the test is "passed" vacuously.

References

M. Friedman, *A Theory of the Consumption Function*, Princeton 1957.

M. Friedman, "The Role of Monetary Policy," *Amer. Econ. Rev.*, Mar. 1968, *58*, 1–17.

D. F. Gordon and A. Hynes, "On the Theory of Price Dynamics," in E. S. Phelps et al., *Micro-economics of Inflation and Employment Theory*, New York 1969.

R. E. Lucas, Jr., "Expectations and the Neutrality of Money," *J. Econ. Theor.*, Apr. 1972, *4*, 103–124.

R. E. Lucas, Jr., "Econometric Testing of the Natural Rate Hypothesis," *Conference on the Econometrics of Price Determination*, Washington 1972, 50–59.

R. E. Lucas, Jr., and L. A. Rapping, "Real Wages, Employment and the Price Level," *J. Polit. Econ.*, Sept./Oct. 1969, *77*, 721–754.

R. E. Lucas, Jr., and L. A. Rapping, "Unemployment in the Great Depression: Is There a Full Explanation?", *J. Polit. Econ.*, Jan./Feb. 1972, *80*, 186–191.

J. F. Muth, "Rational Expectations and the Theory of Price Movements," *Econometrica*, July 1961, *29*, 315–335.

E. S. Phelps, introductory chapter in E. S. Phelps et al., *Micro-economics of Inflation and Employment Theory*, New York 1969.

F. Raines, "Macroeconomic Demand and Supply: an Integrative Approach," Washington Univ. working paper, Apr. 1971.

A. Rees, "On Equilibrium in Labor Markets," *J. Polit. Econ.*, Mar./Apr. 1970, *78*, 306–310.

P. Taubman and M. Wilkinson, "User Cost, Capital Utilization and Investment Theory," *Int. Econ. Rev.*, June 1970,*11*, 209–315.

United Nations, Department of Economic and Social Affairs, United Nations Statistical Office, *Yearbook of National Accounts Statistics, 66 and 68*, New York 1958.

Errata

[Editor's note: the following remarks by the author appeared in *American Economic Review* 66 (December 1976):985] Neil Wallace has pointed out a serious conceptual error in the tests I described in my article published in this *Review*, June 1973. The point is obscured by my decision to discuss estimation in terms of the deviations of log output from trend (y_{ct}) instead of the log of the level (y_t), but it is clear from inspection of the two equations for y_t and P_t stated between (10) and (11). Either of these equations can be obtained from the other using the *identity* $y_t + P_t = x_t$.

Much of the discussion of the within-country results given in Section 2 is marred by my erroneous impression that I was estimating a *two-equation* model; in fact, there is only one equation. Since it is too late to do anything about this, let me just indicate the main ways this error affects Table 2 and its interpretation. First, the columns headed R_y^2 and $R_{\Delta P}^2$ have nothing to do with the ability of the model to explain real output *versus* inflation rate movements. The R_y^2 measures the ability of the one equation in the model, estimated in level form, to explain output. The $R_{\Delta P}^2$ measures the ability of the *same* equation, estimated in first difference form, to explain inflation rates. Viewed in this (that is, the correct) way, a comparison of the two has no obvious interest. Second, the test discussed in note 9 and the column headed R_ω^2 have *no* bearing on "cross-equation" theoretical restrictions; since there is only one equation in the system, there can be no such restrictions.

A correct understanding of the relationship between the "two" equations in my model is obviously essential to an interpretation of the within-country results, and as can be seen from the above paragraph, the necessary revisions are far from minor conceptually. Substantively, however, the main conclusion I reached is not altered. The within-country results, which seemed consistent with the evidence but not particularly impressive invalidly interpreted, appear about the same interpreted validly. The cross-country results, which were the *only* evidence bearing directly on the natural rate hypothesis in the paper, are not affected in any way.

Capacity, Overtime, and Empirical Production Functions

1 Introduction

There are at present two leading theories describing the response of a competitive industry to cyclical fluctuations in product demand, one based on the neoclassical production function, the other on the hypothesis of fixed factor proportions. In this introductory section, the implications of each for cyclical movements in output, inputs, and relative prices are sketched, and the formidable (and largely familiar) empirical cases against both theories are reviewed.[1] In the remainder of the paper, an alternative theory, consistent with the evidence which appears to contradict the first two theories, is articulated.

To review the two theories in their simplest form, consider a competitive industry with many firms producing a single output by means of two inputs: labor and capital. Production is subject to constant returns to scale:

$$y_t = f(x_t), \qquad (1)$$

where y_t is output per unit of capital in period t, and x_t is labor (manhours) per unit of capital. In the current period, capital is fixed at its beginning of period level, so that the current period, short-run decision

Reprinted from *American Economic Review* 60 (1970): 23–27 by permission.
I wish to thank my colleagues L. A. Rapping, Myron Joseph, T. W. McGuire, and Wynn Winkler for their comments and suggestions. I would also like to thank Arvind Jain for his assistance and the National Science Foundation for its support.

problem for each firm is: choose labor and output, subject to (1), so as to maximize profit per unit of capital,

$$p_t y_t - w_t x_t. \tag{2}$$

The wage rate w_t and the output price p_t are regarded as parameters by firms. When a particular production function is specified, solution of this maximum problem yields theories of short-run output supply and labor demand.

If the production function is neoclassical ($f'(x) > 0, f'(x) < 0$ for all $x > 0$) one obtains the following well-known implications: (a) the marginal cost curve is smooth and upward sloping, so that demand shifts induce output and price changes in the same direction; (b) real wages $w/p = f'(x)$, should move countercyclically (be negatively correlated with x); (c) empirical estimates of (1) should yield an output-labor elasticity $xf'(x)/f(x)$ roughly equal to labor's share.

An alternative theory is obtained from maximizing the quantity (2) when f exhibits fixed factor proportions:[2]

$$y_t = \min[x_t, 1]. \tag{3}$$

The principal implications of this theory are: (a) the marginal cost curve is flat, up to capacity output, so that demand increases will lead first to expansions of output, next to price increases; (b) since capital earns a return only if $x_t = 1$, this equality should hold at cyclical peaks; (c) both labor's share and the real wage should move countercyclically; (d) under an optimal policy, $y_t = x_t$, so that empirical estimates of (1) should yield an output-labor input elasticity of unity.

Evidence from direct estimation of production functions clearly favors the fixed proportions theory. Table 1 below reports six estimates of the Cobb-Douglas form of (1), with an exponential trend term added.[3] In each case, the estimated output labor input elasticity differs insignificantly from unity. If the test for a "good" production function is an elasticity near labor's share, these results must be discarded (as one suspects similar results have been by many others). Yet by usual econometric standards, these results are excellent, and they exhibit a satisfying uniformity over a wide variety of samples and time periods. Perhaps it would be more interesting to search for a theory which can account for this regularity.

Table 1 Estimated Production Functions

Sample	Period	Constant	L/K elasticity	Trend	$\hat{\rho}$	DWS	R^2
Kendrick	1891–1953	−.221 (.017)	1.141 (.079)	.0058 (.0003)	.730 (.094)	2.23	.978
Kendrick	1891–1929	−.395 (.047)	1.035 (.167)	.0084 (.0011)	.533 (.145)	2.23	.793
Kendrick	1931–1953	−2.909 (.710)	.973 (.060)	.0193 (.0009)	.345 (.200)	1.78	.993
OBE	1930–1965	−.314 (.018)	1.039 (.027)	.0123 (.0003)	.571 (.110)	1.82	.967
Quarterly (OHS)	1948-II– 1965-IV	.420 (.046)	.992 (.041)	.0027 (.0002)	.579 (.115)	2.13	.996
Quarterly (DB)	1948-II– 1965-IV	.402 (.049)	.974 (.048)	.0026 (.0002)	.580 (.115)	2.10	.990

Evidence on cyclical movements in real wages is inconsistent with both theories. Thus Bodkin concludes his recent review and extension of the evidence on this point with: ". . . the majority of the analyses performed with the U.S. data support the . . . view that real wages are positively related to the cyclical utilization of the labour force."[4] Some tests of my own similarly show a weak relationship between movements in real wages and the labor-capital ratio.[5]

A third source of evidence on the fixed proportions hypothesis (3) is obtained by examining trend-corrected capital-output ratios at successive cyclical peaks. Since the constraint $y_t \leq 1$ must be binding for capital to earn a positive return, the peak observed y_t should be (approximately) attained frequently. This prediction is contradicted by the levels of y_t, relative to trend, attained during and immediately following World War II, which far exceed any previous or subsequent values.[6]

To summarize, there appears to be no evidence of diminishing returns to labor in U.S. time series data, either from real wage movements or from direct estimation of production functions. On the other hand, the fixed factor proportions hypothesis cannot account for fixed output per unit of capital flows attained during wartime, or for the absence of countercyclical real wage movements.

2 An Alternative Model
The evidence summarized in the preceding section and its implications for the two standard production theories are familiar to empirical

students of the business cycle. It is widely thought that the most hopeful route toward a resolution of these difficulties will be to incorporate variations in the rate of capital utilization into the theory. This can be done on two levels. First, some investigators have obtained "improved" empirical production functions (that is, have obtained labor elasticities closer to labor's share) by "correcting" measured capital stock for variations in utilization rates. Second, there have been attempts to reformulate the cost structure of firms to explain why less than full utilization of capital can be, at times, optimal. To account for the observations cited above, an adequate theory must clearly do both.

In this paper we shall pursue the view, advanced and studied in some detail by Marris, in which utilization is defined in terms of the fraction of hours per period (day, week) over which equipment is operated.[7] The rate of utilization, for fixed capital stock, will then depend on the rising schedule of wage rates as the firm moves from the most attractive to the least attractive hours of work. Certainly of the several available explanations for variations in rates of capital utilization, this view is the most relevant for secular movements. The basic reason that much of our capital is operated or occupied roughly 40 of 168 hours in a "normal" week is that people dislike night and weekend work, and the reason utilization in this sense has declined slowly throughout the century is that we have spent some of our increasing wealth on indulging this preference.[8] The fact that both hours worked per week and shift work are pro-cyclical suggests that worker preferences may be important in understanding cyclical variation in capital utilization as well. To determine whether this is so, an explicit model linking preferences and utilization is developed in the remainder of this section.[9]

We think of time as divided into discrete periods, corresponding to the period of observation (e.g., quarters) where each period is of length one. Capital stock is fixed throughout the period at its beginning-of-period level, and output is sold (or added to inventory) at the end of the period. Time within the period is treated as the unit interval, with points ordered from most to least desirable for workers. From the point of view of the firm, these preferences are summarized in a schedule $w(s)$, $0 \leq s \leq 1$, of competitive wage rates for work at time s. This schedule will have an upward slope, reflecting observed premium pay for overtime, night, and weekend work.

The flow of output per unit of capital at the instant s, $y(s)$, depends on workers per unit of capital on duty at s, $x(s)$, according to the "instantaneous" production function, (1). The volume of output, per unit of capital, over the entire period of production, is then:

$$y = \int_0^1 y(s) \, ds = \int_0^1 f(x(s)) \, ds. \tag{4}$$

Similarly, total man-hours per unit of capital are:

$$x = \int_0^1 x(s) \, ds, \tag{5}$$

and compensation of employees, per unit of capital, is:

$$wx = \int_0^1 w(s)x(s) \, ds. \tag{6}$$

An empirical production function, then, is a curve fitted to successive observations y_t and x_t (the left sides of the expressions (4) and (5)). Observed time series on money wages are observations on $(wx)_t$ divided by x_t (the expressions (6) and (5)). If the schedule $w(s)$ were flat, these variables would be related as discussed in the preceding section. The problem of this section is to relate these variables when $w(s)$ has the upward slope we observe.

Clearly, there will be no systematic relationship among these variables if the wage schedule $w(s)$ shifts "arbitrarily" from period to period. Accordingly, assume that $w(s)$ in period t is a base wage w_t times a premium schedule, $\phi(s)$, which remains stable over periods.[10] Under this assumption, a firm which is scheduling labor optimally (or which is "on" its short-run cost curve) solves:

$$\max_{x(s) \geq 0} \int_0^1 f(x(s)) \, ds$$

subject to:

$$\int_0^1 \phi(s)x(s) \, ds \leq c. \tag{7}$$

(That is, it maximizes output per unit of capital for a given total variable cost per unit of capital, cw_t.)

We first consider this problem under the fixed factor proportions
hypothesis (3), or

$$f(x(s)) = \min[x(s), 1],$$ (8)

and:

$\phi(s)$ is strictly increasing. (9)

From [13], Theorem 2″, a solution $x^0(s)$ exists. It is clear that $x^0(s)$ will
take the value 1 on an interval $[0, u]$ and 0 on $(u, 1]$ for some number
$0 \leqslant u \leqslant 1$. Since $\phi(s)$ is increasing, u is uniquely determined by:

$$\int_0^u \phi(s)\,ds \leqslant c, \quad \text{with equality if } u < 1.$$ (10)

The short-run product market implications of this model are exactly
as in the standard, neoclassical case. From (10) one obtains total
variable cost as a function of u and w_t, $w_t c(u)$, where $c(u)$ is strictly
convex and satisfies:

$$c(0) = 0, \quad c(1) = \int_0^1 \phi(s)ds, \quad c'(u) = \phi(u).$$ (11)

From (4), output per unit of capital is $y = \int_0^u ds = u$, so that $w_t\phi(y)$ is the
marginal cost function.

From (5), total man-hours per unit of capital also equal u (and y) so
that the observed output-labor input elasticity is predicted to be unity.
With output per man-hour fixed over the cycle, the real wage and
labor's share are the same variable. Their common value is given by
the ratio of money compensation, $(w_t/u) \int_0^u \phi(s)\,ds$, to output price (or
marginal cost) $w_t\phi(u)$. The derivative of this ratio with respect to u
(which is as good an index of the cycle as any other) is then:

$$\frac{1}{u}\left[1 - \frac{w}{p}\left(1 + \frac{u\phi'(u)}{\phi(u)}\right)\right].$$

Since w/p equals labor's share, it is between zero and one. On the
other hand, $1 + u\phi'(u)/\phi(u)$ exceeds one. Hence the cyclical movement in the real wage rate is not restricted by the theory.[11] In summary, the theory just outlined is consistent with all of the evidence
cited in the preceding section.

The short-run cost structure of the firm is essentially unchanged when the fixed proportions assumption is replaced by a neoclassical production function, as we next show. In place of (8), we require f to be twice differentiable and satisfy:

$$f(0) = 0, \qquad f'(x) > 0, \qquad f'(\infty) = 0, \qquad f''(x) < 0. \tag{12}$$

Again, Theorem 2″ of [13] guarantees the existence of an optimal work schedule $x^0(s)$. The strict concavity of f and the convexity of the set of functions defined by $x(s) \geq 0$ and (7) assure that this optimum is unique. Since f is strictly increasing, (7) holds with equality at $x^0(s)$ and, further, there is a positive number λ such that, for all $0 \leq s \leq 1$,

$$f'(x^0(s)) \leq \lambda\phi(s), \tag{13}$$

with equality if $x^0(s) > 0$. To obtain the cost function of the firm, then, one must solve (7) and (13) for λ and $x^0(s)$.

Inverting (13) gives the optimal workforce at s as a function of $\lambda\phi(s)$: $x^0(s) = \bar{x}(\lambda\phi(s))$. Then since the value of the objective function under $x^0(s)$ is output per unit of capital, y, we have:

$$y = \int_0^1 f[\bar{x}(\lambda\phi(s))]\, ds.$$

This in turn may be solved for $\lambda = \lambda(y)$, where

$$\lambda(0) > 0, \qquad \lambda(\infty) = 0, \qquad \lambda'(y) < 0. \tag{14}$$

Then substitution into (7) yields total variable cost as a function of output:

$$w_t c(y) = w_t \int_0^1 \bar{x}[\lambda(y)\phi(s)]\phi(s)\, ds. \tag{15}$$

By differentiation and the application of (13), one verifies the familiar fact that marginal cost is:

$$w_t c'(y) = \frac{w_t}{\lambda(y)}.$$

Thus, as in the fixed proportions case, the short-run product market implications of the model are identical to those of the standard neoclassical model discussed in the introduction.

This model implies a stable empirical "production function," obtained by substituting the optimal work schedule (which depends on output) into (5):

$$x = \int_0^1 x[\lambda(y)\phi(s)]\,ds. \tag{16}$$

The derivative of output with respect to labor input along this curve is readily calculated, but we can determine nothing about dy/dx except its sign. In particular, the elasticity $(x/y)(dy/dx)$ may be on either side of one, and bears no necessary relation to labor's share. Thus, this theory is consistent with the cyclical observations cited above, in the nearly vacuous sense that it is consistent with any stable empirical production function and with any cyclical pattern in real wages and labor's share.

3 Conclusions
The main point of this paper has been to examine two distinct margins along which a firm may increase its observed labor-capital ratio. The first, and most familiar, margin involves labor-capital substitution in the usual sense: at each point in time, one may work a fixed stock of equipment with more labor. The second corresponds to what is referred to as increasing the intensity of capital use: the fraction of the production period over which capital is used is increased. Along both margins, increasing marginal cost is met: in the first case, due to diminishing returns in a productive sense; in the second, due to a rising schedule of premium wages as operations are extended to hours which workers regard as unattractive. These two sources of diminishing pecuniary returns, separately or in combination, have identical short-run product market implications, the same as those of the simple neoclassical theory of Section 1. In contrast to the standard models, however, the models developed above are consistent with observed cyclical patterns in production and real wages. First, in common with the neoclassical theory, these models predict a stable relationship between output per unit of capital stock and man-hours per unit of capital stock. The elasticity of the former with respect to the latter need not, however, exhibit diminishing returns, even if the instantaneous production function is neoclassical. Thus both forms of the theory are consistent with the production function estimates reported in Section 1. Second, neither of the models developed here requires a countercyclical pattern in average, real compensation per man-hour

(the usual measure of "the" real wage rate). Thus the wage implications of the theory are consistent with the results of Bodkin [2] and others.

Notes

1. The review was suggested by, and resembles, some of Phelps's observations in [9].

2. Equation (3) assumes that capital and labor units have been chosen so that peak output per unit of either input is unity.

3. The results in Table 1, lines 1–3, are based on annual U.S. time series from Kendrick [5]. Line 4 is based on annual data from OBE sources. Lines 5 and 6 use OBE quarterly data. They differ only in the capital variable, line 5 using a one-hoss-shay (OHS) assumption to cumulate investment, and line 6 using declining balance (DB). The series are described in detail in [7], an earlier draft of this paper. (They may be obtained from the author on request.) The estimates are obtained using the two-step method proposed by Durbin in [3], which is appropriate under the hypothesis of first-order autocorrelation in the residuals. The statistic R^2 is one minus the sum of squared errors from the second stage, divided by the sum of squared deviations of the dependent variable from its mean (not the computed R^2 from the second stage).

4. The citation is from Section 7 of [2]. Bodkin uses the unemployment rate as an indicator of the cycle, and deflates money wages with a variety of price indexes. It should be mentioned that on postwar, quarterly U.S. manufacturing data Bodkin obtains results which (as he indicates) appear to be an exception to the results cited here.

5. These tests, based on data described in note 3, are reported in [7].

6. Output per unit of capital exceeded its secular (1890–1954) trend level by more than 20 percent in each of the years 1944–46, and in no other years of this period (using the Kendrick data in [5]).

7. See [8]. The view of utilization taken in this paper is essentially that of Marris, although we shall be concerned with a different set of implications. For alternative formulations, see Taubman and Wilkinson [11] and the "puttyclay" theories of Johansen [4] and Solow [10].

8. See the discussion by Lewis in [6].

9. The debt to Marris is acknowledged above. The following also uses the distinction between a rate and a volume of production in exactly the sense of Alchian [1].

10. There is some support for this assumption in the fact that some premium rates—notably overtime—are specified as a proportion of a base wage. About one-fourth of late shift workers receive a premium specified in percentage terms [12, p. 95]. A deeper analysis of this question would, of course, go behind the schedule $\phi(s)$ to the preference functions of labor suppliers.

11. This is true provided the elasticity $u\phi'(u)/\phi(u)$ is regarded as unobservable. The regression of $\log(w/p)$ on $\log(x)$ yields an estimate, according to the above theory, of the inverse of labor's share (about 1.5) less $1 + u\phi'(u)/\phi(u)$. Hence, a coefficient 0 on $\log(x)$ indicates an elasticity for $\phi(u)$ of .5. This number is not widely out of line with time-and-a-half for overtime or an 8 percent night shift differential [12, p. 86]. But to construct a careful test would involve the actual construction of the schedule $\phi(s)$, and the determination of the appropriate arc elasticity to compare against .5.

References

1. Armen Alchian, "Costs and Outputs," in Moses Abramovitz, ed., *The Allocation of Economic Resources: Essays in Honor of B. F. Haley* (Stanford Univ. Press, 1959).

2. Ronald G. Bodkin, "Real Wages and Cyclical Variations in Employment: A Reconsideration," *Canadian J. of Econ.*, Aug., 1969.

3. J. Durbin, "Estimation of Parameters in Time Series Regression Models," *J. of the Royal Statis. Soc.*, Series B, 1960.

4. Leif Johansen, "Substitution Versus Fixed Production Coefficients in the Theory of Economic Growth: A Synthesis," *Econometrica*, Apr. 1959, pp. 157–176.

5. John W. Kendrick, *Productivity Trends in the United States* (Princeton Univ. Press, 1961).

6. H. G. Lewis, "Hours of Work and Hours of Leisure," *I.R.R.A.*, 1956, pp. 196–207.

7. Robert E. Lucas, Jr., "Capacity, Overtime and Investment," unpublished Carnegie-Mellon research memorandum, Aug., 1969.

8. Robin Marris, *The Economics of Capital Utilisation* (Cambridge Univ. Press, 1964).

9. Edmund S. Phelps, introductory chapter in E. S. Phelps *et al., The New Microeconomics in Employment and Inflation Theory* (W. W. Norton, 1969).

10. Robert M. Solow, "Substitution and Fixed Proportions in the Theory of Capital," *Rev. of Econ. Studies*, June, 1962, pp. 207–218.

11. Paul Taubman and Maurice Wilkinson, "User Cost, Capital Utilization and Investment Theory," *Int. Econ. Rev.* (forthcoming).

12. U.S. Dept. of Labor, Bur. of Labor Statis., *Wages and Related Benefits* (Part ii), Bul. No. 1530–1587. (Washington, 1968).

13. Menahem E. Yaari, "On the Existence of an Optimal Plan in a Continuous Time Allocation Process," *Econometrica*, Oct., 1964, pp. 576–590.

Equilibrium Search
and Unemployment

1 Introduction

Thirty years after the Great Depression, economists have again worked up the nerve to ask an obvious question: Why is it that workers *choose* (under some conditions) to be unemployed rather than to take employment at lower wage rates? Soon after serious attention began to be focused on this question, a variety of models were advanced to illustrate how workers might rationally prefer some other activity to work at wage rates they perceive to be temporarily below normal.[1] A particularly interesting class of models arises when the alternate activity is taken to be job search: The worker is faced with a wage offer which he views as a drawing from a probability distribution; his choices are to accept the offer or to take another drawing.[2] (To be of interest, obviously, these choices must be mutually exclusive: One must be unable to search and work at the same time.)

Most contributors to this literature on search behavior subscribe to some form of the Friedman–Phelps notion that there exists a natural rate of unemployment which either cannot or should not (or perhaps both) be lowered (on average) by monetary and fiscal policies.[3] Yet while the language used in discussing this natural rate suggests that it may have the properties of a competitive equilibrium, there exist no theoretical models in which a nonzero equilibrium unemployment rate

Reprinted from *Journal of Economic Theory* 7 (February 1974):188–209 by permission. Copyright 1974 by Academic Press.

We thank E. S. Phelps for his helpful general comments and, in particular, for pointing out an error in an earlier draft in the discussion of Fig. 2.

is determined and its properties studied.[4] Normatively, this means that there is no framework within which important welfare issues such as those raised by Phelps [11, Chapter 4] and Tobin [14] can be formulated and analyzed. Empirically, it means (for example) that there is no theoretical account as to why average rates of unemployment vary so widely from one advanced capitalist economy to another.

Clearly, one cannot hope to deal with these questions by the study of the optimal search behavior of a single agent in the face of a *given* probability distribution of wage offers. The issues are those of market equilibrium and must be met in a theoretical context in which employment behavior and wages are *simultaneously* determined. As the reader who proceeds into the body of this paper will discover, this problem is more difficult than it sounds. Let us try to indicate why in the remainder of this introduction.

In order for wage rates for a single type of labor to differ at a point in time, labor must clearly be exchanged in spatially distinct markets. (Otherwise, wages would be bid into equality in a period much too short to be of economic interest.) The distribution of wage rates governing the worker's decision problem, referred to above, must then be related to his knowledge of the likely outcome of searching over these distinct markets. On the other hand, the distribution of wages over markets will evidently be influenced by the mobility of labor suppliers. In short, optimal labor supply behavior and the wage distribution on which it is based must be simultaneously determined within a model of *market* (as opposed to individual) behavior.

While quite analogous to the problem of using supply and demand schedules to determine price and quantity in a single market, this simultaneity problem is analytically more difficult for at least two reasons. First, since movement in space takes time, labor market search must be studied in a dynamic context. Second, the outcome of the process at each point in time will be a probability distribution rather than simply a number. The *solution* of the model will then be a *stochastic process*.

The rest of this paper is devoted to the elaboration of a complete "search model" of this general type. To preserve simplicity, the treatment will be abstract and illustrative. Discussion of the relationship of the theory to observed labor market behavior will be deferred to the conclusion of the paper and will there be brief.

2 Structure of the Model

We think of an economy in which production and sale of goods occur in a large number of spatially distinct markets.[5] Product demand in each market shifts stochastically, driven by shocks which are independent over markets (so that aggregate demand is constant) but autocorrelated within a single market. Output to satisfy current period demand is produced in the current period, with labor as the only input. Each product market is competitive.

There is a constant workforce which at the beginning of a period is distributed in some way over markets. In each market, labor is allocated over firms competitively with actual money wages being market clearing. Each worker may either work at this wage rate, in which case he will remain in this market into the next period, or leave. If he leaves, he earns nothing this period but enters a "pool" of unemployed workers which are distributed in some way over markets for the next period. In this way, a new workforce distribution is determined, new demands are "drawn," and the process continues.

In this process, all agents are assumed to behave optimally in light of their objectives and the information available to them. For firms, this means simply that labor is employed to the point at which its marginal value product equals the wage rate. For workers, the decision to work or to search is taken so as to maximize the expected, discounted present value of the earnings stream. In carrying out this calculation, workers are assumed to be aware of the values of the variables affecting the market where they currently are (i.e., demand and workforce) and of the true probability distributions governing the future state of this market and the present and future states of all others. That is, expectations are taken to be *rational*.[6]

The economic interpretation of this assumption of rational expectations is that agents have operated for some time in a situation like the current one and have therefore built up experience about the probability distributions which affect them. For this to have meaning, these distributions must remain stable through time. Mathematically, this means that we will be concerned only with *stationary distributions* of demand and workforce and with behavior rules under these stationary distributions. Although sequences tending toward these stationary distributions will be utilized analytically, these seem to have no counterpart in observed behavior.

The task of the following sections may now be outlined in more detail. In the next section, we study the determination of equilibrium employment and wages in a single market, with the expected return to workers of *leaving* that market taken as a parameter. In Section 4, the stationary joint distribution of demand and workforce in this market is determined. In Section 5, we aggregate the workforce over markets to obtain the total economy-wide workforce as a function of the parametric expected return. This relationship serves as an aggregate demand function for labor; given a fixed total workforce, the *equilibrium* expected return is then determined in the usual way. Finally, Section 6 discusses a certain kind of stability possessed by this equilibrium, and concluding remarks are given in Section 7.

3 Equilibrium in a Single Market

In this section and the next, we study wage and employment determination in a single market, representing the impact of the rest of the economy on this market by certain given parameters. This impact takes three forms: first, product demand functions shift in an exogenously determined, stochastic manner; second, the outside economy offers alternative employment to workers; third, new workers arrive from the rest of the economy, augmenting the local work force. We discuss each effect in turn.

The individual market behaves as a Marshallian industry, faced with a demand function $p = D(s, Q)$, where p is price, Q is industry output, and s is a stochastic shift variable, *realized prior to trading*. Output is supplied by m identical firms, each with the production function $\varphi(n)$ depending on labor input only. The industry is competitive, so that the profit (and present value) maximizing policy for firms is to hire labor to the point at which the marginal value product of labor, $p\varphi'(n)$, equals the wage. When the product market is cleared, then, the function $R(s, n)$ defined by

$$R(s, n) = D(s, m\varphi(n))\varphi'(n)$$

gives the marginal value product of labor when demand is in state s and employment is n. Since R summarizes completely the demand side of the labor market, we shall discard the functions D and φ and place restrictions directly on R, as follows.

The function $R(s, n)$ is positive, differentiable, and bounded; its first derivatives satisfy

$$R_s(s, n) > 0, \qquad R_n(s, n) < 0. \tag{1}$$

For each fixed n,

$$\lim_{s \to 0} R(s,n) = 0. \tag{2}$$

For each fixed w, $0 < w \leqslant R(s, 0)$, the function $\hat{n}(s, w)$ defined by $R(s, \hat{n}(s, w)) = w$ satisfies

$$\lim_{s \to \infty} \hat{n}(s,w) = \bar{n}(w) < \infty. \tag{3}$$

The shift variable s follows a Markov process governed by

$$F(s', s) = \Pr\{s_{t+1} \leqslant s' \,|\, s_t = s\}.$$

For fixed s, F is a cumulative distribution function on $s' > 0$, with the continuous, strictly positive density $f(s', s)$. For fixed s', F is a strictly decreasing function of s on $s > 0$; further, if g is continuous,

$$\lim_{s \to 0} \int g(s')f(s',s)\,ds' = \lim_{s \to 0} g(s), \tag{4}$$

and if g is also positive and nondecreasing,

$$\lim_{s \to \infty} \int g(s')f(s',s)\,ds' \leqslant \lim_{s \to \infty} g(s). \tag{5}$$

The process defined by F is assumed to possess a unique stationary distribution.[7]

The demand shifts s are assumed to be independent *across* markets, and the number of markets is large.[8] Further, the total workforce of the economy is fixed. In consequence, once the workforce has settled down to a stationary distribution over markets, the expected present value of job search is a constant, say λ. In this section and the next, we treat λ as a given parameter; its equilibrium value will be determined in Section 5.

At the beginning of the period, each market has a fixed workforce, y, which serves as an upper bound on current period employment in that market. All currently employed workers remain into the next period; currently unemployed workers leave. In addition, new workers arrive in a stochastic fashion, the exact nature of which depends on the search process which is assumed. In the present paper, we shall impose a particular property on the *outcome* of this process, namely that unemployed workers are allocated over markets in such a way as to equate to the opportunity cost λ the expected return in each market receiving workers. The precise arrival rate which will guarantee this outcome will be specified below.[9]

To summarize, the *state* of a particular market is completely described by its state of demand, s, its beginning of period workforce, y, and the expected present value of search, λ. Of these three variables, only s and y vary from market to market; accordingly, we use (s, y) to index markets (referring, for example, to "market (s, y)"). Then for market (s, y), we seek equilibrium values of wages and employment, $w(s, y, \lambda)$ and $n(s, y, \lambda)$, as functions of the state of the market. An equilibrium must satisfy both the market clearing condition

$$w(s, y, \lambda) = R(s, n(s, y, \lambda)) \tag{6}$$

and the labor supply constraint

$$n(s, y, \lambda) \leq y. \tag{7}$$

Additional equilibrium conditions will be obtained by considering the present value maximizing work–search decision made by workers.

To study this choice, let $v(s, y, \lambda)$ be the expected present value of the wage stream for a worker who finds himself in (s, y) at the beginning of the period. In general, $v(s, y, \lambda)$ will equal the current wage plus the expected present value of the wage stream from next period on, discounted to the present by a constant factor β, $0 < \beta < 1$. Formally,

$$v(s, y, \lambda) = w(s, y, \lambda) + \beta E\{v(s', y', \lambda)\}$$

where the expectation is taken with respect to the distribution (as yet undetermined) of next period's state, (s', y') conditional on the information currently available to workers: (s, y, λ). The value of the terms on the right will vary with (s, y); it is convenient to consider three cases separately, as follows.

Case A.   Some (or all) workers leave; some (or none) remain.

In this case, departing workers earn the expected return from search. Remaining workers earn no less, since they have the option to leave, and no more, since departing workers have the option to remain. Thus

$$v(s, y, \lambda) = \lambda. \tag{8a}$$

Case B1.   All workers remain; no additional workers arrive next period.

In this case, current employment is the total workforce y and the current wage is, from (6), $R(s, y)$. Since the current workforce is maintained into the following period, next period's state is (s', y), with s' given probabilistically by $f(s', s)$. Thus

$$v(s, y, \lambda) = R(s, y) + \beta \int v(s', y, \lambda) f(s', s) \, ds'. \tag{8b1}$$

Case B2.   All workers remain; some additional workers arrive next period.

In this case, the arriving workers, in common with *all* searchers, have an expected present value (discounted to the present) of λ. Thus, for them and for the workers remaining in (s, y), $\beta E\{v(s', y', \lambda)\}$ will have the common value λ, and

$$v(s, y, \lambda) = R(s, y) + \lambda. \tag{8b2}$$

Evidently, these three cases divide the positive quadrant of the (s, y) plane into three mutually exclusive and exhaustive subsets.[10]

Now comparing cases B1 and B2, we observe that if no new workers are expected to arrive (case B1), it must be that expected rent in (s, y) is nonpositive with a future workforce of y, or that $\beta \int v(s', y, \lambda) f(s', s) \, ds' \leq \lambda$. Thus, (8b1) and (8b2) may be combined as

$$v(s, y, \lambda) = R(s, y) + \min[\lambda, \beta \int v(s', y, \lambda) f(s', s) \, ds']. \tag{8b}$$

Finally, comparing cases A and B, we observe that remaining workers in either case have rejected the option to search, so that $v(s, y, \lambda) \geq \lambda$. Thus, (8a) and (8b) may combine to yield a single functional equation valid for all cases:

$$v(s, y, \lambda) = \max\{\lambda, R(s, y) + \min[\lambda, \beta \int v(s', y, \lambda) f(s', s) \, ds']\}. \tag{8}$$

The relevant facts about (8) are given in:

Proposition 1.   *Equation* (8) *has a unique solution* $v(s, y, \lambda)$. *The function v is continuous in* (s, y, λ), *nondecreasing in s and* λ, *nonincreasing in y, and satisfies*

$$|v(s, y, \lambda_1) - v(s, y, \lambda_2)| < (1/\beta)|\lambda_1 - \lambda_2| \tag{9}$$

for any λ_1, λ_2. *For each* y, λ,

$$\lim_{s \to 0} v(s,y,\lambda) = \lambda, \tag{10}$$

and for s sufficiently large,

$$v(s, y, \lambda) \leq R(s, y)/(1 - \beta). \tag{11}$$

Proof. Let T_λ, an operator which maps bounded continuous functions u on (s, y) into the same space, be defined by

$$T_\lambda u(s, y) = \max\{\lambda, R(s, y) + \min[\lambda, \beta \int u(s', y)f(s', s)\,ds']\}.$$

The operator T_λ is monotonic: $u \geq v$ for all (s, y) implies $T_\lambda u \geq T_\lambda v$. For any constant c and function u, $T_\lambda(u + c) \leq T_\lambda u + \beta c$. By a slight modification of Theorem 5 of Blackwell [1], these two facts imply that T_λ is a contraction mapping. Thus, Eq. (8), $T_\lambda v = v$, has a unique, continuous solution and $\lim_{n \to \infty} T_\lambda u = v$ for any continuous u.

If $u(s, y)$ is increasing in s and decreasing in y, so is $T_\lambda u$, using (1). Hence, $v = \lim T_\lambda^n u$ is nondecreasing in s and nonincreasing in y.

Let $\lambda_1 > \lambda_2$. Clearly, $T_{\lambda_1} v(s, y, \lambda_2) \geq v(s, y, \lambda_2)$ for all (s, y). Since the operator T_{λ_1} is monotonic, we have

$$v(s,y,\lambda_1) = \lim_{n \to \infty} T_{\lambda_1}^n v(s,y,\lambda_2) \geq v(s,y,\lambda_2).$$

Hence v is nondecreasing in λ.

To verify (9), let $\lambda_1 > \lambda_2$ and define $u(s, y) = v(s, y, \lambda_2) + (\lambda_1 - \lambda_2)/\beta$. Then from the definitions of T_{λ_1} and $v(s, y, \lambda_2)$, we have, since $\beta < 1$,

$$T_{\lambda_1} u(s, y) = v(s, y, \lambda_2) + \lambda_1 - \lambda_2 < u(s, y).$$

Then by the monotonicity of T_{λ_1},

$$v(s,y,\lambda_1) = \lim_{n \to \infty} T_{\lambda_1}^n u(s,y) < u(s,y) = v(s,y,\lambda_2) + (\lambda_1 - \lambda_2)/\beta.$$

To prove (10), let $v_0 = 0$ and apply T_λ repeatedly, using (2) and (4) at each step.

To prove (11), let $v_0 = 0$ and apply T_λ repeatedly, using (5) at each step.

This proves Proposition 1.

With the value function v determined, we return to the determination of equilibrium employment and wages and of the equilibrium behavior of new arrivals. To determine employment, let $\tilde{n}(s, \lambda)$ be the employment that would occur in a market with demand s if the workforce constraint were not present. Thus, $\tilde{n}$ is the solution to

$$R(s, \tilde{n}(s, \lambda)) + \min[\lambda, \beta \int v(s', \tilde{n}(s, \lambda), \lambda) f(s', s) \, ds'] = \lambda.$$

Since R is positive, the solution cannot occur when the second term on the left is λ, so we may simplify to

$$R(s, \tilde{n}(s, \lambda)) + \beta \int v(s', \tilde{n}(s, \lambda), \lambda) f(s', s) \, ds' = \lambda. \tag{12}$$

Then, clearly, equilibrium employment is

$$n(s, y, \lambda) = \min[\tilde{n}(s, \lambda), y], \tag{13}$$

and equilibrium wages are found using (6). We summarize in

Proposition 2. *For each fixed (s, y, λ), there exist unique equilibrium employment and wage functions $n(s, y, \lambda)$ and $w(s, y, \lambda)$ defined implicitly by (6), (8), (12), and (13). These functions are continuous in (s, y, λ) and satisfy the monotonicity properties*[11]

$$n_s \geq 0, \quad n_y \geq 0, \quad n_\lambda \leq 0, \tag{14}$$
$$w_s \geq 0, \quad w_y \leq 0, \quad w_\lambda \geq 0. \tag{15}$$

Also, for each fixed (y, λ),

$$\lim_{s \to 0} n(s, y, \lambda) = 0 \tag{16}$$

and

$$\lim_{s \to \infty} n(s, y, \lambda) = \min[\bar{n}(\lambda), y], \tag{17}$$

where $\bar{n}(\lambda)$ is a finite bound, varying with λ.

The *proof* of Proposition 2 is facilitated by reference to Fig. 1, which exhibits the left side of (12) as a function of n.

By (1) and Proposition 1, the curves in Fig. 1 are negatively sloped and shift to the right as s increases. As λ increases, these curves shift upward by Proposition 1 but, from (9), by an amount less than the

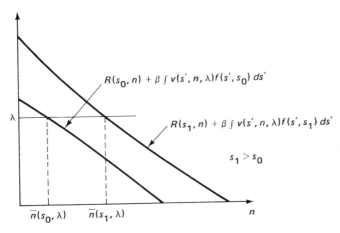

Figure 1

increase in λ. Then, using (13), (14) is proved; (15) follows from (14) and (6).

Applying (2), (4), and (10), (16) is proved.

Applying (3), (5), and (11), (17) is proved.

The results of this section may be illustrated on a conventional supply–demand diagram for labor. The demand curve is simply the marginal productivity condition (6), which shifts with the state of product demand, s. The curve SS is the relation between n and w implicit in (6) and (12): it is the locus of the wage–employment pairs which would be traced out as demand shifts if the workforce y did not constrain employment. The boldface curve is then the labor supply curve associated with the workforce y. The curve SS shifts up with increases in opportunity cost λ.

We remark that SS will not be flat, as would be the case if workers held a fixed "reservation wage" above which they accept employment and below which they do not. The reason this does not occur lies in the fact that as demand varies, wage and price changes convey information about future wage prospects as well as current earnings. Thus, as demand shifts to the left and employment declines, future prospects in (s, y) are affected in two ways: first, lower demand this period increases the probability of a low demand next period as well; second, lower employment this period implies a lower workforce next period. These effects work in opposite directions, which is to say that on any

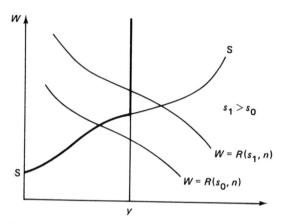

Figure 2

interval, the curve SS may be either upward sloping (as drawn in Fig. 2) or downward sloping.

4 The Equilibrium Distribution of the Workforce

Implicit in the above discussion of equilibrium employment in a single market is the stochastic law relating a market's *next period* workforce to its current period demand and workforce, (s, y). In the present section, we make this law explicit, then develop its implications for the stationary joint distribution of demand and workforce.

In the preceding section, we postulated that all unemployed workers move toward markets with nonnegative expected rents. From the discussion of cases B1 and B2 above, it is clear that a market will attract new workers only if $n(s, y, \lambda) = y$ *and*

$$\beta \int v(s', y, \lambda) f(s', s) \, ds \geq \lambda. \tag{18}$$

If searchers were perfectly directed toward markets, each market satisfying (18) would receive exactly the arrivals a such that $y + a$ would satisfy (18) with equality. Equation (8) remains valid, however, under the somewhat weaker requirement that the search process eliminate rents on average. Specifically, let x be a positive random variable with the strictly positive density ϕ, c.d.f. Φ, and mean 1. We assume that each market (s, y) satisfying (18) receives $a(s, y, \lambda)x$ new workers, where the function $a(s, y, \lambda)$ is defined implicitly by

$$\beta \iint v(s', y + a(s, y, \lambda)x, \lambda) f(s', s) \phi(x) \, ds' \, dx = \lambda \tag{19}$$

if (s, y, λ) satisfies (18), and

$$a(s, y, \lambda) = 0 \tag{19a}$$

otherwise.[12]

The possible transitions from (s, y) are illustrated in Fig. 3. If (s, y) is in region I, current employment and next period's workforce is $n(s, \lambda)$, and $y - n(s, \lambda)$ workers enter the unemployed pool. Markets in region II neither contribute to nor receive from the unemployment pool, maintaining their current workforce into the next period. Markets in region III employ all their workforce and receive new workers for next period, as specified by (19).

Analytically, the transitions from (s, y) are described by[13]

$$\Pr\{s_{t+1} \leq s', y_{t+1} \leq y' \mid s_t = s, y_t = y\}$$
$$= F(s', s)\Pr\{n(s, y, \lambda) + a(s, y, \lambda)\, x \leq y'\}$$
$$= F(s', s)\Phi\left(\frac{y' - n(s, y, \lambda)}{a(s, y, \lambda)}\right).$$

These transition probabilities define an operator P on distribution functions $\Psi(s, y)$ as follows: Suppose that at a point in time, demand and workforce are distributed according to the c.d.f. Ψ; then the demand–workforce distribution next period is

$$P\Psi(s', y') = \int\int F(s', s)\Phi\left(\frac{y' - n(s, y, \lambda)}{a(s, y, \lambda)}\right) \Psi(ds, dy). \tag{20}$$

We wish to show that the (s, y) process has a unique stationary distribution, or to prove

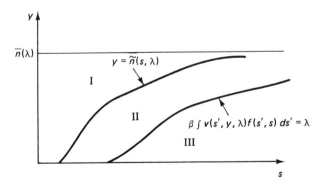

Figure 3

Proposition 3. *With P defined by* (11), $P\Psi = \Psi$ *has a unique solution* Ψ^* *(for each fixed* λ*) and* $\lim_{n\to\infty} P^n\Psi = \Psi^*$ *for all* Ψ. *Further,* Ψ^* *possesses a continuous density* ψ^* *which is strictly positive on* $(s > 0, y \geq 0)$.

The proof of Proposition 3 follows the treatment of Feller [3, pp. 264–268] or Doob [2, pp. 190–221]. The essential elements are the proofs of

Lemma 1. *For any initial distribution* Ψ, *the sequence* $\{P^n\Psi\}$ *is stochastically bounded.*

and

Lemma 2. *For any nondegenerate rectangle R in* $(s > 0, y \geq 0)$ *and any initial distribution* Ψ, *there is some m such that for all* $n > m$, *the distribution* $P^n\Psi$ *assigns positive probability to R.*

The second of these two lemmas specifies that the entire set $(s > 0, y > 0)$ is the ergodic set and contains no cyclically moving subsets; the first assures that most of the probability remains concentrated on a bounded subset of $(s > 0, y \geq 0)$. Together, these facts imply Proposition 3.

Proof of Lemma 1. For probabilities assigned by $P^n\Psi$, we use the notation $\Pr\{(s_n, y_n) \in A\}$. For arbitrary $\epsilon > 0$ and initial distribution Ψ, we wish to find $(\bar{s}, \bar{y})$ such that

$$(P^n\Psi)(\bar{s}, \bar{y}) = \Pr\{s_n \leq \bar{s}, y_n \leq \bar{y}\} \geq 1 - \epsilon$$

uniformly in n. Evidently, it will be sufficient to verify this inequality for $n \geq m$ for some m.
    We have

$$\Pr\{s_n \leq \bar{s}, y_n \leq \bar{y}\} \geq 1 - \Pr\{s_n \geq \bar{s}\} - \Pr\{y_n \geq \bar{y}\}.$$

Since $\{s_n\}$ has a stationary distribution, $\bar{s}$ may be chosen so that $\Pr\{s_n \geq \bar{s}\} \leq \epsilon/2$ for n sufficiently large. Let $\bar{n}(\lambda)$ be the employment bound referred to in (17), Proposition 2. Choose $\bar{y}$ so that

$$\Pr\{x \geq (\bar{y} - \bar{n}(\lambda))/a(\bar{s}, 0, \lambda)\} = 1 - \Phi[(\bar{y} - \bar{n}(\lambda))/a(\bar{s}, 0, \lambda)] \leq \epsilon/2.$$

Then since $a(s, y, \lambda)$ is increasing in s and decreasing in y,

$$\Pr\{y_n \geq \bar{y}\} \leq \Pr\{\bar{n}(\lambda) + a(\bar{s}, 0, \lambda)x \geq \bar{y}\} \leq \epsilon/2.$$

This completes the proof of Lemma 1.

Proof of Lemma 2. We shall show that if the distribution is initially concentrated on an arbitrary point (s_0, y_0), then $\Pr\{\underline{s} \leqslant s_n \leqslant \bar{s}, y \leqslant y_n < \bar{y}\} > 0$ for all $n \geqslant 3$, provided $\underline{s} < \bar{s}$ and $\underline{y} < \bar{y}$.

Let $\tilde{y}$ satisfy $\beta \int v(s', \tilde{y}, \lambda) f(s', \underline{s}) \, ds' = \lambda$ (so that $(\underline{s}, \tilde{y})$ is on the lower curve in Fig. 3), and let $\tilde{s}$ satisfy $\tilde{y} = \tilde{n}(\tilde{s}, \lambda)$ (so that $(\tilde{s}, \tilde{y})$ is on the upper curve of Fig. 3). Then since $f(s', s)$ is strictly positive,

$\Pr\{n(s_1, y_1) \leqslant \tilde{y}, s_1 \leqslant \tilde{s} \mid (s_0, y_0)\} > 0$

for any (s_0, y_0), and, therefore,

$\Pr\{y_2 \leqslant \tilde{y}, \underline{s} \leqslant s_2 \leqslant \tilde{s}\} > 0.$

Then since $\phi(x)$ is strictly positive,

$\Pr\{y \leqslant y_3 \leqslant \bar{y}, \underline{s} \leqslant s_3 \leqslant \bar{s}\} > 0.$

Evidently, the passage thus described may occur in any number of steps greater than three, so the proof is complete.

For each fixed λ, then, the (s, y) process has a unique stationary distribution, described by its c.d.f. $\Psi(s, y, \lambda)$ or its density $\psi(s, y, \lambda)$. In the remainder of this section, we study the behavior of mean values of functions of (s, y) taken with respect to Ψ as the parameter λ varies. The result of this examination is

Proposition 4. *Let $\psi(s, y, \lambda)$ be the stationary density found in Proposition 3, and let $g(s, y)$ be continuous, Then if the integral*

$h(\lambda) = \iint g(s, y)\psi(s, y, \lambda) \, ds \, dy$

exists, it is a continuous function of λ.

The proof begins with the observation that one can always select a closed rectangle R, with the complement $\tilde{R}$ containing the (s, y) pairs with either very small or very large s-values, such that

$\iint_{\tilde{R}} |g(s, y)| |\psi(s, y, \lambda_1) - \psi(s, y, \lambda_0)| \, ds \, dy \leq \delta$

for any λ_0, λ_1 and $\delta > 0$. We shall be concerned, then, only with showing that the above integral taken over R tends to zero with $|\lambda_1 - \lambda_0|$. We do so with heavy reliance on Fig. 3.

As λ increases (say from λ_0 to λ_1), the curves in Fig. 3 both shift down (by Propositions 1 and 2). This implies that $\Phi(s, y, \lambda_1)$ lies everywhere (on the y-axis) to the *left* of $\Psi(s, y, \lambda_0)$. (That is, high λ values are associated with low workforce levels.) Now since the functions $\bar{n}(s, \lambda)$ and $v(s, y, \lambda)$ are continuous, there is a maximum absolute vertical shift, $c(\lambda_0, \lambda_1)$, of the two curves on R. Further, c tends to zero with $\lambda_1 - \lambda_0$.

By the argument used to prove Proposition 3, one can find the c.d.f. $\Psi(s, y, \lambda_0, c)$ implied by a *constant* shift of c in both curves of Fig. 3. Evidently, this c.d.f. lies everywhere to the left of $\Psi(s, y, \lambda_1)$, so that the *horizontal* distance between $\Psi(s, y, \lambda_1)$ and $\Psi(s, y, \lambda_0)$ is bounded from above by the horizontal distance between $\Psi(s, y, \lambda_0, c)$ and $\Psi(s, y, \lambda_0)$. But $\Psi(s, y, \lambda_0, c) = \Psi(s, y - c, \lambda_0)$, so this latter distance is simply c, which tends to zero with $\lambda_1 - \lambda_0$.

Since Ψ possesses a continuous density, this continuity property is sufficient to guarantee the continuity of $h(\lambda)$.

5 Economy-Wide Equilibrium

Propositions 1–4 describe the determination of the stationary distributions of employment, workforce, and wages in a representative market, with the expected return from search, λ, treated as a given parameter. From an economy-wide viewpoint, however, it is the size of the workforce which is fixed and the "price" λ which adjusts to clear the market.

For given λ, the system described above would behave, in the aggregate, as an occupation with a membership elastically supplied at the expected present value λ. The distribution of the workforce over locations (indexed by (s, y)) would in this case be the same as the stationary distribution of (s, y) in any one market. (This follows from our assumptions that the number of markets is large and that demand shifts are independent across markets.) Then the total workforce demanded (per market) in this occupation, at the return λ, is

$$\iint y\Psi(s, y, \lambda)\,ds\,dy. \tag{21}$$

For each fixed λ, the integral (21) converges in view of the facts that employment is bounded for each fixed λ (Eq. (17), Proposition 2), that $a(s, y, \lambda)$ is bounded, and that the random variable x has a finite mean. By Proposition 4, the expression (21) is a continuous function of λ. As observed in Section 4, increases in λ shift the distribution function $\Psi(s, y, \lambda)$ to the left (along the y-axis), so that (21) is a decreasing function of λ. As $\lambda \to 0$, $E(y; \lambda) \to \infty$ since R is a positive strictly decreasing function of n; as $\lambda \to \infty$, $E(y; \lambda) \to 0$. The demand function is thus as shown in Fig. 4.

Now let μ denote the fixed workforce per market *supplied*. This vertical supply function together with the demand function just obtained gives the equilibrium λ: the solution to

$$\iint y\Psi(s, y, \lambda)\, ds\, dy = \mu. \tag{22}$$

We summarize in

Proposition 5. *For all values of workforce-per-market μ, there is a unique positive equilibrium value of λ.*

Thus, Propositions 1–3 and 5 provide a full description of the equilibrium determination of wages, employment, and workforce in all markets of the economy.[14] By Proposition 3, there will always be some markets in region I of Fig. 3, where the workforce y exceeds the equilibrium employment level $\bar{n}(s, \lambda)$. This means that labor market equilibrium necessarily involves positive unemployment.

Numerical calculations of the equilibrium pictured in Fig. 4 are provided in the appendix to this paper.

6 Stability of Equilibrium
The equilibrium obtained for this model economy provides a complete description of the *time paths* of all variables involved, both at an aggregate and the individual market level. Since provision of such a

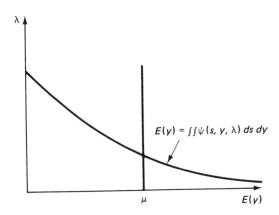

Figure 4

description is frequently thought to be the task of "stability theory" (in the sense of, for example, Samuelson [12]), one may ask whether the latter theory has any applicability to the present model. The answer, we think, is "yes," provided one raises the stability question in its most fundamental sense of determining whether if an equilibrium approximately describes the economy at a point in time, it will continue to do so in the future.

In the present context, this approximation question is particularly pertinent, since we have provided no account as to how workers arrive at the state of perfect knowledge of the probability distributions relevant to their decision problem. Ultimately, this is a question for psychological rather than economic theory, so we do not apologize for framing it here in *ad hoc* "adaptive" terms.

The distributions F and Φ refer to variables exogenous to the markets under study; presumably, they are learned by processing observed frequencies in some sensible fashion, "Bayesian" or otherwise, which has the property that the "true" distributions become "known" after enough time has passed. The distribution $\Psi(s, y, \lambda)$, on the other hand, depends on the behavior of workers, so that as worker perceptions change, so does the "true" Ψ which is being learned. This could, in general, raise insuperable analytical difficulties, but in the present context it does not, since the *only* feature of Ψ which is relevant to worker decisions is the parameter λ. We must describe, then, how the economy operates when the λ perceived by workers differs from the equilibrium value λ^* (say) and how, under this circumstance, perceptions are revised.

For specificity, suppose $\lambda > \lambda^*$. Then the number of workers entering the pool exceeds the number which can be reassigned at an average return of λ. One could modify the reallocation mechanism in many ways, but suppose in particular that the mean of the random variable x varies so as to equate the total number of workers reallocated to the size of the pool. Then both searchers and workers who remain on the job will be disappointed (on average) in their wage expectations. Presumably, this will lead them to revise their perceived λ downward, slowly relative to the passage of trading time t. Thus, we assume

$$d\lambda/dt = g(\lambda - \lambda^*),$$

where g is a decreasing function vanishing at zero. Clearly (from Fig.

4), the equilibrium is stable. Equally clearly, this stability result can have no relevance to the dynamic response to regularly recurring shocks.[15]

7 Concluding Remarks

Although there are (by assumption) no *aggregate* dynamics in the model developed above, it should be obvious that the mechanism we have described is consistent with the now familiar account of the observed Phillips curve in terms of expectations. Thus, an unanticipated change in aggregate demand (a change in $E(s'|s)$) will move unemployment and wage changes in opposite directions. Of course, if aggregate demand changes were a recurrent event, as they are in reality, this fact would become incorporated into the maximum problem facing workers and would result in different equilibrium functions $w(s, y)$ and $n(s, y)$. We leave this nontrivial development for future research.

The implications one *can* draw from the model as it stands are of a comparative static nature, both positive and normative. As an example of the former, suppose a lump-sum cost is imposed on leaving one's market to search, so that the right side of (12) becomes $\lambda - c$ rather than simply λ. This will raise the curve $y = \bar{n}(s, \lambda)$ in Fig. 3 and shift the "demand curve" in Fig. 4 downward. The result is a decrease in unemployment and a decrease in the equilibrium present value of wages, λ. (This example also shows that lower average unemployment is not, in general, associated with higher welfare for workers.) It may well be, though one could hardly demonstrate it at this level of abstraction, that differences of this sort in the actual or perceived costs of changing jobs can help to account for the observed differences in average unemployment across occupations and among countries.

We can also examine Tobin's normative concern [14, p. 8] that "the external effects [of search] are the familiar ones of congestion theory. A worker deciding to join a queue or to stay in one considers the probabilities of getting a job, but not the effects of his decision on the probabilities that others face." Now one could *add* congestion in the usual sense to the search model we have developed (say, by assuming that searching workers travel on a congested route).[16] But it should be clear that congestion of this sort is not a necessary component of an equilibrium search model. In our scheme, the injury a searching worker imposes on his fellows is of exactly the same type as the injury

a seller of any good imposes on his fellow sellers: the equilibrium
expected return λ from job search serves the function of any other
equilibrium price of signalling to suppliers the correct social return
from an additional unit supplied.

The question of whether there exist important external effects in
actual labor markets remains, of course, to be settled. However this
may turn out, it is surely a major advance even to be discussing
unemployment from the point of view of the usual (in better developed
areas of economics) standard of allocative efficiency. Our intention in
this paper has been to indicate the general kind of framework within
which such discussions can be conducted and to begin to develop
suitable analytical methods.

Appendix: Examples

Several examples were analyzed numerically to determine the workforce demand and unemployment rate as a function of the market
parameter λ. In order to compute these solutions, it was necessary to
assume a finite number of market demand states and to permit only
integer values for the workforce. In addition, we assumed that x had
a degenerate distribution concentrated at one.

The method of solution used the T_λ operator, defined in Section 3,
to determine the value function $v(s, y, \lambda)$. The initial approximation
was $v_0(s, y, \lambda) = \lambda$. The nth approximation $v_n(s, y, \lambda)$ was $T_\lambda v_{n-1}(s, y,$
$\lambda)$. With the assumed discount factor $\beta = 0.9$, the convergence to $v(s,$
$y, \lambda)$, the unique fixed point of T_λ, was rapid. Equation (12) was then
solved to determine $\bar{n}(s, \lambda)$, and Eqs. (19) and (19a) were used to
determine $a(s, y, \lambda)$. Next period's workforce, given $x = 1$, will be

$$y' = \min[\bar{n}(s, \lambda), y] + a(s, y, \lambda). \tag{23}$$

The workforce will be bounded, which along with the previous assumptions implies a finite number of possible market states (s, y). Thus,
the stochastic process for a market is a finite-state Markov chain with
some transition probability matrix, say, P. This matrix whose ijth
element specifies the probability that state j will occur next period
given current state i is determined by (23) and the transition probability
matrix of the s-process.

Let u be a function (represented by a vector) defined on the possible
market states. Using the analysis of Feller [3, pp. 264–268], the ex-

pected value of u with respect to the stationary distribution implied by P can be determined by computing

$$\lim_{n \to \infty} P^n u.$$

The limiting vector has elements all of which are equal to the expected value of u. This was the procedure we used to compute

$$\sum_{s,y} y\psi(s, y, \lambda);$$

the average workforce per market, and

$$\sum_{s,y} a(s, y, \lambda)\psi(s, y, \lambda),$$

the average unemployment per market.[17]

Two of the examples considered had the marginal revenue schedules depicted in Fig. 5. There are but two demand states: $s = 1$ or $s = 2$. The transition probability matrix for the s process was

$$\begin{bmatrix} .9 & .1 \\ .1 & .9 \end{bmatrix},$$

so there was a strong persistence in demand. The discount factor β was 0.9.

As the theory predicts, the labor demand curve, pictured in Fig. 5, is downward sloping. On the other hand, the unemployment level, also pictured in Fig. 5, is not monotonic, having maxima. Overall, we found for low and high persistence in demand that unemployment rates were low. In the former case, there was little gained by reallocating workers, while in the latter reallocation occurred infrequently. As expected, the greater the variability of demand, holding the degree of persistence fixed, the greater the level of unemployment. This result is reasonable for more workers should be reallocated when demand conditions change.

Notes

1. A number of these are collected in Phelps *et al.* [10]. The central ideas can be traced at least back to Hicks [5].

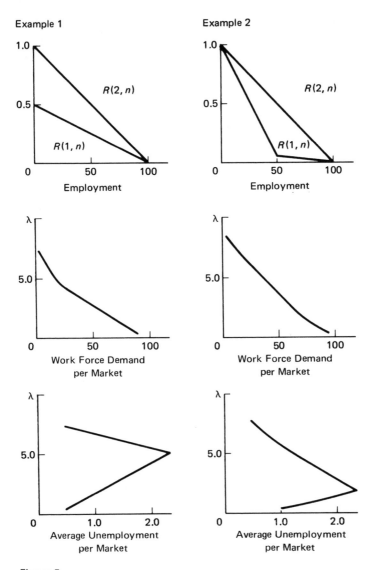

Figure 5

2. For example, the Mortensen and Gordon–Hynes chapters of [10], McCall [8], and Stigler [13]. It is perhaps necessary to emphasize that the class of models in which active job search is the *only* alternative to work by no means exhausts the class of models in which unemployment is viewed as a "rational" choice.

3. In addition to the above references, see Friedman [4].

4. Lucas [7] provides an equilibrium in which employment fluctuates with aggregate demand. In this model, however, "unemployment" as an activity is not differentiated from "leisure" or other nonwork alternatives.

5. See Phelps' introductory chapter in [10] for the description of the "island economy" which is the direct ancestor of the present model.

6. In the sense of Lucas and Prescott [6] and Muth [9].

7. For an example of a Markov process satisfying all these restrictions, including (4) and (5), let (ϵ_t) be a sequence of independent, normal variates, let $0 < r < 1$, and let s_t follow

$$\ln(s_{t+1}) = a + r\ln(s_t) + \epsilon_t.$$

8. By large, we mean either a continuum of markets or a countable infinity. Economically, then, the assumption of independent demand shifts means that *aggregate* demand is taken to be constant through time.

9. In Eq. (19).

10. See Fig. 3 (which we do not at this point in the argument have enough information to draw) for this partitioning of the positive quadrant.

11. We use the usual notation for partial derivatives, recognizing that the monotonicity properties only imply that they exist almost everywhere.

12. The arbitrariness in the search hypothesis (19) seems unavoidable, at least in the absence of a physically described process of search (e.g., the hypothesis that searchers follow a random walk over markets viewed as points in the plane). Our own attempts to formulate processes of the latter type have rapidly led to a complexity uncompensated by additional economic insight.

The hypothesis (19) seems roughly to capture the following sort of process. Unemployed workers are informed (by advertising, word of mouth, etc.) of which markets need workers (are in region III of Fig. 3) and in which of these demand is greatest. All workers move toward a market in this class. Since the search is not coordinated, there is a stochastic element in the relationship between the actual "shortage" and arrivals of new workers.

13. We use the convention that when $a(s,y,\lambda) = 0$, division of a positive (negative) number by $a(s,y,\lambda)$ yields $+ (-)\infty$. A c.d.f. evaluated at $+\infty$ is 1; evaluated at $-\infty$, it is 0.

14. Since the content of this paper consists as much in motivating and explaining a particular definition of equilibrium as in analyzing this equilibrium, we have intermingled definitions and results in a way which may be difficult

for readers to disentangle. A different procedure would be to begin with the following (abbreviated)

Definition. An *equilibrium* for the economy under study consists of a 5-tuple of nonnegative, continuous functions $n(s,y)$, $\bar{n}(s,y)$, $w(s,y)$, $v(s,y)$, and $a(s,y)$, a c.d.f. $\Psi(s,y)$, and a nonnegative number λ such that (6), (8), (12), (13), (19), (20), and (22) are satisfied.

The content of Propositions 1–3 and 5, then, is that a unique equilibrium in the sense of the definition exists. Of course, these propositions also contain information useful in characterizing this equilibrium.

15. For reasons developed by Gordon and Hynes in [10].

16. Phelps [11, Chapter 4, pp. 103–105] also discusses congestion problems, but in a way which makes it clear that these problems arise under nonwage rationing of jobs (i.e., under *dis*equilibrium prices) as opposed to being externalities in the usual equilibrium sense.

17. The computer program used for these calculations is available upon request.

References

1. D. Blackwell, Discounted dynamic programming, *Ann. Math. Statist.* **36** (1965), 226–235.

2. J. L. Doob, "Stochastic Process," Wiley, New York, 1953.

3. W. Feller, "An Introduction to Probability Theory and Its Applications," Vol. ii, Wiley, New York, 1966.

4. M. Friedman, The role of monetary policy, *Amer. Econ. Rev.* **58** (1968), 1–17.

5. J. R. Hicks, "Value and Capital," Clarendon Press, Oxford, England, 1939.

6. R. E. Lucas, Jr. and E. C. Prescott, Investment under uncertainty, *Econometrica* **39** (1971), 659–681.

7. R. E. Lucas, Jr., Expectations and the neutrality of money, *J. Economic Theory* **4** (1972), 103–124.

8. J. McCall, The economics of information and optimal stopping rules, *J. Business* **38** (1965), 300–317.

9. J. F. Muth, Rational expectations and the theory of price movements, *Econometrica* **29** (1961).

10. E. S. Phelps *et al.* "Microeconomic Foundations of Employment and Inflation Theory," Norton, New York, 1969.

11. E. S. Phelps, "Inflation Policy and Unemployment," Norton, New York, 1972.

12. P. A. Samuelson, "Foundations of Economic Analysis," Harvard University Press, Cambridge, 1947.

13. G. J. Stigler, The economics of information, *J. Political Economy* **69** (1961), 213–235.

14. J. Tobin, Inflation and unemployment, *Amer. Econ. Rev.* **62** (1972), 1–18.

An Equilibrium Model
of the Business Cycle

This paper develops a theoretical example of a business cycle, that is, a model economy in which real output undergoes serially correlated movements about trend which are not explainable by movements in the availability of factors of production. The mechanism generating these movements involves unsystematic monetary-fiscal shocks, the effects of which are distributed through time due to information lags and an accelerator effect. Associated with these output movements are procyclical movements in prices, procyclical movements in the share of output devoted to investment, and, in a somewhat limited sense, procyclical movements in nominal rates of interest.

1 Introduction

This paper develops an exploratory business cycle theory in which unsystematic monetary shocks and an accelerator effect interact to generate serially correlated, "cyclical" movements in real output. Associated with these output movements are procyclical movements in prices, in the ratio of investment to output, and, in a rather special sense, in nominal interest rates. In contrast to conventional macro-economic models, the model studied below has three distinguishing characteristics: prices and quantities at each point in time are determined in *competitive equilibrium*; the expectations of agents are *rational*, given the information available to them; information is

Reprinted from *Journal of Political Economy* 83 (December 1979):1,113–1,144 by permission of The University of Chicago Press. Copyright 1975 by The University of Chicago Press.

I would like to thank Robert Barro, Fischer Black, Edward Prescott, and Thomas Sargent for many very helpful comments on an earlier draft.

imperfect, not only in the sense that the future is unknown, but also in the sense that no agent is perfectly informed as to the current state of the economy.

The attempt to discover a competitive equilibrium account of the business cycle may appear merely eccentric or, at best, an aesthetically motivated theoretical exercise. On the contrary, it is in fact motivated entirely by practical considerations. The problem of quantitatively assessing hypothetical countercyclical policies (say, a monetary growth rule or a fiscal stabilizer) involves imagining how agents will behave in a situation which has never been observed. To do this successfully, one must have some understanding of the way agents' decisions have been made in the past *and* some method of determining how these decisions would be altered by the hypothetical change in policy. Insofar as our descriptions of past behavior rely on arbitrary mechanical rules of thumb, adjustment rules, illusions, and unspecified institutional barriers, this task will be made difficult, or impossible. Who knows how "illusions" will be affected by an investment tax credit?[1]

In all of the models discussed in the paper, real output fluctuations are triggered by unanticipated monetary-fiscal shocks. The first theoretical task—indeed, the central theoretical problem of macroeconomics—is to find an analytical context in which this can occur and which does not at the same time imply the existence of persistent, recurrent, unexploited profit opportunities. Section 2 develops a neoclassical monetary growth model, with the aim of illustrating why this problem cannot be resolved within the class of aggregative models which view trade as taking place each period in a single, centralized market. This abstract environment, while analytically convenient, places too much information at the disposal of traders for cyclical behavior to be consistent with rationality.

In sections 3–5, this model is modified by viewing production and trade as occurring in a large number of markets which are imperfectly linked both physically and informationally. This is the analytical device first proposed by Phelps (1969) and since utilized by myself (1972, 1973), Lucas and Prescott (1974), and Barro (1975). As shown in Lucas (1972), this modification of the information structure of an otherwise neoclassical system leads to a real response to a purely nominal disturbance.

In Lucas (1972), and also in Sargent (1973*b*) and Sargent and Wallace (1973), however, these real movements are of no longer duration than the duration of the shock: no forces are present to account for the persistence or cumulation of the effects of the initial disturbance. In the present study, two such forces are introduced: information lags, such as to prevent even relevant past variables from becoming perfectly known, and physical capital, introducing a form of the familiar accelerator effect.

In the model set out in sections 3–5, agents' behavior is described by a pair of asset demand functions relating decisions to expected yields. That is, the link between tastes, technology, and demand behavior is not made explicit. On the other hand, the inference problem solved by agents to relate available information to expected yields is developed in some detail in section 6.

Sections 7–9 develop certain conditions which an equilibrium solution must satisfy. The main novelty lies in the explication of the theoretical links between "structural" and "reduced-form" parameters implied by the rationality of agents' expectations formation: the "reduced form" depends on the "structure" for the usual reasons; and the "reduced form" determines the stochastic behavior of prices, and therefore affects the form of optimal forecast rules, and therefore the "structural equations" (decision rules).

Sections 10–12 describe the nature of the "cycle" produced by the model under three sets of assumptions on the parameters of the model. Section 10 exhibits the model of section 2 as a special case. Section 11 develops a purely monetary cycle in which capital plays no role. Section 12 describes a "monetary over-investment" cycle.[2] It is the latter version which exhibits the qualitative characteristics cited in the first paragraph of this Introduction.

The cycles of sections 11 and 12 occur in a setting which abstracts from the existence of economy-wide securities markets. In view of the importance placed in the model on the partial nature of the information conveyed by the "local" prices at which agents trade, this abstraction may well be crucial. The informational role of economy-wide interest rates is briefly, if inconclusively, discussed in section 13.

Sections 14 and 15 discuss, briefly, some issues of testing and policy implications. Section 16 concludes the paper.

2 A Neoclassical Monetary Growth Model

Though the main concern of this paper is with oscillations of ouput
and prices about a trend path, it will be useful to begin on more
familiar ground with the discussion of a fairly standard, undisturbed
neoclassical growth model. This will permit the fixing of notation and
the early disposal of certain side issues.

Consider, to be specific, an economy producing a single output to
be divided among private consumption, C_t, real government consumption, G_t, and next period's capital, K_{t+1}. The production function is f,
and

$$C_t + G_t + K_{t+1} = f(K_t, N_t) + (1 - \delta)K_t \qquad (1)$$

holds where N_t is employment. The function f has the usual monotonicity and curvature properties and is homogeneous of degree 1; δ is
a depreciation rate.

There is a constant population of identical households which own
all the factors of production. Labor is hired by firms at the wage W_t;
capital is rented at U_t; and output is sold (to households and government) at P_t. All three markets are competitive. Firms maximize current-period profit, so that in equilibrium

$$f_K(K_t, N_t) = \frac{U_t}{P_t}, \qquad (2)$$

$$f_N(K_t, N_t) = \frac{W_t}{P_t}. \qquad (3)$$

Households supply labor inelastically in quantity N, which fact, in
conjunction with (2) and (3), determines equilibrium output, real wage,
and real rental price, each as a function of K_t. In addition to owning
the capital stock, households also hold a stock, M_t, of money balances
and select an end-of-period balance, M_{t+1}.[3] Their budget constraint,
given factor market equilibrium, is then

$$P_t(C_t + K_{t+1}) + M_{t+1} \leq P_t f(K_t, N) + P_t(1 - \delta)K_t + M_t. \qquad (4)$$

The objective of the household is to maximize a subjectively discounted sum of current period utilities, where the latter depend on
consumption and current holdings of real balances, M_{t+1}/P_t.

The model is completed by the specification of fiscal and money
supply behavior. Let all of government consumption be financed by

a monetary expansion at a constant, given rate μ. Then G_t is given implicitly by

$$P_t G_t = M_{t+1} - M_t = \mu M_t. \tag{5}$$

The dynamic behavior of the system will be determined once the demand on the part of households for the two forms of asset accumulation is specified. The most satisfactory way to do this, from some points of view, is to make explicit the household's preference functional and then to derive asset demands from households' infinite period maximum problem. An alternative route, taken here so as to set the stage for subsequent sections, is to postulate these demands directly.[4] Thus, let the demand for capital, K_{t+1}, depend on the expected one-period rates of return on capital and money, r_{kt} and r_{mt}, and the initial state of the household, K_t and M_t/P_t. The demand for money will depend on the same four variables. Given asset demands, consumption is implicit from (4).

Again with an eye toward later developments, both relationships are assumed to be log linear. For the log of a variable, use the corresponding lowercase letter, so that k_t means the *log* of capital, and so forth. Then the second equality in (5) becomes [since $\log(1 + \mu) \approx \mu$]

$$m_{t+1} - m_t = \mu. \tag{6}$$

The two demand functions for assets are postulated as

$$k_{t+1} = \alpha_0 + \alpha_1 r_{kt} - \alpha_2 r_{mt} + \alpha_3 k_t, \tag{7}$$
$$m_{t+1} - p_t = \beta_0 - \beta_1 r_{kt} + \beta_2 r_{mt} + \beta_3 k_t. \tag{8}$$

The elasticities α_1, α_2, α_3 and β_1, β_2, β_3 are assumed to be positive; $\alpha_1 > \alpha_2$; $\beta_2 > \beta_1$; and α_3 and β_3 are less than unity. For completeness, the log of beginning-of-period real balances, $m_t - p_t$, should also appear on the right sides of (7) and (8) (since they figure in the budget constraint [4]). Here and in subsequent sections I shall neglect this "real balance effect" in order to focus on the effects of monetary changes on the two yields, r_{kt} and r_{mt}.[5]

The real one-period rate of return on capital is next period's real rental price, $f_K(K_{t+1}, N)$, less the depreciation rate. Approximating this by a linear function of the log of capital gives

$$r_{kt} = \delta_0 - \delta_1 k_{t+1}, \qquad \delta_1 > 0. \tag{9}$$

The rate of return on money is the percentage rate of deflation:

$$r_{mt} = p_t - p_{t+1}. \tag{10}$$

Since both of these rates of return depend on the values of future variables, both are "expectations" at the time they affect the decisions of traders. In the present context of certainty, it is natural to take these expectations to be correct (or rational). This assumption closes the system (6)–(10).

Substituting (6), (9), and (10) into (7) and (8), one obtains a pair of first-order difference equations in capital and real balances. The usual practice is to obtain the general solution to this system and then apply the boundary conditions that capital equal its historically given initial value and that real balances remain bounded and bounded away from zero as t tends to infinity. A slightly different method is adopted here, one which turns out to be more convenient when uncertainty is introduced.

Given the structure of the economy (the parameters α_i, β_j, δ_k, and μ), the pair (k_t, m_t) describes completely the *state* of the system at the beginning of period t. This leads naturally to *defining* a solution to be a set of functions relating equilibrium decisions and price to these two state variables. Since the system is linear, it is natural to conjecture the existence of solution functions of the form

$$k_{t+1} = \pi_{10} + \pi_{11}k_t + \pi_{12}m_t, \tag{11}$$
$$p_t = \pi_{20} + \pi_{21}k_t + \pi_{22}m_t. \tag{12}$$

Then *solving* means finding numbers $\pi_{10}, \ldots, \pi_{22}$ such that (6)–(12) hold *identically* in (k_t, m_t).

Substituting from (6) and (9)–(12) into (7) and (8) yields the required identities in (k_t, m_t); equating the coefficients yields six equations in the unknown π_{ij}s:

$$\pi_{10} = \alpha_0 + \alpha_1\delta_0 - \alpha_1\delta_1\pi_{10} + \alpha_2\pi_{21}\pi_{10} + \alpha_2\pi_{22}\mu, \tag{13}$$
$$\pi_{11} = -\alpha_1\delta_1\pi_{11} - \alpha_2\pi_{21}(1 - \pi_{11}) + \alpha_3, \tag{14}$$
$$\pi_{12} = -\alpha_1\delta_1\pi_{12} + \alpha_2\pi_{21}\pi_{12}, \tag{15}$$
$$\mu - \pi_{20} = \beta_0 - \beta_1\delta_0 + \beta_1\delta_1\pi_{10} - \beta_2\pi_{21}\pi_{10} - \beta_2\pi_{22}, \tag{16}$$
$$-\pi_{21} = \beta_1\delta_1\pi_{11} + \beta_2\pi_{21}(1 - \pi_{11}) + \beta_3, \tag{17}$$
$$1 - \pi_{22} = \beta_1\delta_1\pi_{12} - \beta_2\pi_{21}\pi_{12}. \tag{18}$$

Equations (14) and (17) involve only π_{11} and π_{21}; their solution is diagrammed in Appendix A. As seen in figure A1, there are two solution pairs. One pair, with $\pi_{11} > 1$ and $\pi_{21} > 0$, has no economic significance and will be discarded.[6] The other is the desired solution; it satisfies

$$\frac{\alpha_3}{1 + \alpha_1 \delta_1} < \pi_{11} < 1, \tag{19}$$

$$\pi_{21} < 0. \tag{20}$$

Inspection of (15) and (18) shows that one solution is

$$\pi_{12} = 0, \tag{21}$$

$$\pi_{22} = 1. \tag{22}$$

Since $\pi_{21} < 0$, there is no solution other than this classical one. Finally, the constants π_{10} and π_{20} are readily calculated from (13) and (16).

With these solution values, equation (11) is a stable first-order difference equation in capital stock. Capital tends monotonically to its stationary value, $\pi_{10}/(1 - \pi_{11})$. The behavior of prices is given by (12), given the paths of capital and money.

Note first the sense in which money is "neutral" in this system. From (21) and (22), a once-and-for-all change in the *level* of money balances leads to a proportional change in the price level in the current and all future periods. There are no real effects. On the other hand, it is evident from (13) that changes in the *rate of increase* of money, μ, *will* have real consequences: the higher μ is the larger π_{10} is and hence the larger capital is all along its time path and at its stationary point. As Tobin (1965) and others have noted, this effect "works" through the real yield on money, which is, from (10) and (12),

$$r_{mt} = \pi_{21}(k_t - k_{t+1}) - \mu,$$

or, in the stationary state, simply the negative of the rate of monetary expansion.[7]

Note, second, the peripheral role played by the "flow variables"— output, private and government consumption, and employment—in determining the dynamic behavior of the system. The model is analyzed by first reducing it to the equations describing the motion of assets and their prices, solving these, and then returning to the determination of flow equilibrium. This characteristic, long familiar in more abstract theory, will carry over into subsequent sections. As a result, I will be discussing business cycles with scarcely a reference to such key magnitudes as employment, consumption, government spending, and real output. This may give an unfamiliar tone to much of what follows, but the translation back into the standard vocabulary is, I think, a straightforward exercise.

In particular, the reader may verify that the introduction of a taste for leisure and, consequently, a variable labor supply into the model of this section is easy to carry out, with no effect on the form of (7) and (8). This modification is obviously essential for business cycle theory and will be taken for granted below.

Finally, and in sharp contrast to traditional macroeconomic models, the solution found above remains valid under very wide variations in what is assumed about the behavior of money. To take one example, suppose $m_{t+1} - m_t$ is a sequence of independent, normal variates, each with mean μ and variance σ^2. If (9) and (10) are reinterpreted as *expected* rates of return, conditional on information available up through t, then (11) and (12) remain a solution, with the *same* coefficients π_{ij} as found above. In view of the emphasis often put on the distinction between anticipated and unanticipated monetary changes, this fact may seem paradoxical. It results from the fact that in a competitive market the current price is part of traders' information sets. Thus, a trader who knows the coefficients of (12) and the current real capital k_t *knows* m_t prior to committing himself, regardless of whether it is announced or not, or anticipated or not.

3 A Cycle Model: Introduction
The above discussion of a monetary growth model concluded with the observation that merely introducing "noise" into monetary policy was not sufficient to induce the sort of responses in real and nominal variables which occur during the observed business cycle. The problem is that in an economy in which all trading occurs in a single competitive market, there is "too much" information in the hands of traders for them ever to be "fooled" into altering real decision variables.

To get away from this analytical difficulty, but not so far away as to preclude a simple description of aggregate behavior, I shall adopt the device proposed by Phelps (1969) and, since utilized in similar contexts by Lucas (1972, 1973) and Lucas and Prescott (1974), of thinking of trading as occurring in distinct markets, or "islands." Such a system is described in this section and analyzed in the remainder of the paper.

At the beginning of a period, traders are distributed in some way over a continuum of markets. Each market has capital in place, as determined by the preceding period's trading. There is a stock of money in the hands of traders; in addition, government purchases introduce new money in a way which varies stochastically from market to market and period to period. Within each market, production, exchange, and asset accumulation take place exactly as described in the preceding section, with the sole difference being that the two yields, r_{kt} and r_{mt}, are conditional expectations rather than known numbers. Once trading is complete, agents select a new market at random, new monetary shocks are realized, and the process continues.[8]

Capital accumulated in a particular market is assumed to remain there into the next period, though its owners move on. The dollar return to capital is then received by shareholders after trading is complete. The size of this one-period "float" is taken to be proportional to the stock of money (though, in fact, this cannot hold exactly) and is neglected in what follows. The financing of investment is entirely "internal": there are no economy-wide markets for capital funds.[9]

All exchange in this economy takes place at competitive market clearing prices. The behavior of each trader is *rational* both in the conventional sense of optimal, given objectives and expectations, and in the Muthian sense (Muth 1961) that available information is optimally utilized in forming expectations. In order that the latter assumption have an operational meaning, the analysis will be restricted to the situation in which the relevant distributions have settled down to stationary values and can thus be "known" by traders.

The central economic ingredients of this model will, as in the preceding section, be the asset demand functions (7) and (8), which will now differ from market to market due to variations in capital stock and in information. The aim of the analysis will, also as above, be to obtain the analogue to the solutions (11) and (12) for the motion of the state variables and their relative price. The major difference induced by the introduction of relative and aggregate "noise" will be in the calculation, by agents, of the expected yields r_{kt} and r_{mt}, which will now be mean values conditioned on limited information rather than perfectly foreseen realizations.

It will be convenient to develop these elements in the reverse of the usual order. In the next section, the information structure of the economy is described and the solution of the model is stated formally. Next, in section 5, the asset demand functions are restated and the two expected yields redefined. The inference problem solved by agents is treated in section 6, completing the statement of the model.

4 Notation and a Formal Solution

To move toward an explicit description of the economy described above, think of trade as occurring in a continuum of separated markets z, $0 < z < 1$, where z is an index of location. The system is driven by stochastic injections of new money (in the form of governmental spending) which vary over time and over markets at a given time. Let the average (over markets) percentage increase in money be x_t, where $x_t \sim N(\mu, \sigma^2)$. Market z receives an increment which deviates from the average by the percentage amount $\theta_t(z)$, where

$$\theta_t(z) = \rho\theta_{t-1}(z) + \epsilon_t(z), \qquad 0 < \rho < 1 \tag{23}$$

and $\epsilon_t(z) \approx N(0, \sigma_\epsilon^2)$. Take $\epsilon_t(z)$ and x_s to be independent for all s, t, z and $\epsilon_t(z)$ and $\epsilon_s(z')$ to be independent, unless $s = t$ and $z = z'$. Then the stationary distribution of $[x_t, \theta_t(z)]$ for any fixed location z will be normal with mean $(\mu, 0)$ and covariance matrix

$$\begin{pmatrix} \sigma^2 & 0 \\ 0 & \sigma_\theta^2 \end{pmatrix},$$

where $\sigma_\theta^2 = \sigma_\epsilon^2/(1 - \rho^2)$. None of the shocks $\epsilon_t(z)$, $\theta_t(z)$, and x_t is ever observed by agents, but their distributions are taken to be constant and known by agents.[10]

As a consequence of these shocks, the only ones affecting the economy, capital stock may be expected to vary over time and across markets. Let $k_t(z)$ denote the log of beginning-of-period capital in z at t and let k_t be the average value of $k_t(z)$ over all markets. Use $u_t(z) = k_t(z) - k_t$ to denote the deviation from average of market z's capital. These three variables will follow a stochastic process to be determined. Denote the stationary distribution of $u_t(z)$ as $N(0, \sigma_u^2)$. One would expect the persistent, relative shocks $\theta_t(z)$ to affect capital movements, so that $\sigma_{u\theta} = E[\theta_t(z)u_t(z)]$ will be nonzero. These distributional facts are also assumed known to agents, though $k_t(z)$ and k_t cannot be directly observed.

Also as a consequence of the disturbances, individuals in different markets will acquire differing amounts of money during a trading period. Think of a large number of agents, each selecting next period's market at random, so that the distribution of agents by their money balances will be the same in all markets. In the normal, log-linear structure to be used below, the only changing feature of this distribution will be its logarithmic mean, denoted (as in sec. 2) by m_t. This average follows the random walk

$$m_{t+1} = m_t + x_t. \tag{24}$$

Assume that m_t is not directly observed by agents. Equations (23) and (24) together give a complete description of the flows of money through the various markets in this economy and all the relevant information on the distribution of money among agents.

According to the above description, then, the aggregate (or average) state of the economy is described by the values k_t, m_t, and x_t of capital stock, money, and nominal government spending. The situation of an individual market z is described by its capital relative to average, $u_t(z) = k_t(z) - k_t$, and the government spending it receives relative to average, $\theta_t(z)$.

As agents diffuse through this system, they observe none of these variables directly. Each period, however, they trade goods for money at a market clearing price $p_t(z)$. The history of prices $p_t(z)$, $p_{t-1}(z')$, $p_{t-2}(z'')$, . . . , observed by an individual is his source of information on the current state of the economy and of the market z in which he currently finds himself; equivalently, this history is his source of information on future prices.[11] Since traders follow different paths, each will have different information in hand, so that in general one would need to describe the informational state of the economy by a distribution of agents by information held. To complicate matters still further, this informational state will influence prices and will then itself be an object of speculation—agents will form expectations about the expectations of others. Two further conventions will help to simplify this complex picture. First, assume that each agent summarizes the price history $(p_{t-1}, p_{t-2}, \ldots)$ observed by him in a pair $(\hat{k}_t, \hat{m}_t)$, his unbiased estimate of the current values of the aggregate state variables, (k_t, m_t).[12] Second, prior to trading each period, these estimates are "pooled" by traders by simple averaging, so that a single pair $(\hat{k}_t, \hat{m}_t)$ of numbers describes the perceptions of *all* agents. Let these perceptions be normally distributed about the actual aggregate state, with the covariance matrix

$$\begin{bmatrix} \sigma_k^2 & \sigma_{mk} \\ \sigma_{mk} & \sigma_m^2 \end{bmatrix}.$$

The *state* of a particular market z, then, is fully described by seven numbers: $\hat{k}_t, \hat{m}_t, k_t, m_t, x_t, \theta_t(z), u_t(z)$. Agents do not know this state, though of course they do know their own expectations $(\hat{k}_t, \hat{m}_t)$. On the basis of the latter, they have a well-formed opinion of the relevant variables they cannot observe: $k_t, m_t, x_t, \theta_t(z), u_t(z)$. Specifically, they believe (correctly) that this random vector is normally distributed with a mean $(\hat{k}_t, \hat{m}_t, \mu, 0, 0)$ and covariance matrix

$$\Sigma = \begin{bmatrix} \sigma_k^2 & \sigma_{km} & 0 & 0 & 0 \\ \sigma_{km} & \sigma_m^2 & 0 & 0 & 0 \\ 0 & 0 & \sigma^2 & 0 & 0 \\ 0 & 0 & 0 & \sigma_\theta^2 & \sigma_{u\theta} \\ 0 & 0 & 0 & \sigma_{u\theta}^2 & \sigma_u^2 \end{bmatrix} \tag{25}$$

This completes the description of both the actual state of the economy and the opinions agents have as to this state.

As in section 2, the aim of the analysis will be to define and study the equilibrium motion of this system from state to state. Also as in section 2, one has the choice of thinking of equilibrium as a set of *time paths* of assets and prices, or as a set of *functions* which specify prices and asset movements, given the current state. Taking the latter route, let an equilibrium take the form[13]

$$k_{t+1}(z) = \pi_{10} + \pi_{11}\hat{k}_t + \pi_{12}\hat{m}_t + \pi_{13}[k_t + u_t(z)]$$
$$+ \pi_{14}m_t + \pi_{15}[x_t + \theta_t(z)], \tag{26}$$
$$p_t(z) = \pi_{20} + \pi_{21}\hat{k}_t + \pi_{22}\hat{m}_t + \pi_{23}[k_t + u_t(z)]$$
$$+ \pi_{24}m_t + \pi_{25}[x_t + \theta_t(z)]. \tag{27}$$

Subsequent sections will be devoted first to developing a set of conditions which these coefficients π_{ij} must satisfy and then to developing the implications of these conditions.

5 Asset Demand Functions

Current-period flow equilibrium is determined in each market exactly as in section 2. I shall focus, then, on the asset demand functions (7) and (8), repeated here in a notation which emphasizes their market specificity but is otherwise unchanged:

$$k_{t+1}(z) = \alpha_0 + \alpha_1 r_{kt}(z) - \alpha_2 r_{mt}(z) + \alpha_3 k_t(z), \tag{28}$$
$$m_t^d(z) - p_t(z) = \beta_0 - \beta_1 r_{kt}(z) + \beta_2 r_{mt}(z) + \beta_3 k_t(z). \tag{29}$$

The parameters α_i, β_j are restricted as in section 2. In addition to (28) and (29), money supply follows (23) and (24), and

$$m_t^d(z) = m_t + x_t + \theta_t(z) \tag{30}$$

holds.

The two asset yields, r_{kt} and r_{mt}, are conceptually as in section 2 but in the present case of uncertainty will be taken to be conditional means. The return on money is, again, the expected deflation rate. Since traders will choose next period's market at random, the expected rate relevant in z at t is

$$r_{mt}(z) = p_t(z) - \bar{p}_{t+1}^e(z), \tag{31}$$

where $p_t(z)$ is the observed current price and $\bar{p}_{t+1}^e(z)$ is the expected value of next period's *average* price level, conditional on information available in z at t.

The return on capital is, as before, the expected real rental price. Since capital accumulated in z remains there into the next period, the nominal rental will be proportional to the *local* price prevailing next period. On the other hand, since dividends will be spent elsewhere, the appropriate deflator is an expected *average* price. In addition to these price effects, the dampening effect of diminishing returns will also, as in section 2, be present. In view of the peripheral role of diminishing returns over the cycle, I shall neglect the latter effect here and write

$$r_{kt}(z) = p_{t+1}^e(z) - \bar{p}_{t+1}^e(z), \tag{32}$$

where $p_{t+1}^e(z)$ is the price expected to prevail locally, next period, on the basis of current-period information.

6 The Formation of Expectations

Since the rates of return which figure in the demand functions, (28) and (29), are not directly observable, they (or the expected prices which comprise them) must be inferred by agents from available information. This inference problem is the subject of this section.

The information sets and "priors" of agents are described in section 4. Agents know the coefficients of the solution (26)–(27) and take the joint distribution of the state vector $[k_t, m_t, x_t, \theta_t(z), u_t(z)]$ to be normal, with mean $(\hat{k}_t, \hat{m}_t, \mu, 0, 0)$ and covariance matrix Σ as given by (25). Then, prior to trading, they observe the equilibrium price, which as a function of the unobserved state vector carries additional information. On the basis of this new information, agents form a posterior distribution on the state vector to be used in forecasting. Denote the mean of this posterior distribution $[\hat{k}_t, \tilde{m}_t, \tilde{x}_t, \tilde{\theta}_t(z), \tilde{u}_t(z)]$.

From (27), the price which, prior to trading, had been expected to prevail was

$$\hat{p}_t = \pi_{20} + \pi_{21}\hat{k}_t + \pi_{22}\hat{m}_t + \pi_{23}\hat{k}_t + \pi_{24}\hat{m}_t + \pi_{25}\mu.$$

Also from (27), the price which in fact prevails is

$$p_t(z) = \hat{p}_t + \pi_{23}(k_t - \hat{k}_t) + \pi_{23}u_t(z)$$
$$+ \pi_{24}(m_t - \hat{m}_t) + \pi_{25}(x_t - \mu) + \pi_{25}\theta_t(z). \tag{33}$$

Thus, $[k_t, m_t, x_t, \theta_t(z)]$ and $p_t(z) - \hat{p}_t$ are, from the point of view of agents, jointly normally distributed variates with a covariance matrix given by Σ and (33). A straightforward calculation yields the conditional means[14]

$$\tilde{k}_t = \hat{k}_t + \sigma_p^{-2}(\pi_{23}\sigma_k^2 + \pi_{24}\sigma_{mk})[p_t(z) - \hat{p}_t], \tag{34}$$
$$\tilde{m}_t = \hat{m}_t + \sigma_p^{-2}(\pi_{23}\sigma_{mk} + \pi_{24}\sigma_m^2)[p_t(z) - \hat{p}_t], \tag{35}$$
$$\tilde{x}_t = \mu + \sigma_p^{-2}\pi_{25}\sigma^2[p_t(z) - \hat{p}_t], \tag{36}$$
$$\tilde{\theta}_t(z) = \sigma_p^{-2}(\pi_{23}\sigma_{u\theta} + \pi_{25}\sigma_\theta^2)[p_t(z) - \hat{p}_t], \tag{37}$$
$$\tilde{u}_t(z) = \sigma_p^{-2}(\pi_{23}\sigma_u^2 + \pi_{25}\sigma_{u\theta})[p_t(z) - \hat{p}_t], \tag{38}$$

where

$$\sigma_p^2 = \pi_{23}^2\sigma_k^2 + 2\pi_{23}\pi_{24}\sigma_{mk} + \pi_{24}^2\sigma_m^2 + \pi_{25}^2\sigma^2$$
$$+ \pi_{23}^2\sigma_u^2 + 2\pi_{23}\pi_{25}\sigma_{u\theta} + \pi_{25}^2\sigma_\theta^2 \tag{39}$$

is the variance of actual price about its prior mean.

One notes that each posterior (conditional) mean is simply the prior mean, corrected by a term which incorporates the new information contained in the market price, $p_t(z) - \hat{p}_t$. In each case the weight attached to the new information $p_t(z) - \hat{p}_t$ in (34)–(38) is the simple regression coefficient of the shock in question on $p_t(z) - \hat{p}_t$. Thus, for example, in (36), $\sigma_p^{-2}\pi_{25}\sigma^2$ is the covariance of $p_t(z) - \hat{p}_t$ and $x_t - \mu$ divided by the variance of price.

The estimates (34)–(38) are now used by traders both to update their estimates $(\hat{k}_t, \hat{m}_t)$ of the aggregate state of the economy and to form unbiased expectations $r_{kt}(z)$ and $r_{mt}(z)$ of the yields which are relevant to the asset demand decision. Using $E_z(\cdot)$ to denote an expectation formed in z in t, one has, from (26),

$$\hat{k}_{t+1}(z) = E_z(\pi_{10} + \pi_{11}\hat{k}_t + \pi_{12}\hat{m}_t + \pi_{13}k_t + \pi_{14}m_t + \pi_{15}x_t)$$
$$= \pi_{10} + \pi_{11}\hat{k}_t + \pi_{12}\hat{m}_t + \pi_{13}\tilde{k}_t + \pi_{14}\tilde{m}_t + \pi_{15}\tilde{x}_t,$$

where $\hat{k}_{t+1}(z)$ is the posterior estimate of k_{t+1} based on market z information. Now substitute from (34), (35), (36), and (33) and average over markets z to obtain the *average* estimate of k_{t+1}:

$$\hat{k}_{t+1} = \pi_{10} + (\pi_{11} + \pi_{13})\hat{k}_t + (\pi_{12} + \pi_{14})\hat{m}_t + \pi_{15}\mu$$
$$+ B_1[\pi_{23}(k_t - \hat{k}_t) + \pi_{24}(m_t - \hat{m}_t) + \pi_{25}(x_t - \mu)], \qquad (40)$$

where B_1 is a function of the elements of Σ and the π_{ij}, given for reference in Appendix B. Similar calculations give

$$\hat{m}_{t+1} = \hat{m}_t + \mu + B_2[\pi_{23}(k_t - \hat{k}_t)$$
$$+ \pi_{24}(m_t - \hat{m}_t) + \pi_{25}(x_t - \mu)], \qquad (41)$$

where B_2 is given in Appendix B.

The expected yields as defined by (31) and (32) are calculated in the same way. For example,

$$r_{mt}(z) = p_t(z) - \bar{p}_{t+1}^e(z)$$
$$= \pi_{20} + \pi_{21}\hat{k}_t + \pi_{22}\hat{m}_t + \pi_{23}[k_t + u_t(z)]$$
$$+ \pi_{24}m_t + \pi_{25}[x_t + \theta_t(z)]$$
$$- E_z(\pi_{20} + \pi_{21}\hat{k}_{t+1} + \pi_{22}\hat{m}_{t+1} + \pi_{23}k_{t+1}$$
$$+ \pi_{24}m_{t+1} + \pi_{25}x_{t+1}), \qquad (42)$$

using the solution for price, (27). Observing that $E_z[\hat{k}_{t+1}] = E_z[k_{t+1}]$ and $E_z[\hat{m}_{t+1}] = E_z[m_{t+1}]$ and using the solution for capital (26) and the monetary rule (24), one finds

$$r_{mt}(z) = \pi_{21}\hat{k}_t + \pi_{22}\hat{m}_t + \pi_{23}[k_t + u_t(z)] + \pi_{24}m_t + \pi_{25}[x_t + \theta_t(z)]$$
$$- (\pi_{21} + \pi_{23})E_z(\pi_{10} + \pi_{11}\hat{k}_t + \pi_{12}\hat{m}_t + \pi_{13}k_t$$
$$+ \pi_{14}m_t + \pi_{15}x_t)$$
$$- (\pi_{22} + \pi_{24})E_z(m_t + x_t)$$
$$- \pi_{25}\mu. \qquad (43)$$

Now using the estimates (35)–(37) and (33) and collecting terms, one finds

$$
\begin{aligned}
r_{mt}(z) = &(\pi_{21} + \pi_{23})[1 - (\pi_{11} + \pi_{13})]\hat{k}_t \\
&- (\pi_{21} + \pi_{23})(\pi_{12} + \pi_{14})\hat{m}_t + (1 - A_1) \\
&\times [\pi_{23}(k_t - \hat{k}_t) + \pi_{23}u_t(z) + \pi_{24}(m_t - \hat{m}_t) \\
&+ \pi_{25}(x_t - \mu) + \pi_{25}\theta_t(z)] \\
&+ C_1,
\end{aligned}
\tag{44}
$$

where A_1 is given in Appendix B and C_1 is a constant which will be ignored in the sequel. An analogous calculation gives an expression for the expected yield on capital:

$$
\begin{aligned}
r_{kt}(z) = &A_2[\pi_{23}(k - \hat{k}_t) + \pi_{23}u_t(z) + \pi_{24}(m_t - \hat{m}_t) \\
&+ \pi_{25}(x_t - \mu) + \pi_{25}\theta_t(z)],
\end{aligned}
\tag{45}
$$

where A_2 is given in Appendix B.

This completes the statement of the model, though a mathematical definition of its solution is still two sections away. The given economic parameters are the coefficients in the asset demand functions, $\alpha_0, \ldots,$ α_3 and $\beta_0, \ldots, \beta_3$, the parameter ρ, and the two variances σ^2 and σ_ϵ^2. The economic assumptions imply a set of conditions relating these parameters to the solution parameters: the coefficients π_{ij} in (26) and (27) and the remaining elements of the covariance matrix Σ. Implications on the slope coefficients will be developed in the following section; those on the covariance matrix in section 8.

7 Implications on Slope Coefficients

Inserting the expressions for expected yields given by (44) and (45) into the capital demand function (28) yields $k_{t+1}(z)$ as a linear function of the current state variables in market z. A second expression of this functional relationship is given by (26). Since these two relationships are equivalent, their right-hand sides must be identically equal in $\hat{k}_t$, $\hat{m}_t$, k_t, m_t, x_t, $\theta_t(z)$, and $u_t(z)$. Equating coefficients gives five conditions:

$$
\begin{aligned}
\pi_{11} = &-[\alpha_1 A_2 - \alpha_2(1 - A_1)]\pi_{23} \\
&- \alpha_2(\pi_{21} + \pi_{23})(1 - \pi_{11} - \pi_{13}),
\end{aligned}
\tag{46}
$$

$$
\begin{aligned}
\pi_{12} = &-[\alpha_1 A_2 - \alpha_2(1 - A_1)]\pi_{24} \\
&+ \alpha_2(\pi_{21} + \pi_{23})(\pi_{12} + \pi_{14}),
\end{aligned}
\tag{47}
$$

$$
\pi_{13} = [\alpha_1 A_2 - \alpha_2(1 - A_1)]\pi_{23} + \alpha_3,
\tag{48}
$$

$$
\pi_{14} = [\alpha_1 A_2 - \alpha_2(1 - A_1)]\pi_{24},
\tag{49}
$$

$$\pi_{15} = [\alpha_1 A_2 - \alpha_2(1 - A_1)]\pi_{25}. \tag{50}$$

Equating money demand and supply (eliminating $m_t^d(z)$ between [29] and [30]) and inserting the yields (44) and (45) give an expression for the current price, $p_t(z)$. Since the expression (27) must be equivalent, one obtains five more conditions:

$$\pi_{21} = [\beta_1 A_2 - \beta_2(1 - A_1)]\pi_{23}$$
$$\quad - \beta_2(\pi_{21} + \pi_{23})(1 - \pi_{11} - \pi_{13}), \tag{51}$$
$$\pi_{22} = -[\beta_1 A_2 - \beta_2(1 - A_1)]\pi_{24}$$
$$\quad + \beta_2(\pi_{21} + \pi_{23})(\pi_{12} + \pi_{14}), \tag{52}$$
$$\pi_{23} = [\beta_1 A_2 - \beta_2(1 - A_1)]\pi_{23} - \beta_3, \tag{53}$$
$$\pi_{24} = [\beta_1 A_2 - \beta_2(1 - A_1)]\pi_{24} + 1, \tag{54}$$
$$\pi_{25} = [\beta_1 A_2 - \beta_2(1 - A_1)]\pi_{25} + 1. \tag{55}$$

The two additional conditions for the constant terms π_{10} and π_{20} will be neglected.

So far, then, we have ten equations involving the ten unknown π_{ij} *and* (via A_1 and A_2) the five unknown elements of Σ: σ_k^2, σ_m^2, σ_{mk}, $\sigma_{u\theta}$, and σ_u^2.

8 Implications on Covariances

Rationality of expectations also implies that the covariance matrix Σ used by agents in forecasting is at the same time the *true* stationary covariance matrix. For the exogenously given moments σ^2 and σ_θ^2, this holds by direct assumption. For the other elements of Σ, some calculations are involved.

From (26) one observes that

$$u_{t+1}(z) = k_{t+1}(z) - k_t = \pi_{13}u_t(z) + \pi_{15}\theta_t(z). \tag{56}$$

Then, using the fact that

$$\theta_{t+1}(z) = \rho\theta_t(z) + \epsilon_t,$$

the stationary moments σ_u^2 and $\sigma_{u\theta}$ are given by

$$\sigma_u^2 = \frac{\pi_{15}^2}{1 - \pi_{13}^2} \frac{1 + \rho\pi_{13}}{1 - \rho\pi_{13}} \sigma_\theta^2, \tag{57}$$

$$\sigma_{u\theta} = \frac{\rho\pi_{15}}{1 - \pi_{13}} \sigma_\theta^2, \tag{58}$$

provided $|\pi_{13}| < 1$.

Averaging both sides of the solution (26) with respect to z gives an expression for k_{t+1}. Subtracting this equation from (40), one obtains

$$\hat{k}_{t+1} - k_{t+1} = (\pi_{13} - \pi_{23}B_1)(\hat{k}_t - k_t) + (\pi_{14} - \pi_{24}B_1)(\hat{m}_t - m_t)$$
$$- (1 - \pi_{25}B_2)(x_t - \mu), \tag{59}$$
$$\hat{m}_{t+1} - m_{t+1} = -\pi_{21}B_2(\hat{k}_t - k_t) + (1 - \pi_{24}B_2)(\hat{m}_t - m_t)$$
$$- (1 - \pi_{25}B_2)(x_t - \mu). \tag{60}$$

Provided the deterministic part of the pair (59)–(60) (that is, the system obtained by setting $x_t = \mu$ for all t) is stable, it is a familiar calculation to obtain three linear equations in the moments σ_k^2, σ_m^2, and σ_{mk}. For reference, write it as

$$\begin{bmatrix} \sigma_k^2 \\ \sigma_{mk} \\ \sigma_m^2 \end{bmatrix} = K_1 \begin{bmatrix} \sigma_k^2 \\ \sigma_{mk} \\ \sigma_m^2 + \sigma^2 \end{bmatrix}, \tag{61}$$

where the 3×3 matrix K_1 is written in Appendix B.

9 Mathematical Solution: Preliminaries

The mathematical problem is now sharpened to: for given $\alpha_1, \ldots, \alpha_3, \beta_1, \ldots, \beta_3, \sigma^2, \sigma_\epsilon^2$, and ρ, find $\pi_{11}, \ldots, \pi_{15}, \ldots, \pi_{21}, \ldots, \pi_{25}$, $\sigma_u^2, \sigma_{u\theta}, \sigma_k^2, \sigma_m^2$, and σ_{mk} which satisfy (46)–(55), (57), (58), and (61) such that the difference equations (56), (59), and (60) are stable. In this section, the size of the system will be drastically reduced by solving for some coefficients in terms of others.

First, adding (46) to (48) and (51) to (53) gives two equations in the sums $\pi_{11} + \pi_{13}$ and $\pi_{21} + \pi_{23}$. These are essentially the same equations solved for π_{11} and π_{21} in section 2; their solution is diagrammed in Appendix A. As in section 2, there are two solution pairs, one of which is of economic interest. Denote these solution values $\pi_1 = \pi_{11} + \pi_{13}$ and $-\pi_2 = \pi_{21} + \pi_{23}$. From figure A1 (Appendix A) one sees that these solutions satisfy

$$\alpha_3 < \pi_1 < 1 \tag{62}$$

and

$$\frac{\beta_3}{1 + \beta_2} < \pi_2 < \beta_3. \tag{63}$$

Next, add (47) and (49) and conclude that

$$\pi_{12} + \pi_{14} = 0. \tag{64}$$

Similarly, add (52) and (54) and conclude that

$$\pi_{22} + \pi_{24} = 1. \tag{65}$$

Neither of these classical neutrality-of-money results should come as a surprise.

Third, from (54) and (55), conclude that

$$\pi_{25} = \pi_{24} \tag{66}$$

and from (49), (50), and (66) that

$$\pi_{15} = \pi_{14}. \tag{67}$$

Fourth, solving (53) and (54) for π_{23} gives

$$\pi_{23} = -\beta_3\pi_{24}. \tag{68}$$

Then, from (48), (49), and (68), one obtains

$$\pi_{13} = \alpha_3 - \beta_3\pi_{14}. \tag{69}$$

Reviewing the facts stated in (62)–(69), one sees that all slope coefficients π_{ij} have been expressed in terms of π_{14} and π_{24} and the now "known" numbers π_1 and π_2. Let me rename π_{14} and π_{24}, π_3 and π_4 respectively. In terms of these parameters $\pi_1, \ldots, \pi_4$, (59) and (60) become

$$\hat{k}_{t+1} - k_{t+1} = (\alpha_3 - \beta_3\pi_3 + \beta_3\pi_4 B_1)(\hat{k}_t - k_t)$$
$$+ (\pi_3 - \pi_4 B_1)(\hat{m}_t - m_t) - (\pi_3 - \pi_4 B_1)(x_t - \mu), \tag{70}$$
$$\hat{m}_{t+1} - m_{t+1} = \beta_3\pi_4 B_2(\hat{k}_t - k_t)$$
$$+ (1 - \pi_4 B_2)(\hat{m}_t - m_t) - (1 - \pi_4 B_2)(x_t - \mu). \tag{71}$$

The motion of aggregate capital and the price level, k_t and p_t, is from (26) and (27):

$$k_{t+1} = \pi_{10} + \pi_1 k_t + (\pi_1 - \alpha_3 + \beta_3\pi_3)(\hat{k}_t - k_t)$$
$$- \pi_3(\hat{m}_t - m_t) + \pi_3 x_t, \tag{72}$$
$$p_t = \pi_{20} + m_t - \pi_2 k_t + (\beta_3\pi_4 - \pi_2)(\hat{k}_t - k_t)$$
$$+ (1 - \pi_4)(\hat{m}_t - m_t) + \pi_4 x_t. \tag{73}$$

The information contained in the 10 equations (46)–(55) may now be conveniently restated as

$$\pi_3 = [\alpha_1 A_2 - \alpha_2(1 - A_1)]\pi_4, \tag{74}$$
$$\pi_4 = [\beta_1 A_2 - \beta_2(1 - A_1)]\pi_4 + 1. \tag{75}$$

The terms A_1, A_2, B_1, and B_2 may similarly be expressed in terms of π_1, π_2, π_3, and π_4; these simplified expressions are given in Appendix B.

The problem of solving for the equilibrium parameter values is now reduced to: find π_3, π_4, σ_u^2, $\sigma_{u\theta}$, σ_m^2, σ_{mk}, and σ_k^2 such that (74), (75), (57), (58), and (61) are satisfied. The fact that the covariance structure and the response coefficients π_3 and π_4 are mutually dependent makes this task difficult, and results have been obtained for special cases only. These will be discussed in detail in subsequent sections.

At this point, however, the general nature of the dynamic system is fairly clear. Equations (70) and (71) describe the consequences of the unsystematic shocks, x_t, on the deviations between the perceived and the actual aggregate state of the economy, $\hat{k}_t - k_t$ and $\hat{m}_t - m_t$. This autonomous, two-equation system converts a one-time pulse of monetary "misinformation" into an extended, distributed lag effect. Equation (72) describes the motion of capital stock as the sum of a "deterministic" part, which is essentially the same as the capital path found in section 2, and autocorrelated deviations about this path, determined by the shocks and their lagged effects from (70) and (71). The effects on price are given in (73).

10   Case 1: Centralized Market Clearing

The case in which the relative demand variance σ_θ^2 is zero corresponds exactly to the situation discussed briefly at the end of section 2 in which monetary shocks are the only exogenous disturbance to which the economy is subject. Since with no variation in θ all markets are identical, an economy with $\sigma_\theta^2 = 0$ may be viewed as one in which all trade takes place in a single market.

The algebra appropriate to this case is given in Appendix C. Briefly, one observes first that the function A_2 is zero when $\sigma_\theta^2 = 0$, implying from (45) that expected real yields on capital do not change with monetary shocks. It follows that $\sigma_k^2 = \sigma_{mk} = \sigma_m^2 = 0$ is the solution to (61). Then, from (74) and (75), the coefficients π_3 and π_4 are 0 and 1, respectively.

Inserting these values into (70) and (71) gives the solution for equilibrium price and capital accumulation. In this case, $k_t(z) = k_t = \hat{k}_t$ for all markets and all periods. Similarly, $m_t = \hat{m}_t$. In short, there is no misinformation. The effect of monetary changes on capital is nil ($\pi_3 = 0$); there is a proportional effect on nominal prices ($\pi_4 = 1$). Monetary changes are accurately conveyed to agents via price movements, even though unanticipated, and the response is simply an adjustment in nominal units.

While this case is of no particular interest substantively, it does serve to "justify" the apparatus set up in preceding sections, to which I shall shortly return. The introduction of separate, informationally distinct markets is not a step toward "realism" or (obviously) "elegance" but, rather, an analytical departure which appears essential (in some form) to an explanation of the way in which business cycles can arise and persist in a competitive economy.

11 Case 2: A Purely Monetary Cycle[15]
The case in which the capital stock does not respond to monetary shocks may, in contrast to the preceding case, be of practical importance, since cyclical variations in capital appear, at least at the casual level, to be of questionable quantitative significance. Arithmetically, this case can be obtained from the present model by setting the elasticities of investment with respect to expected yields equal to zero. If $\alpha_1 = \alpha_2 = 0$ then, from (74), $\pi_3 = 0$ and (see Appendix C) $\sigma_k^2 = \sigma_{km} = 0$. For all markets and all t, $k_t(z) = k_t = \hat{k}_t = \pi_{10}/(1 - \pi_1)$.

The functions A_1 and A_2 are found equal to γ/π_4 and $\rho(1 - \gamma)$, respectively, where

$$\gamma = \frac{\sigma_m^2 + \sigma^2}{\sigma_m^2 + \sigma^2 + \sigma_\theta^2} .$$

Then, from (75),

$$\pi_4 = \frac{1 + \beta_2\gamma}{1 + \beta_2 - \beta_1\rho(1 - \gamma)} . \tag{76}$$

Letting σ_θ^2 range from 0 to infinity, the price response π_4 ranges from the high value of unity to a low value of $(1 + \beta_2 - \rho\beta_1)^{-1}$. In economic terms, as the fraction of demand variation due to aggregate nominal disturbances tends to unity, equilibrium prices tend to move in proportion to demand shifts. As this occurs, the output response tends to zero. Their ratio (the slope of the Phillips curve) tends to infinity.

It remains to determine σ_m^2 as a function of σ^2. For the case under consideration, (61) takes the form

$$\sigma_m^2 = (1 - \gamma)^2(\sigma_m^2 + \sigma^2) = \left[\frac{\sigma_\theta^2}{\sigma_m^2 + \sigma^2 + \sigma_\theta^2}\right]^2 (\sigma_m^2 + \sigma^2). \tag{77}$$

The solution for σ_m^2 and $\sigma_m^2 + \sigma^2$ as functions of σ^2 are diagrammed in figure 1; σ_m^2 is zero when $\sigma^2 = 0$, with a derivative approaching $+\infty$; it reaches a maximum of $\frac{1}{4}\sigma_\theta^2$ when $\sigma^2 = \frac{3}{4}\sigma_\theta^2$; it tends to 0 as $\sigma^2 \to \infty$. The behavior of $\sigma_m^2 + \sigma^2$ is as shown. The coefficient γ increases from 0 to 1 as σ^2 increases from 0; it equals $\frac{1}{2}$ when $\sigma^2 = \frac{3}{4}\sigma_\theta^2$.

The variance σ_m^2 is not, of course, the variance of the money supply (which *has* no stationary value when m_t follows a random walk). It is the average squared value of $m_t - \hat{m}_t$: the difference between the actual money supply and the level perceived, on average, by agents. When the monetary shock is small (σ^2 near zero) this error is small, since past information is a reliable guide to the present state. When σ^2 is very large, σ_m^2 is again small, since contemporaneous price movements provide an excellent indicator of movements in $m_t + x_t$. The error is greatest when σ^2 is of the same order of magnitude as σ_θ^2, so that

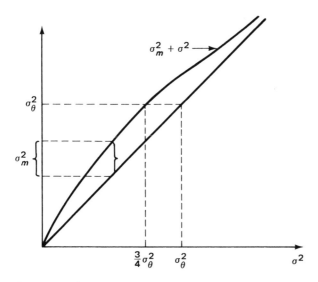

Figure 1

monetary noise is sufficient to be economically interesting yet small enough to be confounded by agents with relative demand movements.

To obtain the dynamic behavior implied by these solution values, rewrite (71) (or [60]) as

$$m_{t+1} - \hat{m}_{t+1} = (1 - \gamma)(m_t - \hat{m}_t + x_t - \mu), \qquad (78)$$

which is implied by the solution found above. Given exogenous money movements as assumed in (24), (78) describes the way agents' beliefs about the state of the economy move through time relative to the motion of the actual state.

To get a more concrete idea of the kind of "cycle" implied by this solution, it is useful to simulate the response to a single once-and-for-all demand shock (even though the occurrence of such a pattern has been assumed to have zero probability). Imagine an initial situation in which perceived and actual states are equal: $\hat{m}_0 = m_0$. There is an initial shock to demand: $x_0 - \mu = S$. Thereafter, money grows smoothly at its average expansion rate: $x_t = \mu = 0$, $t > 1$. From (78), agents will initially underestimate the true stock of money but will "catch on" at an exponential rate through time:

$$m_t - \hat{m}_t = (1 - \gamma)^t S, \qquad t \geqslant 1. \qquad (79)$$

From (73), specialized to this case, the initial shock will induce a price increase above what had been expected in period 0 in the amount $\pi_4 S$. Prices will continue to stay above expectations due to lagged adjustments in $\hat{m}_t$ but by an exponentially decreasing amount. To be exact,

$$p_t - \hat{p}_t = \pi_4 (1 - \gamma)^t S, \qquad t \geqslant 0.$$

This motion will not be affected by changes in the *average* monetary growth rate, although, of course, the path of actual prices will be.

The movements in flow variables—output, employment, and consumption—which parallel these price movements can be inferred from the income-expenditure identity (1), the link between monetary expansion and government spending, (5), and assumptions about households' preferences for labor supplied and goods consumed. For the latter, assume purely for simplicity that consumption does not vary over the cycle, so that fluctuations in government purchases are absorbed by employment fluctuations. In the case under discussion, capital and investment are also constant, so that (1) may then be solved for employment as a function of $g_t = \log(G_t)$. Expanding this function yields the approximation

$$n_t = \eta_0 + \eta_1 g_t, \tag{80}$$

where n_t is the log of employment. The elasticity η_1 is the average ratio of G to output divided by the elasticity of production f with respect to labor input (labor's share).

From (5) and (74), real government spending is in turn given by

$$g_t = x_t - p_t + m_t. \tag{81}$$

With capital fixed, (81) and (73) together yield

$$g_t = (1 - \pi_4)(x_t - \hat{m}_t + m_t) + \text{constant}. \tag{82}$$

Then, combining (79), (80), and (82), the time path of the percentage deviations of employment from its normal level, resulting from a shock S, is given by

$$n_t - n^e = \eta_1(1 - \pi_4)(1 - \gamma)^t S, \qquad t = 0, 1, 2, \ldots . \tag{83}$$

Similarly, the expected yield on money will move in proportion to $m_t - \hat{m}_t$. The exact relationship is, from (44),

$$r_{mt} = \frac{(1 - \gamma)(1 + \beta_1\gamma)}{(1 + \beta_2\gamma)} \pi_4(1 - \gamma)^t S, \qquad t \geq 0, \tag{84}$$

where r_{mt} is the variable part of $r_{mt}(z)$ averaged over markets. The relationship of this pattern in r_{mt} to observed cyclical patterns in interest rates, which is by no means a simple issue, is discussed below (sec. 13).

One notes that the effects of an initial shock, in the purely monetary model, will *persist* but can never *cumulate*: the largest effect must come in the first period. To account for the observed gradual cyclical upswing, it appears that one must introduce systematic patterns in the shocks or modify the internal structure of the model.

12   Case 3: A Monetary Over-Investment Cycle

The preceding section exhibits a unique solution to the system (57), (58), (61), (72), and (73) for the case when $\alpha_1 = \alpha_2 = 0$. In this section, approximate solutions are developed and their properties discussed for the situation where α_1 and α_2 are small but positive. The details of

this expansion are discussed in Appendix D; the main results are as
follows.

For the accelerator coefficient π_3, one finds

$$\pi_3 = \left[\frac{1 - \gamma}{1 + \beta_2 - \beta_1\rho(1 - \gamma)}\right] [\rho\alpha_1 - \alpha_2 + (\alpha_1\beta_2 - \alpha_2\beta_1)\gamma], \tag{85}$$

where γ is the variance ratio defined in the preceding section. A
sufficient condition for a positive accelerator effect, $\pi_3 > 0$, is $\rho\alpha_1 - \alpha_2 > 0$. Since $\alpha_1 > \alpha_2$, this will obtain if ρ is near 1. (If ρ were near
zero, meaning that relative demand shifts were nearly transitory, one
would not *expect* an accelerator effect, since new capital can only be
installed with a one-period lag). As with the other real consequences
of monetary shocks, the accelerator effect on investment is larger the
smaller is the fraction γ of demand variance due to nominal shocks.
In summary, to be induced to vary the investment rate, agents must
(i) be responsive to perceived future relative returns ($\alpha_1 > 0$), (ii) be
convinced that current relative demands are a good indicator of these
future returns (ρ large), and (iii) be convinced that current price movements contain information on current relative demands (γ small).

The effects of introducing a positive accelerator π_3 on the lagged
perceptions of a monetary movement are easy to describe in words.
The increased capacity due to an initial positive shock *retards* the
upward adjustment of the price level to the new money introduced by
the shock. The adjustment of expectations to the shock will then take
place more slowly than the exponential pace described in (78). The
details of these movements in perceptions are given in (70) and (71);
expressions for the coefficients in these equations, valid for α_1 and α_2
small, are given in Appendix D.

The characteristic roots of this system are near α_3 and $1 - \gamma$, both
in the unit interval, so that following a one-time shock, perceptions on
both capital and money will return to "normal" in a nonoscillating
fashion. The "cross effects" are probably both positive: underestimation of capacity ($\hat{k}_t - k_t < 0$) leads to underestimation of aggregate
demand ($\hat{m}_{t+1} - m_{t+1} < 0$), and, similarly, $\hat{k}_{t+1} - k_{t+1}$ increases as $\hat{m}_t - m_t$
increases. In response to a pulse shock S, both $\hat{k}_t - k_t$ and $\hat{m}_t - m_t$ move
proportionally to S. One (but not both) of these errors can continue
to move in the same direction (that is, errors *can* cumulate) while the
other decays. Eventually, both tend to zero.

Given the motion of the perception errors $\hat{k}_t - k_t$ and $\hat{m}_t - m_t$, as just discussed, the motion of *actual* capital stock k_t following an initial shock S is given by (72). The initial effect is $\pi_3 S$; subsequent effects in the same direction are contributed by the term $\pi_3(m_t - \hat{m}_t)$. Offsetting effects arise from $\hat{k}_t - k_t$. Since $\alpha_3 < \pi_1 < 1$, and since all three forcing terms tend to zero, k_t must eventually return to its normal level.

The consequences for employment of these movements in actual and perceived state variables can be obtained as in the preceding section. The presence of capital makes these calculations both more complicated and more interesting. Again, take consumption to be constant, "solve" (1) for the log of employment, and expand to obtain the analogue of (80):

$$n_t = \eta_0 + \eta_1 g_t + \eta_2(k_{t+1} - k_t) + \eta_3 k_t. \tag{86}$$

As before, the elasticity η_1 is the ratio of G to output divided by labor's share; η_2 is the average capital-output ratio divided by labor's share; and η_3 is capital's share divided by labor's share. Real spending, g_t, is obtained from (81) and (73):

$$g_t = \pi_2 k_t - (\beta_3 \pi_4 - \pi_2)(\hat{k}_t - k_t) + (1 - \pi_4)(x_t - \hat{m}_t + m_t). \tag{87}$$

Combining (86) and (87) yields the time path of employment.

The direct "multiplier" effect on employment of a shock $(\eta_1 g_t)$ works much as in the preceding section: there is an initial effect due to a movement in x_t followed by additional effects due to informational lags. The effect new to this section is the accelerator term $\eta_2(k_{t+1} - k_t)$, which can be relatively large even for small values of π_3. Further, since capital returns to normal, the term $\pi_2(k_{t+1} - k_t)$ must eventually make a *negative* contribution to employment, possibly driving employment below its normal level, even in the absence of a downward shock.

Movements in expected yields on both money and capital will, as in the preceding section, be procyclical.[16] These facts may be verified from (44) and (45), but the exact expressions need not be given here.

13   The Role of Interest Rates

The procyclical pattern of interest rate movements has perhaps attracted more theoretical and empirical attention in recent years than any other "stylized fact" concerning business cycles. The procyclical movement of the two expected yields, as shown in (84) and, for the general case, in (44) and (45), raises the hope that this fact too is accounted for by the model developed above. The question is worth examining, although it will turn out that a satisfactory answer remains beyond the scope of this paper.

Formally, the model above considers internal equity financing only, in contrast with the established convention that, in theories which consider one source of financing only, that one source should be bonds. This departure is obviously necessitated by the presence of uncertainty: the claim to an uncertain yield *cannot* be a single type of bond. One could *add* private bonds as an additional source of financing. If bond transactions were localized, as are goods transactions (that is, exchanges among agents in a single market), this would be easy to do, and one can conjecture that bond yields would move as the expected yields in (44) and (45). The interesting issue, however, is to examine the consequences of a single *economy-wide* market for some standardized kind of bond which would clear in an integral sense but not for each fixed market z. This modification would involve a major change in the information structure of the economy, since the equilibrium interest rate (or bond price) would depend only on *aggregate* state variables, and hence its value would convey to agents some aggregate information uncontaminated by local disturbances.

To see the effects of this, return to the inference problem solved by agents in section 6 and suppose that agents also observe the value of a known linear function of $\hat{k}_t - k_t$, $\hat{m}_t - m_t$, and x_t. The extreme consequence occurs when capital movements are unimportant, as in the purely monetary model of section 11. In this case, the interest rate will convey the aggregate state of the economy *perfectly* to agents, eliminating the real part of the cycle altogether.[17] With an accelerator effect present, it seems likely that the existence of an economy-wide bond market would dampen cyclical movements but not eliminate them or alter their qualitative character. Without further analysis, however, the question remains open and, clearly, crucial.

The interest rate question illustrates an interesting analytical tension which must arise in any cycle theory based on incomplete information. On the one hand, it is easy to postulate agents and market institutions which ignore or foolishly waste information: the result is a theory which seriously understates agents' abilities to vary their decision rules with changes in the environment (such as, for example, the theory underlying the major econometric forecasting models). It is equally easy to postulate "efficient" securities markets which rapidly transmit *all* information to all traders: the result is a static general equilibrium model. To observe that one must avoid both extremes to understand the business cycle does not take one very far in discovering the correct "centrist" model, but it seems nonetheless an essential point of departure.

14   Remarks on Testability

The model described in section 12, and any other variant in this general class, ascribes values to all aggregate moments: the complete covariance function of the vector of observable variables. Since there are many more such sample moments than there are free parameters in the system, it is clear that the model has empirical content.

In the absence of an economic theory on the behavior of the shocks, one would in practice begin by describing the shocks stochastically by some ad hoc method, possibly using only past values of the series itself, possibly relating it to movements in other state variables. Then, based on these findings, one would need to redo the theory above (especially the inference problem in sec. 6), assuming that the same pattern in the disturbance is also known to traders. If, as seems likely, a fairly complicated pattern (say, three or four parameters) is required to describe the shocks, this will lead to *more,* not fewer, testable restrictions on the solution parameters.[18] In short, there appears to be little risk of the vacuity which mars so much of distributed lag econometrics.

In addition to aggregate predictions, the theory also "predicts" that deviations from average in the demand for individual products will be independent from product to product and through time. One may (as I did [Lucas 1972]) take these "predictions" metaphorically[19] (as one takes the prediction that all individuals are indistinguishable and live forever), but it is instructive to ask which covariance structures for individual demand shocks will lead to aggregate behavior "like" that described above and which will not. The answer seems to be that one needs each individual market shock to be expressable as a linear combination of a large number of roughly commensurate independent shocks (so that the law of large numbers applies as used above) plus a *single* shock common to all markets. This assumption, namely, that there exists some single random variable identifiable as aggregate demand, *is* testable and surely deserves systematic examination.

15 Remarks on Policy Implications

All aggregate output movements in the models studied above result
from movements in a single monetary-fiscal shock to aggregate demand. Evidently, the key to any stabilization policy in such a setting
would involve the elimination of any avoidable components of the
variance of this shock. The present study, then, provides a rationalization for rules which smooth monetary policy, exactly as did the
earlier studies of Lucas (1972), Sargent and Wallace (1973), and Barro
(1975). Similarly, it rationalizes the analogous fiscal rule of continuous
budget balancing and rules to stabilize the quantity of private money,
such as larger reserve requirements for banks. Though it could be
extended to do so, the present model sheds no light on the relative
importance of monetary and fiscal effects, since all shocks, by assumption, involve both monetary and fiscal elements.

If, as seems likely in fact, some components of aggregate demand
variance are unavoidable, the present model offers the additional possibility of stabilization by affecting the response characteristics of the
private sector. For example, a fiscal stabilizer which reduced the
parameters α_1 and α_2 (the elasticities of investment with respect to
perceived, pretax rate-of-return changes) would convert the economy
of section 12 to the more stable economy of section 11. This *feasibility*
of stable but reactive stabilization policies will obtain, it would appear,
in any model in which the effects of shocks persist through effects on
capital accumulation.

In my view, the *desirability* of reactive policy rules is a more serious
issue than is their feasibility. A tax policy which reduced the responsiveness of investment to aggregate demand changes would, as can be
seen from the analysis in the preceding sections, reduce the variance
of aggregate output and employment. At the same time, such a policy
would necessarily reduce the responsiveness of investment to relative
demand shifts, retarding the movement of resources into the socially
most desirable activities. Since the preferences and production possibilities in this model economy have not been made explicit, one
cannot conclude with the presumption that the balancing achieved by
the private sector in this model is efficient. On the other hand, it has
not been necessary to introduce any of the standard types of "market
failure" in order to account for the main features of the observed
cycle.

16 Conclusion

This paper develops a theoretical example of a business cycle, that is, a model economy in which real output undergoes serially correlated movements about trend which are not explainable by movements in the availability of factors of production. The mechanism generating these movements involves unsystematic monetary-fiscal shocks, the effects of which are distributed through time due to informational lags and an accelerator effect. Associated with these output movements are (i) procyclical movements in prices, (ii) procyclical movements in the share of output devoted to investment, and (iii), in a somewhat limited sense, procyclical movements in nominal rates of interest.

This behavior is obtained under assumptions about expectations formation which seem suited to the study of a recurrent event: agents are well aware that the economy goes through recurrent "cycles" which distort perceived rates of return. On the other hand, the transitory nature of real investment opportunities forces them to balance the risk of incorrectly responding to spurious price signals against the risk of failing to respond to meaningful signals.

Appendix A

Equations (14) and (17) are two equations in the unknown parameters π_{11} and π_{21}. Solving them means essentially finding the roots of a quadratic, which can of course be done in several ways. A particularly convenient way is to add β_2 times (14) to α_2 times (17), obtaining the line

$$\pi_{21} = \frac{\beta_2 + (\beta_2\alpha_1 - \beta_1\alpha_2)\delta_1}{\alpha_2}\pi_{11} - \frac{\alpha_3\beta_2 + \alpha_2\beta_3}{\alpha_2}. \tag{A1}$$

Rewrite (14) as

$$\pi_{21} = \frac{\alpha_3 - (1 + \alpha_1\delta_1)\pi_{11}}{\alpha_2(1 - \pi_{11})}. \tag{A2}$$

The two solutions to (A1) and (A2) (that is, to [14] and [17]) are illustrated in figure A1. The relevant root economically is in the southeast quadrant; it satisfies the inequalities (19) and (20).

To obtain $\pi_1 = k_{11} + \pi_{13}$ and $-\pi_2 = \pi_{21} + \pi_{23}$ (as in sec. 9), one proceeds in the same way. Adding (46) and (48) yields

$$\pi_1 = \alpha_3 - \alpha_2(-\pi_2)(1 - \pi_1). \tag{A3}$$

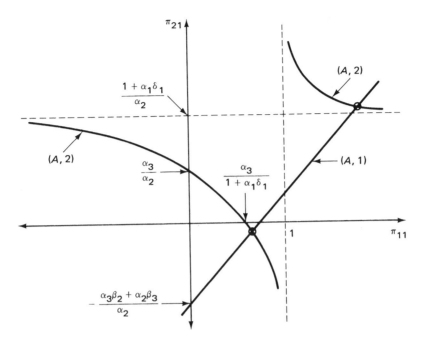

Figure 9.A1

Adding (51) and (53) gives

$$-\pi_2 = -\beta_3 - \beta_2(-\pi_2)(1 - \pi_1). \tag{A4}$$

These are equivalent to (14) and (17), with $\delta_1 = 0$. Thus, $(\pi_1, -\pi_2)$ satisfy (A1) and (A2), with $\delta_1 = 0$, and their solution values appear in figure A1, with $\delta_1 = 0$. The inequalities (62) and (63) are easily verified.

Appendix B
Some expressions which arise in the text are

$$B_1 = \sigma_p^{-2}[\pi_{13}(\pi_{23}\sigma_k^2 + \pi_{24}\sigma_{mk})$$
$$+ \pi_{14}(\pi_{23}\sigma_{mk} + \pi_{24}\sigma_m^2) + \pi_{15}\pi_{25}\sigma^2], \tag{B1}$$
$$B_2 = \sigma_p^{-2}(\pi_{23}\sigma_{mk} + \pi_{24}\sigma_m^2 + \pi_{25}\sigma^2), \tag{B2}$$
$$A_1 = (\pi_{21} + \pi_{23})B_1 + (\pi_{22} + \pi_{24})B_2, \tag{B3}$$
$$A_2 = \sigma_p^{-2}[\pi_{13}\pi_{23}(\pi_{23}\sigma_m^2 + \pi_{25}\sigma u_\theta)$$
$$+ (\pi_{23}\pi_{15} + \rho\pi_{25})(\pi_{23}\sigma_{u\theta} + \pi_{25}\sigma_\theta^2)]. \tag{B4}$$

Define the quantities $M, D_1, \ldots, D_4$ by

$$M = \beta_3^2 \sigma_k^2 - 2\beta_3 \sigma_{mk} + \sigma_m^2 + \sigma^2 + \beta_3^2 \sigma_u^2 - 2\beta_3 \sigma_{u\theta} + \sigma_\theta^2, \qquad \text{(B5)}$$
$$D_1 = M^{-1}(\beta_3^2 \sigma_k^2 - \beta_3 \sigma_{mk}), \qquad \text{(B6)}$$
$$D_2 = M^{-1}(-\beta_3 \sigma_{mk} + \sigma_m^2 + \sigma^2), \qquad \text{(B7)}$$
$$D_3 = M^{-1}(\beta_3^2 \sigma_u^2 - \beta_3 \sigma_{u\theta}), \qquad \text{(B8)}$$
$$D_4 = M^{-1}(-\beta_3 \sigma_{u\theta} + \sigma_\theta^2). \qquad \text{(B9)}$$

Then, after the elimination of parameters described in section 9, (B1)–(B4) can be rewritten

$$B_1 = -\frac{\alpha_3}{\beta_3 \pi_4} D_1 + \frac{\pi_3}{\pi_4}(D_1 + D_2), \qquad \text{(B10)}$$

$$B_2 = \frac{1}{\pi_4} D_2, \qquad \text{(B11)}$$

$$A_1 = \pi_2 \frac{\alpha_3 - \beta_3 \pi_3}{\beta_3 \pi_4} D_1 + \frac{1 - \pi_2 \pi_3}{\pi_4} D_2, \qquad \text{(B12)}$$

$$A_2 = (\alpha_3 - \beta_3 \pi_3)D_3 + (\rho - \beta_3 \pi_3)D_4. \qquad \text{(B13)}$$

To obtain the matrix K_1 used in (61), first abbreviate the coefficients of (59) and (60) by

$$C_{11} = \pi_{13} - \pi_{23}B_1 = \alpha_3 - \beta_3 \pi_3 + \beta_3 \pi_4 B_1,$$
$$C_{12} = \pi_{14} - \pi_{24}B_1 = \pi_{15} - \pi_{25}B_1 = \pi_3 - \pi_4 B_1,$$
$$C_{21} = -\pi_{23}B_2 = \beta_3 \pi_4 B_2,$$
$$C_{22} = 1 - \pi_{24}B_2 = 1 - \pi_{25}B_2 = 1 - \pi_4 B_2.$$

Then

$$K_1 = \begin{bmatrix} C_{11}^2 & 2C_{11}C_{12} & C_{12}^2 \\ C_{11}C_{21} & C_{11}C_{22} + C_{12}C_{21} & C_{12}C_{22} \\ C_{21}^2 & 2C_{21}C_{22} & C_{22}^2 \end{bmatrix}. \qquad \text{(B14)}$$

Provided the matrix (C_{ij}) is stable (as required by the definition of a solution used here), the process (59)–(60) has a unique stationary covariance matrix. Since this covariance matrix is also a solution to (61) (and vice versa), it follows that (61) has a unique solution, or that $K_1 - I$ is a nonsingular matrix.

Appendix C

For the case $\sigma_\epsilon^2 = 0$, $\sigma_u^2 = \sigma_{u\theta}^2 = \sigma_\theta^2 = 0$ from (57) and (58). Then, from (B8)–(B9), $D_3 = D_4 = 0$ so that from (B13) $A_2 = 0$. It also follows that $C_{11} = (\alpha_3/\beta_3)C_{21}$ and $C_{12} = (\alpha_3/\beta_3)C_{22}$, so that by direct inspection of (59) and (60) one sees that $\sigma_k^2 = \alpha_3^2\sigma_m^2$ and $\sigma_{km} = \alpha_3\sigma_m^2$. These facts permit the calculation of M, D_1, and D_2 as functions of the two variances σ_m^2 and σ^2. Inserting these into the third equation of (61), one obtains a cubic in the unknown σ_m^2. The root zero occurs twice; the third root is negative. Thus, the unique solution of (61) is $\sigma_k^2 = \sigma_{km} = \sigma_m^2 = 0$.

With these variance, $D_1 = 0$ and $D_2 = 1$. Inserting these values into the expression for A_1 from (B12), one finds that $\pi_3 = 0$ and $\pi_4 = 1$ is the unique solution to (74) and (75).

For the case $\alpha_1 = \alpha_2 = \alpha_3 = 0$, use (61) to solve for σ_k^2 and σ_{km} as functions of $\sigma_m^2 + \sigma^2$. Evidently, $(0, 0)$ is a solution, since in this case $D_1 = 0$. If $D_1 = 0$, there is no other solution. If $D_1 \neq 0$, one finds that $\sigma_k^2 < 0$, an impossibility. The solution given in the text is thus unique.

Appendix D

Equations (57), (58), (61), (72), and (73) are seven equations in the unknown reduced-form parameters $(\pi_3, \pi_4, \sigma_k^2, \sigma_{mk}, \sigma_m^2, \sigma_u^2, \sigma_{u\theta})$. In section 11 it was found that $(0, \bar{\pi}_4, 0, 0, \bar{\sigma}_m^2, 0, 0)$, with $\bar{\pi}_4$ given in (76) and $\bar{\sigma}_m^2$ by (77), is the unique solution when $\alpha_1 = \alpha_2 = 0$. Let $\alpha_2 = \xi\alpha_1$, where $\xi\epsilon(0, 1)$ is a constant. Then the implicit function theorem implies that for α_1 sufficiently small, a differentiable solution exits. This solution can be approximated for α_1 small by expanding $(\pi_3, \pi_4, \sigma_k^2, \sigma_{mk}, \sigma_m^2, \sigma_u^2, \sigma_{u\theta})$ about the point $(0, \bar{\pi}_4, 0, 0, \bar{\sigma}_m^2, 0, 0)$.

Carrying out this expansion, (85) is immediate from (64) and (76). The approximate coefficients C_{ij} (see Appendix B) of the difference equations (70) and (71) are readily, if tediously, obtained in the same way. The expressions given below are obtained by expanding in α_1 and by discarding terms involving powers of γ of 2 or higher. The full expressions are not difficult to obtain, but there is little to be gained by repeating them here:

$$C_{11} = \alpha_3 - \beta_3(1 - \gamma)\pi_3 + \alpha_3 \frac{\gamma}{1 - \pi_3}\alpha_1,$$

$$C_{12} = (1 - \gamma)\pi_3 - \frac{\alpha_3\gamma}{1 - \alpha_3}\alpha_1,$$

$$C_{21} = \beta_3\gamma(1 - \frac{\beta_3\alpha_1}{1 - \alpha_3} - 2\frac{\beta_3\rho}{1 - \alpha_3}\pi_3),$$

$$C_{22} = 1 - \gamma + \beta_3 \frac{\gamma\alpha_1}{1 - \alpha_3} + 2\beta_3 \frac{\rho\gamma}{1 - \alpha_3}\pi_3.$$

For α_1 (and hence π_3) small, the roots of (C_{ij}) are seen to be near α_3 and $1 - \gamma$ (the two diagonal elements). C_{21} will be positive, as asserted in the text. C_{12}, treated also as positive in the text, can in fact have either sign, even for α_1 small. For γ small, it will be positive.

Notes

1. This argument is much more fully developed in Lucas (1973b).

2. The terminology is taken from Haberler's useful taxonomy of cycle theories (Haberler 1960).

3. Here and in the remainder of the paper there will be only one nominal asset and it will be supplied exclusively by the government. I will call this asset "money" without qualifying this usage each time it arises, but it might as well be called "bonds" or "government liabilities." This means that the analysis will not be able to deal with questions involving the relative importance of monetary and fiscal disturbances, though it could without much difficulty be modified to do so.

4. This is making virtue of analytical necessity, but there are definite intuitive advantages to a parametric, "certainty equivalent" approach as used here: the forecasting and choice problems solved by agents are separated (though we know this separation is artificial), and the distinct effects of each on decision rules are clearly seen (see n. 15).

5. One can easily add a term "$\alpha_4(m_t - p_t)$" to the right of (7), and similarly to (8), and trace out the consequences. This leads to possibly interesting stability problems which are poorly understood (by me) and which I do not wish to confound with the cyclical complications which are introduced later.

6. This discarding of an unstable root is, of course, the step which is customarily "justified" by a transversality condition in models in which agents' maximum problems are made explicit (see, e.g., Brock 1973).

7. This nonneutrality of inflation did not appear in Lucas (1972) or Sargent (1973b), since both papers excluded capital formation. This led Tobin (1973), and perhaps others, to wonder how monetary distortions present in models with certainty and perfect foresight can disappear when uncertainty is introduced. The answer is, they do not. The point of Lucas (1972) and Sargent (1973b) is not that the introduction of uncertainty removes long-familiar neoclassical nonneutralities but, rather, that it does not in itself introduce new ones.

8. The idea behind this island abstraction is not, of course, to gain insight into maritime affairs, or to comment on the aimlessness of life. It is intended simply to capture in a tractable way the fact that economic activity offers agents a succession of ambiguous, unanticipated opportunities which cannot be expected to stay fixed while more information is collected. It seems safe and, for my purposes, sensible to abstract here from the fact that in reality

this situation can be slightly mitigated by the purchase of additional information.

9. See sec. 13 for a discussion of the probable effects of introducing an economy-wide bond market.

10. The assumption that these unobserved distributions are "known" need not be taken as a literal description of the way agents think of their environment. It is just a convenient way of assuming that agents use the data available to them in the best possible way.

11. This neglects, as Sargent has pointed out to me, the information conveyed to traders when they receive the dividend "check" for their investment of two periods earlier.

12. See n. 10 above.

13. With a modest application of intuition, one can specify some of the solution parameters in advance. (E.g., since two markets with the same total $m_t + x_t + \theta$ should look alike, one should have $\pi_{14} = \pi_{15}$ and $\pi_{24} = \pi_{25}$.) There is no harm in carrying along extra parameters, however, and since intuitions differ, one may as well develop such facts formally. This is done in sec. 9.

14. See, e.g., Graybill (1961, theorem 3.10, p. 63).

15. This is essentially a parametric version of the model in Lucas (1972), except that in the present version, monetary changes are perceived with a distributed (rather than a fixed one-period) lag. Setting $\sigma_m^2 = 0$ gives an exact counterpart to the model of Lucas (1972). A comparison of the two gives a good idea of the costs and benefits of working with parametrically specified demand functions rather than with preference functions of agents (see n. 4 above).

16. Friedman (1971, p. 327) observes that cyclical variations in the average marginal productivity of capital are of slight quantitative importance, so that variation in the expected average yield on capital must play a minor cyclical role. This fact, as Friedman suggests elsewhere in the same article, is thus entirely consistent with an important cyclical role for average expected real yields.

17. Could not a given interest rate movement indicate ambiguously either a high x_t or a high $m_t - \hat{m}_t$? As a transient effect, yes, but not in the stationary distribution; see (60) with $\hat{k}_t - k_t = 0$.

18. See Sargent's application of the principle of rationality to the Fisherian interest rate–inflation rate distributed lag (Sargent 1973a).

19. In his persuasive comment on Lucas (1973a), Vining (1974) utilizes a literal interpretation of this assumption to obtain a suggestive empirical test.

References

Barro, Robert J. "Rational Expectations and the Role of Monetary Policy." Working paper, Univ. Chicago, 1975.

Model of the
Business Cycle

Brock, William A. "Money and Growth: The Case of Long-Run Perfect Foresight." Working paper, Univ. Chicago, 1975.

Friedman, Milton. "A Monetary Theory of Nominal Income." *J.P.E.* 79, no. 2 (1971):323–337.

Graybill, Franklin A. *An Introduction to Linear Statistical Models.* Vol. 1. New York: McGraw-Hill, 1961.

Haberler, Gottfried. *Prosperity and Depression.* Rev. ed. Cambridge, Mass.: Harvard Univ. Press, 1960.

Lucas, Robert E., Jr. "Expectations and the Neutrality of Money." *J. Econ. Theory* 4 (April 1972):103–124.

Lucas, Robert E., Jr. "Some International Evidence on Output-Inflation Tradeoffs." *A.E.R.* 63 (1973):326–334. (*a*)

Lucas, Robert E., Jr. *Econometric Policy Evaluation: A Critique.* Carnegie-Mellon University Working Paper. Pittsburgh: Carnegie-Mellon Univ., 1973. (*b*)

Lucas, Robert E., Jr., and Prescott, Edward C. "Equilibrium Search and Unemployment." *J. Econ. Theory* 7 (February 1974):188–209.

Muth, John F. "Rational Expectations and the Theory of Price Movements." *Econometrica* 29 (July 1961):315–335.

Phelps, Edmund S., et al. *Microeconomic Foundations of Employment and Inflation Theory.* New York: Norton, 1969.

Sargent, Thomas J. "Interest Rates and Prices in the Long Run." *J. Money, Credit, and Banking* 5 (February 1973):385–449. (*a*)

Sargent, Thomas J. "Rational Expectations, the Real Rate of Interest, and the Natural Rate of Unemployment." *Brookings Papers Econ. Activity* 2 (1973):429–472. (*b*)

Sargent, Thomas J., and Wallace, Neil. "'Rational' Expectations, the Optimal Monetary Instrument, and the Optimal Money Supply Rule." Working paper, Univ. Minnesota, 1973.

Tobin, James. "Money and Economic Growth." *Econometrica* 33 (October 1965):671–684.

Tobin, James. Discussion of Sargent (1973*b*). *Brookings Papers Econ. Activity* 2 (1973):477–478.

Vining, Daniel R., Jr. "The Relationship between Relative and General Prices." Working paper, Pittsburgh: Carnegie-Mellon Univ., 1974.

Understanding
Business Cycles

1

Why is it that, in capitalist economies, aggregate variables undergo repeated fluctuations about trend, all of essentially the same character? Prior to Keynes' *General Theory,* the resolution of this question was regarded as one of the main outstanding challenges to economic research, and attempts to meet this challenge were called *business cycle theory.* Moreover, among the interwar business cycle theorists, there was wide agreement as to what it would mean to solve this problem. To cite Hayek, as a leading example:

The incorporation of cyclical phenomena into the system of economic equilibrium theory, with which they are in apparent contradiction, remains the crucial problem of Trade Cycle Theory;[1]

By "equilibrium theory" we here primarily understand the modern theory of the general interdependence of all economic quantities, which has been most perfectly expressed by the Lausanne School of theoretical economics.[2]

A primary consequence of the Keynesian Revolution was the redirection of research effort away from this question onto the apparently simpler question of the determination of output at a point in time,

Reprinted from *Stabilization of the Domestic and International Economy,* vol. 5 of Carnegie-Rochester Series on Public Policy, eds. Karl Brunner and Allan H. Meltzer, Amsterdam: North-Holland Publishing Company, 1977, pp. 7–29, by permission.

Paper prepared for the Kiel Conference on Growth without Inflation, June 22–23, 1976; revised, August 1976. I would like to thank Gary Becker, Jacob Frenkel, Don Patinkin, Thomas Sargent, and Jose Scheinkman for their comments and suggestions.

taking history as given.[3] A secondary consequence of this Revolution, due more to Tinbergen than to Keynes, was a rapid increase in the level of precision and explicitness with which aggregate economic theories were formulated. As a result, Keynesian macroeconomics has benefited from several decades of methodological improvement whereas, from this technical point of view, the efforts of the business cycle theorists appear hopelessly outdated.

Yet from another point of view, they seem quite modern. The observation that macroeconomics is in need of a microeconomic foundation has become commonplace, and though there is much confusion about the nature of this need and about what it would mean to satisfy it, it is likely that many modern economists would have no difficulty accepting Hayek's statement of the problem as roughly equivalent to their own. Whether or not this is so, I wish in this essay to argue that it *should* be so, or that the most rapid progress toward a coherent and useful aggregate economic theory will result from the acceptance of the problem statement as advanced by the business cycle theorists, and not from further attempts to refine the jerry-built structures to which Keynesian macroeconomics has led us.

Honoring one's intellectual ancestors is a worthwhile aim in itself, but there is a more immediate reason for interpreting the contemporary search for a theoretically sound aggregative economics as a resumption of the work of pre-Keynesian theorists. Accompanying the redirection of scientific interest occasioned by the Keynesian Revolution was a sharp change in the nature of the contribution to policy which economists hoped to offer and which the public has come largely to accept. The effort to "explain business cycles" had been directed at identifying institutional sources of instability, with the hope that, once understood, these sources could be removed or their influence mitigated by appropriate institutional changes. The process envisaged was the painfully slow one of public discussion and legislative reform; on the other side, there was the hope of long-term or "permanent" institutional improvement. The abandonment of the effort to explain business cycles accompanied a belief that policy could effect immediate, or very short-term, movement of the economy from an undesirable current state, *however arrived at,* to a better state.

The belief that this latter objective is attainable, and that the attempt to come closer to achieving it is the only legitimate task of research in aggregate economics is so widespread that argument to the contrary is viewed as "destructive," a willful attempt to make life more difficult for one's colleagues who are only trying to improve the lot of mankind. Yet the situation is symmetric. If the business cycle theorists were correct, the short-term manipulation on which much of aggregative economics is now focused only diverts attention from discussion of stabilization policies which might actually be effective; such postponement is, moreover, accompanied by the steady and entirely understandable erosion in the belief on the part of noneconomists that aggregative economics has anything useful to say.

In the next section, I will review some of the main qualitative features of the events we call business cycles, and then turn to the Keynesian response to these facts, to the progress made along the line Keynes and Tinbergen initiated, and finally to the severe limits to this progress which have now become apparent. The remainder of the essay will consider the prospects of accounting for cyclical phenomena by an *economic* theory, in the narrow sense in which Hayek and other business cycle theorists have used that term.

2

Let me begin to sharpen the discussion by reviewing the main qualitative features of economic time series which we call "the business cycle." Technically, movements about trend in gross national product in any country can be well described by a stochastically disturbed difference equation of very low order. These movements do not exhibit uniformity of either period or amplitude, which is to say, they do not resemble the deterministic wave motions which sometimes arise in the natural sciences. Those regularities which are observed are in the *comovements* among different aggregative time series.

The principal among these are the following.[4] (i) Output movements across broadly defined sectors move together. (In Mitchell's terminology, they exhibit high *conformity*; in modern time series language, they have high *coherence*.) (ii) Production of producer and consumer durables exhibits much greater amplitude than does the production of nondurables. (iii) Production and prices of agricultural goods and natural resources have lower than average conformity. (iv) Business profits show high conformity and much greater amplitude than other series. (v) Prices generally are procyclical. (vi) Short-term interest rates are procyclical; long-term rates slightly so. (vii) Monetary aggregates and velocity measures are procyclical.

There is, as far as I know, no need to qualify these observations by restricting them to particular countries or time periods: they appear to be regularities common to all decentralized market economies. Though there is absolutely no theoretical reason to anticipate it, one is led by the facts to conclude that, with respect to the qualitative behavior of co-movements among series, *business cycles are all alike*. To theoretically inclined economists, this conclusion should be attractive and challenging, for it suggests the possibility of a unified explanation of business cycles, grounded in the *general* laws governing market economies, rather than in political or institutional characteristics specific to particular countries or periods.

I have omitted the behavior of foreign trade statistics from the above catalogue of phenomena-to-be-explained, in part because, for a large economy like the U.S., trade statistics do not exhibit high enough conformity to be cyclically interesting. For a smaller country, to be sure, export movements would do much to "explain" cycles, but to focus on open-economy explanations would, I think, beg the more difficult and crucial question of the ultimate origins of cyclical movements.

Also omitted, but too striking a phenomenon to pass over without comment, is the general reduction in amplitude of *all* series in the twenty-five years following World War II. At this purely descriptive level, it is impossible to distinguish good luck from good policy. Nevertheless, so long a period of relative stability strongly suggests that there is nothing inherent in the workings of market economies which requires living with the level of instability we are now experiencing, or to which we were subject in the pre-World War II years. That is, attempts to document and account for regular cyclical movements need not be connected in any way to a presumption that such movements are an *inevitable* feature of capitalist economies.

3

The implications of Keynesian macroeconomic models conform well to the time series features reviewed above. Early versions (for example, by Hicks, 1937, and Modigliani, 1944) fit well qualitatively; the econometric models which developed from this theory and from Tinbergen's largely independent early work[5] conform well quantitatively. These models located the primary disturbances in investment behavior, linked via lags (in Tinbergen's U.S. model) to the highly volatile profit series. Movements in these high-amplitude series then induce general movements in output and employment. Since these disturbances were, in Hicks' terms, "IS shifts," they were consistent with procyclically moving interest rates and velocity. The assumption of rigid wages and prices was a good empirical first approximation. Later on, a wage-price sector (still later called a Phillips curve) was added to fit observed procyclical wage and price movements.[6]

In this description, movements in money play no important role in accounting for cycles. This feature certainly did not result directly from the theoretical models; Keynes, Hicks, and Modigliani all gave great emphasis to monetary forces. The de-emphasis on money was on empirical grounds: econometricians from Tinbergen on discovered that monetary factors did not seem very important empirically.[7]

The empirical success of these developments was measured in an original and historically apt way by Adelman and Adelman (1959) in their simulation of the Klein-Goldberger model of the U.S. economy. The Adelmans posed, in a precise way, the question of whether an observer armed with the methods of Burns and Mitchell (1946) could distinguish between a collection of economic series generated artificially by a computer programmed to follow the Klein-Goldberger equations and the analogous series generated by an actual economy. The answer, to the evident surprise of the Adelmans (and, one suspects, of Klein and Goldberger, who had in no way directed their efforts to meeting this criterion) was *no*.[8]

This achievement signaled a new standard for what it means to understand business cycles. One exhibits understanding of business cycles by constructing a *model* in the most literal sense: a fully articulated artificial economy which behaves through time so as to imitate closely the time series behavior of actual economics. The Keynesian macroeconomic models were the first to attain this level of explicitness and empirical accuracy; by doing so, they altered the meaning of the term "theory" to such an extent that the older business cycle theories could not really be viewed as "theories" at all.

These models are not, however, "equilibrium theories" in Hayek's sense. Indeed, Keynes chose to begin the *General Theory* with the declaration (for Chapter II is no more than this) that an equilibrium theory was unattainable: that unemployment was not explainable as a consequence of individual choices and that the failure of wages to move as predicted by the classical theory was to be treated as due to forces beyond the power of economic theory to illuminate.

Keynes wrote as though the "involuntary" nature of unemployment were verifiable by direct observation, as though one could somehow look at a market and verify directly whether it is in equilibrium or not. Nevertheless, there were serious empirical reasons behind this choice, for nowhere is the "apparent contradiction" between "cyclical phenomena" and "economic equilibrium" theory sharper than in labor market behavior. Why, in the face of moderately fluctuating nominal wages and prices, should households *choose* to supply labor at sharply irregular rates through time? Most business cycle theorists had avoided this crucial problem, and those who addressed it had not resolved it. Keynes saw that by simply sidestepping this problem with the unexplained postulate of rigid nominal prices, an otherwise classical model could be transformed into a model which did a fair job of accounting for observed time series.

This decision on the part of the most prestigious theorist of his day freed a generation of economists frc n the discipline imposed by equilibrium theory, and, as I have descri ?d, this freedom was rapidly and fruitfully exploited by macroeconom tricians. Now in possession of detailed, quantitatively accurate replicas of the actual economy, economists appeared to have an inexpensive means to evaluate various proposed economic policy measures. It seemed legitimate to treat policy recommendations which emerged from this procedure as though they had been experimentally tested, even if such policies had never been attempted in any actual economy.

Yet the ability of a model to imitate actual behavior in the way tested by the Adelmans (1959) has almost nothing to do with its ability to make accurate *conditional* forecasts, to answer questions of the form: how *would* behavior have differed had certain policies been different in specified ways? This ability requires *invariance* of the structure of the model under policy variations of the type being studied. Invariance of parameters in an economic model is not, of course, a property which can be assured in advance, but it seems reasonable to hope that neither tastes nor technology vary systematically with variations in countercyclical policies. In contrast, agents' *decision rules will* in general change with changes in the environment. An equilibrium model is, by definition, constructed so as to predict how

agents with stable tastes and technology will *choose* to respond to a
new situation. Any disequilibrium model, constructed by simply cod-
ifying the decision rules which agents have found it useful to use over
some previous sample period, without explaining *why* these rules were
used, will be of no use in predicting the consequences of nontrivial
policy changes.

The quantitative importance of this problem is, of course, a matter
to be settled by examination of specific relationships in specific models. I have argued elsewhere[9] that it is of fatal importance in virtually
all sectors of modern macroeconomic models, primarily because of
the faulty treatment of expectations in these models. Rather than
review these arguments in detail, let me cite the most graphic illustration: our experience during the recent "stagflation."

As recently as 1970, the major U.S. econometric models implied
that expansionary monetary and fiscal policies leading to a sustained
inflation of about 4 percent per annum would lead also to sustained
unemployment rates of less than 4 percent, or about a full percentage
point lower than unemployment has averaged during any long period
of U.S. history.[10] These forecasts were widely endorsed by many
economists not themselves closely involved in econometric forecasting. Earlier, Friedman (1968) and Phelps (1968) had argued, purely on
the basis of the observation that *equilibrium* behavior is invariant
under the units change represented by sustained inflation, that *no*
sustained decrease in unemployment would result from sustained inflation. In this instance, the policy experiment in question was, most
unfortunately, carried out, and its outcome is now too clear to require
detailed review.

It is important that the lesson of this episode not be lost. The issue
is much deeper than the addition of a few new variables to econometric Phillips curves (though this is the only revision in macroeconomic models which has followed from it), as Friedman made clear in
his Presidential Address. Friedman's argument did not proceed on the
basis of a specific aggregative model, with a better "wage-price sector" than the standard models. On the contrary, it was based on a
general characteristic of economic equilibrium: the zero-degree homogeneity of demand and supply functions. Thus, without using any
very specific model, and without claiming the ability to forecast in any
detail the initial response of the economy to an inflation, one can, in
the case of sustained inflation, reason that, if the unemployment rate

prior to the inflation were an equilibrium (or "natural") rate, then the
same rate will be an equilibrium once the inflation is underway.

The case of sustained inflation is a relatively simple one (though
apparently not *too* simple, as it is still highly controversial). For other
kinds of policy questions, one would need a more explicit model. How
would the variance, and other moments, of real output change if a
policy of 4 percent monetary growth were adopted? Under a balanced
budget fiscal rule? Under flexible rather than fixed exchange rates?
One can generate numerical answers to questions of this sort from
current macroeconomic models, but there is no reason for anyone to
take these numbers seriously. On the other hand, neither can quantitative answers be obtained by purely theoretical reasoning. To obtain
them, one needs an explicit, equilibrium account of the business cycle.

4

I have summarized, in section 2, the main features of the cyclical
behavior in quantities and prices. In section 3, I have argued the
practical necessity of accounting for these factors in equilibrium (that
is, non-Keynesian) terms. That is, one would like a theory which
accounts for the observed movements in *quantities* (employment, consumption, investment) as an optimizing response to observed movements in *prices*.

In the next section, I will describe the general point of view toward
individual decision making to be taken in the remainder of the paper,
and will explain, in particular, why the *recurrent* character of business
cycles is of central importance. Given this general view, I shall consider in sections 6 and 7 the way in which *relative* price movements
induce fluctuations in employment and investment. Sections 8, 9, and
10 examine the conditions under which these same quantity responses
may be triggered by movements in general, or nominal, prices. Not
surprisingly, the source of general price movements is located, in
section 11, in monetary changes.

5

The view of the prototypical individual decision problem taken by
modern capital theory is a useful point of departure for considering
behavior over the cycle, though it is in some respects highly misleading. An agent begins a period with stocks of various kinds of capital
accumulated in the past. He faces *time paths* of prices at which he

can trade in the present and future. Based on his preferences over time paths of labor supplied and goods consumed, he formulates a plan. Under certainty, he is viewed as simply executing a single plan without revision; with uncertainty, he must draw up a contingency plan, saying how he will react to unforeseeable events.

Even to begin to think about decision problems of this general form, one needs to imagine a fairly precise view of the future in the mind of this agent. Where does he get this view, and how can an observer infer what it is? This aspect of the problem has received rather offhand treatment in traditional capital theory, and no treatment at all in traditional macroeconomics. Since it is absolutely crucial for understanding business cycles, we must pursue it here in some detail.

At a purely formal level, we know that a rational agent must formulate a subjective joint probability distribution over all unknown random variables which impinge on his present and future market opportunities. The link between this subjective view of the future and "reality" is a most complex philosophical question, but the way it is solved has little effect on the structure of the decision problem as seen by an individual agent. In particular, any distinction between *types* of randomness (such as Knight's (1921) distinction between "risk" and "uncertainty") is, at this level, meaningless.

Unfortunately, the general hypothesis that economic agents are Bayesian decision makers has, in many applications, little empirical content: without some way of inferring what an agent's subjective view of the future is, this hypothesis is of no help in understanding his behavior. Even psychotic behavior can be (and today, is) understood as "rational," given a sufficiently abnormal view of relevant probabilities. To practice economics, we need *some* way (short of psychoanalysis, one hopes) of understanding *which* decision problem agents are solving.

John Muth (1961) proposed to resolve this problem by identifying agents' subjective probabilities with observed frequencies of the events to be forecast, or with "true" probabilities, calling the assumed coincidence of subjective and "true" probabilities *rational expectations*. Evidently, this hypothesis will not be of value in understanding psychotic behavior. Neither will it be applicable in situations in which one cannot guess which, if any, observable frequencies are relevant: situations which Knight[11] called "uncertainty." It will *most* likely be useful in situations in which the probabilities of interest concern a fairly well defined recurrent event, situations of "risk" in Knight's terminology. In situations of risk, the hypothesis of rational behavior on the part of agents will have usable content, so that behavior may be explainable in terms of economic theory. In such situations, expectations are rational in Muth's sense. In cases of uncertainty, economic reasoning will be of no value.

These considerations explain why business cycle theorists emphasized the *recurrent* character of the cycle, and why we must hope they were right in doing so. Insofar as business cycles can be viewed as repeated instances of essentially similar events, it will be reasonable to treat agents as reacting to cyclical changes as "risk," or to assume their expectations are *rational,* that they have fairly stable arrangements for collecting and processing information, and that they utilize this information in forecasting the future in a stable way, free of systematic and easily correctable biases.

6

In moving from these general considerations to more specific theory, it will be helpful to consider as an example a "representative" agent.[12] Imagine a single worker-producer, confronted each period with a given market price for a good which he then makes to order, at a fixed rate of output per hour. That is, he comes to his place of work, observes his current selling price, determines how many hours to work that day, sells his produce, then goes home to relax.

The good he receives in exchange for the effort is "money"; I shall not be concerned with the historical reasons for this arrangement, but simply take it for granted. This money, in turn, is spent on a wide variety of goods, different from day to day. Some purchases he makes on his way home, in an hour's break from work, or several days later. I assume for now that he holds no other securities. I assume also that this agent lives in a cycle-free world, in which the general or average level of prices does not change, though individual prices fluctuate from day to day.

Now let us postulate an increase of 10 percent in today's selling price, as compared to the average of past prices. How will this hypothetical producer respond? The answer given by economic theory must be: who knows? At this point, I have said nothing which would enable one to imagine what the producer thinks this price movement *means.* If he believes the price change signals a permanent change in his selling price, we know from much evidence that he will work no harder, and probably a little less hard. That is, we know that "long run" (very unfortunate terminology, since the "long-run" response to a permanent price change will be *immediate*) labor supply elasticities are zero or negative.

What if, at the opposite extreme, the price change is transitory (as would be the case if each period's price were an independent drawing from a fixed distribution)? The answer in this case amounts to knowing the rate at which the producer is willing to substitute labor today for labor tomorrow. If "leisure" is highly substitutable over time, he will work longer on high price days and close early on low price days. Less is known about actual labor supply responses to transitory price movements than about the "long-run" response, and what we do know indicates that leisure in one period is an excellent substitute for leisure in other, nearby periods. Systematic evidence at the aggregate level was obtained by Rapping and myself (1970); Ghez and Becker (1975) reached the same conclusion at a disaggregative level. The small premiums required to induce workers to shift holidays and vacations (take Monday off instead of Saturday, two weeks in March rather than in August) point to the same conclusion, and this "casual" evidence is somewhat more impressive because of its probabilistic simplicity: holidays are *known* to be transitory. On the basis of this evidence, one would predict a *highly elastic* response to transitory price changes.

Before dealing with complications to this example, let us note its promise for business cycle theory. I have described a producer who responds to small price fluctuations with large fluctuations in output and employment: exactly what we observe over the cycle. The description rests on economically intelligible substitution effects, not on unintelligible "disequilibria." Yet let us go slowly: our aggregative observations refer to co-movements of output and prices *generally*; the example refers to *relative* price movements in a stationary environment.

Before facing this difficult issue, let us consider some variations on the example just considered. First, from a descriptive point of view, it often seems more realistic to think of demand information being conveyed to producers by *quantity* changes: new orders, inventory rundowns, and the like. There seems to be no compelling substantive reason to focus exclusively on *prices* as signals of current and future demand. At this verbal level, it seems to me harmless and accurate to use the terms price increase and sales increase interchangeably. Somewhat surprisingly, however, rigorous analysis of equilibrium determination when producers set prices is extremely difficult, and no examples relevant to business cycle behavior exist.

A second variation is easy to carry out. Rather than consider a worker-entrepreneur, one could separate these functions, introduce firms, and consider labor and product markets separately. In the present context, this would introduce a distinction between wages and prices, and raise the issue of risk-allocating arrangements between employers and workers.[13] It would also permit the study of possibly different information sets for firms and workers. None of these questions is without interest, but all are, in my opinion, peripheral for business cycle theory. Observed real wages are not constant over the cycle, but neither do they exhibit consistent pro- or countercyclical tendencies. This suggests that any attempt to assign systematic real wage movements a central role in an explanation of business cycles is doomed to failure. Accordingly, I will proceed as though the real wage were fixed, using the terms "wages" and "prices" interchangeably.

Additional variations can be obtained by distinguishing among various uses of the worker-producer's time when he is not working. Many writers have attempted, for example, to interpret measured unemployment as time engaged in job search. Certainly, if one substitutes away from work one substitutes *into* some other activity, and experience shows that one's belief in the importance of substitution is bolstered by some plausible illustrations. Nevertheless, there is little evidence that much time is spent in job search, that search is less costly when unemployed than when employed, or, for that matter, that measured unemployment measures any *activity* at all. Economically, the important issue is the magnitude of the elasticity of employment with respect to transitory wage and price movements, not the reasons why that elasticity is what it is.

Indeed, I suspect that the unwillingness to speak of workers in recession as enjoying "leisure" is more a testimony to the force of Keynes' insistence that unemployment is "involuntary" than a response to observed phenomena. One doesn't want to suggest that people *like* depressions! Of course, the hypothesis of a cleared labor market carries with it no such suggestion, any more than the observation that people go hungry in cleared food markets suggests that people enjoy hunger.

7

More complex variations on this example arise when *capital* of various kinds is introduced. Let us do this, retaining still the assumption of stability over time in the general level of prices.

Three possibilities of interest arise. First, suppose that current production can be stored as finished goods inventory. This possibility seems to work *against* the account of price-output co-movements sketched above. The producer will surely produce in low price periods for sale later when price is high, smoothing labor supply relative to the case where storage is precluded. On the industry level, however, this behavior also dampens price movements. The net result is likely to be a reduction in the elasticity of employment-production with respect to price, and an increase in the real sales-price elasticity.

As a second possibility, suppose the producer can use a part of his current production to acquire a machine which will raise his output-per-hour in all future periods. As a third, suppose he can take a course in school which will have the same effect. Since these two possibilities do not differ economically, they may be considered as one. In the example of purely transitory price movements, discussed earlier, it is clear that neither of these options will ever be exercised—provided the producer was satisfied with his original stock of capital. By the time the new capital can be applied to production, the price movement which made it appear profitable will have vanished.

Current relative price movements will have their maximal effect on capital accumulation when, at the opposite extreme, they are regarded as permanent. In this case, however, as I have noted, employment will be insensitive to price movements. Thus, to observe investment and employment moving systematically in the direction of relative price movements, it must be the case that such movements are a *mix* of transitory and permanent elements. In such a situation, the producer will find himself obliged to engage in what engineers call "signal processing": he observes a single variable (price) changing through time; these movements arise from movements in more fundamental variables (the transitory and permanent components of price) which cannot be observed directly; from these observed price movements, together with his knowledge of the relative importance of the two unobserved sources of price change, he imperfectly infers the movements in the two components. Based on his solution to this implied conditional probability calculation, he takes a decision. Not surpris-

ingly, the decision turns out to be an average of the decisions appropriate to the two extremes.

To recapitulate, our hypothetical producer is taken to face stochastic
price variability, which is describable as a mix of transitory and permanent components, both unobserved. His optimal response to price
movements depends on two factors: the way he interprets the information contained in these changes, and his preferences concerning
intertemporal substitution of leisure and consumption. Under assumptions consistent with rational behavior and available evidence, his
response to an unforeseen price increase is a sizable increase in labor
supplied, a decline in finished goods inventory, and an expansion in
productive capital accumulation of all kinds. This behavior is symmetric; the responses to price decreases are the opposite.[14]

8

It is time to think of situating this representative producer in an
economy comprised of similar agents, though of course producing
different goods and subject to different individual price movements.
To do this, one must go behind price movements to the changes in
technology and taste which underlie them. These changes are occurring all the time and, indeed, their importance to individual agents
dominates by far the relatively minor movements which constitute the
business cycle. Yet these movements should, in general, lead to relative, not general price movements. A new technology, reducing costs
of producing an old good or making possible the production of a new
one, will draw resources into the good which benefits, and *away from*
the production of other goods. Taste shifts in favor of the purchase of
one good involve reduced expenditures on others. Moreover, in a
complex modern economy, there will be a large number of such shifts
in any given period, each small in importance relative to total output.
There will be much "averaging out" of such effects across markets.

Cancellation of this sort is, I think, the most important reason why
one cannot seek an explanation of the *general* movements we call
business cycles in the mere presence, per se, of unpredictability of
conditions in individual markets. Yet this argument is not entirely
tight. It is surely *possible* for a large number of agents spontaneously
to feel an urge to increase their work weeks and expand investments.
More seriously, there have been many instances of shocks to supply

which affect all, or many, sectors of the economy simultaneously. Such shocks will not cancel in the way I have described, and they will induce output fluctuations in the aggregate. They will not, however, lead to movements which fit the description sketched in section II: all supply shifts will lead to countercyclical price movements (other things being equal) in contrast to the procyclical movements we observe.

It is, then, possible to situate our hypothetical producer in a general equilibrium setting, in which his price and output fluctuate, yet aggregate levels do not. His responses to these *relative* prices movements will mimic the aggregate responses to general price movements which constitute the business cycle. We have then a coherent model, but not one which as yet accounts for the general phenomena to be explained. This model can, without difficulty, be modified to permit general, supply-induced output fluctuations, but these bear no resemblance to the modern business cycle.

Before leaving this world of stable aggregates, it is worth stressing that most of the risk which troubles and challenges economic agents would be present in such a setting. Will consumers take to a novel automobile design, or will it become a national joke? Will a dozen years of training in piano lead to the concert stage, or just a pleasurable hobby? Will this week's overtime wages help finance a child's education, or tide the family over next month's strike? By the time one has acquired the information necessary to resolve questions like these, it is too late; one way or the other, one is committed.

Compared to risks of this nature and magnitude, the question of whether the hours actually worked in the year ahead will be 1.03 times what one plans for now, or .97, seems a minor one, and seems so because it is. In aggregative economic theory, we are accustomed to think of business cycles as a kind of risk imposed on an otherwise stable environment. Such habits of thought reflect the transfer of abstractions useful for some purposes into contexts where they involve fatal distortions of reality.

9

Let us now drop the assumption of stability in average prices. From the point of view of the individual producer, this involves only a slight change in the nature of the signal processing problem which must be solved. Before, a given movement in his "own price" could mean a permanent relative price change or a transitory one. Now, it can also mean that *all* prices are changing, a situation which, if correctly diagnosed, would lead to no real response on the producer's part. Yet, for the same reason that permanent and transitory relative price movements cannot be sorted out with certainty at the time, neither can relative and general movements be distinguished. General price increases, exactly as will relative price increases, will induce movements in the same direction in employment and investment.

Unlike the responses to taste and technology changes described earlier, these responses to general price increases will not tend to cancel over markets. To be sure, some producers will observe declines in demand even during price expansions, but more will observe increases (this is what a *general* price increase means), and therefore more will be expanding in real terms than will be contracting. The net effect will be co-movements in prices, output, and investment at the aggregate level, just as is observed over the actual cycle.

It is *essential* to this argument that general price movements not be perceived as such as they are occurring. Within the context of the aggregative models ordinarily used, this assumption may seem implausible: how could traders not know *the* price of goods? In the reality of a multi-commodity world, however, no one would want to observe all prices every day, nor would many traders find published price indices particularly useful. An optimizing trader will process those prices of most importance to his decision problem most frequently and carefully, those of less importance less so, and most prices not at all. Of the many sources of risk of importance to him, the business cycle and aggregate behavior generally is, for most agents, of no special importance, and there is no reason for traders to specialize their own information systems for diagnosing general movements correctly.

By the same reasoning, one can see that *sustained* inflation will not affect agents' real decisions in the way that transitory price movements do. Nothing is easier than to spot and correct systematic *bias* in forecasts. Such corrections involve no changes in agents' information systems or in the costs of processing information. There may, of course, be some lag in diagnosing sustained inflation for what it is; about as often, agents will incorrectly perceive a transitory inflation as though it were sustained.

Changes in the degree of price variability will have more fundamental effects on agents' information processing behavior, because they
affect the "weights" placed on price information in forecasting future
prices. The general idea is that one trusts "noisy" price signals less.

10

The aggregate or average response to general price movements becomes more complex as one considers investment as well as employment responses. Investment decisions will be distorted by general
price movements, for the same reasons as will employment, and in the
same direction as the responses induced by relative price movements.

Further complications follow, however, from the observation that
current investment affects future *capacity,* and hence future prices.
This effect can be seen to extend in time, perhaps even to amplify,
the initial effects of general price movements.

To spell this out in more detail, imagine that some event occurs
which would, if correctly perceived by all, induce an increase in prices
generally. Sooner or later, then, this adjustment will occur. Initially,
however, more traders than not perceive a relative price movement,
possibly permanent, in their favor. As a result, employment and investment both increase. Through time, as price information diffuses
through the economy, these traders will see they have been mistaken.
In the meantime, however, the added capacity *retards* price increases
generally, postponing the recognition of the initial shock. In this way,
unsystematic or short-term shocks to prices can lead to much longer
swings in prices.

In addition, there is a downturn automatically built in to this expansion of capacity. When recognition of general inflation does occur,
investment will have to become less than normal for a time while
capacity readjusts downward. There is no reason to expect this read-
justment to come rapidly, or to be describable as a "crash," or "bust."

This scenario, like the earlier description of the employment response, depends crucially on the confusion on the part of agents
between relative and general price movements. This is especially clear
in the case of investment, since optimal investment policy has a great
deal of "smoothing" built into it: since investment is a long-term
commitment, it will respond only to what seem to be relatively permanent relative price shifts.

This observation has led, on serious grounds, to skepticism as to the importance of accelerator effects in the business cycle. How can moderate cyclical movements in prices lead to the high-amplitude movements in durable goods purchases which are observed? Here again, one must insist on the minor contribution of economy-wide risk to the general risk situation faced by agents. For individual investment projects, rates of return are highly variable, often negative, and often measured in hundreds of percent. A quick, current response to what seems to others a weak "signal" is often the key to a successful investment. The agent who waits until the situation is clear to everyone is too late; someone else has already added the capacity to meet the high demand. What appears, at the aggregate level, to be a high-amplitude response pattern to low-amplitude shocks is, at the level at which decisions are made, a high-amplitude response to still higher amplitude movements in returns to individual investments.[15]

11

I began section 2 with a definition of business cycles as repeated fluctuations in employment, output, and the composition of output, associated with a certain typical pattern of co-movements in prices and other variables. Since in a competitive economy, employment and output of various kinds are chosen by agents in response to price movements, it seemed appropriate to begin by rationalizing the observed quantity movements as rational or optimal responses to observed price movements. This has been accomplished in the preceding five sections. I turn next to the *sources* of price movements.

For explaining *secular* movements in prices generally, secular movements in the quantity of money do extremely well. This fact is as well established as any we know in aggregative economics, and is not sensitive to how one measures either prices or the quantity of money.[16] There is no serious doubt as to the direction of effect in this relationship; no one argues that the anticipation of sixteenth-century inflation sent Columbus to the New World to locate the gold to finance it. This evidence has no direct connection to business cycles, since it refers to averages over much longer periods, but the indirect connections are too strong to be ignored: we have accounted for the pattern of co-movements among real variables over the cycle as responses to general price movements; we know that, in the "long run," general price movements arise primarily from changes in the quantity of money. Moreover, cyclical movements in money are large enough to be quantitatively interesting. All these arguments point to a monetary shock as the force triggering the real business cycle.

The direct evidence on short-term correlations between money, output, and prices is much more difficult to read. Certain extreme episodes appear to indicate that depressions and recoveries are money-induced.[17] In general, however, the link between money and these and other variables is agreed to be subject, in Friedman's terms, to "long and variable lags."

Paradoxically, this weakness in the short-term evidence linking money to economic activity, and in particular to prices, is *encouraging* from the point of view of monetary business cycle theory. To see why, recall the theoretical link between general price movements and economic activity as sketched above. This connection rested on the hypothesis that the signal processing problem of identifying general price movements from observations of a few individual prices was *too difficult* to be solved perfectly by agents. Now suppose it were true that one could describe short-term general price movements by a simple, fixed function of lagged movements in some published monetary aggregate. Then, far from being difficult, the signal processing problem to be solved by agents would be *trivial*; they could simply observe current monetary aggregates, calculate the predicted current and future price movements they imply, and correct their behavior for these units changes perfectly. The result would be a very tight relationship between money and prices, over even very short periods, and no relationship at all between these movements and changes in real variables.

These remarks do not, of course, explain *why* monetary effects work with long and variable lags. On this question little is known. It seems likely that the answer lies in the observation that a monetary expansion can occur in a variety of ways, depending on the way the money is "injected" into the system, with different price response implications depending on which way is selected. This would suggest that one should describe the monetary "state" of the economy as being determined by some *unobservable* monetary aggregate, loosely related to observed aggregates over short periods but closely related secularly.

12

Let me recapitulate the main features of the business cycle theory
sketched in the preceding sections. We began by imagining an economy with fluctuating tastes and technology, implying continually
changing *relative* prices, and studied the co-movements in quantities
and prices which would emerge if agents behaved in their own interest
and utilized their incomplete information effectively. We then super-
imposed on this economy sizable, unsystematic movements in a monetary aggregate, adding an additional source of "noise" to individual
price movements. The result is to generate a pattern of co-movements
among aggregate series which appears to match the observations summarized in section 2.

In retrospect, this account seems rather embarrassingly simple: one
wonders why it seems to be necessary to undo a Revolution to arrive
at it. Yet one must be careful not to overstate what has, in fact, been
arrived at. I think it is fairly clear that there is nothing in the behavior
of observed economic time series which precludes ordering them in
equilibrium terms, and enough theoretical examples exist to lend confidence to the hope that this can be done in an explicit and rigorous
way. To date, however, no equilibrium model has been developed
which meets these standards and which, at the same time, could pass
the test posed by the Adelmans (1959). My own guess would be that
success in this sense is five, but not twenty-five years off.[18]

The implications for economic policy of a successful business cycle
theory of the sort outlined here are, I think, easy to guess at even
when the theory itself is in a preliminary state. Indeed, much of the
above is simply an attempt to understand and make more explicit the
implicit model underlying the policy proposals of Henry Simons, Milton Friedman, and other critics of activist aggregative policy. By
seeking an equilibirum account of business cycles, one accepts *in
advance* rather severe limitations on the scope of governmental countercyclical policy which might be rationalized by the theory. Insofar
as fluctuations are induced by gratuitous monetary instability, serving
no social purpose, then increased monetary stability promises to reduce aggregate, real variability and increase welfare. There is no
doubt, however, that *some* real variability would remain even under
the smoothest monetary and fiscal policies. There is no *prima facie*
case that this residual variability would be better dealt with by cen-

tralized, governmental policies than by individual, decentralized responses.[19]

In view of this lack of novelty in the realm of policy, it seems a fair question to ask: why do we need the theory? The general answer, I think, is that in a democratic society it is not enough to believe oneself to be right; one must be able to explain *why* one is right. We live in a society in which the unemployment rate fluctuates between, say, 3 and 10 percent. It follows that both situations are attainable, and it is clear that most people are happier at three than at ten. It is also clear that government policies have much to do with which of these situations prevails at any particular time. What could be more natural, then, than to view the task of aggregative economics as that of discovering which policies will lead to the more desirable situation, and then advocating their adoption? This was the promise of Keynesian economics, and even now, when the scientific emptiness of this promise is most evident, its appeal is understandable to all who share the hope that social science offers more than elegant rationalization of the existing state of affairs.

The economically literate public has had some forty years to become comfortable with two related ideas: that market economies are inherently subject to violent fluctuations which can only be eliminated by flexible and forceful governmental responses; and that economists are in possession of a body of scientifically tested knowledge enabling them to determine, at any time, what these responses should be. It is doubtful if many who are not professionally committed hold, today, to the latter of these beliefs. This in itself settles little in the dispute as to whether the role of government in stabilization policy should be to reduce its own disruptive part or actively to offset private sector instability. As long as the business cycle remains "in apparent contradiction" to economic theory, both positions appear tenable. There seems to be no way to determine how business cycles are to be dealt with short of understanding what they are and how they occur.

Notes

1. Hayek (1933), p. 33n.

2. Hayek (1933), p. 42n.

3. This redirection was conscious and explicit on Keynes' part. See, for example, the first sentence of his chapter on the trade cycle. "Since we claim

to have shown in the preceding chapters what determines the volume of employment at any time, it follows, if we are right, that our theory must be capable of explaining the phenomena of the trade cycle'' (1936), p. 313.

4. The features of economic time series listed here are, curiously, both "well known" and expensive to document in any careful and comprehensive way. A useful, substantively oriented introduction is given by Mitchell (1951), who summarizes mainly interwar, U.S. experience. The basic technical reference for these methods is Burns and Mitchell (1946). U.S. monetary experience is best displayed in Friedman and Schwartz (1963). An invaluable source for earlier British series is Gayer, Rostow, and Schwartz (1953), esp. Vol. II. The phenomena documented in these sources are, of course, much more widely observed. Most can be inferred, though with some difficulty, from the estimated structure of modern econometric models. An important recent contribution is Sargent and Sims (1976), which summarizes postwar U.S. quarterly series in several suggestive ways, leading to a qualitative picture very close to that provided by Mitchell, but within an explicit stochastic framework, so that their results are replicatable and criticizable at a level at which Mitchell's are not.

5. For example, see Tinbergen (1939). This work was not explicitly Keynesian; indeed, it was conceived as an empirical complement to Haberler's review and synthesis of theoretical work on business cycles (1936). Keynes, on his part, was actively hostile toward Tinbergen's work. See Moggridge (1973), pp. 285–320. In referring to those who built in part on Tinbergen's work as "Keynesian" I am, then, contributing to the continuation of an historical injustice.

6. Klein and Goldberger (1955).

7. Tinbergen (1939), pp. 183–185. Tinbergen, as did most subsequent macroeconometricians, used the significance of interest rates to test the importance of money.

8. It is not correct that a search for "good fits" would have led to a model satisfying the Adelmans' criteria; think of fitting polynomials in time to "explain" each series over the sample period.

9. Lucas (1976).

10. Hirsch (1972), de Menil and Enzler (1972).

11. Knight (1921). I am interpreting the risk-uncertainty distinction as referring *not* to a classification of different types of individual decision problems but to the *relationship* between decision maker and observer.

12. Many of the arguments in this and subsequent sections have been developed more explicitly elsewhere. The closest single parallel treatment is in Lucas (1975). See also Phelps, *et al.* (1970), Barro (1976), Sargent and Wallace (1975), Sargent (1976). In what follows, I will not document particular arguments, nor will I attempt to apportion credit (or blame) for ideas discussed.

13. One such arrangement is the practice of "laying off" workers. See Azariadis (1975).

14. What is happening to consumption expenditures as these employment and investment responses take place? In his critique of equilibrium business cycle models, Grossman (1973) argues that consumption must *necessarily* move in the *opposite* direction from labor supplied. Since this is not what is in fact observed over the cycle, it would indeed be a serious paradox if a negative correlation were a consequence of utility theory. One *can* derive it for special cases (see Lucas, 1972, Fig. 1) but this implication is certainly *not* a general fact for optimizing households; it does *not*, for example, follow from Rapping's and my (1970) theory or from that of Ghez and Becker (1975, ch. 4).

15. "Austrian" or "monetary-over-investment" business cycle theory (see Haberler 1936, or Hayek, 1933) was based on this same idea of mistaken investment decisions triggered by spurious price signals. However, the price which this theory emphasized was the rate of interest, rather than product prices as stressed here. Given the cyclical amplitude of interest rates, the investment-interest elasticity needed to account for the observed amplitude in investment is *much* too high to be consistent with other evidence.

16. Friedman and Schwartz (1963).

17. Again, see Friedman and Schwartz (1963).

18. Proceeding further out on this limb, it is likely that such a "successful" model will be a close descendant of Sargent's (1976).

19. That is to say, active countercyclical policy would require the same kind of cost-benefit defense used in evaluating other types of government policies. See Phelps (1972), and also Prescott's review (1975).

References

Adelman, I., and Adelman, F. L., "The Dynamic Properties of the Klein-Goldberger Model," *Econometrica,* 27, No. 4, (October 1959), 596–625.

Azariadis, C., "Implicit Contracts and Underemployment Equilibria," *Journal of Political Economy,* 83, No. 6, (December 1975), 1183–1202.

Barro, R. J., "Rational Expectations and the Role of Monetary Policy," *Journal of Monetary Economics,* 2, No. 1, (January 1976), 1–32.

Burns, A. F., and Mitchell, W. C. *Measuring Business Cycles.* New York: National Bureau of Economic Research, 1946.

Friedman, M., "The Role of Monetary Policy," Presidential Address to the American Economic Association, *American Economic Review,* 58, No. 1, (March 1968), 1–17.

Friedman, M., and Schwartz, A. J. *A Monetary History of the United States, 1867–1960.* Princeton: Princeton University Press for the National Bureau of Economic Research, 1963.

Gayer, A. D., Rostow, W. W., and Schwartz, A. J. *The Growth and Fluctuation of the British Economy, 1790–1850.* Oxford: The Clarendon Press, 1953.

Ghez, G. R., and Becker, G. S. *The Allocation of Time and Goods Over the Life Cycle*. New York: National Bureau of Economic Research, 1975.

Grossman, H. I., "Aggregate Demand, Job Search, and Employment," *Journal of Political Economy*, 81, No. 6, (November/December 1973), 1353–1369.

Haberler, G. *Prosperity and Depression*. Geneva: League of Nations, 1936.

Hayek, F. A. von. *Monetary Theory and the Trade Cycle*. London: Jonathan Cape, 1933.

Hicks, J. R., "Mr. Keynes and the 'Classics': A Suggested Interpretation," *Econometrica*. 5, (1937), 147–159.

Hirsch, A. A., "Price Simulations with the OBE Econometric Model," in *The Econometrics of Price Determination Conference*. (ed. O. Eckstein), Washington, D.C.: Board of Governors of the Federal Reserve System and Social Science Council, 1972.

Keynes, J. M. *The General Theory of Employment, Interest and Money*. London: Macmillan, 1936.

Klein, L. A., and Goldberger, A. S. *An Econometric Model of the United States, 1929–52*. Amsterdam: North Holland, 1955.

Knight, F. H. *Risk, Uncertainty and Profit*. Boston: Houghton Mifflin, 1921.

Lucas, R. E., Jr., "Expectations and the Neutrality of Money," *Journal of Economic Theory*, 4, No. 2, (April 1972), 103–123.

Lucas, R. E., Jr., "An Equilibrium Model of the Business Cycle," *Journal of Political Economy*, 83, No. 6, (December 1975), 1113–1144.

Lucas, R. E., Jr., "Econometric Policy Evaluations: A Critique," in *The Phillips Curve and Labor Markets*, (eds. K. Brunner and A. H. Meltzer), Carnegie-Rochester Conference Series on Public Policy, 1, Amsterdam: North Holland, 1976, 19–46.

Lucas, R. E., Jr., and Rapping, L. A., "Real Wages, Employment, and Inflation," in *Microeconomic Foundations of Employment and Inflation Theory*, (eds. E. S. Phelps, et al.), New York: Norton, 1970.

de Menil, G., and Enzler, J. J., "Price and Wages in the FR-MIT Econometric Model," in *The Econometrics of Price Determination Conference*, (ed. O. Eckstein), Washington, D.C.: Board of Governors of the Federal Reserve System and Social Science Council, 1972.

Mitchell, W. C. *What Happens During Business Cycles*. New York: National Bureau of Economic Research, 1951.

Modigliani, F., "Liquidity Preference and the Theory of Interest and Money," *Econometrica*. 12, No. 1, (January 1944), 45–88.

Moggridge, D. (ed.) *The Collected Writings of John Maynard Keynes*, Vol. XIV. London: Macmillan, 1973.

Muth, J., "Rational Expectations and the Theory of Price Movements," *Econometrica*, 29, No. 3, (July 1961), 315–335.

Phelps, E. S., "Money Wage Dynamics and Labor Market Equilibrium," *Journal of Political Economy*, 76, No. 4, II, (July/August 1968), 687–711.

Phelps, E. S., *Inflation Policy and Unemployment Theory: The Cost-Benefit Approach to Monetary Planning*. London: Macmillan, 1972.

Phelps, E. S., *et al. Microeconomic Foundations of Employment and Inflation Theory.* New York: Norton, 1970.

Prescott, E. C., "Efficiency of the Natural Rate," *Journal of Political Economy,* 83, No. 6, (December 1975), 1229–1236.

Sargent, T. J., "A Classical Macroeconometric Model for the United States," *Journal of Political Economy,* 84, No. 2, (April 1976), 207–237.

Sargent, T. J., and Sims, C. A., "Business Cycle Modeling Without Pretending to Have Too Much A Priori Economic Theory," University of Michigan working paper, March 1976.

Sargent, T. J., and Wallace, N., "'Rational' Expectations, the Optimal Monetary Instrument, and the Optimal Money Supply Rule," *Journal of Political Economy,* 83, No. 2, (April 1975), 241–254.

Tinbergen, J. *Business Cycles in the United States of America, 1919–32.* Geneva: League of Nations, 1939.

Unemployment Policy

The U.S. unemployment rate was certainly too high in 1975, and most economists would agree that it is too high today. It will also be agreed that this observation poses a problem for public policy (in a sense that the observation that winters in Chicago are "too cold" does not). But what exactly is meant by the statement that unemployment is "too high," and what is the nature of the policy problem it poses? This question can be answered in more than one way, and the answer one chooses matters a great deal.

One common answer to this question is that there exists a rate of unemployment—call it "full employment"—which can and should serve as a "target" for economic policy. Unemployment above this rate is regarded as being of a different character from the "frictional" unemployment required to match workers and jobs efficiently, and is treated from a welfare point of view as waste, or deadweight loss. Elimination of this waste is an objective of monetary, fiscal, and perhaps other policies. In the first part of this paper, I will argue that this way of posing the issue does not lead to an operational basis for unemployment policy, mainly on the ground that economists have no coherent idea as to what full employment means or how it can be measured.

An alternative view, prevalent prior to the Great Depression and enjoying something of a revival today, treats *fluctuations* in unem-

Reprinted from *American Economic Review: Papers and Proceedings* 68 (May 1978):353–357 by permission.

I am very grateful for criticism of an earlier draft by Jacob Frenkel, Sherwin Rosen, and Jose Scheinkman.

ployment and other variables as posing a policy problem. On this view, the average (or natural, or equilibrium) rate of unemployment is viewed as raising policy issues only insofar as it can be shown to be "distorted" in an undesirable way by taxes, external effects, and so on. Nine percent unemployment is then viewed as too high in the same sense that 2 percent is viewed as "too low": both are symptoms of costly and preventable instability in general economic activity. In the concluding part of this paper, I will sketch the approaches to unemployment policy which are suggested by this alternative view and some which are not.

1 Full Employment: Definition and Measurement

The idea that policy can and should be directed at the attainment of a particular, specifiable *level* of the measured rate of unemployment (as opposed to mitigating *fluctuations* in unemployment) owes it wide acceptance to John Maynard Keynes' *General Theory*. It is there derived from the prior hypothesis that measured unemployment can be decomposed into two distinct components: "voluntary" (or frictional) and "involuntary," with full employment then identified as the level prevailing when involuntary unemployment equals zero. It seems appropriate, then, to begin by reviewing Keynes' reasons for introducing this distinction in the first place.

Keynes (ch. 2, p. 7) classifies the factors affecting equilibrium employment in a real general equilibrium theory: the mechanics of matching workers to jobs, household labor-leisure preferences, technology, and the composition of product demand. Is it the case, he asks, that spontaneous shifts in any of these four real factors can account for employment fluctuations of the magnitude we observe? Evidently, the answer is negative. It follows that two kinds of theory must be needed to account for observed unemployment movements: granted that real general equilibrium theory may account for a relatively constant, positive component, *some other theory* is needed for the rest.

Accepting the necessity of a distinction between explanations for normal and cyclical unemployment does not, however, compel one to identify the first as voluntary and the second as involuntary, as Keynes goes on to do. This terminology suggests that the key to the distinction lies in some difference in the way two different types of unemployment are *perceived by workers*. Now in the first place, the distinction we are after concerns *sources* of unemployment, not differentiated types.

One may, for example, seek very different theoretical explanations for the average price of a commodity and for its day-to-day fluctuations, without postulating two types of price for the same good. Similarly, one may classify motives for holding money without imagining that anyone can subdivide his own cash holdings into "transactions balances," "precautionary balances," and so forth. The recognition that one needs to distinguish among sources of unemployment does not in any way imply that one needs to distinguish among types.

Nor is there any evident reason why one would *want* to draw this distinction. Certainly the more one thinks about the decision problem facing individual workers and firms the less sense this distinction makes. The worker who loses a good job in prosperous times does not *volunteer* to be in this situation: he has suffered a capital loss.[1] Similarly, the firm which loses an experienced employee in depressed times suffers an undesired capital loss. Nevertheless the unemployed worker at any time can always find *some* job at once, and a firm can always fill a vacancy instantaneously. That neither typically does so *by choice* is not difficult to understand given the quality of the jobs and the employees which are easiest to find. Thus there is an involuntary element in *all* unemployment, in the sense that no one chooses bad luck over good; there is also a voluntary element in all unemployment, in the sense that however miserable one's current work options, one can always choose to accept them.[2]

Keynes, in chapter 2, deals with the situation facing an *individual* unemployed worker by evasion and wordplay only. Sentences like "more labor would, as a rule, be forthcoming at the existing money wage if it were demanded" are used again and again as though, from the point of view of a jobless worker, it is unambiguous what is meant by "*the* existing money wage." Unless we define an individual's wage rate as the price someone else is willing to pay him for his labor (in which case Keynes' assertion above is *defined* to be false), what *is* it? The wage at which he would *like* to work more hours? Then it is *true* by definition and equally empty. The fact is, I think, that Keynes wanted to get labor markets out of the way in chapter 2 so that he could get on to the demand theory which really interested him. This is surely understandable, but what is the excuse for letting his carelessly drawn distinction between voluntary and involuntary unemployment dominate aggregative thinking on labor markets for the forty years following?

It is, to be sure, possible to write down theoretical models in which households are faced with an "hours constraint" limiting the hours they can supply at "the" prevailing wage, and in which, therefore, there is a clear distinction between the hours one can supply and the hours one would like to supply. Such an exercise is frequently motivated as an attempt to "explain involuntary (or Keynesian) unemployment." This misses the point: involuntary unemployment is not a fact or a phenomenon which it is the task of theorists to explain. It is, on the contrary, a theoretical construct which Keynes introduced in the hope that it would be helpful in discovering a correct explanation for a genuine phenomenon: large-scale fluctuations in measured, total unemployment. Is it the task of modern theoretical economics to "explain" the theoretical constructs of our predecessors, whether or not they have proved fruitful? I hope not, for a surer route to sterility could scarcely be imagined.

In summary, it does not appear possible, even in principle, to classify individual unemployed people as either voluntarily or involuntarily unemployed depending on the characteristics of the decision problems they face. One cannot, even conceptually, arrive at a usable definition of full employment as a state in which no involuntary unemployment exists.

In practice, I think this fact has been recognized for some time. Estimates of full employment actually in use have been obtained using aggregate information rather than data on individuals. As recently as the 1960's it was widely believed that there was some level of aggregate unemployment with the property that when unemployment exceeded this rate, expansionary monetary and fiscal measures would be non-inflationary, while at rates below this critical level they would lead to inflation. One could then identify unemployment rates at or below this full-employment level as frictional or voluntary, and unemployment in excess of this level as involuntary. It was understood that only unemployment of the latter type posed a problem curable by monetary or fiscal policy. As Walter Heller wrote, "Gone is the countercyclical syndrome of the 1950's. Policy now centers on gap closing and growth, on realizing and enlarging the economy's non-inflationary potential" (Preface). Later, Heller refers to "the operational concepts of the 'production gap,' 'full-employment surplus,' the 'fiscal drag,' and 'fiscal dividends'" (p. 18).

For the purpose of calculating the production gap to which Heller

referred, it makes little difference whether the voluntary-involuntary
terminology accurately reflects differences in the way unemployed
people view their situations. The issue here is rather whether there
exists an aggregate rate of unemployment (on the order of 4 or 5
percent) which is of use in measuring an economy's noninflationary
potential. If there were, then objections of the sort I have raised above
could be dismissed as merely terminological: if one objected to calling
unemployment above the designated full-employment level involuntary, one could call it something else, perhaps wasteful or unnecessary.

The last ten years have taught us a great deal about this operational
concept of a production gap. In 1975, the U.S. economy attained the
combination of 9 percent inflation and an unemployment rate of 9
percent. Applying the concept of a production gap to these numbers,
does one conclude that the noninflationary potential of the U.S. economy is associated with unemployment rates in excess of 9 percent?
Does one redefine 9 percent inflation to be noninflationary? Or can the
entire episode be somehow pinned on oil prices?

I have reviewed two possible routes by which one might hope to
give the term full employment some operational significance. One was
to begin at the individual worker level, classifying unemployment into
two types, voluntary and involuntary, count up the number classed as
voluntary, and define the total to be the unemployment level associated
with full employment. A second was to determine the operating characteristics of the economy at different rates of unemployment, and
then to define full employment to be the rate at which inflation rates
are acceptable. Neither of these approaches leads to an operational
definition of full employment. Neither yields a coherent view as to
why unemployment is a problem, or as to the costs and benefits
involved in economic policies which affect unemployment rates. The
difficulties are not the measurement error problems which necessarily
arise in applied economics. They arise because the "thing" to be
measured does not exist.

2 Beyond Full-Employment Policy

Abandoning the constraint that any discussion of unemployment must
begin first by drawing the voluntary-involuntary distinction and then
thinking in separate ways about these two types of unemployment
will, I think, benefit both positive and normative analysis. Practicing
social science is hard enough without crippling oneself with dogmatic

constraints. A terminology which precludes asking the question: "Why do people choose to take the actions we see them taking, instead of other actions they might take instead?" precludes any serious thinking about behavior at all.

Whether or not the body of work stemming from the Edmund Phelps volume, and earlier work of George Stigler, John McCall and others, has produced all the right answers about the determinants of employment and unemployment, it has at least begun to pose some of the right questions. By treating all unemployment as voluntary, this work has led to the examination of alternative arrangements which firms and employees might choose to adopt for dealing with fluctuations in product demand, and their reasons for choosing to react to such fluctuations in the way we observe them doing. Pursuit of this question has indicated both how very difficult it is, and even more so how much economics was swept under the rug by "explaining involuntary unemployment" by incompetent auctioneers or purely mechanical wage and price equations.

Practicing normative macroeconomics without the construct of full employment does take some getting used to. One finds oneself slipping into such sentences as: "There is no such thing as full employment, but I can tell you how it can be attained." But there are some immediate benefits. First, one dispenses with that entire meaningless vocabulary associated with full employment, phrases like potential output, full capacity, slack, and so on, which suggested that there was some *technical* reason why we couldn't all return to the 1890 workweek and produce half again the GNP we now produce. Second, one finds to one's relief that treating unemployment as a voluntary response to an unwelcome situation does not commit oneself to normative nonsense like blaming depressions on lazy workers.

The effect it does have on normative discussion is twofold. First, it focuses discussion of monetary and fiscal policy on *stabilization,* on the pursuit of price stability and on minimizing the disruptive effects of erratic policy changes. Some average unemployment rate would, of course, emerge from such a policy but as a by-product, not as a preselected target. Second, by thinking of this natural rate as an equilibrium emerging from voluntary exchange in the usual sense, one can subject it to the scrutiny of modern methods of public finance.

To take one example, as the level of unemployment compensation is varied, an entire range of average unemployment rates, all equally "natural," is available to society. At one extreme, severe penalties to declaring oneself unemployed could reduce unemployment rates to any desired level. Such a policy would result in serious real output losses, as workers retain poor jobs too long and accept poor jobs too readily. An output-maximizing unemployment compensation scheme would, with risk-averse workers, involve a subsidy to being unemployed, else workers retain a poor but relatively sure current wage in preference to the riskier but, on average, more productive return to seeking a new job. In view of the private market's inability to provide sufficient insurance against unemployment risk, still further gains in expected utility could be expected by still higher unemployment compensation, resulting in a deliberate sacrifice in real output in exchange for a preferred arrangement for allocating risk.[3] Notice that as one traces out tradeoffs of this sort, the issue of slack or waste does not arise. Different policies result in different levels of real output, but output increases are necessarily obtained at the expense of something else. Whether any particular level of unemployment compensation is too high or too low is a difficult issue in practice, but it is one that cannot be resolved simply by observing that other, unemployment reducing, compensation levels are *feasible*.

The policy problem of reducing business cycle risk is a very real and important one, and one which I believe monetary and fiscal policies directed at price stability would go a long way toward achieving. The problem of finding arrangements for allocating unemployment risks over individuals in a satisfactory way is also important, and can be analyzed by the methods of modern welfare economics. The pursuit of a full-employment target which no one can measure or even define conceptually cannot be expected to contribute to the solution of either problem.

Notes

1. Given the time-consuming nature of job search and the element of luck involved in finding a good "match," there is a capital-like element in most jobs. With job-specific human capital, the capital loss involved in job (or employee) loss is increased.

2. These observations refer to easily verified features of any sizable labor market. Aggregate statistics on unemployment or on listed vacancies do not bear on their accuracy, since listing oneself as unemployed does not imply

that one would accept *any* employment, nor is an advertised vacancy available to *any* job applicant.

3. See Kenneth Arrow's analysis of medical insurance.

References

K. J. Arrow, "Welfare Analysis of Changes in Health Coinsurance Rates," in Richard N. Rosett, ed., *The Role of Health Insurance in the Health Services Sector*, New York 1976.

Walter W. Heller, *New Dimensions of Political Economy*, Cambridge, Mass. 1966.

John M. Keynes, *The General Theory of Employment, Interest, and Money*, London 1936.

J. McCall, "The Economics of Information and Optimal Stopping Rules," *J. Bus.*, July 1965, *38*, 300–317.

Edmund S. Phelps et al., *Microeconomic Foundations of Employment and Inflation Theory*, New York 1969.

G. J. Stigler, "The Economics of Information," *J. Polit. Econ.*, June 1961, *69*, 213–235.

Rules, Discretion, and the Role of the Economic Advisor

1 Introduction

I take the purpose of this session to be to elicit views on economic policy from economists of different points of view. The particular title of the session, "Macroeconomic Policy, 1974/75: What Should Have Been Done?" does not seem to me useful for this purpose, as I will explain below, so I will adopt a somewhat different approach. I will begin by stating a variation on the policy proposals advanced by Milton Friedman in "A Monetary and Fiscal Framework for Economic Stability" (1948) and *A Program for Monetary Stability* (1959). After some speculations on why the Friedman program has had so limited an impact,[1] I will identify and discuss some recent developments suggesting that its acceptance and influence may be greater in the near future. The paper concludes with an assessment of the case for the Friedman program as it stands today, a brief discussion of problems of transition, and some concluding remarks.

In centering the discussion around a proposal Friedman formulated, in its essentials, thirty years ago, I run an admitted risk of locking myself and others into positions we may have taken up years ago and not rethought seriously since. The alternative strategy of repackaging this proposal in more current language is one I find distasteful, and,

Reprinted from *Rational Expectations and Economic Policy*, ed. Stanley Fischer, Chicago: The University of Chicago Press, 1980, pp. 199–210, by permission of The University of Chicago Press. Copyright 1980 by The University of Chicago Press.

The revision has benefited from the suggestions of Stanley Fischer, Milton Friedman, and Robert Weintraub.

in any case, it would quickly be found out. I will begin, then, on familiar ground and, for the most part, remain there.

1. a 4% annual rate of growth of M1, maintained as closely as possible on a quarter-to-quarter basis;

2. a pattern of real government expenditures and transfer payments, varying secularly but not in response to cyclical changes in economic activity;

3. a pattern of tax rates, also varying secularly but not in response to cyclical changes in economic activity, set to balance the federal budget *on average*;

4. a clearly announced policy that wage and price agreements privately arrived at will not trigger governmental reactions of any kind (aside from standard antitrust policies and the general policy of government preference for low over high bids).

The first three of these policy rules are taken directly from Friedman's writings.[2] The fourth is simply a recognition of the fact that, since the time Friedman's proposals were originally formulated, intervention in the details of private price and wage negotiations has ceased to be viewed as an emergency measure so that a position on the generally accepted aspects of aggregative policy cannot omit mention of this fact.

In restating these recommendations, I have tried to follow Friedman in being concrete and operational concerning exactly which policies are being advocated. Under the principle that *natura non facit saltum*, these particular policies must have neighbors that would have nearly the same consequences, and one would certainly like to have an analytical framework within which one could assess the consequences of variations on them. The provision of such a framework is far beyond the scope of the present paper. I will proceed, instead, in an entirely different direction: first by recalling some of the main features of the intellectual environment, both within and without our profession, into which Friedman's framework was introduced and then by tracing some of the changes since in this environment.

2 The Employment Act of 1946

The dominant events influencing the minds of the intended readers of Friedman's "Framework" were the Great Depression of the 1930s

and the "prosperity" (as measured by unemployment rates) of the
Second World War. It is difficult to imagine a sequence of events that
could more forcefully illustrate both the costs of high unemployment
and the ability of government policy to affect unemployment. In all
capitalist countries, this "lesson" had profound influences on policy.
In the United States, it was embodied in the Employment Act of 1946.

To some contemporaries, the Employment Act was "a weak and
meaningless wraith" (Bailey 1950, p. 253), and in some respects it is
easy to see why. The act granted the executive no powers which had
not been fully assumed during the New Deal period preceding, nor did
it specify either the economic targets to be achieved or the policy tools
to be utilized. The act did, however, require the executive in very
explicit terms to forecast the state of the economy in the coming year
and to prescribe policies designed to alter this state in a desirable
direction. Moreover, it was clear in specifying exactly where the expertise required to carry out this task could be found: The Council of
Economic Advisors was established by the act as the channel by which
this expertise could be brought to bear on practical policy.

It would be a difficult and subtle task to trace the effects of the
Employment Act on the policy performance of the U.S. government
in the postwar years. There is nothing subtle, however, in the effects
of the act (or of the events immediately preceding it) on the practice
of monetary economics in the postwar period. Renamed *macroeconomics,* this subdiscipline *defined* itself to be that body of expertise
the existence of which was presupposed in the Employment Act, and
its practitioners devoted themselves to the development and refine-
ment of forecasting and policy evaluation methods which promised to
be of use in the annual diagnosis-prescription exercise called for by
the act.

In many respects, the assumption of this rather specific, applied
role had a very healthy effect on monetary economics. The set of
common, agreed-upon substantive objectives helped to unify the field
and lent it a quantitative, operational character in sharp contrast with
the literary, doctrinal emphasis of so much prewar monetary and
business cycle theory. A great number of talented scientists found this
new character congenial.

The highly productive, collective effort to make the Employment
Act "work" was just getting underway when Friedman's "Framework" was published in 1948. This was a proposal "concerned . . .

with structural reform [which] should not be urged on the public unless and until it has withstood the test of professional criticism" (Friedman 1948 [1953, p. 156]). Perhaps this description may be taken as a comment on the haste with which Keynesian theory, at that time regarded as difficult and controversial, understood by only a handful of American economists, had been embodied in federal legislation. In any case, it is an accurate description of the proposals which are, implicitly, a prediction that the diagnosis and prescription process called for in the Employment Act *cannot* be made to work, given the level of scientific understanding of monetary dynamics at the time. The proposals are offered rather as a *compromise,* promising economic performance superior to that which had been observed historically, yet promising less than the performance goals which are implicit, if vague, in the Employment Act. They constituted, Friedman hoped, "a minimum program for which economists of the less extreme shades of opinion can make common cause" (Friedman 1948 [1953, p. 135]).

In retrospect, it is clear that Friedman underestimated by far the extent to which his colleagues were united in the belief that the Employment Act, together with the Federal Reserve Act as supplemented by changes in the 1930s, provided a workable policymaking apparatus. Post-World War II macroeconomics has shown little interest in reforms of the institutional framework within which economic policy is conducted, and virtually no concern with formulating legislative guidelines or limits on monetary, fiscal, and now, "incomes," policy. The professional forum for debating alternative monetary institutions to which Friedman addressed his proposals did not analyze them, consider them, reject them in favor of others. It simply passed out of existence. Instead, within the existing institutional framework, the role of the economic expert as day-to-day manager expanded rapidly, and the role of the academic macroeconomist became that of equipping these experts with ideas, principles, formulas which gave, or appeared to give, operational guidance on the tasks with which these economic managers happened to be faced.

From the perspective of this new role for aggregative economics, the difficulty with the Friedman proposals was not so much that they were demonstrably dominated by others, but that they were irrelevant. They speak to the question: Under what rules of the game, remaining predictably in force over long periods, can we expect satisfactory economic performance? The economic manager responsible for advis-

ing on, say, the size of the coming fiscal year deficit is simply unin-
terested in this question: it seems to him merely an academic exercise,
unrelated to the tasks he has taken it upon himself to perform.

On one level, this reaction to the Friedman proposals is understandable. General economic performance in the twenty years following the
passage of the Employment Act was, by any historical standard, highly
successful. It is not surprising, then, that there was little general
discussion of institutional change during this period and that this lack
of interest was reflected in economists' choice of research problems.
Yet the history of monetary and fiscal institutions, in the United States
and elsewhere, is one of repeated failure, and failure at very high
social cost. One is not surprised that a large fraction of the profession
found it worthwhile to attempt to provide the expertise presupposed
by the existing institutions. Similarly, it should surprise no one that
others continued to question the viability of these institutions and
focused their work on the design of alternative frameworks which
might ultimately replace them.

3 Some Signs of Change
Events of the current decade have brought about important changes
in both public and professional confidence that economic expertise can
deliver satisfactory performance within the framework provided by
the Employment and Federal Reserve acts. They also provide examples of mechanisms, quite outside those established by this legislation,
by which public opinion may be brought to bear on economic policy.
In this section, I will briefly review a few of these, beginning with
what is surely the most important: the experience of stagflation.

In a first course in econometrics, students discover upward-sloping
demand curves and production functions which impute negative productivity to capital. Students find these shocking experiences for which
nothing in their theory courses has prepared them. This is a standard
developmental crisis, like discovering that one's parents are not perfect, and experience shows that if it occurs in a reasonably protected
and supportive environment, it can be survived and resolved with no
lasting harm done.

There is a tendency on the part of many economists involved with
Keynesian macroeconometric models to view the inflation and un-
employment rate forecast errors of the 1970s in much the same terms.
That is, the error itself is not denied (this is hardly a possibility) but

is interpreted as indicating nothing deeper than a neglect in controlling for some other factors which, when properly taken into account, reveal the original basic structure to be sound. Thus we show our econometrics students that by controlling for income and other variables and by reducing contamination from supply side effects, the law of demand is revealed as clearly in the data as it is in the theory chapters of their textbooks.

I have argued elsewhere, most recently and comprehensively in collaboration with Thomas Sargent (Lucas 1975, Lucas and Sargent 1978), that these two cases are not at all analogous scientifically and that the misforecast of the stagflation period is in fact a symptom of much deeper problems. But a second, even clearer, difference in these two cases involves the context in which the error occurred. The stagflation error did not occur in the privacy of the seminar room, a puzzle of interest to professionals only. It occurred *after* the idea of a stable inflation-unemployment trade-off had become accepted by the public generally as *the* central construct in discussing macroeconomic policy, and *after* wide public acceptance of the idea that movements along the Phillips curve were technically within the control of economic managers. Even if it were true (and I believe it is not) that the sources of this error are easily correctible and unlikely to be repeated, an enormous and far-reaching change has already taken place in the political climate in which economic issues are discussed.

Two early symptoms of this change are Arthur Laffer's influential "Laffer curve" and Arthur Okun's proposal for controlling inflation by a complex system of taxes and subsidies on individual producers. Though both can be supported by theory of sorts, provided one uses the term "theory" with sufficient looseness, neither follows in any way from any widely accepted theoretical framework, neither has received serious analysis by either proponents or critics, neither was even *mentioned* in the academic literature prior to the last year or so.

This is the legacy of stagflation: a general loss of confidence, whether scientifically warranted or not, in the formerly accepted framework guiding discretionary economic management. Since the demand for discretionary policies remains strong, we are seeing the proliferation of new "solutions" to "short-run" policy problems, defended by the promise of particular results but without basis in either theory or historical experience. Given the entry costs into economic advising of this sort, is there any real doubt what the future holds if economists continue to view themselves in a day-to-day management role?

The experience of stagflation has, then, brought about important changes in the nature of the postwar dialogue by means of which policy-oriented economists attempt to advance their ideas and to satisfy the immediate needs of economic managers. Recently, there have been a number of important developments occurring outside the now-traditional dialogue among experts and economic managers, the most striking of which has been the passage of California's Proposition 13, limiting property taxes. Similar measures are under consideration in other states and there are analogous attempts underway to influence the federal budget at the constitutional level.

The main impetus for this "tax revolt" is surely dissatisfaction over the general level of taxes and government spending, and not over the nature of stabilization policy. Yet there is a clear and instructive connection at the political level. In policies of either type, it is evidently impossible for large numbers of people to form opinions and exercise influence at anything like the level of detail at which legislators and economic managers and their advisors carry on their discussion. In contrast, it is clearly possible for people to impose limits on these technical discussions, to *bound* levels and rates of change of economic aggregates. Public opinion generally can do little to *guide* the exercise of discretionary economic authority, but it has enormous potential to limit its scope.

To this point I have stressed developments external to the economics profession, as opposed to internal, scientific developments, as influences on the way economists and noneconomists view the possibilities open to us for influencing economic policy. This choice of emphasis reflects the opinion that public opinion generally (or what used to be called "political feasibility") was far more important than were scientific considerations in influencing professional reaction to Friedman's "Framework," and that this situation is not at all unusual. (This observation is not intended as a lament: there is little to be said for isolating economics from general contemporary social thought, and the consequences of trying to do so tend to lead to reliance on sterile aesthetic criteria in guiding theoretical work.)

Nevertheless, research based on the idea of *rational expectations* has played a role in buttressing the case for thinking about policy, as

Friedman argued we should, as a problem in selecting stable, predictable policy *rules*. The main argument turns out to be a positive (as
opposed to normative) one: our ability as economists to predict the
responses of agents rests, in situations where expectations about the
future matter, on our understanding of the stochastic environment
agents believe themselves to be operating in. In practice, this limits
the class of policies the consequences of which we can hope to assess
in advance to policies generated by fixed, well understood, relatively
permanent rules (or functions relating policy actions taken to the state
of the economy).

I have developed the reasoning underlying this point elsewhere
(Lucas 1975). (Indeed, it follows from modern control-theoretic views
of policy evaluation almost independently of one's view on expectations formation.) I have been impressed both with how noncontro-
versial it seems to be at a general level and with how widely ignored
it continues to be at what some view as a "practical" level. One could
ask for no better illustration of this than the question motivating this
session: "Macroeconomic Policy, 1974/75: What Should Have Been
Done?" The question presupposes one of two possible situations. The
first is that households and firms in 1974/75 were describable by a
fixed set of decision rules, so that given any hypothetical selection of
1974/75 policies, one could simply read private-sector responses off
these fixed curves to determine the response of the economy as a
whole. The second situation under which this question is meaningful
imagines firms and households attempting to solve maximum problems
involving not only current policy actions but expected, future actions
as well. The economist evaluating 1974/75 policy is in this case required to understand what these expectations about the future were,
and how they would have been influenced by policy actions taken in
1974/75.

Does anyone seriously argue that either of these two situations
prevails in fact? If so, on what scientific ground? If not, then why are
we discussing this spuriously practical question at all?

This seems to me by far the most fundamental sense in which recent
work on expectations reinforces the viewpoint toward policy which
Friedman espoused in his 1948 paper. It emphasizes the fact that
analysis of policy which utilizes economics in a scientific way *necessarily* involves choice among alternative stable, predictable policy

rules, infrequently changed and then only after extensive professional and general discussion, minimizing (though of course never entirely eliminating) the role of discretionary economic management.

Though an agreement to focus on alternative policy *rules* would, in my view, be the major step toward restoring some degree of rationality to aggregative policy discussions, it does not necessarily follow that the particular set of rules advocated by Friedman would dominate others. On the one hand, several researchers have developed particular examples in which a 4% monetary growth rule is not dominated by monetary policies which react to the state of the economy (Sargent and Wallace 1975, Barro 1976, Lucas 1972). Moreover, Sargent (1976) has shown that one can find models of this class which account very well for the behavior of postwar, U.S. time series. On the other hand, John Taylor (1979) has developed an empirically implemented example in which monetary policies which react to the state of the system dominate (in a particular sense) a fixed monetary growth rule, though the latter is also shown, in this context, to dominate actual postwar policies. It seems clear at this point that the choice among alternative sets of policy rules will necessarily depend on the answer to difficult substantive questions involving the sources of business cycles and the nature of business cycle dynamics. Though there seems good reason to expect that the principle of rational expectations will prove to be a powerful tool in attacking these questions, it is clearly not sufficient in itself to dictate the nature of desirable countercyclical policies.

4   The Case for the Friedman Program

I began this paper with a brief summary of a variant of Milton Friedman's well-known program for stabilization policy, and then advanced some conjectures of a sociological nature about why professional discussion of this program has been so unsatisfactory in the past and some reasons for believing that the terms of the discussion may now be shifting toward those which Friedman presupposed in his 1948 paper. Yet beyond an unelaborated endorsement of this program, I have devoted no space to its defense or to an assessment of its likely consequences, if adopted.

To an extent which, until a recent rereading, I had forgotten, this absence of a clear defense and assessment also characterizes Friedman's "Framework." There, in outlining his strategy, Friedman says that "I deliberately gave primary consideration to long term objec-

tives. That is, I tried to design a framework that would be appropriate
for a world in which cyclical movements other than those introduced
by 'bad' monetary and fiscal arrangements, were of no consequence.
I then examined the resulting proposal to see how it would behave in
respect to cyclical fluctuations. It behaves *surprisingly* well . . .''
(Friedman 1948 [1953, p. 133]; italics mine). How well is this? "The
proposal may not succeed in reducing cyclical fluctuations to tolerable
proportions. . . . I do not see how it is possible to know now whether
this is the case" (Friedman 1948 [1953, p. 156]).

The strategy, then, was to design a workable stabilization policy not
dependent in any way on detailed knowledge of business cycle dynamics. The program would (I think on this there is no serious professional
disagreement) *fully* protect the economy against sustained inflation. It
would *fully* insure against the kind of monetary collapse which was so
important a factor in the early stages of the Great Depression of the
1930s. It would entirely eliminate erratic monetary and fiscal shocks
as independent sources of instability. Surely these are modest claims
when compared with what can be accomplished via the application of
optimal control to purely hypothetical economies which provide a
complete description of business cycle dynamics. Yet as compared
with actual performance in both the distant and recent past, their
appeal is evident.

In my view, recent research has added little to strengthen Friedman's case, except in what might be called a negative way. Friedman's
case was built largely on the presumption of *ignorance* of the nature
of business cycles. Many of us confused the methodological advances
in economic dynamics that took place in the 1950s and 1960s with the
substantive narrowing of this ignorance and consequently with the
increasing feasibility of sophisticated, reactive countercyclical policy.
We have learned, I believe, that the list of economic propositions
sufficiently well grounded in theory and evidence to be useful in formulating aggregative policy is no longer now than it was in 1948. This
situation is discouraging and also, I think, improvable, but in the
meantime we should be grateful that, in the face of our ignorance, we
can still do "surprisingly well."

5   The Problem of Transition
From the point of view of those involved in economic management,
the position that policy should be dictated by a set of fixed rules seems

at best a partial response to the question: What should be done, now? To one with some responsibility for monetary policy in 1974, say, it is not very helpful to observe that monetary growth "should have" proceeded at a constant 4% rate for the 25 years preceding. Moreover, even if a move toward a policy of fixed rules were desired, it could be done in innumerable ways, presumably with different consequences, and a criterion based on long-run average performance offers no help in choosing among them. What advice, then, do advocates of rules have to offer with respect to the policy decisions before us *right now*?

This question does have a practical, men-of-affairs ring to it, but to my ears, this ring is entirely false. It is a king-for-a-day question which has no real-world counterpart in the decision problems actually faced by economic advisors. In the current system of discretionary economic management, no one or no small group has the job of deciding what to do right now and into the middle distance with respect to the main aggregative decision variables. None of these managers is in a position to influence the economy in any significant way toward a regime of fixed, nonreactive policy rules. They are simply reacting, sometimes well, sometimes badly, to current difficulties, with no more capability of affecting policy five years hence than of affecting what happened five years before.

Economists who pose this "What is to be done, today?" question as though it were somehow the acid test of economic competence are culture-bound (or institution-bound) to an extent they are probably not aware of. They are accepting as *given* the entirely unproved hypothesis that the fine-tuning exercise called for by the Employment Act is a desirable and feasible one. In criticizing Friedman's 1948 proposal from this point of view, they are simply missing its main point. It is not a recipe for making the Employment Act "work" but rather a prediction that it *cannot* be made to work, and an outline of an alternative set of policy arrangements.

If one does try to think in a politically serious way about possible scenarios leading to a fixed-rule regime, one is led to assign the primary roles to actors *outside* the executive–central bank system of economic management. An encouraging example is provided by the House Concurrent Resolution 133, requiring that the Federal Reserve Board announce monetary growth targets in advance and account for deviations afterward.[3] One can imagine this resolution hardening into legally binding limits on monetary growth rates. A second example is politi-

cally less advanced: movements for constitutional limits on the federal
budget deficit.[4]

In cases such as these, existing economic managers will not program
a transition in any formal way, though they could certainly help to
minimize disruption. But the inherent gradualism of the legislative and
constitutional processes will mean that any actual move toward fixed
rules will necessarily occur with ample advance warning and a great
deal of prior adjustment on the part of both government and the private
sector. Analytical elegance will clearly not be one of the virtues of
such a transition, but I see no reason to expect large economic disruption, at least by the sorry standards of the past decade, to be an
inevitable or even a likely consequence.

6 Concluding Remarks

As an advice-giving profession we are in way over our heads. The
Employment Act of 1946 placed heavy demands on the ability of
economists to guide executive authority granted very broad powers.
In the early postwar years, and even through the sixties, it appeared
that the framework provided by the Keynesian theory of income determination was, intelligently applied, capable of meeting these demands. As confidence has ebbed in our ability to use general monetary
and fiscal policy to carry out the aims of the Employment Act, professionals and nonprofessionals alike have turned to a wide variety of
complex, selective interventions in individual markets. Even to begin
to assess the likely consequences of these policies in anything like a
scientific way is clearly well beyond the current limits of our discipline.

One response to this situation is to attempt to deal with this ever
broadening range of management questions, working and hoping for
advances sufficiently dramatic to enable us to regain the intellectual
control we thought we had in the sixties. If, as I believe to be the
case, this will require scientific improvements of a fundamental or
basic nature, then this response is not likely to succeed. Basic research, to be successful, requires some degree of control over the
questions to be asked and the results that can be delivered. Though
stimulated by practical demands, it is rarely carried out by those in an
active managerial role, even at one remove.

An alternative response is to attempt to make clear to our fellow
citizens the questions that currently available expertise can hope to
answer successfully, to base policy recommendations on the well-

understood and empirically substantiated propositions of monetary economics, discouragingly modest as these may be, and to make it as clear as possible that the main task of monetary and fiscal policy is to provide a stable, predictable environment for the private sector of the economy.

Notes

1. Of course, Friedman's work in general has had an enormous impact on many dimensions. I am here referring only to his recommendation that monetary and fiscal policy be conducted according to fixed rules.

2. Rules 2 and 3 are paraphrases of those in Friedman 1948 (1953, pp. 136–137). Rule 1 is from Friedman 1959, pp. 87–92, there presented as a desirable but second-best alternative to the requirement of 100% reserve banking advocated in Friedman 1948.

3. The substance of this resolution became an amendment to the Federal Reserve Act in 1977. See Weintraub 1978.

4. For a proposed amendment to this effect, together with an economic and political analysis, see Buchanan and Wagner 1977.

References

Bailey, S. K. 1950. *Congress Makes a Law*. New York: Columbia University Press.

Barro, R. J. 1976. "Rational Expectations and the Role of Monetary Policy." *Journal of Monetary Economics* 2:1–32.

Buchanan, J. M., and Wagner, R. E. 1977. *Democracy in Deficit*. New York: Academic Press.

Friedman, M. 1948. "A Monetary and Fiscal Framework for Economic Stability." *American Economic Review* 38:245–264. Reprinted in *Essays in Positive Economics*. Chicago: University of Chicago Press, 1953.

Friedman, M. 1959. *A Program for Monetary Stability*. New York: Fordham University Press.

Lucas, R. E., Jr. 1972. "Expectations and the Neutrality of Money." *Journal of Economic Theory* 4:103–24.

Lucas, R. E., Jr. 1975. "Econometric Policy Evaluation: A Critique." In *The Phillips Curve and Labor Markets*, edited by K. Brunner and A. H. Meltzer, pp. 19–46. Carnegie-Rochester Conference Series no. 1. New York: North-Holland.

Lucas, R. E., Jr., and Sargent, T. J. 1978. "After Keynesian Macroeconomics." In *After the Phillips Curve: Persistence of High Inflation and High Unemployment*, pp. 49–72. Conference Series no. 19. Boston: Federal Reserve Bank of Boston.

Sargent, T. J. 1976. "A Classical Macroeconomic Model for the United States." *Journal of Political Economy* 84:207–254.

261   Rules, Discretion,
and the Role of the
Economic Advisor

Sargent, T. J., and Wallace, N. 1975. "'Rational' Expectations, the Optimal Monetary Instrument, and the Optimal Money Supply Rule." *Journal of Political Economy* 83:241–254.

Taylor, J. B. 1979. "Estimation and Control of a Macroeconomic Model with Rational Expectations." Econometrica, forthcoming.

Weintraub, R. E. 1978. "Congressional Supervision of Monetary Policy." *Journal of Monetary Economics* 4:341–362.

A Review:
Paul McCracken et al.,
Towards Full Employment and Price Stability, A Report to the OECD by a Group of Independent Experts OECD, June 1977

Towards Full Employment and Price Stability is a report to the Organization for Economic Cooperation and Development (OECD) authored by a committee of eight economists, under the chairmanship of Paul McCracken. The Committee met nine times and utilized the efforts of staff members of the OECD Secretariat. The Report contains descriptive and evaluative material on the performance of the OECD economies in the period since 1965, presented as background for a variety of recommendations or guidelines for economic policy in these countries over the decade we are now entering.

The structure of the OECD Report invites the reader to view it as the transmission to "policymakers" of a professional or scientific consensus. It begins with a 33-page Summary, self contained, and surely the only part likely to be read by its primary audience. Each paragraph in this summary references, by number, corresponding paragraphs of the 207 pages which follow, apparently intending to convey the impression that the latter provide analytical support for the conclusions of the Summary. Next come nine pages of dissents by three of the eight authors. Last come 75 pages of notes, mainly references to the technical "literature." One's overall impression is of a voluminous body of technical, scientific research being distilled for the benefit of readers who, if they lack the technical sophistication re-

Reprinted from *Policies for Employment, Prices, and Exchange Rates,* vol. 11 of Carnegie-Rochester Series on Public Policy, eds. Karl Brunner and Allan H. Meltzer, Amsterdam: North-Holland Publishing Company, 1976, pp. 161–168, by permission.

quired to follow the reasoning, are at least able to understand the recommendations and act on them.

The policy objectives emerging from the study are standard, if somewhat vague: to "return to reasonable rates of growth" (p. 17), to "minimize average unemployment over the [five-year] recovery period as a whole" (p. 18), while avoiding "policies which will permit or accommodate high rates of inflation" (p. 18).

How can this be accomplished? To keep on the "correctly-judged recovery track" (p. 18) a "relatively active demand management policy may be needed" (p. 19). This policy will involve "publicly announced targets for the growth of monetary aggregates" (p. 18), "a fiscal policy geared to a budget target designed to avoid giving an inflationary stimulus over the medium term" (p. 18) together with "a prices and incomes policy" (p. 18). It is likely that these tools will be insufficient to keep us on the correctly-judged recovery track, in which case "there may be no alternative to policies which involve more detailed intervention" (p. 19), such as "quasi-selective action to influence broad categories of demand–business investment, housebuilding, inventories, consumption, etc." (p. 23), "additional employment in the public sector" (p. 23), "temporary subsidies to cover part of the cost of taking on new employees" (p. 29), or "vigorous steps to facilitate sectoral adjustment" (p. 29). "More vigorous energy policies are required" (p. 30). The authors also "agree on the desirability of building up security stocks of cereals" (p. 30). "Exchange rate policy may also have a useful role to play" (p. 18). This should be directed at achieving the "desired blend of flexibility and viscosity" (p. 32). Though the authors "are against going back to a formal pegging of exchange rates" (p. 31), "only time will tell how much collective management will be needed" (p. 32).

There does not, unfortunately, exist an "easy and simple formula" (p. 32) to assist those governments which are willing to take on the manipulation of the hundreds, perhaps thousands, of control variables which are implicit in these recommendations. "The right mix of policies will vary between countries" (p. 18). "Policy should be cautious" (p. 19). It should be "pursued in a pragmatic and moderately flexible way" (p. 20). Timing is crucial, so "governments should be ready to act reasonably promptly" (p. 19). Little wonder that "policy makers" are advised to "communicate and consult with one another as a matter

of intelligent self-interest'' (p. 30). One only wonders where they will
find the time.

A curious feature of the Report, not reflected in these citations, is
the fact that much of this advice is delivered in a tone of sad resig-
nation. The term ''market'' is used frequently, and though it is not
made entirely clear why, it appears that the authors view free markets
with a good deal of warmth, or perhaps nostalgia. Thus, they are
aware of ''all the difficulties and dangers'' (p. 19) involved in ''more
detailed intervention in the process of price and income determination'' (p. 27). Alas, ''there may be no alternative.'' They believe that
''it is essential that full use be made of the market mechanism'' (p.
30). (This followed ''more vigorous energy policies are required''[!])
They favor ''determined government efforts'' promoting ''better functioning of markets'' (p. 28). ''This calls in some areas for the removal
of obstacles to a freer play of market forces, in others for action by
the authorities to supplement market signals'' (p. 28). ''Capital markets
are generally innovative and competitive'' but, of course, ''regulations
[are] necessary to protect borrowers and lenders'' (p. 29). Apparently,
the ''better functioning of markets'' is also to be ''pursued in a pragmatic and moderately flexible way.''

The method of selective citation has its limitations, but I know of
no other way to convey the Report's undisciplined eclecticism. It
meanders through the long list of issues which have been defined in
popular debate as ''policy problems,'' accepting all as equally suited
to treatment by government action and equally amenable to economic
expertise, offering ambiguous and unsupported opinion on each. Nowhere can one discern a consistent set of economic principles underlying either the choice of questions to be addressed or the policy
stances which are recommended.

As an economist, I find this alarming, but not because I believe the
Report will in any direct way contribute to a worsening in economic
policy in the OECD countries. On the contrary, the Report is so nearly
vacuous that it will be difficult to tell which governments are attempting to follow its guidance and which are not. It is alarming because of
the vision of economics it presents, to the public and to us: an economics limited to the writing of safely ambiguous lines for insertion in
the speeches of treasury officials and central bankers. It is opportun-
ism posing as pragmatism.

What is the explanation for this? This seems to me a serious question, for the Committee includes, in addition to its chairman, some very distinguished economists. Indeed, two of these, Professors Giersch and Komiya, commented very unhappily on the Report's vagueness in their individual comments. In attempting to find an answer, I found it helpful to reexamine an earlier attempt to articulate to a general audience the main themes of Keynesian macroeconomic policy: Walter Heller's 1966 Godkin Lectures, published as *New Dimensions in Political Economy*.

Heller wrote with an authority which differs so sharply from anything in the main text of this OECD Report that almost any paragraph, inserted into the Report, would stand out as if printed in red ink. His lectures convey an infectious sense of the power of economic ideas to effect fundamental changes in the way noneconomists think about economic policy. Moreover, Heller was explicit as to the *source* of this authority: His lectures were built on the "bedrock," as he called it, of Keynesian macroeconomic theory. This theory and its wide acceptance permitted him to write "of the increasing power and reliability of the tools that economists bring to their trade; a growing consensus on the analytical core of economics; lessons of performance well done that will not easily be undone" (p. 14). It is a sad but accurate reflection on the decade since, that Part I of the OECD Report is titled: "What Went Wrong?"

What went wrong, in brief, is that Keynesian macroeconomic theory failed. Only when one reads the OECD Report as a response to this failure, do the causes of its deficiencies begin to become understandable and alternative responses suggest themselves. Before developing this theme, however, I want to clarify what I mean by the assertion that "Keynesian macroeconomic theory failed."

It is not uncommon to see the modifier "Keynesian" used to mean "consistent with the observed behavior of economic time series." Brevity aside, it is difficult to see the advantages of this usage, but certainly if this is what is meant by Keynesian theory, then one cannot say it has "failed." Similarly, it seems certain that Keynes's thought will continue to stimulate economic theorists in various and unpredictable ways for the foreseeable future, so much so that many economists will think of themselves as "Keynesians." In advance of seeing these developments, one cannot presume to pronounce them failed. I am here using the term "Keynesian" much more narrowly, to refer to the multiplier calculations which all of us understood Heller to be discussing and applying, together with the underlying if less precisely specified theory which provided guidance as to the range of circumstances under which these calculations might be expected to yield accurate answers.

Briefly, the idea was to begin with a target rate of unemployment (around 4 percent in the U.S.) for, say, the coming year, and use Okun's law to find the level of real GNP consistent with this target. Standard multipliers together with short-term forecasts of private spending behavior then yield estimates of fiscal policies which will attain the target. Now it is easy to dismiss these as "easy and simple formulas," but they are more appropriately described as meaningful and operational. Their advantage over a concept like "the correctly judged recovery track" is that they provide quantitative guidance and have the property that if two different economists are asked to work out the details, both will arrive at about the same answer.

In applying these formulas, several important qualifications were understood. First, the stimulus or restraint of a particular fiscal policy could be offset by interest rate movements. An interest-stabilizing monetary policy would need to accompany the fiscal policy selected and, in view of the difficulty in forecasting other forces acting on interest rates, this policy could not be specified in advance. Second, it was understood that if the unemployment target used to initiate these calculations were too low, stimulus would result in inflation, either in addition to or even instead of, a real output response. All of this is well developed in Heller's book, and, of course, in many other places.

I want to use the term "Keynesian theory" narrowly, focusing on the quantitative formulas which were actually used to generate policy advice, so as to be as clear as possible as to what I mean by failure. The theory failed in the sense that it produced quantitative answers that turned out to be wrong. Its *central* premises that monetary policy could stabilize interest rates and that inflation could be ignored at high rates of unemployment turn out to be sufficiently bad approximations to reality that the multipliers whose application rested on them are, quite simply, useless. This conclusion is not, I think, especially controversial and it is certainly not original. But it must be insisted on, as it is both important and difficult for us macroeconomists not to confuse the operational theory we would like to have with the theory we actually do have. In 1966, it seemed to many that we had one theory which could quantitatively link fiscal policy to economic performance with sufficient accuracy that it could be responsibly applied to policymaking. In 1977, we know we have none.

Yet in reading the OECD Report, the untrained reader would get exactly the opposite impression. Whereas Walter Heller claimed only to have a theory which could provide rough guides for full employment fiscal policy, the OECD authors appear to be in possession of a much more powerful theory, capable of dealing not merely with full employment and price stability, but with energy, agricultural inventories, exchange rates, securities regulation, and a host of other "problems," all of which they see as interrelated. How is it that the *failure* of the model on which the economic activism of the sixties was based can lead macroeconomists to offer advice on a much *wider* range of issues? The answer, I think, requires an understanding of the "conservative" role of Keynesian activism.

Whatever may be the intellectual roots of the general public approval of widespread government economic intervention, or "activism," it is clear that they antedate by far the introduction of Keynesian economics in the sense which I have sketched above. The role of Keynesian theory was to *rationalize* this activism, where I mean "rationalize" not in the sense of "apologize for," but rather in the sense of "bring order to" or "bring under rational control." The politically serious opponents of the application of Keynesian doctrine in the U.S., in the 1960s, were not advocates of fixed monetary growth rules and laissez faire; they were "structuralists" concerned about "automation," and they entered the debate armed with long lists of specific interventions in particular product and labor markets. The intended role of Keynesian theory was not to *introduce* activist policy, but to provide an alternative to a miscellany of incoherent and ineffective interventions. Heller looked forward to the time when, "if we manage to solve tolerably well the macroeconomic problem of keeping the economy moving along the path of its noninflationary potential, both President and public will have no choice but to learn their microeconomic lessons" (p. 49).

And if we do *not* solve this problem tolerably well? Heller did not say it, but the OECD Report does, with unmistakable clarity: Then we shall have to put off this lesson in microeconomics, accept the problem definitions offered us by Presidents and publics, and in the meantime do our best to persuade both that their confidence in us was not misplaced. The OECD Report represents not an extension and advance over the "easy and simple formulas" of the operational form of Keynesian economics, but rather a reversion to the unprincipled activism which Keynesian theory seemed to promise, for a brief period, to channel in a socially productive direction.

The OECD Report serves as a sobering lesson to economists who believed that when Keynesianism stumbled influence would somehow be passed to "monetarism." Indeed, some of the Report's oddest features result from the authors' attempts to digest recent monetarist criticism, to utilize it in support of a new, more sophisticated activism. The Report contains many monetarist sounding phrases, many references to "expectations," and insists (incredibly, given its "advice") that it opposes "fine tuning" in favor of more predictability in government policy. The idea seems to be that one can somehow synthesize Keynesian and monetarist views into a new framework as operational as that within which Heller operated. The fact is, however, that no one has worked such a synthesis out, and this fact shows, in lines like: "Governments can and should help to promote healthier expectations" (p. 19). The modern activist demand manager is in the position of a motorist lost in Illinois but possessing only a roadmap of Pennsylvania. It is no help to say: "Well, we must just modify our map to fit Illinois." The sentiment is attractively upbeat and "constructive," but it makes no sense.

The failure of this attempted synthesis to yield a coherent policy program is not, I believe, a reflection on the analytical abilities of the McCracken Committee but of the intractability of the problem itself. Professor Komiya puts this (and much else) clearly in his individual comments: "Dynamic optimisation in an uncertain world requires constant adjustment of the trajectory, as with rockets and satellites" (pp. 250–251). "For example, a statement such as 'the general case for "feeling one's way" along gingerly is rather compelling' is not acceptable to me. I believe it is most important that the medium-term targets themselves be revised frequently, taking into consideration latest developments which are to some extent different from what was predicted earlier" (p. 251).

The predictability obtained by the "public announcements of targets for the rate of growth of the money supply" (p. 20), desirable from a monetarist point of view, is both immaterial and undesirable from a Keynesian point of view. From a modern Keynesian viewpoint, target unemployment rates, interest rates, and inflation rates can be maintained (and hence made predictable) by constant adjustment of policy instruments to new shocks. Of course, this means that the policy instruments themselves will be unpredictable, but what difference does this make to anyone? The clarity of Komiya's remarks stems from the fact that he is working within an internally consistent (Keynesian) framework, and is willing to accept the policy implications which follow from it.

From a monetarist point of view, price stability and predictability *are* important, and are approximately attainable under a well-chosen and predictable monetary growth rule. On this view, unemployment and interest rates are unpredictable, and this is accepted as a fact of economic life, curable only at a prohibitive cost. These two views of the world are mutually incompatible, and lead, therefore, to quite different recommendations for policy. The McCracken Committee has tried to compile a program by taking some objectives which are desirable and attainable under a Keynesian view and advocating Keynesian policies to attain them. It has taken a few others which monetarists claim to know how to achieve, and advocated monetarist policies to do so. The hope, I suppose, was to please everyone, but the inevitable result was a report full of contradiction, partially but not fully hidden by ambiguous language.

It seems certain that economic policy in the OECD countries in the coming ten years will involve a wide variety of government interventions in particular sectors and industries. The particular interventions which emerge will, looked at in the right way, presumably exhibit some pattern. (For a social scientist, this much must be taken as an article of faith.) The chances that it will be *economic* theory which provides coherence to these policies must be judged, however, to be near zero. In these circumstances, the McCracken Committee is attempting to create the appearance that economic advisors are technically in control of developments, guiding them in a spirit of flexibility and pragmatism, supported by the technical research efforts of an entire profession.

Yet is it in the interest of economics that these political developments be viewed as being supported by a consensus of professional opinion? The main reason to answer in the negative, stressed in this review, is also the simplest: it is not true. There is also a second reason, of a more "pragmatic" nature. There is every reason to believe that the economic policies of the coming decade will, being guided by no economic principles, lead to very bad results. What can be the benefit of claiming for economic theory the blame for a collection of policies which in no way follow from it?

References

McCracken, P. et al. (1977). *Towards full employment and price stability: a report to the OECD by a group of independent experts*. Paris: Organization for Economic Co-operation and Development.

Heller, W. (1966). *New dimensions in political economy* (Godkin Lectures). Cambridge: Harvard University Press.

Methods
and Problems
in Business Cycle
Theory

1 Introduction

One of the functions of theoretical economics is to provide fully articulated, artificial economic systems that can serve as laboratories in
which policies that would be prohibitively expensive to experiment
with in actual economies can be tested out at much lower cost. To
serve this function well, it is essential that the artificial "model"
economy be distinguished as sharply as possible in discussion from
actual economies. Insofar as there is confusion between statements of
opinion as to the way we believe actual economies would react to
particular policies and statements of verifiable fact as to how the model
will react, the theory is not being effectively used to help us to see
which opinions about the behavior of actual economies are accurate
and which are not. This is the sense in which insistence on the "realism" of an economic model subverts its potential usefulness in thinking about reality. Any model that is well enough articulated to give
clear answers to the questions we put to it will necessarily be artificial,
abstract, patently "unreal."

Reprinted from *Journal of Money, Credit, and Banking* 12 (November 1980, Part 2)
by permission. Copyright 1980 American Enterprise Institute for Public Policy
Research.

This paper was prepared for the American Enterprise Institute Seminar on Ra-
tional Expectations, held on February 1, 1980, in Washington, D.C. Many of the
ideas in it were developed under the stimulus of Don Patinkin's course on the
History of Monetary Thought, taught at the University of Chicago, winter 1979.
Allan Drazen, Sherwin Rosen, and Nasser Saïdi provided very helpful criticism of
an earlier draft. A version of this paper entitled "Economic Policy and the Business
Cycle" was presented at The Ohio State University as the Money, Credit, and
Banking Lecture, on May 8, 1980.

At the same time, not all well-articulated models will be equally useful. Though we are interested in models because we believe they may help us to understand matters about which we are currently ignorant, we need to test them as useful imitations of reality by subjecting them to shocks for which we are fairly certain how actual economies, or parts of economies, would react. The more dimensions on which the model mimics the answers actual economies give to simple questions, the more we trust its answers to harder questions. This is the sense in which more "realism" in a model is clearly preferred to less.

On this general view of the nature of economic theory then, a "theory" is not a collection of assertions about the behavior of the actual economy but rather an explicit set of instructions for building a parallel or analogue system—a mechanical, imitation economy. A "good" model, from this point of view, will not be exactly more "real" than a poor one, but will provide better imitations. Of course, what one means by a "better imitation" will depend on the particular questions to which one wishes answers.[1]

In this paper I wish to review some recent developments in business cycle theory, taking the point of view suggested above. On this view, one would expect developments to arise from two quite different kinds of forces outside the subdisciplines of monetary economics or business cycle theory. Of these forces the most important, I believe, in this area and in economics generally, consists of purely technical developments that enlarge our abilities to construct analogue economies. Here I would include both improvements in mathematical methods and improvements in computational capacity. The neglect in traditional history of doctrine of this force for change in our thinking is a serious omission, and contributes to the common but mistaken sense that everything has been said before or "it's all in Marshall." Marshall's world was enough like ours and Marshall was an astute enough observer of his world that it is difficult to make general observations about our economy which do not have close precedent in some Marshallian observation about his. Our ability to construct analogue economies is, however, much greater, so that we have the capacity to study in detail market interactions about which Marshall could only conjecture.

The second source of theoretical developments is changes in the questions we want models to answer, or in the phenomena we wish to

understand or explain. To the journalist, each year brings unprecedented new phenomena, calling for unprecedented new theories
(where "theory" amounts to a description of the new phenomena
together with the assertion that they are new). Since there is an obvious sense in which this view carries some truth, I will not attempt
to refute it. I have argued elsewhere [23] that it is in our interest to
take exactly the opposite viewpoint in the study of business cycles, or
as close to an opposite view as we can get by with, and will maintain
this attitude below. The Great Depression, however, remains a formidable barrier to a completely unbending application of the view that
business cycles are all alike.

There is, of course, a third source of developments in our understanding of business cycles: the activities of economists specializing
in the field. Making the connections between the technical innovations
discovered by our colleagues and the difficult questions thrown at us
by the real world is no easy task, and I do not wish to minimize the
importance of these efforts. Yet I do think that both amateur and
professional historians have tended to go too far in attempting to
understand developments in monetary economics in terms entirely
internal to the subdiscipline, and that some leaning in the other direction may therefore be useful.

In the next section of the paper, I will review what seem to me the
main features of the Keynesian Revolution from the view set out
above. There is, I know, a growing feeling that such skeleton rattling
is becoming tiresome and old hat. Yet the advancement of theoretical
constructs from this era as though they were facts to be explained
continues to be a standard mode of debate in macroeconomics, suggesting the existence of still more deeply buried bones. The remainder
of the paper will be an attempt to diagnose more recent developments,
and perhaps even to extrapolate a little way into the future.

2 Business Cycle Theory through Keynes
Business cycle theory (as distinct from monetary economics) is mainly
a twentieth century product. For the most part, the major nineteenth
century economists set short-term fluctuations to one side in order to
focus attention on other issues. The general underlying idea (one might
call it a "natural rate hypothesis") must have been that one could
understand the main determinants of the average levels and rates of
growth in economic activity without understanding the fluctuations.

The task of making precise exactly which aspects of economic life had been so set aside by this fruitful nineteenth century strategy was undertaken at the beginning of the present century by Wesley Mitchell. Mitchell sought an empirical definition of business cycles through the systematic exclusion of those movements in economic time series that appeared likely to be explicable by then existing theory: the general level and pattern of growth in economic activity, and movements in individual series that seemed to arise from supply or demand conditions specific to individual markets. Neither of these exclusion principles is without ambiguity, so Mitchell proceeded cautiously and experimentally, trying a wide variety of data-summarizing techniques on the broadest available collection of series.

For two reasons, it is easy to forget the remarkable character of the regularities that Mitchell succeeded in discovering and documenting. On the one hand, we have lived with them for so long that they seem not so much the product of an imaginative and abstract way of organizing economic time series as simply "facts" that "everyone knows." On the other, they are regularities that, from the point of view most widely adopted since the 1930s, are not especially noteworthy or suggestive. The central finding, of course, was the similarity of all peacetime cycles with one another, once variation in duration was controlled for, in the sense that each cycle exhibits about the same pattern of co-movements among variables as do the others.

Not surprisingly, these empirical findings (guided theoretically in the sense I have indicated), corroborated by other evidence and a variety of less systematically organized impressions, stimulated a great deal of theoretical work. The idea that one could, with a firm empirical basis, speak of something like a "typical business cycle," divided into stages invariant in character (if not in duration) suggested that a substantial part of observed fluctuations might be explainable at a fairly abstract, or "simple" level, with a single theoretical explanation of *the* (i.e., of all) business cycle(s). This is the organizing principle Gottfried Haberler employed, for example, in *Prosperity and Depression* [11]. That so wide a variety of theories as discussed in this book could be fit with such ease into so tight a logical pattern is testimony, I think, to the power of the abstraction in the idea of a single or typical business cycle.

Another example of pre-Keynesian business cycle theory (here I suppose I am inexcusably abusing the language), which is useful for

two of my purposes, is John Maynard Keynes's *Treatise on Money*
[16]. Comparison of this work with the *General Theory* [17] is useful
both in illustrating the way that limits on our technical ability to
construct explicit theory limit our ability to think productively about
phenomena, and in illustrating the extent to which thinking in monetary economics is subject to outside or "real world" shocks.

The *Treatise* is sometimes described (and was even by Keynes[2]) as
a kind of initial, clumsy groping toward the ideas presented in the
General Theory. I suppose there must be some psychological truth to
this view, but emphasizing this aspect of the *Treatise* leads to a very
strained reading of what seems to me a fairly straightforward example
of pre-Depression thinking on business cycles. The main objective of
the book is to try to understand fluctuations in economic activity about
a secular trend in which real magnitudes are determined by the real
considerations of neoclassical value theory and in which nominal
prices are governed by the quantity theory of money. Keynes was
convinced, correctly I believe, that attempting to discuss fluctuations
in terms of fluctuations in *velocity* would not be productive and sought
instead a point of view that stressed changes in the composition of
expenditures over the cycle. He then showed that this point of view
could be reconciled with a quantity-theoretic view of longer-term
changes.

The accounting system, or set of notational conventions, embedded
in his "fundamental equations" was designed to facilitate this reconciliation, and served this function well enough. Beyond this, however,
Keynes's apparatus could not go. He states an identity and discusses
it; then he moves a term from the left to the right and discusses the
result of that operation; he defines a new variable in terms of previously defined ones and discusses that; then he talks about the identity
restated in terms of this new variable; and so on and on. The problem
is not that the underlying ideas are trivial, though the algebra certainly
is. On the contrary, the book deals in an intelligent way with the
fundamental problems business cycles raise. The difficulty is that
Keynes has no apparatus for dealing with these problems. Though he
discusses them verbally about as well as his contemporaries, neither
he nor anyone else was well enough equipped technically to move the
discussion to a sharper or more productive level.

The onset of the Great Depression did nothing to improve Keynes's
equipment for understanding the business cycle, viewed as a recurrent

sequence of booms and depressions. Instead, it permitted him to reformulate the problem itself as one of accounting for the level of output and employment at a point in time, as opposed to one of accounting for a particular pattern repeated in the time series. So reformulated, the problem could productively be studied simply by discarding an equation of static equilibrum theory (the labor supply curve) in contrast to the much more difficult task, undertaken in the *Treatise,* of supplementing this static theory with suitable short-run dynamics. This simpler problem was one on which progress could be made at the Marshallian level of analysis on which Keynes was a master.[3]

In reading the *General Theory* in this way, I am of course simply following the classic exegesis of John Hicks [14] (as well as Hicks's initial view of the *General Theory* as "slump economics") and Franco Modigliani's [29] pioneering step toward a "neoclassical synthesis." There is, certainly, much of interest in the *General Theory* that is not captured either in Hicks's diagram or Modigliani's equation system, a fact that led Axel Leijonhufvud (and others, perhaps even Hicks and Modigliani) to view the "Keynesian economics," which was later based mainly on these early interpretations, as a kind of vulgarization of the *General Theory*. While there is some truth, forcefully developed in Leijonhufvud's monograph [18], in this view, it misses what I believe to be the more essential truth, stressed in my introduction, that progress in economic thinking means getting better and better abstract, analogue economic models, not better verbal observations about the world.

The *General Theory* is, to be sure, a mine of acute and well-phrased remarks about the trials of conducting one's affairs in an uncertain world. Perhaps there are some, though I would not like to have the task of documenting this, that are both central to business cycle behavior and not prefigured in, say, Mitchell [28], or even a century before in Henry Thornton's writings. Certainly the likely, central role of profit expectations and investment behavior was stressed by virtually every economist who devoted more than superficial thought to business cycles. Economists who find Keynes's style congenial will continue to use his writings as Dennis Robertson did Lewis Carroll's, but surely there is more to the cumulative nature of economics than this!

To extract from the *General Theory* a simple graphical method for thinking about national income determination is not, I believe, to vulgarize its contribution. Vulgarity in economics would more appropriately be defined as criticizing or caricaturing an abstract (and hence potentially useful) model because it leaves something out.

3   The Neoclassical Synthesis

The *General Theory* was, if the argument of the preceding section is accurate, more successful than the *Treatise* not because of theoretical advances within monetary economics but because the event of the Great Depression permitted Keynes to restate the problem posed by the business cycle into a form such that the theoretical methods at his disposal admitted genuine progress. It was a fortunate historical accident that at about the same time, and for reasons unrelated to contemporaneous economic events, technical advances in statistical and economic theory occurred which transformed "Keynesian economics" into something very different from, and much more fruitful than, anything Keynes himself had foreseen.

One of these advances, which one may date from the work of Tinbergen [47] or perhaps from Slutsky [44], was the idea that one might describe an economy as a system of stochastically disturbed difference equations, the parameters of which could be estimated from actual time series. Indeed, in describing a "business cycle theory" as a "fully articulated imitation economy," I have presupposed the objective of these early econometricians to have by now become common property. The rapid progress of the econometric models toward something that appeared close to imitative perfection was, I have argued elsewhere [22], illusory. Sargent and I [26] have subsequently argued in some detail that useful analogue systems will not be found among variations within the class of these pioneering econometric models. The issues touched on in these earlier papers still seem to me at the center of the question of what we can hope for from a theory of business cycles, but there is no reason to take them up again here.

The second of these advances, like the first, has roots the disentangling of which would challenge an objective scholar's career. Instead, I will take a subjective course, identifying this development with Paul Samuelson's *Foundations of Economic Analysis* [36] and advising the more serious historian to pursue the copious references in that text.

In so doing, I follow Don Patinkin's practice in his *Money, Interest, and Prices* [32], perhaps the most refined and influential version of what I mean by the term "neoclassical synthesis." Samuelson advanced, in the first place, the main ingredients for a mathematically explicit theory of general equilibrium: an artificial system in which households and firms jointly solve explicit, "static," maximum problems, taking prices as parametrically given. He took for granted that such equilibria were nonvacuous in the mathematical sense, a supposition that was later confirmed under fairly broad conditions. Such equilibria can be shown to be equivalent to Pareto-optimal resource allocations.

I refer to this theory as "static" following Samuelson, despite the ambiguity involved in specifying an empirical counterpart to this modifier. The underlying idea seems to be taken from physics, as referring to a system "at rest." In economics, I suppose such a static general equilibrium corresponds to a prediction as to how an economy would behave should external shocks remain fixed over a long period, so that households and firms would adjust to facing the same set of prices over and over again and attune their behavior accordingly. It is not difficult to think of modifying this idea of "rest" to accommodate slow and fairly predictable secular changes, and this accommodation will be taken for granted in what follows, as it seems to have been in the monetary economics literature.

Now economies experiencing recurrent business cycles are quite evidently not "at rest" so that static general equilibrium theory, though a genuine model in the sense of being explicit and complete, is not a good imitation of reality for the purpose of understanding these events. To deal with this disparity, the *Foundations* offered a solution too (though there advanced, it seems to me, as an answer to an entirely different kind of question[4]). Samuelson proposed a dynamic model of price adjustment in which the rates of change of prices offered in each market were related to the level of "excess demands" in all markets. Whatever the history or underlying objectives of this model of price dynamics (and, implicitly, of quantity dynamics) this theory introduced sufficient additional (to those needed to describe tastes and technology) parameters to the equilibrium system so that, given an initial shock to the system, a wide variety of paths were consistent with its eventual return to equilibrium.

This introduction of additional (to those used to describe preferences and technology) free parameters held out the promise that one could construct a theoretical system the stationary point of which was a general equilibrium in the neoclassical sense but whose movements, out of equilibrium, might replicate the "Keynesian" behavior captured so well by the econometric models. Spelling out these connections became the main program of theoretical research in macroeconomics from the 1940s through the 1960s. The task seemed to involve somehow motivating the introduction of "money" and other financial elements into "real" general equilibrium theory, modifying the purely theoretical system in the direction of the applied econometric theory, and simultaneously reworking the structural equations of the econometric models so as to clarify their theoretical underpinnings. The objective of the enterprise was widely agreed to be "unification" of the two types of theories into which Keynesian ideas were translated in the 1930s and 1940s.

Reviewing the vast amount of useful economics that came out of this attempt at unification would be much too ambitious a task for this paper. Instead, I will make a few general remarks on the attitudes toward stabilization policy that were fostered by the neoclassical synthesis. First, since the synthesis was formed by the addition of free parameters to a static general equilibrium system, the general class of models it suggested admitted a wide variety of possibilities for business cycle behavior. Thus it seemed a framework open enough to contain virtually any point of view toward policy as a special case, an attractive feature to the nondogmatic. I suspect this is one reason why those economists, like Milton Friedman, who made no use of this framework were treated with some impatience by its proponents. Why could he not simply specify which particular parameter values corresponded to the case *he* believed to fit the facts, let others do likewise, and then the matter could be handed over to the econometricians for a definitive resolution?

Second, since fluctuations about the system's equilibrium represented disequilibrium behavior, standard welfare propositions could be applied only to the average behavior of the system, and not to fluctuations about the average. This left one free to apply other criteria in evaluating stabilization policies: "gaps" instead of "triangles," as James Tobin [50] puts it. The general idea was to use policy tools to keep the actual path of the system "close" in one sense or another to its equilibrium path. Proponents of various stabilization policies were thus free of the burden under which the ordinary welfare economist labors—of "justifying" intervention by some specific "market failure" and tailoring the nature of the intervention to the nature of the failure. Under the neoclassical synthesis, the business cycle was *defined* to be market failure, and any policy that promised to move the system toward "full employment equilibrium" was viewed as an improvement.

So widely endorsed was the general idea of the neoclassical synthesis described above that its central constructs have become a common shorthand for describing "the facts." Now when the success, actual and potential, of this synthesis is once again at issue, these constructs no longer facilitate discussion, but rather get in the way. Two examples will illustrate what I mean.

The first is from James Tobin [50], who in summarizing what he calls "the central propositions of the *General Theory*" begins with: "In modern industrial capitalist societies, prices and wages respond slowly to excess demand or supply, especially slowly to excess supply. Over a long short run, ups and downs of demand register in output; they are far from completely absorbed in prices." He goes on to cite evidence for this proposition from British economic behavior in the 1920s and the U.S. Great Depression.

What I take Tobin to mean by this complex proposition is something like the following. *If* one were to try to interpret the British experience of the 1920s, America's of the 1930s, and business cycles generally, in terms of a static general equilibrium (allowing for secular trend) and dynamic adjustment in prices of the sort described by Samuelson, then we would need to postulate "slow" (say, half-life of many quarters) coefficients describing wage and price responses to excess supply. Qualified in this way, the statement seems to me a true one. Yet qualified in this way, Tobin's argument cannot shed light on the desirability of attempting to account for business cycles within the framework provided by the neoclassical synthesis as opposed to using some other framework, which is the intended subject of his paper.

In a similar vein, Franco Modigliani [30] characterizes Thomas Sargent's [38] econometric model of the U.S. as one in which employment declines can be accounted for only by "severe attack[s] of contagious laziness." He goes on to say that "equally serious objections apply to Friedman's modeling of the commodity market as a perfectly competitive one . . . and to his treatment of labor as a homogeneous commodity traded in an auction market, so that, at the going wage there is never any excess demand by firms or excess supply by workers."

As in Tobin in [50], Modigliani is here thinking of a competitive equilibrium in the static sense of the neoclassical synthesis, so that an equilibrium decrease in employment would necessarily have to arise either from a spontaneous technology or taste shift ("an attack of laziness") and so that a model in which labor markets are continuously cleared is patently in contradiction with observed employment and unemployment fluctuations. Later on, he refers to the "substantial agreement that in the United States the Hicksian mechanism [his overly modest term for what I am here calling the neoclassical synthesis] is fairly effective in limiting the effect of shocks and that the response of wages and prices to excess demand and supply will also work *gradually* toward eliminating largely, if not totally, any effect on employment." "These inferences are supported by simulations with econometric models like the MPS."

Now both Modigliani and Tobin are, in the papers from which I have quoted, explicitly defending (via the time-honored tactic of counterattack) their preferred framework for studying business cycles against "monetarist" or "rational expectations" alternatives. Yet both take the correctness of the framework they defend as *given* and use it as a point of departure in criticizing alternatives. The failure of a simulation of Sargent's econometric model to reproduce the results of simulations of the MPS model is viewed as evidence that Sargent's model does not "fit the facts!" It seems clear that debate at this level cannot advance matters.

4 Recapitulation and Assessment
It will be useful at this stage to attempt a summary of the theses advanced in the sections above. I began by sketching a view of an economic theory (by which I mean a theory that purports to account for specific observed and as yet unobserved aspects of behavior) as a mechanical, analogue economy. It follows from this view that developments in a particular substantive field, such as the study of business cycles, will be influenced strongly by technical developments in our ability to construct explicit model economies, and by real world de-

velopments that alter our view as to the questions we think such models can and ought to be able to help us to answer.

Viewed from this perspective, the main features of the Keynesian Revolution and the neoclassical synthesis into which it evolved in the United States seemed to be the following. They include, in the first instance, the onset of the Great Depression and the consequent shift of attention from explaining a recurrent pattern of ups and downs to explaining an economy apparently stuck in an interminable down. Keynes's *General Theory* is then seen as, first, a recognition of the importance of this change of circumstances, and second, at least as read by Hicks, Modigliani, and others, as the proposal for a simple aggregative account of output and employment determination at a point in time. Developments in British Keynesian macroeconomics since the 1930s give, I think, a reasonably accurate view of what would have become of the revolution had these elements and no others been involved.

In the United States and on the continent, two other elements were involved in essential ways, both of a technical character. One was the development of explicit stochastic descriptions of economic systems. The other was the development of a static general equilibrium theory together with an associated theory of disequilibrium price dynamics. These elements were rapidly combined to provide rigor and clarity to Keynes's account of short-term equilibrium determination, and to add to this theory explicit dynamic elements, which permitted it to fit actual time series in a fairly literal way. Moreover, they held out a definite promise for additional "unification," a task that occupied some of the profession's best talent for three decades.

Toward the close of the 1960s, this orderly progress toward unity was disturbed by two theoretical developments. One of these, Milton Friedman's presidential adddress to the American Economic Association [8], was written from the "monetarist" viewpoint which had continued to pursue the study of business cycles along the line initiated by Mitchell. The other, Edmund Phelps's [33] and the subsequent "Phelps volume" [34] seemed initially an attempt to complete the unity promised by the neoclassical synthesis through discovery of a microeconomic foundation to the labor market and product pricing side of the standard models. However differently motivated, the papers of Friedman and Phelps both carried the clear implication that "excess demand" was neither necessary nor sufficient for price or

wage inflation, and that *any* average inflation rate was consistent theoretically with *any* level of unemployment. This conclusion, arrived
at via impeccable neoclassical reasoning, conflicted with the prediction
of a real output-inflation trade-off, which was at the center of all
models based on the neoclassical synthesis.

In attempts to formalize the Friedman-Phelps natural rate hypothesis, it was soon discovered that then-conventional ways of modeling
expectations-formation were both central to the issues involved and
fundamentally defective. John Muth's [31] hypothesis of rational expectations, formulated originally to deal with an entirely different set
of substantive questions, turned out to be a natural way to formalize
the Friedman-Phelps arguments. Subsequent research in macroeconomics has revealed the sweeping implications of this hypothesis, and
the extent to which it proves subversive of the main positive and
policy presumptions underlying the neoclassical synthesis.

At the present time, these developments retain enough novelty to
make them difficult to assess with detachment. Yet I believe it is
possible, indeed necessary, to attempt to understand them in terms
similar to those I have used in trying to understand earlier developments in monetary economics and business cycle theory. If it was in
fact the conjunction of real world shifts in the questions to which
people wanted answers together with technical improvements in economic theory which led to the major rethinking of business cycle
theory that I have been here calling the neoclassical synthesis, then
it is not unlikely that more recent developments can be similarly
attributed to forces to these two categories.

The real world event from the recent past which first comes to mind
is the combination of inflation with higher than average unemployment
that characterized the 1970s. While consistent with the Friedman-
Phelps logic, these events were badly misforecast with 1960s vintage
econometric models. To what extent this forecast error should be
interpreted as a "fatal" error in models based on the neoclassical
synthesis or simply as one suggesting some modifications is not so
easy to determine.[5] The idea that virtually all of this period was
characterized by "excess supply" and hence that virtually all of the
inflation must be attributable to "supply shocks" does not seem to be
worth taking seriously and I have yet to see a quantitative case for
this position made. (This is, of course, not to say that there have not
been serious supply shocks over the decade.) On the other hand, some

recent models stressing the role of contractually fixed nominal prices
permit prices to respond to secular or "anticipated" demand without
"excess demand" necessarily ever emerging, while retaining a "short-
term" role for "excess demands" and supplies.[6] Perhaps these may
be interpreted as an attempt to reconcile the experiences of the 1970s
with *some* key features of the neoclassical synthesis. In short, events
of the 1970s have been provocative, but perhaps not decisive.

A less spectacular but perhaps ultimately more influential feature of
post-World War II time series has been the return to a pattern of
recurrent, roughly similar "cycles" in Mitchell's sense. If the magnitude of the Great Depression dealt a serious blow to the idea of the
business cycle as a repeated occurrence of the "same" event, the
postwar experience has to some degree restored respectability to this
idea. If the Depression continues, in some respects, to defy explanation by existing economic analysis (as I believe it does), perhaps it is
gradually succumbing to the Law of Large Numbers.

These new observations have been influential (as new observations
should be to empirical researchers), but it seems to me the main
outside influences have been, and will continue to be, changes in
available theoretical methods. In business cycle theory, it appears not
to be the problem that changes but rather the way we look at it. Of
changes in methods, certainly the most central have been postwar
developments in general equilibrium theory.

5   Postwar General Equilibrium Theory

The general equilibrium theory which Modigliani, Patinkin, and others
hoped to integrate with an operational business cycle theory did not
remain frozen in the form it had assumed in the 1930s and 1940s.
Indeed, much of what has since developed was sketched out in some
detail by John Hicks, in *Value and Capital* [15]. There Hicks proposed
reinterpreting the maximum problems solved by firms and households
as involving choices over sequences of dated goods, with choices of
specific future goods interpreted as plans and with their prices interpreted as price expectations. Hicks noted that if future goods were
viewed as contracted for in advance, the prices of future goods would
simply be known numbers, and general equilibrium in a dynamic economy, so modeled, would be equivalent formally to equilibrium in a
"static" model. Hicks believed that the presence of uncertainty in real
situations rendered a model stressing forward contracts inapplicable

in most dynamic situations of real interest, and so put most of his emphasis on a discussion of a sequence of "spot" equilibria.

Kenneth Arrow [2] and Gerard Debreu [5] observed that uncertainty could be incorporated into "static" general equilibrium theory by exactly the same device that Hicks proposed to incorporate the passage of time: namely by indexing goods both by the date on which they are to be exchanged *and* by the (perhaps stochastically selected) "state of nature" contingent on which the exchange is to occur. Like Hicks's, the innovation was not initially an extension of general equilibrium theory in a mathematical sense, but rather the observation that the *range of applicability* of this body of theory could be vastly broadened by some ingenuity in specifying what is meant by a commodity.

One way to interpret a "contingent claim" equilibrium is as a description of an economy in which all state-contingent prices are determined in advance, in the clearing of a single grand futures market. On this interpretation, individual traders may assess the probabilities of the occurrence of future states of nature, but with prices determined in advance, the issue of price *expectations* does not arise. Alternatively, one may sometimes (though certainly not always) think of a contingent-claim equilibrium as being determined via a sequence of "spot" markets, in which current prices are set given certain expectations about future prices. On this second interpretation, one needs a principle to reconcile the price distributions implied by the market equilibrium with the distributions used by agents to form their own views of the future. John Muth [31] noted that the general principle of the absence of rents in competitive equilibrium carried the particular implication that these distributions could not differ in a systematic way. His term for this latter hypothesis was rational expectations.[7]

As originally proposed by Arrow and Debreu, this contingent-claim interpretation of a competitive equilibrium model took all information to be simultaneously and freely available to all traders, and many important results (e.g., the extension of the main theorems of welfare economics to uncertain environments) are crucially dependent on this assumption. It was soon recognized by many researchers that the idea of viewing a commodity as a function of stochastically determined shocks is an invaluable one also in situations in which information differs in various ways among traders. Indeed, it is this idea that permits one to use economic theory to make precise what one *means* by information, and to determine how it is valued economically.

When originally proposed, the contingent-claim formulation tended
to be viewed as highly esoteric and remote from practice, no doubt
because it arose at the most abstract end of the discipline. However,
this formulation rapidly and easily absorbed and clarified a variety of
special results in the economics of uncertainty, and facilitated their
unification and extension. It is now in standard use in virtually every
applied field of economics. It is also in use, though I would not as yet
say "standard," in business cycle theory.

Would it not be surprising if this were not so? The idea that speculative elements play a key role in business cycles, that these events
seem to involve agents reacting to imperfect signals in a way which,
after the fact, appears inappropriate, has (as I remarked in section 3)
been a commonplace in the verbal tradition of business cycle theory
at least since Mitchell [28]. Now for the first time we have at our
disposal methods for constructing artificial model economic systems
in which these elements play a well-defined role. It is now entirely
practical to view price and quantity paths that follow complicated
stochastic processes as equilibrium "points" in an appropriately specified space. This is a development that will make a difference in the
way we think.

To ask why the monetary theorists of the 1940s did not make use
of the contingent-claim view of equilibrium is, it seems to me, like
asking why Hannibal did not use tanks against the Romans instead of
elephants. There is no reason to view our ability to think as being any
less limited by available technology than is our ability to act (if, indeed,
this distinction can be defended). The historical reason for modeling
price dynamics as responses to static excess demands goes no deeper
than the observation that the theorists of that time did not know any
other way to do it. It is, of course, conceivable that theorists in full
command of newer methods will nonetheless conclude that there are
sound reasons for continuing to use the older technology for some
purposes (just as there are some purposes for which we continue to
prefer elephants to tanks). This seems to me most unlikely if the
purpose is to understand business cycles. That a powerful model-
building apparatus specifically designed to help us deal with problems
involving choice under uncertainty should simply be passed over in
favor of an older apparatus which is (for the most part) incapable of
taking these problems into account,[8] would, should it occur, certainly

refute rather decisively the point of view toward the development of economic thought that I have advanced in this paper.

6 Future Developments

Even if one is persuaded, as am I, that the theoretical advances sketched in the last section will have a major impact on our thinking about business cycles, it is obviously impossible to forecast with any accuracy the form this impact will take. What is already clear, however, is that certain characteristics of earlier theories, adopted originally (I have argued) for convenience, are no longer analytically necessary. In particular, it is possible to construct systems in competitive equilibrium, in a contingent-claim sense, which exhibit a vast variety of dynamic behavior. The idea that an economic system in equilibrium is in any sense "at rest" is simply an anachronism.

For a modern theoretical economist, surely the most natural way to read the original Friedman and Phelps articles is as attempts to conjecture some of the properties that a successful general-equilibrium model of business cycles will be likely to possess. Indeed, Friedman refers to the natural rate of unemployment as "the level that would be ground out by the Walrasian system of general equilibrium equations, provided there is imbedded in them the actual structural characteristics of the labor and commodity markets" though he is not able to put such a system down on paper. In his introduction to [34], Phelps sketches a specific general equilibrium system in some detail. Much of the research that has been done since may be interpreted as efforts to cast these ideas more explicitly into the contingent-claim framework.

In recent years, a number of economists have worked to develop what I prefer to call *equilibrium* models of business cycles.[9] These are models that utilize the contingent claim point of view described in the last section in an essential way, and in which prices and quantities are taken to be always in equilibrium. In these models, the concepts of excess demands and supplies play no observational role and are identified with no observed magnitudes. In contrast to the static equilibrium models available in the 1940s, equilibrium models of this new class seem to do about as well in fitting time series as do models based on the neoclassical synthesis.

Now it is clear that these new equilibrium models can, in principle, be "synthesized" with a Samuelson-like model of disequilibrium price adjustment just as could the older equilibrium models.[10] This must be true of *any* equilibrium model. Moreover, since a synthesis of this kind involves the addition to the model of free parameters, the synthesized version cannot fit facts worse than the original equilibrium version on which it is based. One seems to be led, then, not to equilibrium models as a class, but to a vastly larger class of synthesized disequilibrium models. Now I am attracted to the view that it is useful, in a general way, to be hostile toward theorists bearing free parameters, so that I am sympathetic to the idea of simply capitalizing this opinion and calling it a Principle. In evaluating economic theories that claim to be useful in guiding policy in the way sketched in my introductory section, however, there are important substantive considerations supporting such an attitude of hostility, which seem to me to put it on a sounder basis that can be afforded by a general prejudice in favor of parsimony. I will try to spell these considerations out.

Our task as I see it (to restate my introduction somewhat more bluntly and operationally) is to write a FORTRAN program that will accept specific economic policy rules as "input" and will generate as "output" statistics describing the operating characteristics of time series we care about, which are predicted to result from these policies. For example, one would like to know what average rate of unemployment would have prevailed since World War II in the United States had Ml grown at 4 percent per year during this period, other policies being as they were. (One would like to know the answers to a lot of other questions, too, but this came to mind first, and gives a concrete idea of where this argument is headed.) It must be taken for granted, it seems clear, that simply attempting various policies that may be proposed on actual economies and watching the outcome must not be taken as a serious solution method: Social Experiments on the grand scale may be instructive and admirable, but they are best admired at a distance. The idea, if the marginal social product of economics is positive, must be to gain some confidence that the component parts of the program are in some sense reliable prior to running it at the expense of our neighbors.

How is confidence of this sort earned? This is a question on the answer to which economists are fairly well agreed, yet I cannot recall where I have seen the nature of this agreement articulated. The central idea is that *individual* responses can be documented relatively cheaply,

occasionally by direct experimentation, but more commonly by means
of the vast number of well-documented instances of individual reactions to well-specified environmental changes made available "naturally" via censuses, panels, other surveys, and the (inappropriately
maligned as "casual empiricism") method of keeping one's eyes open.
Without such means of documenting patterns of behavior, it seems
clear that the FORTRAN program proposed above cannot be written.
Suppose, on the contrary, that such means are available, or that we
have some ability to predict how individual behavior will respond to
specified changes. How, if at all, can such knowledge be translated
into knowledge of the way an entire *society* is likely to react to changes
in its environment?

To be more concrete, consider the question: How will a monkey
that has not been fed for a day react to a banana tossed into its cage?
I take it we have sufficient previously established knowledge about
the behavior of monkeys to make this prediction with some confidence. Now alter the question to: How will five monkeys that have
not been fed for a day react to one banana thrown into their cage?
This is an entirely different question, on which the knowledge of
preferences (each monkey wants as much of the banana as he can get)
and technology (banana consumption in total cannot exceed unity)
gives us scarcely a beginning. We clearly need to know something
about the way a group of monkeys interacts, in addition to their
individual preferences, in order to have any hope of progress on this
complicated question.

People interested in the way groups of monkeys solve problems of
allocating scarce resources satisfy their curiosity by assembling groups
of monkeys and tossing them scarce resources. I have taken it as
given that we economists cannot proceed in this way, yet the allocation
of scarce resources is something we are admired for being experts at.
Economics is sometimes characterized as the working out of the implications of the idea that individuals pursue their self-interest, yet we
have just observed how empty an idea this is, applied in isolation to
even the most trivial animal experiment. Can we imagine that it gains
power in some mysterious way when applied to human societies with
millions of participants?

The ingredient omitted so far is, of course, *competition*. Let us take
our banana, cut it into five pieces, give each of the five monkeys one
piece, and impose on them the rule they may interact only by exchang-

ing banana pieces for minutes of backscratching, at some fixed rate.
(I confess to having no idea how this imposition might be effected in
practice.) Now in this situation, and given sufficient information as to
how individual monkeys are willing to trade-off backscratching and
banana eating, we can predict the outcome of this interaction (equilibrium price and quantities exchanged), at least given sufficient computational ability. Notice that, having specified the rules by which
interaction occurs in detail, and in a way that introduces *no* free
parameters, the ability to predict individual behavior is nonexperi-
mentally transformed into the ability to predict group behavior.[11]

I have emphasized that it is the hypothesis of competitive equilibrium which permits group behavior to be predicted from knowledge of
individual preferences and technology without the addition of any free
parameters. This needs further illustration, in contexts closer to our
interests than animal experiments. Employment and nominal wages
are, in an immediate sense, determined by some very complicated
labor market interactions involving employees and employers. It is
possible, we know, to mimic the aggregate outcome of this interaction
fairly well in a competitive equilibrium way, in which wages and
manhours are generated by the interaction of "representative" households and firms.[12] The parameters in this model describe either households' willingness to substitute goods and leisure contemporaneously
and intertemporally or the technology available to firms.

It is also possible, in the manner of the neoclassical synthesis, to fit
a quite different model—a Phillips curve—to these same aggregate
outcomes. Here one also uses a parametric description (different, of
course, in this case) of preferences and technology and, *in addition,*
a parameter describing the speed with which an "auctioneer" adjusts
the nominal wage to excess demands and supplies. Now the introduction of a fictional auctioneer is not a defect of this second way of
looking at things, relative to the first. All models are fictions according
to the viewpoint I am taking, and in any case, an auctioneer is presupposed in the first model too, but one operating so rapidly that he
is not noticed. Nor can it be a disadvantage of this second way of
modeling wage and employment determination that it cannot fit data
as well as the first: the addition of a free parameter cannot hurt in this
sense.

The disadvantage of the second model is this: there is no way to obtain information on the rate at which the wage is adjusted, this added parameter, except by observing the entire system in operation. If this parameter changes in reaction to changes elsewhere in the system (as we know that in fact it does), there is no way to predict the nature of these responses short of experimenting with the system as a whole. Yet it is precisely the attempt to avoid having to do this that leads us to use economic theory in the first place.

In the case of the equilibrium account of wage and employment determination, parameters describing the degree of intertemporal substitutability do the job (in an empirical sense) of the parameter describing auctioneer behavior in the Phillips curve model. On these parameters, we have a wealth of inexpensively available data from census cohort information, from panel data describing the reactions of individual households to a variety of changing market conditions, and so forth. In principle (and perhaps before too long, in practice, for there is a good deal of very promising research going on on just this topic[13]) these crucial parameters can be estimated independently from individual as well as aggregate data. If so, we will know what the aggregate parameters mean, we will understand them in a sense that disequilibrium adjustment parameters will *never* be understood. This is exactly why we care about the ''microeconomic foundations'' of aggregate theories.[14]

Researchers familiar with current work alluded to in the preceding paragraph will appreciate the extent to which it describes hopes for the future, not past accomplishments. These hopes might, without strain, be described as hopes for a kind of unification, not dissimilar in spirit from the hope for unification which informed the neoclassical synthesis. What I have tried to do above is to stress the empirical (as opposed to the aesthetic) character of these hopes, to try to understand how such quantitative evidence about behavior as we may reasonably expect to obtain in society as it now exists might conceivably be transformed into quantitative information about the behavior of imagined societies, different in important ways from any which have ever existed. This may seem an intimidatingly ambitious way to state the goal of an applied subfield of a marginally respectable science, but is there a less ambitious way of describing the goal of business cycle theory?

7 Concluding Remarks

This paper has been an attempt to understand and clarify the nature and origins of some recent developments in business cycle theory. In taking an historical point of view, it may be that I have inadvertently adopted the Marxist tactic of describing what I would like to have happen as something that History has already ordained. I have, certainly, emphasized what seems to me the decisive importance of improvements in the analytical equipment we have at our disposal, but with the intent of stressing the expansion of our opportunities these improvements offer, not particular directions they dictate. For this reason, I have tried to avoid claiming too much for the particular examples of equilibrium models that now exist. There is no point in letting tentative and, I hope, promising first steps harden into positions that must be defended at all cost.

If an historical approach cannot guarantee an ability to foresee the future, it does seem to me to aid in distinguishing those elements in past thinking that remain useful from those that do not. The neoclassical synthesis arose, as does all useful economics, from a compromise between what we would like to have known and what the methods at our disposal seemed to make it possible to know. Nothing could be more detrimental to the productive use of methods more recently developed than to view the categories and constructs that were produced by this compromise as constraints on the way we think about business cycles today.

Notes

1. I do not know the background of this view of theory as physical analogue, nor do I have a clear idea as to how widely shared it is among economists. An immediate ancestor of my condensed statement is [43].

2. In the preface to the *General Theory,* pp. vi–vii.

3. Again, from the preface to the *General Theory,* p. viii: "The difficulty lies, not in the new ideas, but in escaping from the old ones." But it would take more work, I know, than locating a single quotation to convince a sceptic on this point.

4. Samuelson's correspondence principle proposed the use of his stability theory as a criterion to aid in deciding which stationary equilibrium points might actually be observed, and which not: "How many times has the reader seen an egg standing on its end?" Here the idea is clearly to decide which static egg-equilibria are empirically interesting, not to offer an empirically useful dynamic model of rolling or wobbling eggs. Indeed, Gordon and

Hynes's [10] criticism of the use of Samuelsonian disequilibrium price dynamics as a description of observed price paths received central support from [37].

5. An argument for fatality is in [26].

6. See [7, 35, 45]. One way to interpret these models is as attempts to modify the price dynamics of the neoclassical synthesis so as to permit monetary expansion to share at least *some* of the blame for the 1970s inflation with OPEC, etc. (and for inflation in Argentina, Chile, and innumerable other examples in which high inflation has been associated with subtrend real output and employment). Another way is discussed in note 14.

7. Muth formulated the hypothesis of rational expectations using the Simon [42]-Theil [46] idea of *certainty-equivalence* though his introductory discussion makes it clear that the idea is applicable in situations where certainty-equivalence may not be. Its basic logic is not difficult to restate within the Arrow-Debreu contingent claim framework: see [24] for one example.

8. I do not mean to suggest that considerations of choice under uncertainty played no role in the neoclassical synthesis. Both portfolio theory and inventory theory were used, for example, to motivate particular hypotheses about demands for money and other assets [4, 48, 49]. Nevertheless, the concept of *market equilibrium* used was that of static, deterministic general equilibrium theory.

9. Some early examples are [20, 21, 41, 38, 3]. Of these, only [20] utilizes the contingent-claim general equilibrium formalism throughout. The others use linear approximations, motivated informally by reference to the contingent-claim models. It seems clear that econometrically operational models will necessarily have to rely on liberal use of approximate, linear methods.

10. I have in mind the line of research described by Malinvaud in [27] and recently surveyed by Drazen in [6].

The lesson that two models may be "close" in the sense of fitting the same data about equally well yet have radically different implications for policy was brought home forcefully in [41] and elaborated in a more general way in [39].

11. This is a case for the use of explicit game theory in general, not for the use of competitive theory in particular. The case for the use of competitive theory in modeling business cycles would, if I were to develop it here, be based entirely on convenience, or on the limits imposed on us by available technology for working out the implications of other equilibrium definitions.

This qualification to the text must also qualify the claim that equilibrium theory requires the introduction of no free parameters other than those used to describe individual tastes and technology. That is to say, insofar as there is considerable latitutde as to *which* equilibrium concept is being used, one can think of selecting one of them as the fixing of a "free parameter." This does not seem to me a serious issue in practice at the present time, but one can imagine it becoming so through further development in theories of noncompetitive games.

This observation that noncompetitive games may someday prove to be of use in business cycle theory, which seems difficult to quarrel with, is sometimes used to rationalize wholly arbitrary models unrelated to *any* well defined game. I hope it is clear that this note is not intended as a defense of this practice.

12. See [25] though parts of this study need updating. A modern replication of this study would utilize ideas in [40, 12].

13. For example, [9, 13, 19, 1]. I hasten to add that these and related studies were not motivated or intended as support or confirmation of Rapping's and my results, nor is at all clear at this stage that they are leading to estimates consistent with ours. My point is simply that *equilibrium* aggregate models carry implications for a variety of other kinds of data, raising the possibility of independent confirmation (and contradiction) of estimates from aggregative time series.

14. Do the models cited in note 6 constitute a third class, intermediate to those just discussed? I do not believe so. If contract length in these papers is viewed simply as a free parameter (as note 6 interprets them) then this parameter is as unintelligible (in the sense of this paragraph) as that describing the rapidity of an auctioneer's adjustment. If, on the other hand, contract length is viewed as emerging from a decision problem solved by agents then these models, so elaborated, would be equilibrium models (with a different commodity space than those discussed above) and would not necessarily serve to reinforce the point of view toward policy taken by the neoclassical synthesis.

Whether this observation should be taken as severe criticism of contract-based models depends, of course, on one's views as to the likelihood of our being able to account for business cycles using *no* free adjustment parameters. Certainly this question must be regarded as open at present, and however it may be resolved, it must surely be the case that models with one or two free adjustment parameters represent analytical progress over models with dozens, or hundreds, of them.

References

1. Altonji, Joseph G., and Orley C. Ashenfelter. "Wage Movements and the Labor Market Equilibrium Hypothesis." Princeton University, Industrial Relations Section, Working Paper No. 130, November 1979.

2. Arrow, Kenneth J. "The Role of Securities in the Optimal Allocation of Risk-Bearing." *Review of Economic Studies,* 31 (April 1964), 91–96.

3. Barro, Robert J. "Rational Expectations and the Role of Monetary Policy." *Journal of Monetary Economics,* 2 (1976), 1–32.

4. Baumol, William. "The Transactions Demand for Money—An Inventory Theoretic Approach." *Quarterly Journal of Economics,* 66 (November 1952), 545–56.

5. Debreu, Gerard. *Theory of Value.* New Haven, Conn.: Yale University Press, 1959.

6. Drazen, Allan. "Recent Developments in Macroeconomic Disequilibrium Theory." *Econometrica,* 48 (March 1980), 283–306.

7. Fischer, Stanley. "Long-Term Contracts, Rational Expectations, and the Optimal Money Supply Rule." *Journal of Political Economy,* 85 (February 1977), 191–206.

8. Friedman, Milton. "The Role of Monetary Policy." *American Economic Review*, 58 (March 1968), 1–17.

9. Ghez, Gilbert R., and Gary S. Becker. "The Allocation of Time and Goods over the Life Cycle." *New York: National Bureau of Economic Research, 1975.*

10. Gordon, Donald F., and J. Allan Hynes. "On the Theory of Price Dynamics." In *Macroeconomic Foundations of Employment and Inflation Theory,* edited by Edmund S. Phelps, pp. 369–93, New York: Norton, 1970.

11. Haberler, Gottfried. *Prosperity and Depression.* Geneva: League of Nations, 1937.

12. Hansen, Lars P., and Thomas J. Sargent. "Formulating and Estimating Dynamic Linear Rational Expectations Models." *Journal of Economic Dynamics and Control,* 2 (1980), 7–46.

13. Heckman, James J. "Longitudinal Studies in Labor Economics: A Methodological Review." Working Paper, University of Chicago, September 1978.

14. Hicks, John R. "Mr. Keynes and the 'Classics': A Suggested Interpretation." *Econometrica,* 5 (1937), 147–59.

15. Hicks, John R. *Value and Capital: An Inquiry Into Some Fundamental Principles of Economic Theory.* Oxford: Clarendon Press, 1939.

16. Keynes, John M. A. *Treatise on Money.* New York: Harcourt Brace and Co., 1930.

17. Keynes, John M. A. *The General Theory of Employment, Interest and Money.* London: Macmillan, 1936.

18. Leijonhufvud, Axel. *On Keynesian Economics and the Economics of Keynes.* New York: Oxford, 1968.

19. Lillard, Lee A., and Robert J. Willis. "Dynamic Aspects of Earning Mobility." *Econometrica* (September 1978), 985–1012.

20. Lucas, Robert E., Jr. "Expectations and the Neutrality of Money." *Journal of Economic Theory,* 4 (1972), 103–24.

21. Lucas, Robert E., Jr. "An Equilibrium Model of the Business Cycle." *Journal of Political Economy,* 83 (1975), 1113–44.

22. Lucas, Robert E., Jr. "Econometric Policy Evaluation: A Critique." *Journal of Monetary Economics,* 2, Supplement (1976), Carnegie-Rochester Conference Series, Vol. 1.

23. Lucas, Robert E., Jr. "Understanding Business Cycles." *Journal of Monetary Economics,* Supplement (1977), Carnegie-Rochester Conference Series, Vol. 5.

24. Lucas, Robert E., Jr., and Edward C. Prescott. "Investment Under Uncertainty," *Econometrica,* 39 (1971), 659–81.

25. Lucas, Robert E., Jr., and Leonard A. Rapping. "Real Wages, Employment, and the Price Level." *Journal of Political Economy,* 77 (1969), 721–54.

26. Lucas, Robert E., Jr., and Thomas J. Sargent. "After Keynesian Macroeconomics." In *After the Phillips Curve: Persistence of High Inflation and High Unemployment,* Conference Series no. 19, pp. 49–72. Boston, Mass.: Federal Reserve Bank of Boston.

27. Malinvaud, Edmund. *The Theory of Unemployment Reconsidered,* New York: Wiley, 1977.

28. Mitchell, Wesley C. *Business Cycles,* Berkeley, Calif.: University of California Press, 1913.

29. Modigliani, Franco. "Liquidity Preference and the Theory of Interest and Money." *Econometrica,* 12 (1944).

30. Modigliani, Franco. "The Monetarist Controversy or, Should We Forsake Stabilization Policies?" *American Economic Review*, 67 (1977), 1–19.

31. Muth, John F. "Rational Expectations and the Theory of Price Movements." *Econometrica*, 29 (July 1961), 315–35.

32. Patinkin, Don. *Money, Interest, and Prices*. Second edition. New York: Harper and Row, 1965.

33. Phelps, Edmund S. "Money Wage Dynamics and Labor Market Equilibrium." *Journal of Political Economy*, 76 (July/August 1968), 687–711.

34. Phelps, Edmund S., et al. *Microeconomic Foundations of Employment and Inflation Theory*. New York: Norton, 1970.

35. Phelps, Edmund S., and John B. Taylor. "Stabilizing Powers of Monetary Policy under Rational Expectations." *Journal of Political Economy*, 85 (1977), 163–89.

36. Samuelson, Paul A. *Foundations of Economic Analysis*. Cambridge, Mass.: Harvard University Press, 1947.

37. Samuelson, Paul A. "Proof that Properly Anticipated Prices Fluctuate Randomly." *Industrial Management Review*, 6 (1965), 41–49.

38. Sargent, Thomas J. "A Classical Macroeconomic Model for the United States." *Journal of Political Economy*, 84 (1976), 207–38.

39. Sargent, Thomas J. "The Observational Equivalence of Natural and Unnatural Rate Theories of Macroeconomics." *Journal of Political Economy*, 84 (June 1976), 631–40.

40. Sargent, Thomas J. "Estimation of Dynamic Labor Demand Schedules under Rational Expectations." *Journal of Political Economy*, 86 (December 1978), 1009–44.

41. Sargent, Thomas J., and Neil Wallace. "'Rational' Expectations, The Optimal Monetary Instrument, and the Optimal Money Supply Rule." *Journal of Political Economy*, 83 (1975), 214–54.

42. Simon, Herbert A. "Dynamic Programming under Uncertainty with a Quadratic Criterion Function." *Econometrica*, 24 (1956), 74–81.

43. Simon, Herbert A. *The Sciences of the Artificial*. Cambridge, Mass.: MIT Press, 1969.

44. Slutsky, Eugenio. "The Summation of Random Causes as the Source of Cyclic Processes." *Econometrica*, 5 (1937), 105–46.

45. Taylor, John G. "Estimation and Control of a Macroeconomic Model with Rational Expectations." *Econometrica*, 47 (September 1979), 1267–86.

46. Theil, Henri. "A Note on Certainty Equivalence in Dynamic Programming." *Econometrica*, 25 (1957), 346–49.

47. Tinbergen, Jan. "Business Cycles in the United States of America 1919–1932." *Statistical Testing of Business Cycle Theories*, Vol. 2. Geneva, League of Nations, 1939.

48. Tobin, James. "The Interest Elasticity of the Transactions Demand for Cash." *Review of Economics and Statistics*, 38 (1956), 241–47.

49. Tobin, James. "Liquidity Preference as Behavior towards Risk." *Review of Economic Studies*, 2 (1958).

50. Tobin, James. "How Dead is Keynes?" *Economic Inquiry*, 16 (1977), 459–68.

Index